HISTORICAL MEMOIR

OF

THE WAR

IN

WEST FLORIDA AND LOUISIANA

IN 1814–15.
With an Atlas.

Expanded Edition

ARSÈNE LACARRIÈRE LATOUR

Edited with an introduction by Gene Allen Smith

The Historic New Orleans Collection
and University Press of Florida

Gainesville · Tallahassee · Tampa · Boca Raton · Pensacola
Orlando · Miami · Jacksonville · Ft. Myers · Sarasota

First cloth printing, 1999
First paperback printing, 2008
Printed in the United States of America on acid-free paper

13 12 11 10 09 08 6 5 4 3 2 1

Library of Congress Cataloging-in-Publication Data
Latour, Arsène Lacarrière, 1778–1837.
Historical memoir of the war in West Florida and Louisiana in 1814–15: with an atlas / Arsène Lacarrière Latour: edited with an introduction by Gene A. Smith. — Rev. ed.
p. cm.
"Historic New Orleans Collection."
Includes English translation of documents assembled by Latour for a second edition, never before published.
Includes bibliographical references and index.
ISBN 978-0-8130-1675-7 (acid-free paper)
ISBN 978-0-8130-3335-8 (pbk.)
1. New Orleans (La.), Battle of, 1815. 2. United States—History—War of 1812—Naval operations. I. Smith, Gene A., 1963–. II. Historic New Orleans Collection. III. Title.
E356.N5L38 1999
973.5'239—dc21 98-44742

The University Press of Florida is the scholarly publishing agency for the State University System of Florida, comprising Florida A&M University, Florida Atlantic University, Florida Gulf Coast University, Florida International University, Florida State University, New College of Florida, University of Central Florida, University of Florida, University of North Florida, University of South Florida, and University of West Florida.

University Press of Florida
15 Northwest 15th Street
Gainesville, FL 32611
http://www.upf.com

HISTORICAL MEMOIR

OF

THE WAR

IN

WEST FLORIDA AND LOUISIANA

IN 1814–15.

UNIVERSITY PRESS OF FLORIDA

Florida A&M University, Tallahassee
Florida Atlantic University, Boca Raton
Florida Gulf Coast University, Ft. Myers
Florida International University, Miami
Florida State University, Tallahassee
New College of Florida, Sarasota
University of Central Florida, Orlando
University of Florida, Gainesville
University of North Florida, Jacksonville
University of South Florida, Tampa
University of West Florida, Pensacola

CONTENTS

The maps have been moved to the Web site of The Historic New Orleans Collection and may be accessed at the following address: http://www.hnoc.org/latour/latour.php

FOREWORD

The Historic New Orleans Collection and the Battle of New Orleans

The origins of the Historic New Orleans Collection can be traced to General L. Kemper Williams's interest in the Battle of New Orleans. Between 1943 and 1971, General Williams assembled a vast collection of manuscripts, books, pamphlets, maps, drawings, and paintings focusing on the American victory over the British on the plains of Chalmette on January 8, 1815. Primary material collected by General Williams presents contemporary perspectives—both British and American—on the campaign and its significance. The Memorandum of James Stirling, the Edward Nicholls and William H. Percy Letters, and the Robert Aitchison Memoir reflect the British position, while various letters, orders, and papers of such individuals as Willie Blount, William Carroll, John Coffee, Andrew Hynes, Andrew Jackson, and Bartholomew Schaumburg reveal the American point of view. General Williams's initial interest in the battle led him to collect a wide variety of material documenting the history of New Orleans, the State of Louisiana, and the Gulf Coast. To ensure the growth and care of his collection, General and Mrs. Williams founded the Kemper and Leila Williams Foundation, which operates as the Historic New Orleans Collection.

The Collection has continued to add to its holdings on the Battle of New Orleans. The acquisition in early 1997 of Arsène Lacarrière Latour's papers relating to his *Historical Memoir of the War in West Florida and Louisiana in 1814–15* was an important addition to these primary resources on the battle. On the death of Latour in 1839, his papers concerning the *Historical Memoir* became the property of his daughter; his son received the extant copies of the book. The papers were passed down through the family until they were acquired by the Collection from Latour's descendants. Covering the years

1814–1817, the papers largely consist of material received by Latour too late to be included in his 1816 publication. Included are letters and documents that reveal a great deal about the battle, as well as the process of writing the book and the initial response of readers. Latour received much of the information for his initial publication from questionnaires sent to men who took part in the battle. One letter, written in response to such a questionnaire, explains that the soldiers from Tennessee were able to participate only because rains at the last moment permitted them to navigate the rivers to New Orleans. The copy letters of Secretary of State James Monroe to the governors of Kentucky, Georgia, and Tennessee reveal that he probably would have preferred that Latour focus more attention on the political maneuvers during the fall of 1814 than on the battle itself. Copies of his letters to the governors of Tennessee and Kentucky dated January 20, 1815, indicate that Monroe was not sure of the outcome of the battle. These letters are missing from Monroe's copybook in the Library of Congress.

Documentation in Latour's papers indicates that the book met with criticism in Louisiana for a variety of reasons, including the lack of attention given to Governor William C. C. Claiborne. The *Historical Memoir*, sold by subscription for five dollars, was also delivered late. Individuals such as Benjamin H. Latrobe were upset by its tardiness, while others were disturbed by the poor quality of the engraving of Andrew Jackson; some copies did not include the engraving.

The Latour acquisition supplements important research material already held by the Collection. James Monroe's desire to have a greater accounting of preparations for the battle is seen in his letter dated October 10, 1814. In it, Monroe asks Governor Willie Blount of Tennessee to send 7,500 militiamen to New Orleans in view of an anticipated attack on the city. A glimpse of how Latour assembled his book is seen in his previously acquired letter of April 10, 1815. Writing to Major General David B. Morgan in New Orleans concerning the defeat of Morgan's forces on the West Bank during the American battle with the British, Latour asked Morgan to defend his actions in writing and to forward his response for inclusion in the forthcoming account of the battle. A Bartholomew Schaumburg letter of January 25, 1815, describes the animosity between William C. C. Claiborne and Andrew Jackson.

Aside from the Latour Papers, the most significant recent addition to The Collection's related manuscript holdings is unquestionably the William C. Cook War of 1812 in the South Collection. It contains over a thousand published works, original documents, rare prints, and artifacts related to the southern theater of the war, particularly the Creek War, British operations along the Gulf Coast, and the Battle of New Orleans. Published works in the Cook Collection include early histories by Latour's contemporaries, such as Robert B. McAfee, Thomas O'Connor, Henry M. Brackenridge, and Gilbert J. Hunt. The Cook Collection also includes various important U.S. Army and state militia documents, as well as materials concerning the southern Indian tribes and manuscripts from the British perspective.

Following the addition of so much new material to its War of 1812 holdings, the Historic New Orleans Collection made available a dedicated guide to these resources, in the form of an Internet research "pathfinder." This guide can be accessed via the Collection's Web site: www.hnoc.org. Interested researchers can browse detailed finding guides to the archival collections such as the Latour papers, as well as a chronologically arranged bibliography of selected published works, and detailed descriptions of pictorial and three-dimensional items.

The Latour papers complement the holdings of the Historic New Orleans Collection on the Battle of New Orleans, shedding critical new light on the events and providing valuable insight into Latour's research methodology. Latour's *Historical Memoir* was, and still is, the most important firsthand account of the battle. With the publication of this revised edition of Latour's *Historical Memoir*, the information that Latour was unable to include in his 1816 book has been incorporated into the original publication, adding greatly to the available documentation on one of the landmark battles of American history.

Alfred E. Lemmon
Director, Williams Research Center
The Historic New Orleans Collection

EDITOR'S ACKNOWLEDGMENTS

After the Battle of New Orleans, Arsène Lacarrière Latour worked diligently to publish his *Historical Memoir*, only to find that it did not appeal to the public. Disappointed and financially drained, Latour planned a revised edition, which would be assembled under the guidance of his friend Peter Stephen DuPonceau. The revision would address the complaints concerning his earlier edition; it was to include additional documents collected from James Monroe and Andrew Jackson, would have a new chapter organization, and would eliminate some of the French idioms. Unfortunately, the improved edition never appeared and Latour faded into obscurity.

Although the documents assembled for the second edition were not published, they nonetheless shed light on both the Battle of New Orleans and Latour. All of the new documents added to the Appendix have been reproduced as true to the original as possible. Misspellings in the documents and Latour's text have been retained without the use of *sic*, unless they impede the understanding of the text. In such instances brackets have been added with the correct spelling of a word. Other silent changes have been made to allow for correct identification of individuals and to correct awkwardly translated French idioms. Other than these minor alterations, Latour's text with his additional documents remain true to form.

Just as Latour did not write his *Historical Memoir* without the help of his compatriots, I too have relied heavily on the help of others for this edition. First, the Texas Christian University Research Foundation and my colleagues have been very gracious with their support, time, and advice; Don Worcester, Mark Gilderhus, Don Coerver, Todd Kerstetter, and Ken Stevens have read my work, answered my questions, and endured my anxiety. Dr. Harry Redman of Tulane University translated Latour's letters while TCU History Department Administrative Assistant Dana Summers typed them, thereby saving me invaluable time. My students J. Nathan Campbell and Carol Terry were forced to learn more about Latour and the Battle of New Orleans than they cared, and for that I thank them heartily. Harold D.

Moser of the Jackson Papers and William Cook of Nashville, Tennessee, provided me with important manuscript materials that helped complete Latour's story.

Several libraries, historical societies, and archives have offered invaluable assistance: the Library of Congress and National Archives, the Chicago Historical Society, the Henry E. Huntington Library, the Louisiana State University Library, the Maryland Historical Society, and the Texas Christian University Library deserve special thanks. I am also appreciative of the interest of Meredith Morris-Babb and the staff members of the University Press of Florida.

This project would not have been except for the interest of former Historic New Orleans Collection Director Jon Kukla, who saw its importance and offered his support. Director of Publications Patricia Brady cheerfully encouraged this project from the beginning, and she extended her able services as copyeditor; her efforts have reconfirmed my belief in the importance of an editor. On more than one occasion archivist Alfred Lemmon eased my fears with the right words—he is the quintessential professional, and these simple words cannot convey how much I truly appreciate all his efforts. Mark Cave, David Dressing, and the other HNOC staff members have also helped in immeasurable ways. Without the support of the board of directors and the help and encouragement of the Historic New Orleans Collection this project would never have been accomplished.

Two other people were essential to this project. My wife, Tracy, listened patiently, soothed my anxieties, and gave me cheer when all seemed lost. She, like my students, has endured my fascination with Latour, learning far more than she cares about him or the Battle of New Orleans. Last, I must thank Arsène Lacarrière Latour, the man who wrote the book, collected the materials for the revised edition, and most important, lived the life. For the most part forgotten by the past, perhaps he will be remembered by the future.

Editor's Introduction

"The War that was . . . Glorious to the Nation"

General Andrew Jackson's victory over the British at New Orleans on January 8, 1815, is one of the most important battles of the War of 1812 and one of the watershed events in U.S. history. No other military engagement in the years between George Washington's victory at Yorktown and the Confederate attack on Fort Sumter did more to intensify American patriotism or to ensure independence. American authors, as well as the Frenchman Arsène Lacarrière Latour, eulogized the glorious triumph on the plains of Chalmette as a pivotal event in the country's history; it represented the American ability to persevere and prevail despite overwhelming odds.

The victory also became a nationalistic symbol for a growing, vibrant country, confirming the American character after Jackson's motley force of regulars, Kentucky and Tennessee volunteers, Louisiana Creoles, Baratarian privateers and pirates, Choctaw Indians, African-American slaves and freemen confronted and defeated a force of British veterans seasoned by long service in the Napoleonic Wars. Although the battle occurred after the Treaty of Ghent had officially ended the conflict, the American victory removed all uncertainties about the end of the war as both nations quickly ratified the treaty. Perhaps more important, the battle proved conclusively that the United States would never again be a British colony or dependent. The country had survived a "Second War of Independence" against the greatest power of the world and made it clear that the new republic would endure. Americans had secured psychological and political independence, and economic independence would soon follow.[1]

The Battle of New Orleans was one of the few high points in an otherwise disappointing conflict. Americans had initially expected easy victories against an enemy preoccupied with war in Europe. Instead, during the fall of 1812 they suffered setbacks in the Northwest, along the Niagara frontier, and in the Lake Champlain region. Although the following year the country began to reverse its fortunes with important victories on Lake Erie and at the Battle of the Thames, in the fall of 1814 the United States suffered its greatest indignity when British forces captured and burned the capital city of Washington. This episode represented the nadir of the American war effort, and only subsequent victories at Lake Champlain, Baltimore, and New Orleans dispelled the stigma of complete humiliation. Thereafter the selective American memory viewed the isolated defeats as necessary setbacks, ultimately culminating in a "war that was . . . glorious to the nation."[2]

Soon after the end of the war authors and editors, politicians and polemicists, all tried to find meaning in the event. They examined the conflict and debated whether it was glorious or disgraceful, advantageous or ruinous. Throughout their discussions different conclusions emerged, none of which offered a completely satisfactory explanation. Authors—then as now—were unable to agree on either the causes or the consequences of the war. Even the Treaty of Ghent, which ended the war, offered nothing about the causes, nor did it provide evidence of American accomplishments. The conflict simply ended in a *status quo ante bellum*.[3]

Despite the uncertainty about causes and consequences, one fact could not be ignored: The war produced a pantheon of new American heroes whose names became synonymous with the growing republic. Andrew Jackson and William Henry Harrison capitalized on their wartime fame to capture the presidency, while Richard M. Johnson—the killer of Tecumseh—later won the vice-presidency. A host of politicians (James Monroe, John Quincy Adams, Henry Clay, John C. Calhoun), military officers (Winfield Scott, Oliver Hazard Perry, Thomas MacDonough, Jacob Brown), and countless others also used their service to advance their careers. During the revolutionary growth of the American economy after the War of 1812, veterans, particularly if they were closely associated with the conflict's heroes, were granted remarkable opportunities in many fields; indeed wartime service became an indispensable criterion for success in politics or the military during the postwar period.[4]

Jackson, the general who saved New Orleans and the country by snatching victory from defeat, unquestioningly benefitted most from the War of 1812. The battle enhanced his reputation and propelled him into national prominence, ultimately catapulting him to the presidency. He was quickly dubbed "The Hero," which aptly fitted the first man of a forthcoming new American age. Jackson reveled in the public attention and flattery, surrounding himself with supporters and family who reminded him of his status. Many of the general's friends, associates, and subordinates attempted to attach their fortunes to his, while still others celebrated him in the hope of profiting from his loyalty and affection.[5]

Perhaps no one praised Jackson as much or offered a more fitting and lasting tribute than did Arsène Lacarrière Latour, author of the first historical account of the Battle of New Orleans. Latour celebrated Jackson's defense of the Crescent City in glowing terms. He related "in detail, with the utmost exactness and precision, the principal events which took place in the course of this campaign." He also substantiated his story with copies of original letters, reports, and documents that provided "the vouchers [evidence] of the facts which [he] related." Throughout his memorial, or what he called his "inadequate tribute," he insisted that the victory at New Orleans was "due to the energy, ability and courage of a single man." According to Latour, Jackson had preserved the country, and the "voice of the whole nation" acknowledged his selfless sacrifice and service. His book, which also included an engraved portrait of a confident, distinguished, yet approachable Andrew Jackson, showed as well as told the American people that Jackson was their hero and the savior of their country.[6]

What is surprising about this tribute is that so little is known about its author. Major Arsène Lacarrière Latour is not a name synonymous with the Battle of New Orleans; his name does not evoke the same emotion or have the same connotation as Andrew Jackson or even Jean Lafitte. Although his name is not immediately recognizable, Latour was one of the most important participants at New Orleans during the crucial period of December 1814–January 1815. His importance, however, was not because he led men into battle. He did not display great military prowess during the heat of the conflict, nor did his activities turn the tide of the engagement in favor of the Americans on the plains of Chalmette. In fact, at first glance Latour's true significance seems mundane and perhaps even trivial. But such is not the case. He made vital contributions in the battle—providing Jackson with needed information and designing important defenses—that ultimately helped shape the destiny of New Orleans, Louisiana, and the trans-Mississippi West. Despite his noteworthy contributions, history has forgotten this Frenchman.

Arsène Lacarrière Latour, a "little sharp looking frenchman"

Major Latour appears to posterity as a shadowy figure, and there is little about him available upon first examination. He was a Frenchman, the "Principal Engineer of the Seventh Military District" during the Battle of New Orleans, and the author of the important *Historical Memoir of the War in West Florida and Louisiana in 1814–15*. Other than this basic information, his life before and after the climactic event seems to be a mystery. Had he not written his book, he probably would have been completely forgotten.

Géraud-Calixte Jean-Baptiste Arsène LaCarrière was born in the village of Aurillac on October 13, 1778, to Guillaume LaCarrière (Seigneur de Latour and Falhiès) and his wife, Louise Marguerite Daudin. Located in the mountainous province of Auvergne, the south-central French town's livelihood came mainly from raising goats in communal mountain pastures. It was a small agricultural community that offered little opportunity. Shortly after his son's birth, Guillaume LaCarrière became a local magistrate, holding the positions of general-lieutenant and police-lieutenant. These positions provided the family with some financial security and, for Guillaume, the respect of the community; in 1787 the family was important enough to host the Marquis de Lafayette during his celebrated visit to Aurillac.[7]

As the oldest son, Arsène would have inherited the family title and all the family lands had it not been for the French Revolution beginning in May 1789. Later that summer the price of grain, the basis of the ordinary people's diet, soared to prohibitively high levels. In the provinces the price climbed to four times the level of that in Paris; in the capital city a pound of bread cost a peasant one-half a week's earnings. Unemployment became rampant in both city and countryside. Across France peasants rose against their manor lords and all was chaos. Although calm returned briefly to the countryside by the fall of 1789, France was soon at war with Austria and Prussia and, by 1793, also with itself as the Reign of Terror swept the country. The world as Arsène knew it was crumbling before his eyes; his uncle Antoine, the priest of Lascelle, was deported in the fall of 1793, and by early 1794 a guillotine had been erected in the public square of Aurillac.[8]

The disruption in France, however, provided opportunities for many young men to advance. In 1799 Latour accepted an apprenticeship with a local architect—Citizen Lallié—who designed and built houses in Aurillac. This work prepared him well for further study in Paris. He enrolled at the Academy of Fine Arts in 1801 and studied with the noted Charles Percier, the architect who designed the Arc de Triomphe as well as additions to the Louvre and the Tuileries. Latour worked diligently as a student and gained the attention of his instructors. Even so, he believed that he needed to work harder to advance. He claimed that the Revolution had put him seven or eight years behind his peers.[9]

Latour's engineering and architectural training in Paris taught him valuable skills that would be useful for his future, but it was not the reason for his departure to the New World. That motivation came after his January 1798 marriage to Marie-Anne Caroline de Montal. The arranged marriage brought to Latour a sizable dowry, including an estate in Saint Domingue that in 1788 had produced a profit of 10,000 francs. And while the union appeared to be amicable—resulting in the birth of a son, Emile, in 1799 and a daughter, Coralie, in 1800—there was no indication of a deep loving relationship. It was the prospect of property that provided a strong incentive for a young man constantly beset by financial woes while living in Paris. On September 1, 1802, Latour boarded *L'Alphonse* bound for Saint Domingue, where he planned to recover the property belonging to him and his wife's family.[10]

Saint Domingue did not provide the prosperity or stability that Latour anticipated. Beginning in August 1791 the island suffered a twelve-year insurrection in which slaves ultimately defeated the local whites and French General Victor Emmanuel Leclerc's 34,000-man expeditionary force sent by Napoleon Bonaparte to retake the island. When Latour arrived in Cap François in late October 1802, the country had been ravaged by years of fighting. The city had been burned shortly before Leclerc's army arrived, hospitals teemed with the sick and wounded, and the French attempt to quell the rebellion floundered. Latour also found the same money problems he had experienced in Paris. In fact, he insisted that his condition was worse in the Caribbean than it had been in Paris because he had to purchase, in addition to food and shelter, books and drawing materials for his profession; there was no library in Saint Domingue.[11]

Latour's fortunes briefly changed for the better. On November 1, 1802, General Leclerc died of yellow fever, and only a few days later Latour learned that two of the army's three engineers had also died. By the time General Donatien Rochambeau assumed command of the expedition in late November, the army had only one engineer and sickness prevented him from performing his duties. On Christmas day Latour wrote to his wife that Rochambeau had offered him a position in the Corps of Engineers, which would allow him to eat at the general's table, be housed at government expense, and earn 200 francs per month.[12]

When Rochambeau took command, he escalated the island's racial war in his attempt to subdue the population. He asked Napoleon for authorization to reinstate slavery, and while awaiting a response he waged a brutal war of extermination against blacks and mulattoes. French troops burned, hanged, drowned, and tortured blacks in a policy of terror that by March 1803 drove the island's population to insurrection. Further compounding Rochambeau's problems, only two months later Napoleon decided to break the Peace of Amiens and renew his war with Great Britain; he massed men and ships along the English Channel for a planned invasion of England as Rochambeau begged for additional troops, supplies, and relief. Rochambeau became desperate as insurgents in the southern part of the island, supported by the British, waged a devastating guerrilla war that slowly decimated and demoralized French soldiers and terrified the white population who expected to suffer an exacting revenge. Every night privateers, including brothers Jean and Pierre Lafitte, sailed from the island with wealthy white refugees bound for Cuba and Louisiana. Rochambeau, having lost control of the countryside, sought refuge in the fortified city of Le Cap, where he was quickly surrounded by black insurgents. Meanwhile British ships blockaded the harbor and awaited the inevitable. On November 29, 1803, Rochambeau surrendered to the British the remnants of his force; nearly all of those who surrendered soon languished in English prisons.[13]

Latour escaped the horrors of those last days in Saint Domingue, and there is no indication that he was taken prisoner along with Rochambeau. If he was taken prisoner by the British, he apparently was not held for long because in May 1804 he wrote his son that he had been working in the United States for a few months. One story maintains that Latour fled Saint Domingue for Cuba with General Charles François Antoine Lallemand aboard a privateer, maybe even Lafitte's. He remained with Lallemand in Havana for a short time where the two mingled in local society before traveling on to Louisiana. Even if Latour did not meet the Lafittes prior to his arrival in Havana, he probably did so while in the city, which was a center for privateering activity. He probably also met other French exiles who would play important roles in Louisiana, such as the engineer Barthélemy Lafon.[14]

Exactly when Latour arrived in Louisiana is subject to speculation. Some authors maintain that he came in 1810, others as early as 1802. In the introduction to his *Historical Memoir*, Latour declared that he had helped Lafon prepare maps of New Orleans and its Gulf Coast environs, most likely as advance agents for Napoleon's projected occupation of the Louisiana territory in 1803. If so, he had to have left Saint Domingue prior to Rochambeau's capitulation, and in that case he certainly had not been a British prisoner.[15]

Another interesting point that prompts many questions is the association between Latour and Lafon. While Latour remains a shadowy figure, Lafon appears in better focus. For example, Lafon was appointed lieutenant in the Louisiana militia, received votes in 1806 for the territorial house of representatives, and became deputy surveyor for Orleans County. After this respectable start he later became a privateer captain operating for the Lafittes in Louisiana waters. He also became active in smuggling and the slave trade. During the summer of 1813 the Spanish minister to the United States, Don Luis Onís, reported that French agents Lafon and H. L. V. Ducoudray-Holstein were involved in a filibustering attempt against Spanish Texas. A year later, in September 1814, Master Commandant Daniel Todd Patterson's naval expedition captured Lafon and other privateers as well as vessels, money, merchandise, and stores from the Lafitte's Baratarian stronghold at Grande Terre. The story becomes even more intriguing as Lafon again entered the Louisiana militia during the Battle of New Orleans, later joined other soldiers of fortune at Galveston, and along with the Lafittes enlisted as a Spanish agent in the southwest. It is apparent that Lafon, and perhaps even Latour, was willing to share his loyalties, especially when the price was right.[16]

Regardless of Latour's loyalties, in 1804 he and Lafon turned over the maps they had prepared to U.S. Army General James Wilkinson, who had arrived in New Orleans with the acting governor of Louisiana, William C. C. Claiborne, to receive the territory for the United States. Unknown to Claiborne or other American officials, Wilkinson was also working for the Spanish, and his trip to the Crescent City gave him a chance to renew his connections and receive back pay. His intrigue while in New Orleans ultimately delayed his departure to Washington by three weeks, and to cover his tracks he informed Secretary of War Henry Dearborn that he was collecting material for a report on the territory.[17]

Wilkinson's subsequent essay, "Reflections on Louisiana," and his monograph, *The Topography of Louisiana*, combined hard-to-get reliable information about the territory with a number of excellent maps, obviously prepared by Latour and Lafon. He gave copies of this work, which he claimed as his own, to the Spanish governor of West Florida, Vicente Folch, and received 12,000 pesos in return; coincidently this copy of Wilkinson's summary fell into British hands when they seized Pensacola during the War of 1812. The report offered important information about the perceived boundaries of the territory, the military situation in the region, and the U.S. government's intentions concerning the Gulf Coast. Finally, it warned Spanish officials to maintain control over the Floridas since they were the key to American commerce in the Gulf; the maps illustrated Wilkinson's point.[18]

When Wilkinson returned to Washington he gave a copy of his monograph to Secretary Dearborn, who was so impressed with the work that he passed it along to President Thomas Jefferson; Governor Claiborne gave copies of the maps to the postmaster general, who was considering a postal route to New Orleans. The president praised Wilkinson for his zeal, determination, and foresight. Moreover, when the general insinuated that he had gathered the materials in his report at great personal cost, Jefferson reimbursed him with money from the presidential contingency fund. Wilkinson ultimately received money from both the U.S. and Spanish governments for the same report, and although he was accused of treachery on several occasions his critics could never assemble the necessary evidence to prove his guilt. In hindsight it is evident that Wilkinson was working both sides of the fence, but it remains unclear whether Latour and Lafon were willing agents in the general's subterfuge. The activities of each after the War of 1812 suggest that they were.[19]

By January 1805, Latour had moved to New York City, where he joined Jean Jacques Chauveau in a limited partnership to operate a trading business. The enterprise, Lacarrière, Chauveau and Company, did not fare well. Apparently the U.S. government rejected an order of imported French hats that did not meet the standards demanded by the American army, creating a financial hardship for Latour's company and prompting an unsuccessful lawsuit that continued for several years.[20]

Faced with limited business success, Latour turned to his chosen profession of architect and engineer. During the first decade of the nineteenth century, New York City experienced considerable growth and development and a resulting need for additional roads, public works, and port developments. The city also needed additional forts because the harbor had become a haven for privateers and European naval vessels which used the port to lay in water and supplies. More often than not, British warships refitted in the harbor and then hovered off the coast in American waters, awaiting their chance to capture privateers or to impress seamen. In 1805 the citizens of New York City had demanded protection from British depredations while Congress debated whether the country needed warships or additional fortifications for the harbor. Latour took the opportunity to draft for the city an unsolicited plan for harbor defense, which he submitted to War Secretary Henry Dearborn. Not surprisingly, Dearborn later returned the plans and informed Latour that he would not be compensated for his work, "however meritorious," because he had not been appointed by the president or Congress to prepare such a survey.[21]

It may have been during Latour's stay in New York that he first met Edward Livingston. The former mayor and district attorney had fled New York City for New Orleans because of debt. Arriving in the Crescent City in February 1804, he quickly became one of the most prominent lawyers of the region, representing a wide array of clients including U.S. naval commander David Porter and privateers Jean and Pierre Lafitte; he was popular with both Creoles and Anglos. He further solidified his ties to Louisiana by marrying a French refugee from Saint Domingue who was the sister of August de Castera Davezac, a prominent Creole and aide to Jackson during the Battle of New Orleans. Soon after his arrival in the city, Livingston became involved in a series of prolonged land (batture) cases, and these may have prompted him to use Latour's services to bolster his legal arguments. In any case Latour became an associate of one of the most influential men in Louisiana, which placed him in good company and opened doors for future advancement.[22]

By the beginning of 1806, Latour had returned to Louisiana; later that summer he drafted for Elias Toutant Beauregard, the retired military captain of Spanish Louisiana, a city plan for Baton Rouge. Laying it out in the classical French tradition, Latour's design used grid and radial streets around a proposed cathedral square; he surrounded the city to the north, south, and east with boulevards and on the west with the Mississippi River. The Spanish commandant of the district, Carlos Grand Pré, a former French commandant who had gained recognition as a fair-minded administrator, approved his plan. Although Grand Pré had volunteered his services to Spain when France ceded the territory in 1763, his superior, Governor Folch, was constantly suspicious of his enlightened rule and of his association with alleged French agents; Grand Pré's connection in 1808 to General Octaviano Davilmar—a Napoleonic agent sent to foment revolution in Spanish Texas—brought about his recall. Nonetheless, it was surprising that Latour, a young

French engineer who had recently arrived in the remaining Spanish territory of Louisiana, was able to secure such an important project. His architectural and engineering talents may have helped him win the position, but undoubtedly such influential supporters as Livingston or a commandant at Baton Rouge with French predilections were the deciding factors.[23]

During the years 1806 to 1810, while Louisiana experienced the growing pains of a new territory, Latour spent much of his time moving between Baton Rouge and New Orleans, probably performing land surveys for Beauregard and for Livingston's on-going batture cases. Latour also worked for the Marquis de Lafayette. In 1803, Congress had voted a sizable land grant for the French hero of the American Revolution, and Lafayette expressed interest in Louisiana. By March 1806, Lafayette's business agent, M. Duplantier, had arrived in New Orleans to locate a suitable site. Unable to secure title to an entire tract of land on the Carondelet Canal, Duplantier chose 10,000 acres at Point Coupée across the river from Baton Rouge; once located, the land had to be surveyed and private claims settled. During the summer of 1806, Latour apparently surveyed some of the land in question. In 1808, his father, Guillaume LaCarrière, asked Lafayette to use his influence to secure the French consulship at New Orleans for his son. Latour did not receive the position, but Lafayette did respond that he would speak with his "friends about M. Lacarrière de Latour."[24]

By the fall of 1810 Latour was devoting himself full time to architecture in New Orleans. On September 22, 1810, the *Gazette de la Louisiane* reported that Latour and Jean-Hyacinthe Laclotte had opened an engineering and architectural firm at the widowed Madame Guillemard's house at the corner of Royal and Orleans. According to the notice the partners would draw plans and offer estimates, oversee construction, and erect both public and private buildings. Also, beginning on September 20, they had opened a day and evening school that taught drawing and painting, architecture and carpentry, as well as interior design and decoration.[25]

Apparently the partners' business quickly prospered. By January 1811 they had moved their operations to a building they had purchased at 625 Dauphine Street. They also designed Tremoulet's Hotel and began construction on the first Orleans Street Theatre, which was not completed until 1814; Latour probably won the contract because of his experience with the St. Philip Street Theatre, located between Royal and Bourbon, which he had designed and constructed. The architects' most famous project was the renovation of the house of Doctor Yves Lemonnier, also known as the "First

Skyscraper," at the corner of Royal and St. Peters. During their work they heightened the walls of the first two floors, built a third story, and added a roof level of rooms. Before collecting their $7,600 fee in November 1811, the architects installed an ornate iron girded railing, complete with the doctor's monogram, "Y L M," on the third-floor balcony. The doctor's oval room on the third floor supposedly offered the best possible view of the city. The following year they designed a house for Pierre Rogers at 619 Bourbon Street and began several other buildings in the city's French Quarter.[26]

Latour also won the respect and admiration of Benjamin Henry Latrobe, the famous Washington architect who had designed the U.S. Capitol. Latrobe's son Henry came to New Orleans in the spring of 1811 on business for his father, who had the contract to build the city waterworks. Henry's ability to speak French, as well as his French-sounding name (he styled himself H. Boneval Latrobe), afforded him the chance to meet many of the region's creole politicians and leading professionals, including Latour, who took the young man under his wing. Latour offered friendship and professional advice on dealing with the political difficulties the project faced. While this help eased Henry's stay in New Orleans, it did little to complete his father's project.[27]

Despite becoming a U.S. citizen in the spring of 1812 and a seemingly auspicious professional beginning, Latour and Laclotte were facing financial ruin by the spring of 1813. On May 7, 1813, the two architects filed a petition for bankruptcy. When they offered an inventory a month later, it revealed that they possessed only the property on Dauphine Street, a slave, construction tools, and an assortment of building materials. Perhaps their financial failure was tied to Napoleon's declining fortunes in Russia, although such an explanation would imply that Latour was still in the service of Napoleon Bonaparte. Given Latour's association with the French military, this explanation is plausible but highly unlikely. The demise of such a seemingly prosperous business likely resulted from the economic problems caused by the War of 1812.[28]

While the War of 1812 brought disruption and uncertainty to the United States and especially to the Gulf Coast, it created a new opportunity for Latour to demonstrate his talents. After two years of fighting, the war moved to the Gulf of Mexico, and by mid-November 1814 General Andrew Jackson, commander of the Seventh Military District, had obtained positive information via the West Indies that New Orleans was the primary British objective in the South.[29]

Throughout the fall of 1814, Jackson had heard rumors of an impending British attack along the Gulf. The Crescent City was clearly the most valuable and vulnerable point, but Jackson had not been sure that New Orleans would be the British objective. He initially believed Mobile would provide the best route of attack against the Mississippi Valley and ultimately north to Canada. Mobile would also give the British a staging area as well as a central location for linking up with their Spanish and Indian allies. Jackson was so confident in his hunch that he spent much of the fall of 1814 at Mobile preparing for the anticipated attack. Although he did not concentrate his efforts in New Orleans, Jackson made preliminary preparations to defend the city as he waited. He appointed Latour as principal engineer and Lewis Livingston—Edward's son—and Henry Latrobe as assistant engineers of the Seventh Military District.[30]

Once Jackson arrived in New Orleans on December 1, 1814, he immediately met with the influential Citizens' Defense Committee and its chairman, Edward Livingston. The two men had known each other for years, as they had served together in Congress during the 1790s; both men's names had also been associated with Aaron Burr. Jackson recognized that Livingston was an influential local leader whose knowledge of French was a particular asset. He valued Livingston's opinions regarding the area, including his suggestion that New Orleans needed additional defenses. On November 21, Livingston had heartily recommended Latour as a "man of perfect honor and integrity [who] speaks both French and English fluently," qualities that Jackson required if he were to bridge the gap between French Louisiana Creoles and Anglo-Americans while he prepared the city for an attack.[31]

Jackson desperately needed Latour's services as most of the country's military engineers trained at West Point were engaged on the northern frontier or superintending coastal defenses. The shortage of military engineers along the Gulf forced Jackson to turn to Latour; he knew that Latour was qualified because he had helped Lafon prepare maps in 1805 for Wilkinson and again in 1813 for General Thomas Flournoy (then commander of the Seventh Military District). Jackson also knew that these maps were accurate and the best available. Moreover, his situation by December 1814 was perilous. Latour informed him that there were seven possible water routes for a British attack, including Bayou Lafourche, Barataria Bay, River Aux Chenes and Bayou Terre Aux Boeufs, the Mississippi River itself, and three via Lake Borgne.[32]

Bayou Lafourche, a deep narrow stream running from the Mississippi River north of New Orleans to the Gulf, would not serve as the British route of attack because of its length, narrowness, and ease of obstruction. Nor was Barataria Bay feasible—it was seventy miles west of the mouth of the Mississippi with numerous channels running north to the river across from New Orleans—unless the British procured experienced pilots familiar with the narrow, shallow, treacherous passages. River Aux Chenes and Bayou Terre Aux Boeufs, small streams running almost from English Turn and emptying into the Gulf of Mexico just east of the river's mouth, were also winding, narrow, and easily defended.[33]

The main channel of the Mississippi River provided a possible alternative and, given hindsight, would probably have been the best route the British could have taken since they could have used their ships for artillery support and to transport men. The river was the only option where British deep-draft vessels could be used, but even so its shallow mouth denied access to large ships-of-the-line. A strong current also forced vessels to make a long beat upstream, leaving them exposed to fire from the riverbanks. Since this was the most viable route of attack, Fort St. Philip had been constructed about thirty miles from the river's mouth and Fort St. Leon seventy miles upstream. Moreover, Fort St. Leon commanded English Turn, an S-shaped turn where sailing vessels had to wait for a change in wind before proceeding upstream. While it was possible to sail upriver, the time spent tacking and waiting for favorable winds would have left the British flotilla exposed to a constant barrage.[34]

Considering the various routes, Latour assured Jackson that Lake Borgne offered the most feasible alternative for a British attack. The saltwater estuary provided three possible approaches. The first was through the Rigolets from Lake Borgne into Lake Pontchartrain. This avenue, combined with Bayou St. John, would have permitted the English to move by water to within two miles of New Orleans, but it necessitated many light, shallow-draft vessels that the British had problems securing. It also was guarded by Fort Petite Coquilles, which the British believed to have more than 500 men and 40 guns. The second alternative was through Lake Borgne to the plain of Gentilly; from there British troops could march to the city along the Chef Menteur Road. Jackson initially believed that the British would take this route. Because of its accessibility, it was defended by both men and artillery, and a pitched battle there would have allowed the Americans to fall back and construct other lines of defense well away from the city.[35]

The last route, and ultimately the one chosen, called for using Bayou Bienvenu, which drained the area east of New Orleans and stretched from Lake Borgne to within a mile of the Mississippi River. From there the British could proceed north nine miles along the river levee, a narrow strip of land through the region's sugar plantations, toward New Orleans. While this approach appeared to be the path of least resistance, it too was fraught with obstacles. The route was more shallow than expected, preventing British ships from entering the estuary and providing gunfire support to cover their barges' advance. Furthermore, the distance from Cat Island, at the mouth of Lake Borgne, to Bayou Bienvenu was sixty-two miles, and it took thirty-six hours of hard rowing to reach it. But the most serious obstacle, according to British midshipman Robert Aitchison who was present at Lake Borgne, was the "five American gunboats, of great strength" that commanded the shoal waters.[36]

Soon after his consultation with Latour, Jackson ordered that all of the water routes to the city be blocked. Early on the morning of December 4, he joined the commander of the New Orleans naval station, Daniel Todd Patterson, and engineers Howell Tatum and Latour as they traveled downriver to Fort St. Philip. During the trip, Latour provided Jackson with diagrams of the bastion, which appeared to be in good shape. After arriving Jackson saw first-hand the fine condition of the fort and ordered only minor alterations. He instructed Latour to destroy the wooden barracks within the fort and add more artillery on both sides of the river. During their return trip Latour pointed out to Jackson that marshes and swamps dominated the landscape and afforded the British only a few locations to land troops below New Orleans. A week later Jackson, Latour, and Lewis Livingston inspected the Chef Menteur Pass and the Gentilly Road to the east of the city, which Jackson believed the most probable route of attack.[37]

Over the next several days Jackson received disturbing news. On December 15 he learned that Lieutenant Thomas ap Catesby Jones's five-gunboat flotilla stationed on Lake Borgne had been captured the previous day by an overwhelmingly superior British force; the victory placed Jackson at a severe disadvantage because it allowed the British to choose their point of attack. This information was substantiated by news of more than 80 British warships in the area. All the intelligence Jackson received seemed to indicate that the attack was at hand. Jackson needed more time and additional troops as he had—on paper—about 700 men; in reality he had fewer.[38]

The situation was becoming desperate for Jackson. On December 16 he declared martial law, and two days later in the square at the cathedral he reviewed troops, including two battalions of free men of color. This ceremony showed Jackson's confidence, or perhaps a desperation masked as confidence, in the black troops. Jackson was even willing to use Jean Lafitte's "hellish banditti" (pirates/privateers), along with their important cache of powder, shot, and flints. Jackson had been unwilling to seek help from the black troops or Lafitte's pirates, but he could not refuse their assistance when it was offered, given the critical state of affairs.[39]

Latour or Livingston likely arranged the meeting between Jackson and Lafitte. When Jackson initially arrived in the city, he found strong sentiment in favor of accepting the pirates' help. His aide and friend Edward Livingston was a strong advocate. Soon thereafter the Louisiana legislature asked Jackson to secure a pardon for Lafitte and his band should they help defend the city, and a group of distinguished citizens petitioned Jackson to the same effect. Latour knew Lafitte, and he likely also weighed in on the subject. The meeting between the two took place December 18 at Jackson's headquarters on Royal Street. According to Latour, during the meeting Lafitte solicited the "opportunity of proving that if they had infringed the revenue laws, yet none were more ready than they to defend the country and combat its enemies." Jackson apparently was "persuaded that the assistance of these men could not fail being very useful . . . [and] accepted their offers." Although somewhat romantic and patriotic, Latour's brief description provides the only contemporary account of that meeting.[40]

On the evening of December 22, Jackson received intelligence that British sails had been sighted off the three bayous behind Terre aux Boeufs. Such a report meant that the British were within striking distance of the city. The following morning Jackson sent Latour and Tatum to investigate the report. As they traveled south along the river, they encountered several people rushing toward New Orleans. Latour learned from them that British forces had occupied General Jacque Villeré's plantation and had captured the general's son, Major Gabriel Villeré. Tatum immediately returned to tell Jackson of the recent developments while Latour continued south to reconnoiter Villeré's plantation. Cautiously approaching "within rifle shot of those troops," Latour estimated that the British had between 1,600 and 1,800 men. He immediately returned and by 2:00 P.M. had offered Jackson this precise information about the enemy's disposition, location, and strength.[41]

Latour's report prompted Jackson to launch a surprise attack later that evening. In the nighttime operation against the British position some seven miles below the city, Jackson lost more than 10 percent of his force (24 killed, 115 wounded, 74 missing or captured). He also had to retreat without destroying the British advance guard. Historian Henry Adams charged that "the record of American generalship offered many examples of misfortune, but none so complete as this. Neither Hull nor Harrison, Winder or Samuel Smith, had allowed a large British army, heralded long in advance, to arrive within seven miles unseen and unsuspected. . . . The disaster was unprecedented." Such a characterization is unfounded because Jackson had little opportunity to react until he was certain of British intentions. He attacked once he knew, and the surprise subsequently forced the British to delay their operations and to exercise caution. The attack also bought Jackson extra time and could well have been the turning point in the New Orleans campaign. Regardless, during that important operation Jackson reported that "Major Latour, having no command, volunteered his services, and was of great assistance to me."[42]

On December 24, the same day that American and British diplomats signed the Treaty of Ghent ending the war, Jackson moved his army north along the river levee to the old Rodriguez Canal millrace. It was here that Latour supervised the emplacement of artillery and the construction of earthen ramparts on the north side of the canal. After four days of backbreaking, nonstop work, Latour's "formidable" line was ready for use. To strengthen the defenses yet further, Jackson ordered Latour to cut the levee south of the canal, which flooded the ground in front of the American line. Jackson also instructed Major Barthélemy Lafon to do the same below the British lines, surrounding the British with water. Unfortunately, Jackson's plan did not work as well as he hoped, for the temporary swell of the river quickly subsided. The torrent did provide a week's worth of protection as Jackson's troops bolstered their defenses, and the water saturated the ground, creating a quagmire that hindered future British operations.[43]

On that same day Jackson also received an alarming report from the Chef Menteur. Apparently British troops had landed, and this news prompted Jackson to reevaluate enemy operations south of the city. In fact, he almost convinced himself that the troops on Villeré's plantation were but a diversion for a major British attack along Chef Menteur highway. Wanting to corroborate the story before he acted, Jackson sent Latour and 200 Tennesseans to erect batteries at the confluence of the Bayou Sauvage and the Chef Menteur

Pass. When Latour arrived, he did not find a full-scale British assault but rather news that a group of British sailors had set fire to the dry grass of the peninsula; smoke and flames had forced the withdrawal of American forces. Latour returned immediately to New Orleans and informed Jackson that the news had been a rumor and there was no British attack.[44]

Latour arrived at Jackson's headquarters south of the city just as the British launched a frightening rocket attack against the American left. For the better part of a day the British fired Congreve rockets with the expectation that the "noise would strike terror" into the inexperienced Americans. Latour reported, however, that the rockets only wounded ten men and destroyed two caissons. The attack convinced Jackson that the main British army lay before him and that he should strengthen his defensive position. Latour was given responsibility for widening the ditch, raising the height of the rampart, and placing more guns along the length of Jackson's line.[45]

Although Latour had played an important role during the preliminary operations, he was removed from the center of activity just as the British intensified their efforts against Jackson's main line of defense. Jackson dispatched Latour to the west bank of the Mississippi River on December 28 with instructions to build a defensive line stretching west from the river to a cypress swamp. Quickly surveying the area, Latour chose Boisgervais's canal about three miles south of New Orleans. For six days Latour supervised 150 African Americans as they worked on the parapet, but the line was never completed.[46]

Latour did not have enough time to build redoubts or bastions at the canal before Jackson requested a more advanced position. Apparently Jackson wanted a line more closely parallel to the one constructed on the east side of the river. Latour quickly examined a series of advanced positions that were far inferior to the one he had almost finished. Even so, he found a suitable location—a plain between Raguet's and Jourdan's Canals in which the distance between the river and a thicket of woods to the west was 900 yards. Latour believed this position could be adequately manned with General David B. Morgan's limited number of troops and light artillery.[47]

Unfortunately, this defensive line, too, was never completed. Morgan wanted a position farther south, closer to Daniel Patterson's naval batteries on the river. Against Latour's advice he chose a location about a mile below Jackson's line. According to Latour, Morgan made a poor decision and the subsequent "disaster might perhaps have been avoided, had another point for defense been adopted." Morgan's site was a plain about 2,000 yards wide, about twice the length of Jackson's line. Morgan then impressed a band of slaves to dig the breastwork, while his militia watched impassively. When the British finally launched their main assault on January 8, only 200 yards of the line had been completed; the remaining 1,800 yards of Morgan's right flank were guarded only by a canal ditch. This position could not be defended with Morgan's 500 Louisiana militia and his recently arrived 400 Kentucky troops, only 250 of whom were armed.[48]

The beginning of the new year brought a reinvigorated British attack against Jackson's main line. On January 1, 1815, Jackson scheduled a full-dress parade in an attempt to bolster the sagging morale of his troops. Shortly after 10:00 A.M., when the morning fog finally broke, British artillery began concentrating their fire on Jackson's headquarters, the McCarty house. Latour reported that "in less than ten minutes upwards of one hundred balls, rockets and shells struck the house . . . [with] bricks, splinters of wood and furniture, rockets and balls . . . flying in all directions." Everyone within—Jackson and his entire staff, including Latour—was covered with dust and plaster, but no one was injured. This impressive display of British firepower had little impact on Jackson's force.[49]

At dawn on January 8, British General Sir Edwin Pakenham, who had distinguished himself during the Peninsula campaign while serving with his brother-in-law the Duke of Wellington, ordered his veteran troops to make a frontal assault at Chalmette against Jackson's entrenched force. During his two advances that morning against Jackson's line, Pakenham's close ranks ran into a withering flurry of American artillery and rifle fire, which produced devastating British casualties. Within thirty minutes 2,000 redcoats, including Pakenham himself, had been killed. Moreover, British survivors scurried rather than face such murderous fire again. Jackson's makeshift defensive line and heterogeneous force had easily withstood the arrogance of a British frontal attack. Ironically, only a few months earlier similar tactics had brought British forces an overwhelming victory at Bladensburg, allowing them to march uncontested into the American capital of Washington. This time, however, the scenario played out differently.[50]

Latour had played an important contributing role during the events leading up to the major British operation on January 8. Yet one question remains: Where was he on the day of the famous battle at Chalmette? It may never be answered satisfactorily because Latour's account of the engagement does not state his exact location. It is possible that he was with Jackson at Chalmette, especially since the general was aided by his staff during the battle. Yet upon a closer reading of his book, Latour tells readers where he was at given times when he uses first person pronouns. During the battle he proclaims that "all of *us* who were at Jackson's line" felt concern and fear because of the disaster on the west bank; this simple statement may actually provide evidence as to where he was during the event. Yet Latour could have also been on the west bank of the Mississippi River, as he had designed and supervised the construction of defenses there. His subsequent account of the battle may have been an attempt to exonerate himself from the blame associated with the disastrous retreat. Even though he had designed the defenses, Latour makes it clear that it was not his fault the troops fled. In fact, he reminds readers that his defensive line along the Boisgervais's canal ultimately provided the point where American troops rallied. His defensive line had held while Morgan's had failed.[51]

Morgan's feeble force had been completely unprepared for the British attack, and his untrained Kentucky and Louisiana troops broke and ran. They ultimately secured a safe cover at Latour's unfinished line at the Boisgervais's canal. This event was the most controversial one of the campaign, but Latour did not impugn the bravery of the Kentuckians. Instead he blamed their withdrawal on a lack of arms and ammunition, on hunger and exhaustion, and on Morgan's poorly chosen position. Latour insinuated that the affair on the west bank was Morgan's fault, but he decided to leave the decision "to the judgment of the reader."[52]

On the morning after the battle at Chalmette, British naval vessels began bombarding the still unsupported Fort St. Philip downriver. Jackson authorized Latour to recruit skilled laborers from the army and proceed to Fort St. Philip; all who volunteered for this duty received extra pay. The workmen, despite enemy shells and a driving rain, built covers between the guns to shelter the soldiers and strengthened the powder magazines with additional dirt. Although British forces withdrew after an unsuccessful nine-day siege, Latour continued working in the area. In late January he inspected the bayous around New Orleans and offered plans for their defense. Those plans were never implemented, as his tenure with the American army ended on March 17, 1815. The order informing Latour of his discharge also extended his pay for three extra days. Perhaps this was Jackson's way of rewarding Latour for his invaluable service to the American cause.[53]

Latour began to fade again from public view in the months after the Battle of New Orleans, and had it not been for his *Historic Memoir* he might well have been overlooked altogether. During the spring and summer of 1815,

Latour gathered information for his book. By September that "little sharp looking frenchman" was passing through Baltimore on his way to Philadelphia, where his book was published in early March 1816.[54]

In late May of that year, Latour returned to New Orleans, beginning a third professional life—as an agent for Spain. It seems that he joined the Spanish service during the fall of 1815 while in Philadelphia. During his stay there he met with Jean Lafitte, who probably introduced him to the Spanish minister, Luis de Onís. Latour asserted that he met at least twice with Secretary of State James Monroe, with whom he had discussed a second edition of his book. More important, the two had discussed the territorial ambitions of the United States in the Southwest, information that Latour passed along to Spanish officials, who dispatched him on a special expedition into the "Internal Provinces."[55]

From June to November 1816, Latour and Lafitte made a trip on which they supposedly examined the gold region of Arkansas. In reality, the two agents traveled extensively throughout the Southwest, surveyed the region, and prepared maps; they visited the headwaters of the Red, Sabine, Arkansas, and Colorado Rivers, and Latour wrote an exhaustive report concerning American designs on the region. After returning to New Orleans, Latour presented his report to Father Antonio Sedella, head of the Spanish spy network in the Crescent City, who forwarded the information to his superiors; in March 1817 Latour, alias John Williams, traveled to Cuba to meet with Captain General José Cienfuegos and Intendant of the Army Alejandro Ramírez.[56]

While in Cuba, Latour provided Cienfuegos and Ramírez with a copy of his *Historical Memoir* and two reports on conditions within the Spanish empire. The first discussed American plans to foment a slave insurrection in the West Indies as well as pirate and privateer operations in the western Gulf of Mexico. This information offered nothing new to Spanish officials. His second report, the lengthy account of affairs in the "Internal Provinces," warned that should Spain not do something, "the time will come, and unfortunately is not . . . far off, when the Americans . . . will pour in myriads into Mexico." This information, substantiated by other agents, was disseminated to Madrid, to the Spanish minister in Washington, to the viceroy of Mexico, and to the provincial governors of Mexico's northern frontier. Although Latour's report received careful consideration and produced considerable commentary, Spanish officials were unable to counter the threat Americans presented in the borderlands.[57]

Ramírez was nonetheless impressed with the thoroughness of Latour's report and offered him an opportunity to serve Spain as consul in New Orleans. Latour declined, preferring instead to settle in Cuba. By 1818 he had moved to Havana, where he continued his association with the Lafittes and Lafon and with certain French operatives such as Lallemand who planned a colony for Napoleonic emigrés in Texas. Latour opened an architectural firm in Cuba that built the famous Neptune fountain, paved roads and squares, constructed a sewer system in Havana, and erected bridges over the Canimar and Armendariz (now known as the Almendares) Rivers. He also proposed a steamship company that would operate between Havana and Pensacola, Florida.[58]

Latour prospered until January 1829, when his business suddenly went into liquidation; his case was finally resolved five and a half years later, in June 1834, and shortly afterward Latour returned to his native country. When he arrived in France, his friend Charles Lallemand, the governor of Corsica and new Peer of the Kingdom of France, invited him to become his assistant. Although honored by the loyalty of his friend and former associate, Latour declined. His health was deteriorating, and, more important, he wanted to rejoin his son and daughter in Aurillac. During the next two years Latour enjoyed a quiet and peaceful reunion with his family. Ironically, the man who had experienced some of the most exciting and tumultuous events of the age died quietly and unremarkably. On March 21, 1837, at the house of an old aunt in LaCombaldie, near Aurillac, Arsène Lacarrière Latour—engineer, architect, businessman, soldier, historian, and foreign agent—succumbed to a flu epidemic that also killed hundreds of others in the region.[59]

"Fighting the War at My Own Expense"

During the spring of 1815, Latour published a copy of his proposed book abstract in the New Orleans paper *L'Ami des Lois* and collected materials to substantiate his account of the battle of New Orleans; he had actively served during the campaign, and he knew firsthand of the dramatic events and the people involved. He wrote to naval, army, and militia officers as well as state and federal government officials for reports regarding the engagement. He also interviewed eyewitnesses and sent questionnaires to those who had participated requesting information on their activities during the battle.[60]

Latour gathered an impressive array of documents on all facets of the campaign, yet they shed no light on his reasons for writing a book about the battle. Perhaps he had the historical foresight and acumen to understand the importance of the drama in which he had acted. He may even have comprehended that the victory would enhance Jackson's reputation. He had spent much of his life trying to find financial security and might have envisioned the profits a successful book could yield. He had spent a considerable sum of his own money during the battle and even more to publish his book and no doubt hoped that the book would help him recoup his losses.[61]

Another compelling reason for Latour to publish this book was his desire "to perpetuate the memory of Deeds, which will always be considered as an honor to the present generation." Since he wanted posterity to judge the campaign accurately, he assembled many documents relating to the humiliating retreat of David Morgan's Louisiana and Kentucky militia on the west bank. Latour had designed the defenses on the west bank, and this disaster reflected poorly on him. He went to great lengths to explain the reasons for the retreat, insisting that "justice requires that it should be ascertained on which side lies the misconduct, that it may not be wrongfully imputed." He carefully documented the number of troops, their lack of equipment and food, and their exhaustion. After presenting these facts, he wondered "what could be expected from men thus dispirited, ill armed and exhausted with inanition and fatigue?" After all, "veteran troops of the line, in a less perilous situation, have not unfrequently been seized with a panic, and given way." Not surprisingly, this portion of the book reads like an attempt to exonerate the Kentuckians, and perhaps himself, from the charge of cowardice—a damaging one in the early nineteenth century.[62]

Latour was not the only one concerned about his standing. In the following months, several participants contacted him when they learned he was writing a book on the campaign; a frank account could make or break their reputations. General John Adair, commander of the Kentucky militia at Chalmette, was particularly uneasy. Jackson had instructed Adair to send troops to the west bank on the evening of January 7, and it was those men who bolted in the face of enemy fire the following day. Although the troops were exonerated by a court of inquiry, presided over by General William Carroll, Adair nonetheless wanted to be sure that Latour's work backed up that verdict. Adair scrutinized Latour's charts and maps to ensure that the Kentuckians were portrayed in a favorable light. Later A. R. Ellery contacted Latour on Adair's behalf to discuss the project further and to insure that Latour had no "unfavorable idea of Gen. Adair." Adair also wrote to Jackson in March 1815, and Latour secured a copy of the letter, which explained in some detail the circumstances of the Kentuckians' actions. Despite such special pleadings, Jackson still blamed the Kentuckians for the debacle on the west bank. Latour's account acknowledged a disorderly retreat but placed the blame elsewhere.[63]

The court of inquiry that exonerated Adair also found that "the causes of the retreat [were] attributed to the shameful flight of the command of major [Paul] Arnaud, sent to oppose the landing of the enemy." Latour did not concur with those findings. Arnaud had commanded about one hundred ill-equipped and unarmed Louisiana militia—an assessment confirmed by other accounts—who were supposed to prevent the British from landing on the west bank. These men, Latour insisted, had never confronted an enemy in combat, which prompted him to conclude that "it is little strange, then, that they retreated." The book does not condemn the Louisianians or Arnaud. Instead, it blames Morgan for the disaster because he chose a poor defensive position; Latour's assessment reiterates Arnaud's criticism that "the position our troops were occupying was not a good one." Latour was a Frenchman who had made his home in Louisiana, as were those men in Arnaud's 6th Louisiana militia, and he refused to disparage or blame them for Morgan's failures. An interesting note is that Latour dedicated his book to Jackson yet blamed Morgan for the defeat on the west bank, whereas Jackson blamed the Kentuckians and not Morgan or the Louisiana troops.[64]

During the summer of 1815 Latour began composing his book and seeking a publisher. He originally wrote the manuscript in French and asked a friend in Paris to find him a publisher. He soon learned that the costs of printing the text, maps, and portrait of Jackson would be high—almost 2,000 francs without the cost of binding. Latour's friend insisted that he reconsider publishing the book in Paris since "circumstances are not favorable as far as American dealings are concerned." Moreover, the book was "too big"—it should "have several editions"—and would not "have many sales in France." Such reports likely prompted Latour to seek an American publisher.[65]

Latour had H. P. Nugent translate his manuscript into English, and during the fall of 1815 he traveled to the east coast to find a publisher. He spent time in Baltimore with Benjamin Henry Latrobe before "going to Philadelphia about his work on the campaign." He apparently had difficulty finding an American publisher, and later that fall he sent a copy of his prospectus to Thomas Jefferson, who was always willing to offer advice and provide assistance. The former president was so impressed with Latour's outline that he wanted to subscribe for a copy "published in the original language"; al-

changes in style, perhaps correcting some French idioms and eliminating biased epithets such as one referring to the British as "atrocious, ferocious, savage." He also planned to divide the book into chapters, which would strengthen its organization. Otherwise, the only major changes DuPonceau indicated would have been the addition of new documents to the appendix. These materials would have shed further light on the campaign and helped to substantiate the story Latour had told so ably. Although Latour never published a second edition, his book nonetheless has remained a "valuable addition" for historians as well as an indispensable source for studying the New Orleans campaign.[71]

Latour's volume appeared within months of a number of other books on the War of 1812. None of these generally patriotic works focused solely on the Battle of New Orleans; a collection of letters between Adair and Jackson concerning the charge of cowardice was published in Kentucky in 1816, and a treatment of the battle appeared twenty years later. Otherwise, they all concentrated on the war in general and tried to paint it in the best possible terms. Latour's was the first to chronicle the events along the Gulf Coast during the war and the first to capitalize on Andrew Jackson's growing fame afterward.[72] Two years later, John Reid and John Henry Eaton's biography of Jackson, written under the general's personal supervision, further glorified the man who had saved the Crescent City, and the battle served as the backdrop for his rise to prominence. By 1820, interest in the war had declined, even though Jackson's continued popularity carried him to the presidency. Several other biographical tomes would favorably chronicle Jackson's career, but it would not be until after the Mexican War that a second wave of "popular" books emerged about the War of 1812, one of which focused entirely on the battle of New Orleans.[73]

As the mid-nineteenth century approached and as the aging veterans of the War of 1812 died, Americans began to forget about the Second War for Independence. The 1850s brought increased sectional tensions as Americans looked warily toward an uncertain future. Most had little desire to dwell on their glorious past with a national crisis looming. Only after the Civil War did studies such as Benson J. Lossing's *Pictorial Field-Book of the War of 1812* (1869) and Henry Adams's *History of the United States during the Administrations of Thomas Jefferson and James Madison* (1891) reintroduce the reading public to the patriotic War of 1812 and its significance. Both authors relied heavily on Latour as a source of information for their descriptions of the Battle of New Orleans. Ironically, Latour's book had been overshadowed and for the most part forgotten, but it remained the most important firsthand account of military operations during the Battle of New Orleans.

Lossing's *Pictorial Field-Book* was the last American book devoted exclusively to the War of 1812 for almost one hundred years. Not until 1949 did Francis F. Beirne's *The War of 1812* bring the forgotten conflict to twentieth-century readers. Beirne not surprisingly cited Lossing and Adams liberally, both of whom had relied exclusively on Latour for their information on the New Orleans campaign.

The sesquicentennial of the War of 1812 during the early 1960s brought renewed patriotic interest in the conflict, the Battle of New Orleans, and Latour's *Historical Memoir*. In 1964 the University of Florida Press produced a handsomely bound facsimile reprint of Latour's book edited by noted historian Jane Lucas De Grummond. The reprint, one of twelve published in the Florida Quadricentennial Edition under the general editorship of Rembert W. Patrick, was designed to celebrate the historical and cultural heritage of Florida. The reprint had a limited run and soon went out of print, much like Latour's original volume.

The years since the appearance of the De Grummond edition have witnessed a growing interest in the Battle of New Orleans and its importance for the development of the United States as a nation and for Americans as an independent people. In 1965, the Battle of New Orleans Sesquicentennial Commission published a series of pamphlets, under the general editorship of Charles L. Dufour and Leonard V. Huber, to celebrate the momentous occasion. The subsequent nine essays offered views of much-neglected aspects of the battle—the roles of the U.S. Navy, African Americans, and Louisianians and Tennesseans—and they were valuable in raising public consciousness.

The years since have also witnessed a number of important studies related generally to the War of 1812 and specifically to the Battle of New Orleans. Historians Harry L. Coles, Reginald Horsman, John K. Mahon, and, most recently, Donald Hickey have written books entitled *The War of 1812*. Although they all have their individual merits, none of these distinguished scholars offered a comprehensive account of Spanish, British, American, and Native American activities along the Gulf Coast. Wilburt S. Brown's *Amphibious Campaign for West Florida and Louisiana, 1814–1815* (1969) and Robin Reilly's *The British at the Gates* (1974) provide excellent descriptions of the British offensive along the Gulf Coast, but Brown fails to employ extensive manuscript materials and is limited in scope and Reilly does not fully grasp the role of the Spanish, Indians, or African Americans; both have their merits and drawbacks. The most balanced and best researched study since the sesquicentennial is Frank L. Owsley, Jr.'s *Struggle for the Gulf Borderlands: The Creek War and the Battle of New Orleans, 1812–1815*. Using little-known primary sources from England, Spain, and the United States, Owsley offers a comprehensive view, integrating the struggle for the Crescent City into the larger North American conflict.

Numerous other authors have contributed articles and books, all of which advance our knowledge of the Battle of New Orleans. Despite all the new studies on the engagement, Latour's *Historical Memoir* remains a useful and important guide. Anyone undertaking a study of this topic must still consider Latour's remarkably accurate and insightful book. Perhaps the most significant value of the book was and is the impressive collection of primary documents reproduced in the appendix, the firsthand accounts of many individuals who participated in the conflict. Latour served as Jackson's principal engineer and he had access to the accounts and reports of many of the primary participants in the drama. No author can ever have personal access to so many individuals or so much material again. For this reason, if for no other, no new study will ever replace Arsène Lacarrière Latour's *Historical Memoir of the War in West Florida and Louisiana in 1814–15*.

Notes

1. Robert V. Remini, *Andrew Jackson and the Course of American Empire* (New York: Harper and Row, Publishers, 1977), 294–95; Joesph C. Tregle, Jr., "Andrew Jackson and the Continuing Battle of New Orleans," *Journal of the Early Republic* 1 (Winter 1984): 373–74.

2. *The North American Review and Miscellaneous Journal* 3 (July 1816): 233.

3. Ibid., 233; Donald R. Hickey, *The War of 1812: A Forgotten Conflict* (Urbana: University of Illinois Press, 1989), 23; Reginald Horsman, *The Causes of the War of 1812* (New York: A.S. Barnes and Company, 1962), passim.

4. Hickey, *The War of 1812*, 2–3; Charles B. Sellers, *The Market Revolution: Jacksonian America, 1815–1846* (New York: Oxford University Press, 1991), 3–4; Remini, *Andrew Jackson*, 295–97.

5. Remini, *Andrew Jackson*, 317–21.

6. Arsène Lacarrière Latour to Andrew Jackson, 16 August 1815, printed in preface of Arsène Lacarrière Latour, *Historical Memoir of the War in West Florida and Louisiana, 1814–15* (Philadelphia: John Conrad and Company, 1816); also see Latour, xix–xx.

7. Jean Garrigoux, *Un Aventurier Visionnaire: L'étrange parcours d'un Français aux Amériques* [A visionary adventurer: The strange course of a Frenchman in America] (La Haute-Auvergne: Société des lettres, sciences et arts, 1997), 9, 20–22, 28–29.

8. Ibid., 35–37.

9. Ibid., 37–40.

10. Ibid., 57; Martine Bardon, presentation, "Arsène Lacarrière Latour: His Life in Paris in 1802," 2–3, The Historic New Orleans Collection, New Orleans.

11. Garrigoux, *Un Aventurier Visionnaire*, 68–69.

12. Ibid., 72–73.

13. C. L. R. James, *The Black Jacobins: Toussaint L'Ouverture and the San Domingo Revolution* (New York: Vintage Books, 1963), 358–61, 366–69.

14. Garrigoux, *Un Aventurier Visionnaire*, 72–73.

15. Edwin H. Carpenter, Jr., "Latour's Report on Spanish-American Relations in the Southwest," *Louisiana Historical Quarterly*, 30 (July 1947): 716; George W. Cullum, *Campaigns of the War of 1812–15 Against Great Britain* (New York: James Miller, Publisher, 1879), 310; Latour, *Historical Memoir*, 8; Samuel Carter III, *Blaze of Glory: The Fight for New Orleans, 1814–1815* (New York: St. Martin's Press, 1971), 106–7.

16. Militia Returns, January 21, 1806, 4:633, July 1, 1806, 4:698, and H. Molier to William C. C. Claiborne, January 21, 1806, 4:574, in Clarence Edwin Carter, ed., *The Territorial Papers of the United States: Territory of Orleans* (Washington: Government Printing Office, 1940); Frank Lawrence Owsley, Jr., and Gene A. Smith, *Filibusters and Expansionists: Jeffersonian Manifest Destiny, 1800–1821* (Tuscaloosa: University of Alabama Press, 1997), 54–55; Harris Gaylord Warren, *The Sword Was Their Passport: A History of American Filibustering in the Mexican Revolution* (Baton Rouge: Louisiana State University Press, 1943), 19; Stanley Clisby Arthur, *Jean Laffite: Gentleman Rover* (New Orleans: Harmanson, 1952), 81; Robert C. Vogel, "Jean Lafitte, the Baratarians, and the Historical Geography of Piracy in the Gulf of Mexico," *Gulf Coast Historical Review* 5 (1990): 67–68.

17. Royal Ornan Shreve, *The Finished Scoundrel: General James Wilkinson* (Indianapolis: Bobbs Merrill Company, 1933), 132–33; Dumas Malone, *Jefferson the President: Second Term, 1805–1809* (Boston: Little, Brown and Company, 1974), 218–19.

18. James Wilkinson, "Reflections on Louisiana by Vincente Folch," in *Louisiana Under the Rule of Spain, France, and the United States, 1785–1807*, edited by James Alexander Robertson, (Cleveland: Arthur H. Clark Company, 1911), 325–47 (Folch's signature was on the document to protect Wilkinson's identity); Shreve, *The Finished Scoundrel*, 132–33; Malone, *Jefferson the President*, 218–19; David Hart White, *Vincente Folch, Governor in Spanish Florida, 1787–1811* (Washington: University Press of America, 1981), 76.

19. William C. C. Claiborne to Post Master General, June 17, 1805, in *Official Letterbooks of W.C.C. Claiborne, 1801–1816*, edited by Dunbar Rowland (Jackson: Mississippi Department of Archives and History, 1917), 96–98; Shreve, *The Finished*

Scoundrel, 132–33; Malone, *Jefferson the President*, 218–19; Isaac Joslin Cox, "General Wilkinson and his Later Intrigues with the Spaniards," *American Historical Review* 19 (July 1914): 800–801.

20. Garrigoux, *Un Aventurier Visionnaire*, 78–80.

21. Gene A. Smith, *"For the Purposes of Defense": The Politics of the Jeffersonian Gunboat Program* (Newark: University of Delaware Press, 1995), 39–40, 45–46; Garrigoux, *Un Aventurier Visionnaire*, 78–82; Henry Dearborn to A. Lacarrière Latour, November 1, 1805, Miscellaneous Letters Sent by the Secretary of War, 1800–1809, National Archives, RG 107, M370.

22. William B. Hatcher, *Edward Livingston: Jeffersonian Republican and Jacksonian Democrat* (Baton Rouge: Louisiana State University Press, 1940), 106–7, 119, 123, 144–85; Garrigoux, *Un Aventurier Visionnaire*, 82–83.

23. A. Lacarrière Latour, "Plano de la villa de Baton Rouge," map published in 1809, Louisiana State University, Baton Rouge; Garrigoux, *Un Aventurier Visionnaire*, 84–85; Rose Meyers, *A History of Baton Rouge, 1699–1812* (Baton Rouge: Louisiana State University Press, 1976), 75, 82–83; Stanley Clisby Arthur, *The Story of the West Florida Rebellion* (St. Francisville, La.: St. Francisville *Democrat*, 1935), 26; Isaac J. Cox, *The West Florida Controversy, 1798–1813* (Baltimore: Johns Hopkins University Press, 1918; reprint, New York: Peter Smith, 1967), 150–51, 314.

24. Claiborne to Jefferson, March 18, 1806, 3:270, June 22, 1806, 3:343, and Claiborne to James Madison, June 8, 1808, 4:176–77, all in Claiborne, *Official Letterbooks;* Garrigoux, *Un Aventurier Visionnaire*, 97–98; Latour to Mr. Peret, July 10, 1806, Latour to Marquis de Lafayette, n.d., both in Marquis de Lafayette Papers, The Henry E. Huntington Library, San Marino, California.

25. *Gazette de la Louisiane*, 22 September 1810; *Louisiana Courier*, 17 October 1810; Edwin H. Carpenter, Jr., "Arsène Lacarrière Latour," *Hispanic American Historical Review* 18 (May 1938): 222.

26. Carpenter, "Arsène Lacarrière Latour," 222–23; Benjamin Henry Boneval Latrobe, *Impressions Respecting New Orleans*, edited by Samuel Wilson, Jr. (New York: Columbia University Press, 1951), 23, 41; Harnett T. Kane, *Queen New Orleans: City by the River* (New York: William Morrow & Company, 1949), 360; Samuel Wilson, Jr., ed., *Southern Travels: Journal of John H. B. Latrobe, 1834* (New Orleans: The Historic New Orleans Collection, 1986), 49n., 76n.; Stanley Clisby Arthur, *Old New Orleans* (New Orleans: Harmanson, 1936), 61.

27. Claiborne to Benjamin H. Latrobe, May 24, 1811, Claiborne, *Official Letterbooks*, 5:255; Talbot Hamlin, *Benjamin Henry Latrobe* (New York: Oxford University Press, 1955), 355–58; Benjamin Henry Latrobe to Latour, September 17, 1811, June 5, 1814, and Latrobe to Andrew Jackson, September 3, 1815, all in Benjamin Henry Latrobe Papers, Maryland Historical Society, Baltimore.

28. Carpenter, "Arsène Lacarrière Latour," 223; Jane Lucas de Grummond, introduction to reprint of Latour's *Historical Memoir* (Gainesville: University of Florida Press, 1964), xxxvi.

29. Remini, *Andrew Jackson*, 244–46.

30. Ibid., 236–45; Thomas Butler to Latour, December 17, 1814, file 1, Arsène Lacarrière Latour Archives, Historic New Orleans Collection.

31. Remini, *Andrew Jackson*, 249–50; Edward Livingston to Andrew Jackson, November 5, 21, 1814, Andrew Jackson Papers, Library of Congress.

32. Charles Gayarré, *History of Louisiana* (New York: William J. Widdleton, Publisher, 1866), 4:385; Remini, *Andrew Jackson*, 249–51; Andrew Jackson to William C. C. Claiborne, September 30, 1814, in *The Papers of Andrew Jackson*, edited by Harold D. Moser et al. (Knoxville: University of Tennessee Press, 1991), 3:151–52; Arthur, *Jean Laffite*, 99–100; Carter, *Blaze of Glory*, 106; Wilburt S. Brown, *The Amphibious Campaign for West Florida and Louisiana 1814–1815* (Tuscaloosa: University of Alabama Press, 1969), 63.

33. John Shaw to Daniel Patterson, December 21, 1813, Letters Received by the Secretary of the Navy: Captains' Letters, 1805–61, National Archives, RG45, M125; Frank Lawrence Owsley, Jr., *Struggle for the Gulf Borderlands: The Creek War and the Battle of New Orleans, 1812–1815* (Gainesville: University Press of Florida, 1981), 126–27.

34. Owsley, *Struggle for the Gulf*, 126–27.

35. Carter, *Blaze of Glory*, 135–36; Owsley, *Struggle for the Gulf*, 126–27; Brown, *The Amphibious Campaign*, 83.

36. Brown, *Amphibious Campaign*, 48; Gene A. Smith, "Floating a Republican Idea: Jefferson's Gunboats at New Orleans," *Military History of the West* 24 (Fall 1994): 104–5; Alexander Cochrane to John Wilson Coker, March 9, 1815, *The Naval Chronicle* 23 (1815): 337; "Autobiography of Admiral R. Aitchison," 64, original manuscript in the Historic New Orleans Collection.

37. Remini, *Andrew Jackson*, 251; Arthur, *Jean Lafitte*, 101; Cullum, *Campaigns of the War of 1812–15*, 310–11; Howell Tatum, *Major H. Tatum's Journal while Acting Topographical Engineer to General Jackson* (Northampton, Mass.: Smith College Studies in History, 1922), 98–101; Thomas Butler to Latour, December 17, 1814, file 1, Latour Archives; Andrew Jackson to William C. C. Claiborne, December 10, 1814, *Papers of Andrew Jackson*, 3:201–3.

38. Remini, *Andrew Jackson*, 251; Tatum, *Journal*, 102–3; Andrew Jackson to John Coffee, December 16, 1814, *Papers of Andrew Jackson*, 3:205–6.

39. Remini, *Andrew Jackson*, 257–59; Tatum, *Journal*, 104; Andrew Jackson to New Orleans Citizens, December 16, 1814, *Papers of Andrew Jackson*, 3:206–7.

40. Remini, *Andrew Jackson*, 253; Latour, *Historical Memoir*, 71–72.

41. Latour, *Historical Memoir*, 87–88; Tatum, *Journal*, 107; Robin Reilly, *The British at the Gates: The New Orleans Campaign in the War of 1812* (New York: G.P. Putnam's Sons, 1974), 240.

42. Latour, *Historical Memoir*, 91–101; Tatum, *Journal*, 107–10; Henry Adams, *History of the United States during the Administration of Thomas Jefferson and James Madison* (reprint; New York: Literary Classics of the United States, Inc., 1986), 2:1147; Jackson to the Secretary of War, December 27, 1812, in Latour, *Historical Memoir*, xlv–xlvii.

43. Latour, *Historical Memoir*, 112–13; Tatum, *Journal*, 111–12; Carter, *Blaze of Glory*, 188.

44. Latour, *Historical Memoir*; 114–17; Carter, *Blaze of Glory*, 197.

45. Latour, *Historical Memoir*; 121–22.

46. Ibid., 124–25; Carter, *Blaze of Glory*, 236; Tessier to Latour, April 12, 1815, file 18, Latour Archives.

47. Latour, *Historical Memoir*; 166–67; Carter, *Blaze of Glory*, 236; Owsley, *Struggle for the Gulf*, 154.

48. Latour, *Historical Memoir*; 167–70; Carter, *Blaze of Glory*, 236–37; Reilly, *British at the Gates*, 297; Paul Arnaud to Latour, July 27, 1815, file 21, Tessier to Latour, April 15, 1815, file 18, and testimony of Lefebvre concerning work on the Fortifications of Camp Jourdan, March 15, 1815, file 3, all in Latour Archives.

49. Latour, *Historical Memoir*; 132; Tatum, *Journal*, 121; Carter, *Blaze of Glory*, 222.

50. William Priestly to Latour, March 4, 1816, including a sketch of the part Major General William Carroll and his division played during the campaign, file 26, Latour Archives.

51. Latour, *Historical Memoir*; 164, 173.

52. "Proceeding of a court of Inquiry concerning the conduct of Dejean and Cavelier, officers in the army of General Morgan," February 9–12, 1815, file 46, Latour Archives; Latour, *Historical Memoir*; 174–75; Carter, *Blaze of Glory*, 266–67.

53. Latour, *Historical Memoir*; 187–97; Henri Chotard to Latour, January 10, file 2, March 17, 1815, file 4, and Latour to Andrew Jackson, January 30, 1815, file 33, all in Latour Archives; John Reid to Howell Tatum and Latour, January 27, 1815, Chicago Historical Society.

54. Paul Arnaud to Latour, July 27, 1815, file 21, Tessier to Latour, April 12, 1815, file 18, and testimony of Lefebvre concerning work on the Fortifications of Camp Jourdan, March 15, 1815, file 3, all in Latour Archives; Benjamin Henry Latrobe to Henry Latrobe, September 18, 1815, Latrobe Papers.

55. Benjamin Henry Latrobe to Latour, May 3, 1816, Latrobe Papers; Carpenter, "Arsène Lacarrière Latour," 224; Carpenter, "Latour's Report on Spanish-American Relations in the Southwest," 716; Luis de Onís to Pedro de Cevallos, January 29, 1816, Archivo Histórico Nacional (AHN), Estado Legajo 5559, Expediente 26, 388; James Monroe to Andrew Jackson, July 3, 1816, Andrew Jackson Papers.

56. Dr. and Mrs. T. L. Hodges, "Jean Lafitte and Major L. Latour in Arkansas Territory," *Arkansas Historical Quarterly* 7 (Winter 1948): 237–56; Carpenter, "Arsène Lacarrière Latour," 224–27; Carpenter, "Latour's Report on Spanish-American Relations in the Southwest," 715–37; Ruíz de Apodaca to the Minister of State, June 3, 1818, AHN, Est. Leg. 5562, Exp. 5, 234–235; José Cienfuegos to León, April 29, 1817, AHN, Est. Leg. 5559, Exp. 26, 427–28; Luis de Onís to Pedro Cevallos, January 29, 1816, ibid., 388.

57. Carpenter, "Arsène Lacarrière Latour," 225–27; Carpenter, "Latour's Report on Spanish-American Relations in the Southwest," 730; Arthur, *Jean Lafitte*, 146–47.

58. Carpenter, "Arsène Lacarrière Latour," 224–25; Carpenter, "Latour's Report

on Spanish-American Relations in the Southwest," 730; Garrigoux, *Un Aventurier Visionnaire*, 262–66.

59. Garrigoux, *Un Aventurier Visionnaire*, 301–15; Carpenter, "Latour's Report on Spanish-American Relations in the Southwest," 717.

60. *Friend of the Laws*, March 21, 1815; Questionnaire Regarding Kentucky Troops Movements, n.d. [1815], file 11, Tessier to Latour, April 12, 1815, file 18, Jackson to Latour, May 19, 1815, file 19, Cholester to Morton, August 15, 1815, file 22, Edward Livingston to General Mason, n.d., file 25, all in Latour Archives.

61. Triquer to Latour, August 19, 1815, file 23, Latour to Edward Livingston, November 1, 1816, file 29, both in Latour Archives.

62. Peter S. DuPonceau to James Monroe, July 20, 1816, Monroe Papers, Library of Congress; manuscript containing troop information under General Morgan, 1815, file 8, narrative of [?] Thomas concerning the army under General Morgan, 1815, file 9, document abstract of troop strength of William C. C. Claiborne's force, December 25, 1814, files 12 and 13, a report of the strength of General Morgan's force, January 12, 1815, file 14, all in Latour Archives; Latour, *Historical Memoir*, 170, 173–75.

63. John Adair to Latour, n.d., file 10, A. R. Ellery to Latour, June 12, 1815, file 20, Adair to Jackson, March 20, 1815, file 34, and Jackson to Adair, April 2, 1815, file 35, all in Latour Archives; Remini, *Andrew Jackson*, 287–88.

64. "Extracts of the Proceedings of a Court of Inquiry into the retreat on the right bank of the Mississippi on 8 January 1815," Latour, *Historical Memoir*, cxxxii, 168–69; Tessier to Latour, April 12, 1815, file 18, Paul Arnaud to Latour, July 27, 1815, file 21, Morgan to Jackson, January 17, 1815, file 32, fragment of a copy of testimony concerning the Louisiana militia, n.d., file 47, all in Latour Archives; Remini, *Andrew Jackson*, 288.

65. "Manuscript fragments of the *Historical Memoir* with annotations, in French," files 5, 6, and 7, Triquer to Latour, August 19, 1815, file 23, all in Latour Archives.

66. Edward Livingston to Lewis Livingston, July 1815, in Charles Havens Hunt, *Life of Edward Livingston* (New York: D. Appleton and Company, 1864), 213–15; Benjamin Henry Latrobe to Henry Latrobe, September 18, 1815, Latrobe Papers; Thomas Jefferson to Latour, October 26, 1815, file 24, Latour to M. Livingston, November 1, 1816, file 29, both in Latour Archives.

67. Peter S. DuPonceau to Latour, June 17, 1816, file 27, James Workman to Latour, September 15, 1816, file 28, both in Latour Archives; *The North American Review and Miscellaneous Journal* 3 (July 1816): 265–66.

68. Benjamin Henry Latrobe to Henry Latrobe, May 3, 1816, Latrobe Papers; James Workman to Latour, September 15, 1816, file 28, Peter S. DuPonceau to Latour, June 17, 1816, file 27, Triquer to Latour, August 19, 1815, file 23, D. E. Williams to Latour, January 7, 1817, file 31, James Monroe to Jackson, September 5, 27, October 10, 21, December 7, 10, 1814, February 5, 13, March 13, 1815, file 15, Monroe to the Governor of Tennessee, seven letters, file 16, Monroe to the Governor of Kentucky, seven letters including January 20, 1815, file 17, Monroe to the Governor of Georgia, 4 letters, file 17, all in Latour Archives.

69. Latour to M. Livingston, November 1, 1816, file 29, invoice for Dr. Major A. L. Latour, April 26, 1816, file 30, both in Latour Archives.

70. DuPonceau to Latour, June 17, 1816, file 27, Latour to M. Livingston, November 1, 1816, file 29, both in Latour Archives; Peter Stephen DuPonceau to James Monroe, July 20, 1816, Monroe Papers; James Monroe to Andrew Jackson, 3 July 1816, Jackson Papers; James Monroe to [?] [probably Peter Stephen DuPonceau], June 3, 1816, in private collection of William C. Cook, Nashville, Tennessee.

71. *The North American Review and Miscellaneous Journal* 3 (July 1816): 266; Peter S. DuPonceau to James Monroe, July 20, 1816, Monroe Papers.

72. American books that appeared at about the same time as Latour's include Thomas O'Connor, *Impartial and Correct History of the War* (New York: John Low, 1815); *History of the American War of 1812* (Philadelphia: William M'Carty, 1815); H. M. Brackenridge, *History of the Late War Between the United States and Great Britain* (Baltimore: Joseph Cushington, 1816); Gilbert J. Hunt, *The Late War Between the United States and Great Britain* (New York: David Longworth, 1816); J.C. Gilleland, *History of the Late War between the United States and Great Britain* (Baltimore: Schaeffer and Maund, 1817); *Letters of Gen. Adair and Gen. Jackson relative to the charge of cowardice made by the latter against the Kentucky troops at New Orleans* (Lexington, 1816); and Paris M. Davis, *Official and full detail of the great battle of New Orleans* (New York, 1836). William C. Cook, "Early Iconography of the Battle of New Orleans, 1815–1819," *Tennessee Historical Quarterly* 48 (Winter 1989): 218–37, is the best examination of early printed and illustrative work on the Battle of New Orleans.

73. Examples of post–Mexican War literature on the War of 1812 include Charles J. Ingersoll, *Historical Sketch of the Second War between the United States and Great Britain*, 2 vols. (Philadelphia: Lea and Blanchard, 1845–49); Charles J. Peterson, *The Military Heroes of the War of 1812* (Philadelphia: W. A. Leary, 1848); John S. Jenkins, *The Generals of the Late War with Great Britain* (Auburn, N.Y.: Derby, Miller and Company, 1849); Richard Hildreth, *The History of the United States of America, from the Adoption of the Federal Constitution to the End of the Sixteenth Congress*, 3 vols. (New York: Harper and Brothers, 1852), vol. 3; Joel T. Headley, *The Second War with England* (New York: Charles Scribner, 1853); and *An Authentic Narrative of the memorable achievements of the Amer. Army before New Orleans* (New York: J. C. Darby and H. W. Darby, 1856).

HISTORICAL MEMOIR

OF

THE WAR

IN

WEST FLORIDA AND LOUISIANA.

MAJ.R G.AL ANDREW JACKSON

Entered according to act of Congress

HISTORICAL MEMOIR

OF

THE WAR

IN

WEST FLORIDA AND LOUISIANA.

IN 1814–15.

WITH AN ATLAS

BY MAJOR A. LACARRIERE LATOUR
Principal Engineer in the late Seventh Military District United States' Army,

WRITTEN ORIGINALLY IN FRENCH, AND TRANSLATED FOR THE AUTHOR,
BY H. P. NUGENT, ESQ.

Bis Tusci Rutulos egere ad *castra* reversos,
Bis rejecti armis respectant terga tegentes.
Turbati fugiunt Rutuli——————
Disjectique duces, desolatique manipli,
Tuta petunt.—————— *Virg.*

PHILADELPHIA:
PUBLISHED BY JOHN CONRAD AND CO.
J. Maxwell, printer.
1816.

TO

MAJ. GEN. ANDREW JACKSON.

SIR,

Allow me to offer you the following pages, in which I have endeavoured to record the events of that memorable campaign which preserved our country from conquest and desolation. The voice of the whole nation has spared me the task of showing how much of these important results are due to the energy, ability and courage of a single man.

Receive, sir, with this inadequate tribute to your high merits, the assurance of respect and devotion with which I have the honour to be,

Sir,

Your most obedient

and humble servant,

A. LACARRIERE LATOUR.

New Orleans, August 16, 1815.

PREFACE.

THE immense debt of Great Britain, and the expenses of a war carried on for nearly twenty years with hardly any intermission, having exhausted the ordinary sources of her riches, while the war continued to rage with greater fury than ever, she found herself compelled to create new resources to enable her to persevere in the arduous struggle in which she was engaged. For this purpose the rights of neutral nations, founded on the principles of natural equity, established for many ages by the unanimous consent of civilized nations, and secured by the faith of a long succession of treaties, were openly violated by the English government, which, prompted by its inordinate ambition, wished to appropriate to itself the lives and fortunes of their peaceable citizens. To accomplish this purpose, it became necessary to set aside those principles which, until then, had been universally acknowledged, and to substitute new political axioms in their stead. By the mere arbitrary declaration of the British cabinet, the right of blockade was extended over the most extensive coasts, which all the maritime power of the world combined could not have blockaded with effect.* The obsolete right of searching neutral

*The pretended right of blockade never appeared in so ridiculous a light as immediately after the departure of the emperor Napoleon from the island of Elba. It was then strongly surmised, and not without some probability, that the British government had connived at his escape, and to refute this charge, lord Liverpool was compelled to declare in the house of lords, on the 7th of April, 1815, (see the newspapers of the times) *that the whole British navy would be insufficient to blockade the island of Elba;* it is true, he added the qualifying sentence: *so as to prevent the escape of an individual who chose to leave it.* But when we consider the manner in which Napoleon sailed from that island, with several armed vessels, and a considerable body of troops, who will not laugh at the blockading pretensions of Great Britain, if it is true, as lord Liverpool clearly meant to intimate, that *the whole British navy* was insufficient to prevent *such an escape* from a *small island*?

Mathematical truth is not to be looked for in the speeches of British ministers; the blockade of the port of Rochefort by a single squadron, which afterwards so effectually prevented the same individual from escaping, *even in an open boat*, is an incontestible proof

ships for enemy's property, this absurd remnant of the barbarous jurisprudence of the dark ages, justly rejected by the more enlightened policy of later times, was revived and enforced with increased severity, and the right of pressing seamen on board of neutral vessels was claimed as a consequence of the same principle, while, by a further extension of the rights of belligerents, the trade of neutrals with the colonial possession of enemies, was at times entirely prohibited, and at others partially tolerated, by decrees which the belligerent government could construe at pleasure, and which only served to allure the unwary, and secure a certain prey to the hungry swarm of British cruisers. Thus the plunder of neutrals, and the impressment of their seamen, were erected into a system, the true principles of which could only be discovered from its effects.

The United States of America, whose industrious citizens carried on a regular and immense commerce with all the nations of the globe, which had long excited the jealousy of their powerful rival, experienced more than any other nation the pernicious effects of the new system, conceived and executed by this overbearing state; and indeed it appeared to have been established principally with a view to check their commercial pursuits. The American vessels were plundered, detained, or confiscated. The mariners were impressed upon the most frivolous pretences, put on board the ships of war of His Britannic majesty, and subjected to the most rigorous treatment, in order to compel them to shed their blood in a cause which they were not interested. On the high seas, in neutral harbours, upon the coasts, and even in the waters exclusively subject to the jurisdiction of the United States, the American seamen were seized by the petty officers of the British navy, who constituted themselves judges, *de facto*, of the most sacred prerogatives of man, and from the mere similarity of names, or, as their caprice dictated, transformed a free citizen into a slave, without regard to the place of his birth, or to the natural and unalienable right, that all men have to choose their country. The sacred flag of the government itself was no longer a sufficient protection; the sanctuary of a ship of war was violated—freemen were dragged by force and carried away, in savage triumph, from an American frigate sailing quietly, in the midst of a profound peace;—the most ignomini-

---

of lord Liverpool's exaggeration; but it is not the less true, that his assertion, exaggerated as it is, will ever remain the most cutting satire against the absurd claims of his government on the subject of blockade.

ous punishment—But I forbear.—This unheard of outrage, which then, for the first time, astonished the world, has been since sufficiently avenged.

The American government at first only opposed to these enormous violations of the law of nations mild and conciliating representations, and pacific measures, which produced only some partial and momentary disavowals and reparations. With the humane view of saving the country from the horrors of war, and in hopes of inducing England to adopt principles of equity and moderation, by making her government perceive that the people of America would never submit to measures so tyrannical and degrading, the national legislature resolved to interdict every sort of foreign commerce, and laid an embargo on all the ports of the United States.

This measure received the approbation of the whole nation. The citizens no longer deceived themselves with respect to the views and motives of the British government. They preferred submitting for a time to the inconveniences which the stagnation of commerce would naturally produce, to seeing their country exposed to endless humiliations, or compelled to engage in a war, the effects of which could not be calculated. For it was believed by many, that the constitution of the United States was only suited for a state of peace, and that war would infallibly produce a dissolution of the union. These considerations were weighty, and might well induce a nation to pause before it involved itself in a contest which seemed to threaten such a fatal issue.—The embargo was then a wise measure, as there appeared no alternative between it and war. Indeed it is probable that if it had been continued, we might have avoided a recourse to arms, and compelled Great Britain to return to the practice, if not to the principles of justice.

But it was not so ordered, and after little more than one year the embargo was removed. Let us throw a patriotic veil over the causes which produced this unexpected step. It does not belong to me to inquire into its expediency or its motives. Such an inquiry is entirely foreign to the purposes of this work. As it was to be expected, the resumption of maritime commerce was followed by a renewal of spoliations on the part of Great Britain, who mistook our patience for weakness, and ascribed to timidity and other unworthy motives, a conduct which merely arose from an earnest and laudable desire to preserve peace, and avoid the effusion of human blood. Far from foreseeing the privations and hardships to which the people of America would submit, and the exertions which they were capable of making, if driven to extremity, Britain, blinded by her pride, saw in the removal of the embargo nothing else than the result of an inordinate thirst for maritime commerce, and an effeminate attachment to the luxuries with which she had been in the habit of supplying us. As little she foresaw how much she would have to suffer before she discovered her mistake—how much of her treasure was to be spent, and of her blood was to be spilt, before she should be taught to know the spirit and perseverance of a nation which she affected to view with contempt. At last the repetition of injuries filled the measure of American long-animity, and WAR was solemnly declared by the United States, on the 18th of June, 1812. So little premeditated was this measure—so much was it produced by a sudden burst of the national indignation, that no preparations had been made to support the dreadful contest that was now about to take place. Our military establishment was hardly sufficient to afford garrisons for the most exposed points of our widely-extended frontier—the numerous ports upon our sea-board were left exposed, unguarded and unfortified, and our marine consisted only of a few ships of war. But the bravery and energy of our citizens promised abundant resources for our military operations on the land side, and the skill and martial ardour of our seamen, and particularly their excellent commanders, presaged certain and glorious triumphs on the ocean. The riches of an immense soil, and the activity and patriotism of its inhabitants, gave a sufficient pledge to the government to justify the reliance which they had placed on the aid and co-operation of the nation, which, on another and ever-memorable occasion, had proved to the world that there are no sacrifices that it is not ready to make in support of its independence, and in the defence of its just rights.

Thus the United States were forced into a war which they had not provoked;—America took up arms in support of her rights, and for the preservation of her national honour, with a firm determination not to lay them down until the object should be attained. Providence blessed our efforts, and our arms were crowned with the most brilliant triumphs over those of our enemy. The army and navy exhibited a noble rivalship of zeal, devotion, and glory. In the one Lawrence, Bainbridge, Decatur, Perry, M'Donough, Porter;—in the other Pike, Scott, Brown, Jackson, and many more, proved to the enemy, and to the world, that we possessed resolution to defend our rights, and power to avenge our injuries.

The relation of these various exploits is the proper province of history. An abler pen than mine will one day consecrate to posterity this monument of American fame. My humble task has been to collect a part of the materials that may serve to erect it, and which I offer in the present work.

The volume which I present to the public is devoted to the relation of the campaign of the end of 1814 and beginning of 1815: that is to say, from the first arrival of the British forces on the coast of Louisiana, in September, until the total evacuation, in consequence of the treaty of peace, including a period of about seven months. During that space of time, particularly from 14th of December to the 19th of January, events of the highest importance succeeded each other with rapidity; but it was in the short period, from the 23d of December, the day of the landing of the British troops, to the memorable 8th of January, that the American arms acquired that lustre which no time can efface.

Nec poterit tempus, nec edax abolere vetustas.

The preparations which the British government had made for the conquest of Louisiana were immense. So certain were they of complete success, that a full set of officers, for the administration of civil government, from the judge down to the tide-waiter, had embarked on board of the squadron with the military force. The British speculators, who are always found in the train of military expeditions, had freighted a part of the transports for conveying the expected booty, which they estimated beforehand at more than fourteen millions of dollars. The British government well knew that they could not keep Louisiana, even if they should obtain the possession of it. They were not ignorant that the western states could pour down, if necessary, one hundred thousand men to repel the invaders; they therefore could only rely on a momentary occupation, which they hoped, nevertheless, to prolong sufficiently to give them time to pillage and lay waste the country. Therefore they had neglected no means of securing the plunder which they expected to make. Such, indeed, was their certainty of success that it was not thought necessary in Europe to conceal the object of the expedition. At Bordeaux, at the time of the embarkation of the troops, the conquest of Louisiana was publicly spoken of as an enterprize that could not fail of succeeding, and the British officers spoke of that campaign as of a party of pleasure, in which there was to be neither difficulty nor danger. It is even asserted, (though I will not vouch for the truth of the assertion) that the prime minister of Great Britain, lord Castlereagh, being at Paris when the news of the capture of Washington arrived there, boasted publicly that New Orleans and Louisiana would soon be in the power of his countrymen.* Yet this formidable expedi-

**Niles's Historical Register*, vol. vii. p. 389.

tion had already sailed from Europe when its precise object and destination were not known in America. It will be seen, in the course of this memoir, that about the beginning of December, the greatest part of the British force had arrived on our coast, when general Jackson had hardly sufficient time to make the first preparations for defence. Without fearing to be accused of flattery, we may justly call him (under God) *the saviour of Louisiana:* for, in the space of a few days, with discordant and heterogeneous elements, he created and organized the little army which succeeded so well in humbling the British pride. It is true, that the love of country, the hatred of England, the desire of avenging the outrages which we had suffered from that haughty power, fired every heart;—but all this would have availed nothing without the energy of the commander-in-chief: which will appear so much the more extraordinary, when it is considered that he was constantly sick during this memorable campaign, so much so that he was on the point of being obliged to resign his command. Although his body was ready to sink under the weight of sickness, fatigue, and continual watching, his mind, nevertheless, never lost for a moment that energy which he knew so well how to communicate to all that surrounded him. To obstacles, which to others would have appeared insurmountable—to the want of the most indispensable supplies for the army, he opposed the most constant perseverance, until he succeeded either in obtaining what was required, or in creating supplementary resources.

I have already said, that the energy manifested by general Jackson spread, as it were, by contagion, and communicated itself to the whole army. I shall add, that there was nothing which those who composed it did not feel themselves capable of performing, if he ordered it to be done; it was enough that he expressed a wish, or threw out the slightest intimation, and immediately a crowd of volunteers offered themselves to carry his views into execution. Such perfect harmony—so entire and reciprocal a confidence between the troops and their commander, could not fail to produce the happiest effects. Therefore, although our army was, as I have already observed, composed of heterogeneous elements, of men speaking different languages, and brought up in different habits, the most perfect union and harmony never ceased for a moment to prevail in our camp. No one can better than myself bear testimony to the good understanding that reigned among our troops. In the course of the labours at the fortifications, which were erected under my direction, I had occasion to employ soldiers in fatigue duty, who were drafted by detachments from each of the several corps. These men were kept hard at work even to the middle of the night, and by that means lost the little portion of sleep which they could have snatched in the interval of their military duties. I was almost constantly with them, superintending their labours; but I may truly say, that I never heard among them the least murmur of discontent, nor saw the least sign of impatience. Nay, more, four-fifths of our army were composed of militia-men or volunteers, who, it might be supposed, would with difficulty have submitted to the severe discipline of a camp, and of course would often have incurred punishment; yet nothing of the kind took place; and I solemnly declare, that not the smallest military punishment was inflicted. This is a fact respecting which I defy contradiction in the most formal manner. What, then, was the cause of this miracle? The love of country, the love of liberty. It was the consciousness of the dignity of man—it was the noblest of feelings, which pervaded and fired the souls of our defenders—which made them bear patiently with their sufferings, because the country required it of them. They felt that they ought to resist an enemy who had come to invade and to subdue their country;—they knew that their wives, their children, their nearest and dearest friends were but a few miles behind their encampment, who, but for their exertions, would inevitably become the victim and the prey of a licentious soldiery. A noble city and a rich territory looked up to them for protection; those whom their conduct was to save or devote to perdition, were in sight, extending to them their supplicating hands. Here was a scene to elicit the most latent sparks of courage. What wonder, then, that it had so powerful an effect on the minds of American soldiers—of Louisianian patriots! Every one of those brave men felt the honour and importance of his station, and exulted in the thought of being the defender of his fellow citizens, and the avenger of his country's wrongs. Such are the men who will always be found, by those who may again presume to insult a free nation, determined to maintain and preserve her rights.

I have in this work endeavoured to relate in detail, with the utmost exactness and precision, the principal events which took place in the course of this campaign. I have related facts as I myself saw them, or as they were told me by credible eye-witnesses. I do not believe, that through the whole of this narrative I have swerved from the truth in a single instance; if, however, by one of those unavoidable mistakes to which every man is subject, I have involuntarily mis-stated, or omitted to state, any material circumstance, I shall be ready to acknowledge my error whenever it shall be pointed out to

The ministerial papers denounced the Americans as rebels, the devoted objects of vengeance. British publications now breathed the same rage as at the period of the declaration of our independence; and the ministerial writers had recourse to the grossest scurrilities in their endeavours to vilify our government. As they pretended that it was not against France that they had waged so long a war, but against the chief who presided over her councils; so now they affected to proclaim that their hostilities were not directed against the people of the United States, nor against the American nation, but merely against the leader of a dominant faction. It was to restore to our nation the enjoyment of prosperity, that they were determined to overturn our government! It was obvious that the cessation of hostilities in Europe, would afford Britain the means of executing a part of her threats; and reflecting men considered the fall of the emperor of the French (so long wished for by the friends of Britain) as a sure presage that we should soon have to contend with a formidable British force by sea and land; nor was it long before these apprehensions were realized.

On the frontiers of Canada, the British had hitherto conducted the war with much dexterity and intrigue, but without any considerable number of troops. The courage of our soldiers could not remedy the faults of our generals, and the two first campaigns produced nothing more than some brilliant exploits, some particular instances of bravery, that could have no influence on great military operations. Courage without military tactics, an ill-disciplined army conducted without any fixed plan, with a defective system of organization, were the means with which we long opposed the British troops; and it may be truly said that the two first campaigns in Canada were consumed in a war of observation, and in the taking and retaking of a few posts. The British, by all possible means of seduction, had stirred up against us a great number of Indians on the north-western confines of the United States, and excited them to commit depredations on our frontiers, and massacre our citizens. History cannot record all the atrocities committed by those allies of Great Britain, some of which are of such a description that the most credulous would disbelieve them, were not the facts supported by the most creditable witnesses and the most authentic proofs.

Experience at last opened the eyes of our government, and more numerous armies, under able and faithful officers, were sent into Canada, to carry on the war more effectually. It is foreign from the design of this work, to enter into any discussion on that subject; and I will merely observe that it was in some measure owing to a defect in the law then in force for calling out the militia, that our military operations in Canada, during the two first campaigns, were attended with so little success. I allude to the law which called out certain portions of the militia for six months only, at the expiration of which term the men were allowed to return home. Independently of the time necessary to repair from the middle states to the frontiers of Canada, or to Louisiana, six months are hardly sufficient to train a soldier to military discipline and evolutions, so as to render him fit to contend in the field against veteran troops. A subsequent law has, indeed, partly remedied this evil, by prolonging the time of service to twelve months; but even this term would probably be insufficient, had we to carry on a war with vigour.

The arrival of reinforcements to the British army in Canada, was the prelude to more extensive operations. The taking of Washington, and the several attacks made on different points of the Chesapeake, sufficiently evinced the intention of the British government, to endeavour to execute the threats denounced against us through their newspapers. The burning of Havre-de-Grace, the excesses committed at Hampton, and at Frenchtown, enabled us to form a just idea of the men who professed the intention of delivering us from a "government ridiculously despotic," and who in the meantime insulted our wives and daughters, destroyed or plundered our property, and indiscriminately set fire to humble cottages and stately palaces. The capitol itself, that noble monument that might have commanded respect even from barbarians, became a prey to the flames; and that we should not remain in doubt as to the fate we were to expect, the commander of the British naval forces, in an official communication to the secretary of state, explicitly avowed his determination to continue the same system of inhuman warfare, and to lay waste and destroy the American coast, wherever assailable.* From that moment all eyes were opened; the cry of indignation was heard from one extremity of the union to the other, and all minds were now bent on an obstinate and determined resistance. It was evident to all that we had no longer to contend for the precarious possession of an inconsiderable extent of country, but that we were called on to defend our wives and children from British insult and brutality; our fortunes from the rapacity of British invaders, and our homes from pillage, fire and devastation. Those who had hitherto considered the war only as an honourable contest between two nations, mutually esteeming each other, but set at variance by conflicting interests, were now convinced that our enemies were determined to wage against us a

*See admiral Cochrane's letter in the Appendix, No. 1.

war of extermination, and that we had to repel a savage foe, who came to cover our country with mourning and desolation. The Halifax papers announced the embarkation of troops that had composed part of lord Wellington's army. In the list of the regiments and of the general officers, appear several of the former and of the latter who since came to the banks of the Mississippi. The expedition against New Orleans was to consist of *eighteen thousand men*. The same papers predicted that the calamities of war would be severely and extensively felt by the inhabitants of the United States.

From that time it was generally believed that the British would attack the southern states in the ensuing autumn or winter, and Louisiana was particularly pointed out as their most probable object of invasion: yet so ill does the general government appear to have been served by its agents in that remote part of the union, that as late as in the month of September, nothing had been done in the way of effectual preparations, to put that country in a state of defence. (For the government's actions see Appendix, No. 1-a.)

Louisiana, which was particularly marked out as the principal point against which was to be directed a formidable British force, with a considerable extent of coast, numerous communications by water, and with hardly any fortified points, open on all sides, having in its neighbourhood a Spanish settlement freely admitting the enemy's ships, and a great proportion of whose population was disposed to aid him, had no force on which to rely for the defence of her shores, except six gun-boats and a sloop of war. From the gallant defence made by the brave crews of these vessels, we may judge what would have been effected by a number proportionate to the extent of coast to be defended. Fort Plaquemines, that of Petites Coquilles, and fort Bowyer at Mobile point, were the only advanced points fortified; and none of them capable of standing a regular siege.

It may now be made known, without any other danger than that of its appearing incredible, that Louisiana, whose coasts are accessible to such flat-bottomed vessels as are used in conveying mortars, had but two of these engines which belonged to the navy, and which were landed from bomb-ketches that had been condemned. Nor is this all: there were not a hundred bombs of the calibre of those mortars; nor, indeed, could much advantage be derived from them, however well served or supplied. Professional men will understand, that from the construction of their carriages, they were only fit to be mounted on board of vessels, and by no means calculated for land batteries.

The fort of Petites Coquilles was not finished at the time of the invasion, nor was it in a condition to make an ordinary resistance. As to fort Bowyer, at Mobile point, it will appear from the particular account given in this work of the two attacks it sustained, that the brave garrison defending it did all that could be reasonably expected from its local situation and means of resistance. Such was the inconsiderable defence that protected the shores of Louisiana, and covered a country that has an extent of coast of upwards of six hundred miles, and of which even a temporary possession by an enemy might be attended with consequences baneful to the future prosperity of the western states. The general government might and ought to have been well informed of the vulnerable points of Louisiana. Accurate maps of the country on a large scale had been made, by the engineer B. Lafon and myself, and delivered to brigadier-general Wilkinson, who, it is presumable, did not fail to forward them to the secretary of war. That part of the state, in particular, by which the enemy penetrated, was there laid down, and in 1813 brigadier-general Flournoy ordered major Lafon, then chief engineer of the district, to draw up an exact account of all the points to be fortified for the general defence of Louisiana. The draughts, which were numerous, and formed an atlas, were accompanied with very particular explanatory notes. That work, which reflects great credit on its author, pointed out in the most precise and clear manner what was expedient to be done, in order to put the country in a state of security against all surprise. I have always understood that those draughts were ordered and executed for the purpose of being sent to the then secretary of war, to enable the government to determine in their wisdom the points proper to be fortified. To what fatality then was it owing, that Louisiana, whose means of defence were so inadequate; which had but a scanty white population, composed, in a great proportion, of foreigners speaking various languages; so remote from any succours, though one of the keys of the union—was so long left without the means of resisting the enemy? I shall be told that to fortify the coast in time of peace, were to incur an unnecessary expense. This position I by no means admit; but I further observe that the war had already existed two years; and we ought to have presumed, had positive proof been wanting, that the British, having numerous fleets, and every means of transporting troops to all points of the coast of the United States, would not fail to make an attempt against Louisiana;—a country which already by its prodigious and unexampled progress in the culture of sugar, was becoming a dangerous rival to the British colonies. The city of New Orleans contained produce to a vast amount. The cotton crops of the state of Louisiana and the Mississippi territory, accumulated during several years, were stored in that city, surrounded with considerable plantations, having numerous gangs of slaves. It was, in a word, the emporium of the produce of a great portion of the western states. The Mississippi on which it lies, receives the streams that water upwards of a million of square miles, and wafts to New Orleans the annually increasing productions of their fertile banks.—It is by the Mississippi and the rivers emptying into it, that the communication is kept up between the western and northern states.—And by the Mississippi and the Missouri, there will, at no distant period, be carried on, without difficulty, or with very little obstruction, the most extensive inland navigation on the globe.

All these advantages were calculated to excite the cupidity of the British, and inspire them with the desire of getting possession of a country which, besides its territorial wealth, insured to whoever might hold it, an immediate control over the western states. In possessing themselves of Louisiana, the least favourable prospect of the enemy was the plunder of a very considerable quantity of produce, the destruction of a city destined to become commercial, and opulent in the highest degree, and the ruin of numerous plantations which must one day rival in their productions, those of the finest colonies of European nations. Their other prospects, less certain indeed, but in which they were not a little sanguine, were the separation of the western states from the rest of the union; the possibility of transferring the theatre of war to the westward, by the possession of the Mississippi, and effecting a junction with their army in Canada; and lastly, being masters of Louisiana, to import by the river their various manufactures, and secure to themselves the monopoly of the fur trade. (See Appendix, No. 1-b.)

Let us now see in what manner the British began to execute their hostile designs against Louisiana: In the course of the summer of 1814, the brig Orpheus had landed arms and officers in the bay of Apalachicola, and entered into arrangements with the Creeks, to act against fort Bowyer at Mobile point, justly looked upon as a place the possession of which was of the greatest importance towards the execution of the grand operations projected against Louisiana. The British officers diligently executed the object of their instructions, and had completely succeeded in rallying under their standard all the tribes of Indians living to the east of the Chactaws, when an expedition of some troops on board the sloops of war Hermes and Caron, sailed from Bermuda under the command of colonel Nicholls, of the artillery, an enterprising, active, and brave officer, and on the 4th of August touched at the Havanna, in hopes of obtaining the co-operation of the Spanish governor, the assistance of some gun-boats and small vessels with permission to land their troops and artillery at Pensacola. On the refusal of the captain-general, they sailed for Pensacola, determined to land there; although the captain-general had positively refused to grant them permission. (See Appendix, No 2.)

Colonel Nicholls accordingly landed at Pensacola, where he established his head-quarters, and enlisted and publicly drilled Indians, who wore the British uniform in the streets.

The object of that inconsiderable expedition appears to have been to sound the disposition of the inhabitants of the Floridas and Louisiana; to procure the information necessary for more important operations, and to secure pilots to conduct the expedition on our coast and in our waters, rather than to attempt any thing of importance.

Colonel Nicholls directed captain Lockyer of the brig Sophia, to convey an officer to Barataria with a packet for Mr. Lafitte, or whoever else might be at the head of the privateers on Grande Terre.

To give a correct idea of that establishment at Barataria, of which so much has been said, it is necessary to enter into some details, by a digression which will naturally bring us back to our subject.

CHAPTER 1

BARATARIA.

At the period of the taking of Guadaloupe by the British, most of the privateers commissioned by the government of that island, and which were then on a cruise, not being able to return to any of the West-India islands, made for Barataria, there to take in a supply of water and provisions, recruit the health of their crews, and dispose of their prizes, which could not be admitted into any of the ports of the United States; we being at that time in peace with Great Britain. Most of the commissions granted to privateers by the French government at Guadaloupe, having expired some time after the declaration of the independence of Carthagena, many of the privateers repaired to that port, for the purpose of obtaining from the new government, commissions for cruising against Spanish vessels. They were all received by the people of Carthagena with the enthusiasm which is ever observed in a country that for the first time shakes off the yoke of subjection; and indeed a considerable number of men, accustomed to great political convulsions, inured to the fatigues of war, and who by their numerous cruises in the Gulf of Mexico and about the West-India islands, had become well acquainted with all those coasts, and possessed the most effectual means of annoying the royalists, could not fail to be considered as an acquisition to the new republic.

Having duly obtained their commissions, they in a manner blockaded for a long time all the ports belonging to the royalists, and made numerous captures, which they carried into Barataria. Under this denomination is comprised part of the coast of Louisiana to the west of the mouths of the Mississippi, comprehended between Bastien bay on the east, and the mouths of the river or bayou la Fourche on the west. Not far from the sea are lakes called the great, the small, and the larger lake of Barataria, communicating with one another by several large bayous with a great number of branches. There is also the island of Barataria, at the extremity of which is a place called the Temple, which denomination it owes to several mounds of shells thrown up there by the Indians, long before the settlement of Louisiana, and which from the great quantity of human bones, are evidently funereal and religious monuments.

The island is formed by the great and the small lakes of Barataria, the bayou Pierrot, and the bayou or river of Ouatchas, more generally known by the name of bayou of Barataria; and finally the same denomination is given to a large basin which extends the whole length of the Cypress swamps, lakes, prairies and bayous behind the plantations on the right bank of the river, three miles above New Orleans, as far as the Gulf of Mexico, being about sixty miles in length and thirty in breadth, bounded on the west by the highlands of la Fourche, and on the east by those of the right bank of the Mississippi. These waters disembogue into the gulf by two entrances of the lake or rather the bayou Barataria, between which lies an island called Grande Terre, six miles in length and from two to three miles in breadth, running parallel with the coast. In the western entrance is the great pass of Barataria, which has from nine to ten feet of water. Within this pass, about two leagues from the open sea, lies the only secure harbour on all that coast, and accordingly this is the harbour frequented by the privateers, so well known by the name of Baratarians. Social order has indeed to regret that those men, mostly aliens, and cruising under a foreign flag, so audaciously infringed our laws as openly to make sale of their goods on our soil; but what is much more deplorable and equally astonishing is, that the agents of government in this country so long tolerated such violation of our laws, or at least delayed for four years to take effectual measures to put a stop to these lawless practices. It cannot be pretended that the country was destitute of the means necessary to repress these outrages. The troops stationed at New Orleans were sufficient for that purpose, and it cannot be doubted but that a well conducted expedition would have cleared our waters of the privateers, and a proper garrison stationed at the place they made their harbour, would have prevented their return. The species of impunity with which they were apparently indulged, inasmuch as no rigorous measures were resorted to against them, made the contraband trade carried on at Barataria, be considered as tacitly tolerated. In a word, it is a fact no less true than painful for me to assert, that at Grande Terre, the privateers publicly made sale, by auction, of the cargoes of their prizes. From all parts of Lower Louisiana people resorted to Barataria, without being at all solicitious to conceal the object of their journey. In the streets of New Orleans it was usual for traders to give and receive orders for purchasing goods at Barataria, with as little secrecy as similar orders are given for Philadelphia or New-York. The most respectable inhabitants of the state, especially those living in the country, were in the habit of purchasing smuggled goods coming from Barataria. The frequent seizures made of those goods, were but an ineffectual remedy of the evil, as the great profit yielded by such parcels as escaped the vigilance of the custom-house officers, indemnified the traders for the loss of what they had paid for the goods seized; their price being always very moderate, by reason of the quantity of prizes brought in, and of the impatience of the captors to turn them into money, and sail on a new cruise. This traffic was at length carried on with such scandalous notoriety, that the agents of government incurred very general and open reprehension, many persons contending that they had interested motives for conniving at such abuses, as smuggling was a source of confiscation, from which they derived considerable benefit.

It has been repeatedly asserted in the public prints throughout the union, that most of those privateers had no commissions, and were really pirates. This I believe to be a calumny, as I am persuaded they all had commissions either from Carthagena or from France, of the validity of which it would seem the government of those respective countries were alone competent judges.

The privateers of Barataria committed indeed a great offence against the laws of the United States in smuggling into their territory goods captured from nations with which we were at peace; and for this offence they justly deserved to be punished. But in addition to this acknowledged guilt, to charge them with the crime of piracy, when on the strictest inquiry no proof whatsoever of any act amounting to this species of criminality has been discovered, and though since the pardon granted to them by the president of the United States, they have shown their papers and the exact list of the vessels captured by them, to every one who chose to see them, seems evidently unjust. Without wishing to extenuate their real crime, that of having for four years carried on an illicit trade, I again assert that the agents of government justly merit the reproach of having neglected their duty. The government must surely have been aware of the pernicious consequences of this contraband trade; and they had the means of putting a stop to it. It is true that partial expeditions had been fitted out for that purpose; but whether through want of judgment in the plan, or through the fault of the persons commanding those expeditions, they answered no other purpose than to suspend this contraband trade in one part, by making it take a more western direction. Cat island, at the mouth of the bayou or river la Fourche, became the temporary harbour of the privateers, whose vessels were too well armed to apprehend an attack from land troops in ordinary transports. Hence the troops stationed at Grande Terre, la Fourche, &c. could do no more than prevent the continuance of the illegal trade, while they were on the spot; but on their departure, the Baratarians immediately returned to their former station.

There have been those who pretended that the privateers of Barataria were secretly encouraged by the English, who were glad to see a commerce carried on that must prove so injurious to the revenue of the United States. But this charge is fully refuted by this fact, that at different times the English sought to attack the privateers at Barataria, in hopes of taking their prizes, and even their armed vessels. Of these attempts of the British, suffice it to instance that of the 23d of June, 1813, when two privateers being at anchor off Cat island, a British sloop of war anchored at the entrance of the pass, and sent her boats to endeavour to take the privateers; but they were repulsed after having sustained considerable loss.

Such was the state of affairs when on the 2d of September 1814, there appeared an armed brig on the coast opposite the pass. She fired a gun at a vessel about to enter and forced her to run aground; she then tacked and shortly after came to an anchor at the entrance of the pass. It was not easy to understand the intentions of this vessel, who having commenced with hostilities on her first appearance, now seemed to announce an amicable disposition. Mr. Lafitte, the younger, went off in a boat to examine her, venturing so far that he could not escape from the pinnace sent from the brig and making towards the shore, bearing British colours and a flag of truce. In this pinnace were two British naval officers, captain Lockyer, commander of the brig, and an officer who interpreted for him, with captain Williams of the infantry. The first question they asked was, where was Mr. Lafitte? He, not choosing to make himself known to them, replied that the person they inquired for was on shore. They then delivered him a packet directed "To Mr. Lafitte—Barataria;" requesting him to take particular care of it, and to deliver it into Mr. Lafitte's own hands. He prevailed on them to make for the shore, and as soon as they got near enough to be in his power, he made himself known, recommending to them at the same time to conceal the business on which they had come. Upwards of two hundred persons lined the shore, and it was a general cry amongst the crews of the privateers at Grande Terre, that those British officers should be made prisoners and sent to New Orleans, as being spies who had come under feigned pretences to examine the coast and the passages, with intent to invade and ravage the country. It was with much difficulty that Mr. Lafitte succeeded in dissuading the multitude from this intent, and led the officers in safety to his dwelling. He thought, very prudently, that the papers contained in the packet might be of importance towards the safety of the country, and that the officers, being closely watched, could obtain no intelligence that might turn to the detriment of Louisiana. He took the earliest opportunity, after the agitation among the crews had subsided, to examine the contents of the packet; in which he found a proclamation addressed by colonel Edward Nicholls, in the service of his Britannic Majesty and commander of the land forces on the coast of Florida, to the inhabitants of Louisiana, dated *Headquarters, Pensacola, 29th August, 1814*; a letter from the same, directed to Mr. Lafitte, or to the commandant at Barataria; an official letter from the honourable W. H. Percy, captain of the sloop of war Hermes, and commander of the naval forces in the Gulf of Mexico, dated September 1st, 1814, directed to himself; and finally, a letter containing orders from the same captain Percy, written on the 30th of August on board the Hermes, in the road of Pensacola, to the same captain Lockyer commanding the sloop of war Sophia. (For these different papers see Appendix, No. 3.)

When Mr. Lafitte had perused these papers, captain Lockyer enlarged on the subject of them, and proposed to him to enter into the service of his Britannic majesty with all those who were under his command, or over whom he had sufficient influence; and likewise to lay at the disposal of the officers of his Britannic Majesty the armed vessels he had at Barataria, to aid in the intended attack of the fort of Mobile. He insisted much on the great advantages that would thence result to himself and his crews; offered him the rank of captain in the British service, and the sum of thirty thousand dollars, payable, at his option, in Pensacola or New Orleans, and urged him not to let slip this opportunity of acquiring fortune and consideration. On Mr. Lafitte's requiring a few days to reflect upon these proposals, captain Lockyer observed to him that no reflection could be necessary, respecting proposals that obviously precluded hesitation, as he was a Frenchman, and of course now a friend to Great Britain, proscribed by the American government, exposed to infamy, and had a brother at that very time loaded with irons in the jail of New Orleans. He added, that in the British service he would have a fair prospect of promotion; that having such a knowledge of the country, his services would be of the greatest importance in carrying on the operations which the British government had planned against Lower Louisiana; that, as soon as possession was obtained, the army would penetrate into the upper country, and act in concert with the forces in Canada; that every thing was already prepared for carrying on the war against the American government in that quarter with unusual vigour; that they were nearly sure of success, expecting to find little or no opposition from the French and Spanish population of Louisiana, whose interests, manners and customs were more congenial with theirs than with those of the Americans; that finally, the insurrection of the negroes, to whom they would offer freedom, was one of the chief means they intended to employ, being confident of its success.

To all these splendid promises, all these ensnaring insinuations, Mr. Lafitte replied, that in a few days he would give a final answer; his object in this procrastination being to gain time to inform the officers of the state government of this nefarious project. Having occasion to go to some distance for a short time, the persons who had proposed to send the British officers prisoners to New-Orleans, went and seized them in his absence, and confined both them and the crew of the pinnace, in a secure place, leaving a guard at the door. The British officers sent for Mr. Lafitte; but he, fearing an insurrection of the crews of the privateers, thought it advisable not to see them, until he had first persuaded their captains and officers to desist from the measures on which they seemed bent. With this view he represented to the latter that, besides the infamy that would attach to them, if they treated as prisoners, persons who had come with a flag of truce, they would lose the opportunity of discovering the extent of the projects of the British against Louisiana, and learning the names of their agents in the country. While Mr. Lafitte was thus endeavouring to bring over his people to his sentiments, the British remained prisoners the whole night, the sloop of war continuing at anchor before the pass, waiting for the return of the officers. Early the next morning, Mr. Lafitte caused them to be released from their confinement, and saw them safe aboard their pinnace, apologizing for the disagreeable treatment they had received, and which it had not been in his power to prevent. Shortly after their departure, he wrote to captain Lockyer the letter that may be seen in the Appendix, No. 4.

His object in writing the letter was, by appearing disposed to accede to their disposal, to give time to communicate the affair to the officers of the state government, and to receive from them instructions how to act, under circumstances so critical and important for the country. He accordingly wrote on the 4th of September to Mr. Blanque, one of the representatives of the state, sending him all the papers delivered to him by the British officers, with a letter addressed to his excellency W. C. C. Claiborne, governor of the state of Louisiana. (See Appendix, No. 5.) The contents of these letters do honour to Mr. Lafitte's judgment, and evince his sincere attachment to the American cause.

Persuaded that the country was about to be vigorously attacked, and knowing that at that time it was little prepared for resistance, he did what his duty prescribed; apprising government of the impending danger; tendering his services, should it be thought expedient to employ the assistance of his crews, and desiring instructions how to act; and in case of his offers being rejected, he declared his intention to quit the country, lest he should be charged with having co-operated with the invading enemy. On the receipt of this packet from Mr. Lafitte, Mr. Blanque immediately laid its contents before the governor, who convened the committee of defence lately formed, of which he was president; and Mr. Rancher, the bearer of Mr. Lafitte's packet, was sent back with a verbal answer, of which it is understood that the purport was to desire him to take no steps until it should be determined what was expedient to be done; it is added, that the message contained an assurance that, in the meantime, no steps should be taken against him for his past offences against the laws of the United States.

At the expiration of the time agreed on with captain Lockyer, his ship appeared again on the coast with two others, and continued standing off and on before the pass for several days.

Mr. Lafitte now wrote a second letter to Mr. Blanque, urging him to send him an answer and instructions. (See Appendix No. 6.) In the meantime he appeared not to perceive the return of the sloop of war, who, tired of waiting to no purpose, and mistrusting Mr. Lafitte's intentions, put out to sea and disappeared.

About this time, Mr. Lafitte received information that instead of accepting his services, and endeavouring to take advantage of the confidence the British had in him, to secure the country against an invasion, and defeat all their projects, the constituted authorities were fitting out at New-Orleans a formidable expedition against Barataria. He then retired to the German coast, where, strictly adhering to the principles he had professed, he warned the inhabitants of the danger with which they were threatened from the means intended to be employed by the enemy.

About this time, there fell into Mr. Lafitte's hands an anonymous letter directed to a person in New Orleans, the contents of which left no doubt as to the intentions of the British, and which is the more interesting, as all that it announced has since been fully verified. (See Appendix, No. 2.)

Such are the particulars of the first attempt made by the British against Louisiana—an attempt in which they employed such unjustifiable arts, that it may fairly be inferred that the British government scruples not to descend to the basest means, when such appears likely to contribute to the attainment of its ends. Notwithstanding the solemn professions of respect for the persons and property of the inhabitants, so emphatically made in the proclamation of colonel Nicholls, we see that one of their chief reliance for the success of operations in Louisiana, was on the insurrection of the negroes. It is not then evident from this, that the British were bent on the destruction of a country whose rivalship they feared in their colonial productions, and that the cabinet of St. James had determined to carry on a war of plunder and devastation against Louisiana?

In coming to Barataria, to endeavour to gain over the privateers to their interests, they acted consistently with their known principles, and on a calculation of probabilities; for it was an obvious presumption that a body of men proscribed in a country whose laws they had violated, reflecting on their precarious existence, would embrace so favourable an opportunity of recovering an erect attitude in society, by ranging themselves under the banners of a powerful nation. But this calculation of the British proved fallacious; and in this instance, as in every other, they found in every individual in Louisiana, an enemy to Britain, ever ready to take up arms against her; and those very men, whose aid they so confidently expected to obtain, signally proved throughout the campaign, particularly in the service of the batteries at Jackson's lines, that the agents of the British government had formed a very erroneous opinion of them. (See Note No. 1, at the end of the volume.)

The British finding themselves disappointed in their expectation of drawing over to their interests the privateersmen of Barataria, concentrated their preparations at Pensacola and Apalachicola. In this latter place, they had landed not only troops, but also twenty-two thousand stand of arms, with ammunition, blankets, and clothing, to be distributed among the Indians; and it was generally reported at that time, that several of their vessels had already sailed for Jamaica, to take in black troops.

General Armstrong, the then secretary of war, by a circular letter of the 4th of July, had informed the different state governments of the quota of militia they were respectively to furnish, pursuant to the president's requisition of the same date. (See Appendix, No. 7.) On the 6th of August, the governor of the state of Louisiana published, conformably to that requisition, militia general orders, in which, after having laid before his constituents the views and intentions of the general government, to employ an adequate force to maintain with honour the contest in which our country was engaged, he exhorted the citizens of the state zealously to stand the necessary draught for completing the thousand men demanded by the above mentioned requisition. (See Appendix, No. 8.)

All the western and southern newspapers were at that time loudly inveighing against the shameful assistance afforded by the governor of Pensacola to the British, at least inasmuch as he suffered the character of his nation to be sullied, by permitting them publicly to make hostile preparations in that town, where they had established their head-quarters, and where they were, if not the nominal, at least the virtual masters. Such repeated violations, and the succours constantly furnished to the Indians, who were evidently the allies of our enemy, contributed not a little to rouse the national spirit in that part of the union. I cannot refrain from giving here an extract from one of the papers that appeared about that time, in which the writer, after having enumerated all the grievances that the United States had to complain of against the Spanish governor of Florida, says: " who of us would not prefer to take his fortune as a common soldier, to remaining at home in affluence, while the community of which he is a member, submits tamely, silently and unresistingly to such indignities."

The commander-in-chief of the 7th district, wrote to the governor of the state, from fort Jackson, on the 15th of August, announcing to him the necessity of holding all the forces of Louisiana militia in readiness to march at the first signal, in consequence of the preparations making at Pensacola, of which he had received certain information. (See Appendix, No. 9.) Conformably to this order, the governor published in militia general orders, an extract from his letter to the commanders of the two divisions of state militia, in which he gave them instructions and regulations for their respective divisions. Commodore Patterson, commanding the station of New Orleans and its dependencies, received intelligence of the appearance of five British ships of war, which had landed a small number of men on the point at Dauphine island.

General Jackson had at this time removed his head-quarters to Mobile, from which place he wrote to the governor, on the 22d of August, a letter of which the following is an extract:

"I have no power to stipulate with any particular corps, as to particular or local service; but it is not to be presumed at present, that the troops of Louisiana will have to extend their services beyond the limits of their own state. Yet circumstances might arise, which would make it necessary they should be called to face an invading enemy beyond the boundary of the state, to stop his entry into their territory."

In consequence of this letter, the governor published, on the 5th of September, militia general orders, and afterwards general orders, directing the militia of the two divisions of the state, to hold themselves in readiness to march, the first division under major-general Villeré, being to be reviewed on the 10th of the same month, by major Hughes, assistant inspector-general of the district, in the city of New Orleans; and the second, under the command of major-general Thomas, to be reviewed at Baton Rouge on the first of October. (See Appendix, No. 10.)

By another general order, dated New Orleans, 8th September, governor Claiborne ordered the different militia companies in the city and suburbs of New Orleans, to exercise twice, and those of the other parts of the state, once a week. He also recommended to fathers of families, and men whose advanced age exempted them from active service in the field, to form themselves into corps of veterans, choose their own officers, procure arms, and to exercise occasionally. The governor announces to his fellow citizens the dangers with which the country is threatened, urging to them that the preservation of their property, the repose and tranquility of their families, call on every individual to exert all his efforts and vigilance; his order enters into minute details as to the precautions and police to be observed in the existing circumstances; it recommends the greatest diligence to be exerted in procuring arms, and the greatest care to be taken of them; and finally prescribes the conduct to be observed by all the militia officers, in case of the enemy's penetrating into the state. (See Appendix, No. 11.)

About that time, there appeared a Spanish translation of an order of the day published at Pensacola, addressed to a detachment of the royal marines at the moment of their landing. This piece, written in a style of importance that might be used in addressing a numerous army, from which might be expected the most brilliant military achievements, breathes inveterate hatred against the Americans, loudly announcing that the object of the expedition is to avenge the Spaniards for the pretended insults offered them by the United States.

That document, replete with invectives against the American character, contains moreover a strong recommendation to sobriety; and from the earnest manner in which the author insists on that subject, one would be led to believe that the soldiers whom he addresses, stood in great need of his exhortations. This piece requires no further comment, as it speaks for itself; the tone of falsehood and duplicity that pervades it, has induced me to publish it, especially as it may furnish some features in the portrait of our enemy. (See Appendix, No. 12.)

On the 16th of September, a meeting of a great number of the citizens of New Orleans was held at the Exchange Coffee-house, in that city, and by them was appointed a committee of defence to co-operate with the constituted authorities of the state, and with the general government, towards the defence of the country. The president of that committee, Mr. Edward Livingston, after an eloquent speech, in which he showed the expediency of making a solemn declaration of the patriotic sentiments which prevailed among the inhabitants of Louisiana, who had, on several occasions, been calumniated, and represented, as disaffected to the American government, and disposed to transfer their allegiance to a foreign power, proposed a spirited resolution which was unanimously adopted. (See Appendix, No. 13.)

This resolution was, within a few days, followed by an address from the committee of defence to their fellow citizens. The patriotic sentiments expressed in this address, were such as need no comment, as the mere perusal of it will suffice to evince the spirit which animated the people, of whom the committee of defence were on that occasion the organ. (See Appendix, No. 14.)

CHAPTER 2

FIRST ATTACK ON FORT BOWYER.

The preparations which the British had been long making at Pensacola, where, regardless of the rights of neutrality, the Spanish governor permitted the enemy of a nation with which his government was at peace, publicly to recruit, nay, even exercise his troops and the savage Indians whom he had enlisted, and whom he excited by every means of seduction, to renew the horrid scenes exhibited at fort Mims; the little care they took in their proud and frantic spirit to conceal their projects; the advantageous situation of the point of Mobile, as a military post, were among the circumstances which made it probable that fort Bowyer was the object of the expedition the British were fitting out at Pensacola.

Major Lawrence, who commanded that fort, was well aware of the means which the enemy intended to employ against him; and accordingly he made the utmost exertions to put the post confided to him, in a condition to make a vigorous resistance; while the brave garrison under his command ardently longed for an opportunity of evincing their zeal and devotedness for the honour and interest of their beloved country.

Before I enter on the glorious defence made by that garrison, it seems proper that I describe the situation of fort Bowyer, and that of Mobile point. It is indeed unnecessary to show how important the occupation of that spot must necessarily have been towards the success of military operations intended against Louisiana, as that will sufficiently appear from the bare inspection of the map. I will, therefore, merely observe that the point of the Mobile commands the passes at the entrance of the bay, and consequently the navigation of the rivers which empty into it; that on the eastern side it commands the species of archipelago which extends in a parallel direction as far as the passes Mariana and Christiana; that from its situation advancing into the gulf, it must ever afford to those who hold it, the means of exercising an almost exclusive control over the navigation of the coast of West Florida; and that its proximity to Pensacola secures to it a prompt an easy communication with that town.

This point, forming the extremity of a peninsula, joined to the continent by an isthmus four miles wide, between the river and bay of Bonsecours and the bay Perdido, extends in an east and west direction, inclining a little towards the south, for the space of twenty-nine miles in length, from the mouth of the Perdido. A large oblong lake, called Borgne, occupies the greater portion of its interior towards the east, which, independently of the narrow neck of land formed by the two bays, affords in several points the facility of cutting off all communication with the continent. The breadth of the peninsula decreases as it extends towards the west, so that three miles from the point it is only half a mile wide. This part affords another means of defence, of which the British availed themselves when they encamped on the peninsula during their last attack; I mean a ditch or coulée, communicating with a lagoon, the whole occupying upwards of half the breadth of the peninsula. Some briars and stunted fir trees and live oaks grow here and there on a soil almost entirely formed of sand and shells, which mixture gives it a very firm consistency. Within two miles of the point vegetation ceases almost entirely, and the soil becomes a succession of downs, ditches, ravines, and hillocks of sand, arid and moving in some places, and in others as hard as beaten ground. These ditches are from four to eight feet deep, forming several sinuosities, where one sees here and there a few tufts of grass. It is nearly at the extremity of this tongue of land, on the point rounding towards the northeast, that fort Bowyer is situated. The part that is nearest the shore is the angle of the north curtain and the semi-circular battery facing the pass, and opening a little at the distance of fifty yards, contiguous to a bluff which skirts the peninsula on both sides, nearly in its whole length.

Fort Bowyer is a redoubt formed on the seaside, by a semi-circular battery of four hundred feet in development, flanked with two curtains sixty feet in length, and joined to a bastion whose capital line passes through the centre of the circular battery. This bastion has but thirty-five feet in its gorge, with two flanks, each capable of receiving but one piece of artillery, and fifty feet in length on its front and rear aspects.

Its interior dimensions are one hundred and eighty feet in length from the summit of the bastion to the parapet of the circular battery, and two hundred feet for the length of the cord of the arc described by the battery. The receding angles formed by the curtains with the flanks of the bastion and those of the battery, considerably diminish the dimensions of this fort, the superficies of which may be estimated at twenty-two thousand feet.

The circular parts and the flanks which join it to the curtains, have a parapet fifteen feet thick at the summit, and in all the rest of the perimeter of the fort, the parapet does not exceed the thickness of three feet above the platforms; a fosse twenty feet wide surrounds the fort, and a very insufficient glacis without a covered way completes the fortification. The interior front of the parapet is formed of pine, a resinous wood which a single shell would be sufficient to set on fire. The fort is destitute of casemates (the only shelter from bombs) even for the sick, the ammunition or provisions. To these inconveniences may be added the bad situation of the fort, commanded by several mounds of sand, as above described, at the distance of from two to three hundred yards. On the summit of those mounds it would be very easy to mount pieces of artillery, whose slanting fire would command the inside of the fort.

From the first information of the preparations making by the British at Pensacola, until the 12th of September, on which day four large vessels were discovered in the offing, the garrison of the fort had been constantly employed in putting the fortifications in a condition to resist the enemy. Major Lawrence now ordered all the men of the garrison to enter within the fort, and to keep themselves in readiness for action. From that moment the garrison passed each night under arms, every man at his post.

Before I enter on the particulars of the events posterior to the 12th, it may be proper to give a statement of the strength of the garrison, and of the means of defence.

The garrison consisted of one hundred and thirty men including officers, and the whole artillery of the fort was twenty pieces of cannon, distributed in the following manner: two twenty-fours; six twelves, eight nines, and four fours; the twenty-fours and the twelves being alone mounted on coast carriages, and all the others on Spanish carriages little fit for service. One nine-pounder and three fours were mounted on the bastion, all the rest on the circular battery and its flanks. Those guns in the rear bastion and on the flanks, were on temporary platforms, and the men exposed from their knees upwards.

On the 12th of September, the sentinel stationed towards Lake Borgne, reported that on the morning of that day the enemy had landed six hundred Indians or Spaniards, and one hundred and thirty marines, and on the evening of the same day, two English sloops of war, with two brigs, came to anchor on the coast, within six miles east of the fort.

On the 13th, the enemy sent reconnoitring parties towards the back of the fort, who approached to within three quarters of a mile of it. At half after twelve, the enemy approached within the distance of seven hundred yards, whence they threw against the fort three shells and one cannon ball. The shells did no injury, having exploded in the air; but the ball, which was a twelve pound shot, struck a piece of timber that crowned the rampart of the curtain, part of which it carried away and then rebounded. The fort returned a few shots in the direction of the smoke of the enemy's guns, they being covered by the mounds of sand.

Meanwhile, the enemy, under cover of those mounds, retired a mile and a half behind the fort, and appeared to be employed in raising intrenchments. Three discharges of cannon were once more sufficient to disperse them. In the afternoon, several light boats having attempted to sound the channel nearest the point, were forced, by the balls and grape-shot fired against them, to return to their ships.

On the 14th, at six in the morning, the enemy still continued at the same distance, apparently employed in some works of fortification; the ships likewise remained at the same anchorage.

On the 15th of September, a day ever memorable for the garrison of fort Bowyer, the enemy by his movements gave early indications of his intention to attack; for by break of day, a very active communication was perceived between the ships and the troops on shore.

Towards noon, the wind having slackened to a light breeze from the southeast, the ships weighed anchor and stood out to sea: at two o'clock they tacked and bore down against the fort before the wind in line of battle, in the channel, the foremost ship being the Hermes, on board of which was the commodore, captain Percy.

Major Lawrence seeing the enemy determined on making a regular attack, called a council of all his officers. They unanimously agreed to make the most obstinate resistance, vigorously exerting every means of defence, and came to the following resolution:

"That in case of being, by imperious necessity, compelled to surrender (which could only happen in the last extremity, on the ramparts being entirely battered down, and the garrison almost wholly destroyed, so that any further resistance would be evidently useless,) no capitulation should be agreed on, unless it had for its fundamental article that the officers and privates should retain their arms and their private property, and that on no pretext should the Indians be suffered to commit any outrage on their persons or property; and unless full assurance were given them that they would be treated as prisoners of war, according to the custom established among civilized nations."

All the officers of the garrison unanimously swore, in no case, nor on any pretext, to recede from the above conditions; and they pledged themselves to each other, that in case of the death of any of them, the survivors would still consider themselves bound to adhere to what had been resolved on.

By 4 o'clock in the afternoon, the commodore's ship being within the reach of our great guns, a fire was opened on her from two twenty-four-pounders, but with little effect. The ship then fired one of her fore guns, but her shot did not reach the fort. As the ships appeared, all the guns that could be brought to bear opened on them a brisk fire.

At half past four, the Hermes came to anchor under our battery, within musket shot of the fort; and the other three took their station behind that ship, forming a line of battle in the channel. The engagement now became general, and the circular, battery kept up a dreadful fire against the most advanced ships, whilst, on the other hand, the four ships discharged against the fort whole broadsides, besides frequent single shots. Meanwhile captain Woodbine, the person who had enlisted and trained the Indians in Pensacola, opened the fire of a battery that he had established behind the bluff on the southeast shore, at the distance of seven hundred yards from the fort. That battery had one twelve-pounder and a six-inch howitzer, firing balls and shells: these the south battery of the fort soon silenced. It was now that the fire on both sides raged with the greatest fury; the fort and the ships being enveloped in a blaze of fire and smoke, until half past five, when the haliards of the commodore's flag were carried away by a ball, and the flag fell.

On this major Lawrence, with his characteristic humanity, instantly caused the firing to cease, with a view to ascertain the real intention of the enemy, who discontinued firing for five minutes; at the expiration of which, the brig next to the Hermes, discharged a whole broadside against the fort, and at the same time the commodore hoisted a new flag. All the guns of the battery being at that moment loaded, they were all fired at once, and produced such a commotion that it shook the ground. A few moments of silence succeeded. The enemy began to perceive the effect his conduct had on the minds of the garrison, who indignant at the manner in which the British made war, resolved, from the moment of the flag's being replaced, to bury themselves under the ruins of the fort, rather than surrender. The fire being renewed, continued for some time on both sides with the same violence. The Hermes having had her cable cut, was carried away by the current, and presented her head to the fort, and in that position she remained from fifteen to twenty minutes, whilst the raking fire of the fort swept fore and aft almost every thing on deck. At the moment when the fire was most intense, the flagstaff was carried away. This the British plainly perceived; but instead of following the example of major Lawrence, in suspending their fire, they redoubled it, and each of the ships discharged her whole broadside against the fort.

Major Lawrence immediately hoisted another flag on the edge of the parapet, having fastened it to a sponge-staff.

No sooner had the flag of the fort fallen, than the enemy's troops on shore advanced towards the fort, believing it had surrendered; but a few discharges of grape-shot soon convinced them of their error, and forced them to retire again behind the mounds of sand. The Hermes no longer holding by her cable, drifted with the current about half a mile, and having run aground on the bank, the commodore set her on fire. The brig that was next in the line to the Hermes, had suffered so much, that it was with difficulty she could retire beyond the reach of the guns of the fort; but at last the three remaining ships got out to sea. The fort continued firing on the Hermes until night, by which time she appeared in flames, and burned until eleven, when the fire having reached the powder, she blew up with a tremendous explosion.

During the action, two of the guns of the fort were dismounted, and one broken off by a thirty-two pound ball and another burst. I must observe, that of the whole number of guns that were in the fort, eight could not be brought to bear on the ships, and that the greater part of the men who served at the guns, belonged to the infantry, and had never seen artillery service before they were stationed at fort Bowyer: several of their officers also were little acquainted with artillery. (See Atlas, plate No. 3.)

To form a just estimate of the merit of the brave garrison of fort Bowyer, it is necessary to know the force they had to contend against; I therefore give here the statement of that force, as follows:

The ship Hermes of	28 32-pound carronades
The ship Caron	28 do.
The brig Sophia	18 do.
The Anaconda	16 do.
	——90 guns
A land battery, one 12 pounder and a 6 inch howitzer.	2
Total pieces of artillery	92

The enemy's force in men was as follows:

The Hermes had	175 men
The Caron	175 do.
The Sophia	125 do.
The Anaconda	115 do.
	——600
Marines	130
Indians	600
	——730
The whole effective force	1330 men.

From the above statement, the proportion appears to have been above ten to one; and five to one pieces of artillery.

The loss sustained by the garrison was four killed and four wounded. That of the enemy was:

On board the four ships killed	160
Wounded	70
On land killed	2
Total	232

The proportion appears thus to be twenty-nine killed on the side of the British to one on the side of the garrison.

Such was the result of the expedition fitted out at Pensacola with the greatest care, and with all manner of assistance on the part of the Spaniards. (See Appendix, No. 14-a.)

This victory of the American arms over the British troops under such circumstances, with so extraordinary a disproportion of force and of loss, was but the harbinger of the brilliant successes which the sons of liberty were very soon to obtain on the banks of the Mississippi, and of the humiliation that awaited British pride.

Commodore Percy relied so much on the superiority of the number of troops with which he was about to attack fort Bowyer, that he made no secret of his intention to allow the garrison but twenty minutes to capitulate. But how wofully he was disappointed in his expectations!

Instead of the laurels he was so confident of gathering, he carried off the shame of having been repulsed by a handful of men, inferior by nine-tenths to the forces he commanded. Instead of possessing himself of an important point, very advantageous for the military operations contemplated by his government, he left under the guns of fort Bowyer the wrecks of his own vessel, and the dead bodies of one hundred and sixty-two of his men. Instead of returning to Pensacola in triumph, offering the Spaniards, as a reward of their good wishes and assistance, a portion of the laurels obtained, and the pleasure of seeing the American prisoners he was confident of taking, he brought back to that port, which had witnessed his extravagant boasting, nothing but three shattered vessels full of wounded men.

The Spaniards, too timid and too weak to dare to attempt any thing by themselves, saw in the British avengers sent to realize the chimerical dreams with which they had fondly suffered themselves to be deluded. At the Havanna, in Pensacola, and even in New Orleans, six months before the attack on fort Bowyer, it had been currently reported that the time was not far off when the Spanish government was to recover possession of that part of Florida annexed to the state of Louisiana and to the Mississippi territory.

Too prudent to attempt any thing without being sure of success, too weak for any undertaking by themselves, the Spaniards relied on the English for the recovery, without danger to them, of that which, with so little foundation, they claimed as a portion of their territory.

This guile and duplicity of the Spaniards, was seen through by the Americans, and it will hereafter appear that the commander of the seventh military district of the United States, thought it his duty to put a stop to their infamous proceedings.

The important service rendered by the garrison of fort Bowyer could not fail to be justly estimated. On the 17th general Jackson, then at Mobile, wrote a complimentary letter to major Lawrence, expressive of the joy he felt on hearing of the glorious defence made by the garrison under his command, and acquainting him that he had despatched information of it to the general government, who would not fail duly to reward the brave defenders of the rights and honour of the American people.

The New Orleans committee of defence resolved that their president, Edward Livingston, esqr. should be directed to write in their name to major Lawrence, to assure him of the sentiments of gratitude and joy with which the inhabitants of that city had learned the gallant defence of fort Bowyer, and the important service rendered by the garrison, not only to Louisiana, but to the whole union, in preserving to them so important a point. At the same time it was resolved that, in testimony of these sentiments, there should be presented to major Lawrence a sword adorned with suitable emblems. (See Appendix, No. 15.)

On the 21st of September, major-general Jackson, whose head-quarters were at that time at Mobile, issued a proclamation to the inhabitants of Louisiana, in which he sets forth the perfidious conduct of the British on our coasts, and the proposal made to the privateers of Barataria, to join them, and rally round their standard. That proclamation announces to the Louisianians that the government and the general rely on their zealous assistance in repelling the enemy, should he dare to set foot on our soil. (See Appendix No. 16.) On the same day, general Jackson issued a proclamation addressed to the free men of colour of Louisiana, inviting them to unite under the banners of their country for the purpose of contributing to its defence. That proclamation refers them to governor Claiborne for instructions as to the mode of forming corps. (See Appendix, No. 17.)

The spirit of patriotism and zeal which had been evinced with so much ardour for the defence of the country, in Tennessee, by the levying of the troops that had already joined general Jackson, and were encamped on the Alabama, under the command of general Coffee, was again manifested in the further levy of five thousand men, which took place in that state about the middle of October. (See Appendix, No. 17-a.) The general government had received information that the enemy was preparing an expedition against the state of Louisiana, by the way of Mobile, and that his intention was to obtain possession of all the coast, from cape Florida, as far as the Spanish provinces to the west of the Mississippi.

CHAPTER 3

EXPEDITION AGAINST PENSACOLA.

THE Creek Indians in the year 1813 had been defeated and routed by a body of the Tennessee militia commanded by major general Andrew Jackson, and deputies of the Creek nation having sued for peace, had agreed to meet him or some American commissioners on the 10th of August 1814, to determine the boundaries of their nation with the United States. The treaty, as now in force, was settled; but a certain proportion of the Creeks having refused to participate in it, remained still at war with the United States, committing depredations on our settlements on the Alabama, the Tombigbee, and Mobile bay, and they were aided and abetted by the Spaniards, who supplied them with arms and ammunition, and received in Pensacola the property plundered from our citizens. General Jackson demanded satisfaction from the Spanish governor of Pensacola, who in a haughty answer said, that he would protect, clothe and arm, *his* Indians (as he termed them)—that in the ensuing fall he would expatiate more largely on the subject, evidently alluding to the intended attack of the southern states by the British. The messenger who brought this answer had hardly arrived, when a British force, allied with the Creek Indians, came from Pensacola and attacked, on the 15th September 1814, fort Bowyer on Mobile Point; and after having been repulsed, as has been above related, with the loss of a ship and a great number of men, they returned to Pensacola, and there were received, as the friends and allies of the Spaniards, who suffered them to garrison their forts, and even arrested and confined some American citizens, who were suspected of being unfriendly to the British government.

Major-general Jackson, to put an end to this breach of the law of nations, determined to take possession of Pensacola, thereby to deprive the Indians and their British allies of a place of shelter and refuge, after their aggressions on our territory. He accordingly assembled, near fort Montgomery on the

Alabama, an army of about four thousand men, composed of detachments of the 3d, 39th, and 44th regiments of infantry, the militia of Tennessee, and a battalion of volunteer dragoons of the Mississippi territory.

A detachment of cavalry under lieutenant Murray of the Mississippi dragoons were sent to reconnoitre. They made prisoners of a Spanish advanced picket, but could perceive nothing; and lieutenant Murray having imprudently followed alone an Indian whom he saw at some distance, was shot by him. He was regretted as a brave and excellent officer. The army arrived on the 6th of November 1814, within two miles of Pensacola. (See Atlas, plate No. 2.)

Major-general Jackson despatched major Peire to the governor with a summons; but when that officer was at about two or three hundred yards distance of fort St. Michael, in defiance of the sacred laws of nations, he was fired upon from a twelve-pounder, although his character, as a flag of truce, could not be mistaken, he having a large white flag and approaching alone; major Peire, after having reconnoitred the fort and seen it occupied by British troops, reported to the commanding general, who had been previously informed that two flags (one Spanish the other British) had been displayed on the walls of the fort, and that the latter had only been withdrawn the day before the arrival of the American army; and making no doubt that this wanton behaviour towards the sacred character of a flag of truce, was only to be attributed to the British, who, doubtless, did not wish to be seen in the act of violating the neutrality of the Spanish territory, the major-general impelled by a sense of humanity towards the oppressed Spaniards sent a letter by a prisoner, to the governor, demanding an explanation and satisfaction of the affront offered to his flag.

The army was at the same time encamped one mile and a half from the town. The Spanish governor immediately despatched an officer with assurances of his not having had any participation in the transaction of the morning, and added that if the major-general was pleased to renew the communication, he pledged himself that his messenger should be received with due respect. Major Peire went again at midnight, with instructions. The governor having assembled his principal officers, was informed of the conditions proposed by general Jackson, viz: to receive an American garrison in the forts St. Michael and Barrancas, until the Spanish government could procure a sufficient force to enable them to maintain their neutrality against its violation by the British who had possessed themselves of the fortresses, notwithstanding the remonstrances and protest of the Spanish governor. That the

American forces should be withdrawn as soon as such a respectable force should arrive. These conditions having been refused, major Peire declared, agreeably to his instructions, that however reluctant to the feelings of the general, recourse would be had to arms.

On his return, the 7th November, 1814, three thousand men were marched from the encampment in three columns: the centre, composed of detachments of the 39th and 44th regiments of infantry, commanded by major Woodruff, and two pieces of artillery. The right column, composed of general Coffee's volunteers of Tennessee, and the left of the drafted militia of Tennessee and the Chactaw Indians, commanded by major Blue, marched in the rear, with a battalion of volunteer dragoons of the Mississippi territory, under major Hinds.

The column was directed to proceed along the sea beach towards the eastward of the town, to avoid passing under the fire of fort St. Michael; when in sight of the town, the sand proving too heavy for the artillery to make any progress, the centre column was ordered to charge, which was done in the most gallant manner. As soon as the head of the column appeared in the principal street, a Spanish battery of two pieces was opened against them, but was immediately carried at the point of a bayonet, with the loss of eleven men killed and wounded; amongst the latter were the gallant captain Laval of the 3d, and lieutenant Flournoy of the 44th regiment. The Spaniards lost only a few men, four killed and six wounded; the American soldiers, with that mild disposition which characterizes the brave, having spared the vanquished.

The governor of Pensacola, don Gonzales Manriques, having sent a flag of truce to the American general, hostilities immediately ceased, and it was agreed that the block houses in town, fort St. Michael, and Barrancas, should receive an American garrison. But the commandant of fort St. Michael refused to obey the order of the governor. The general sent him a summons offering him the same advantageous propositions which had been made the night before, and giving him half an hour to determine; and having given the command of the town to major Peire and left him eight hundred men, with instructions to get possession of the fort before night, either by negociating or by force, retired to his camp with the remainder of the troops. As he left the town, the British shipping attempted to annoy him with long guns, but without effect.

It was of the utmost importance that the forts should be taken possession of before morning, as the British frigate the Seahorse, the Sophia sloop of war, and the ——— had springs to their cables and were ready either to set fire to the town or effect a landing. The following measures were taken. Two companies, with three pieces of cannon, under the command of captain Denkins, were placed on mount St. Bernard, a position which commands fort St. Michael, and five hundred men were placed on the beach to oppose a landing if attempted. At six o'clock P. M. colonel Sotto, commandant of fort St. Michael, after having sent by two captains a verbal acceptance of the conditions offered him, refused to receive captain Denkins with his command, whom major Peire had sent to take possession of the fort, saying they could not evacuate it before morning. These delays and the bad faith of the Spanish commandant were evidently designed to give the British time to prepare to come to their assistance. This did not escape the American commandant, who ordered captain Denkins to commence an attack upon the fort immediately, and was about to march his forces to storm the place, when colonel Sotto, aware of the consequences, surrendered, under the same conditions proposed at first by the general in chief—and possession was taken of the fort at eleven o'clock P. M. On the same afternoon a battery called St. Rose, situated opposite fort Barrancas at the entrance of the bay, was blown up by the Spaniards.

It is here worthy of remark that property was respected and good order and decorum as much observed as if the American troops had entered a friendly town; and although it had been taken by storm, not a single act of insubordination was complained of. The Spaniards were so much pleased with this behaviour, that they expressed their admiration and astonishment, at being better treated by the Americans, who seemingly had entered their town as foes, than by their British allies and friends, who used them very cavalierly and secreted on board their ships nearly four hundred slaves, who had ran away from their masters, and who, notwithstanding severe remonstrances and repeated applications from the Spanish authorities, refused to restore them.

Next morning, the 8th, the governor having been applied to, for his order to the commandant of the Barrancas to receive an American garrison, refused to give it, alleging that it would not be obeyed. General Jackson then resolved to go down and take that fortress. The Barrancas is a strong battery, of ——— twenty-four pounders, and together with fort St. Rose, on a small island situated opposite, commands effectually the entrance of Pensacola bay; but on the land side it is not so well defended. Preparations were making to march the army down to take that fort; when in the evening, an explosion was heard and flames were seen proceeding from the same direction. General Jackson soon heard by a prisoner, (which afterwards proved to be the fact, the general having sent to the spot to reconnoitre) that the British had persuaded the Spanish commandant to blow up the fortifications, and to retreat to the Havanna, with all his force, amounting to three or four hundred men.

The British shipping by this occurrence dropped down unmolested, and put to sea. The following was the situation of affairs. The British expelled from Pensacola bay; the Indians wandering in those low islands, perishing for want of food; the Spaniards punished for their want of good faith, and taught by sad experience, that they could not expect to injure their peaceable neighbours with impunity. On the other hand, the American army, composed of about four thousand men, of whom one thousand were mounted, could be supplied only by land conveyance (the British commanding the sea) from a country which was itself in want of provisions:—the winter was setting in.—The object of the expedition being accomplished, the major-general seeing that the presence of most of the troops would be wanted for the defence of New Orleans, determined to withdraw them from the Spanish territory, and march the army back to Mobile and New Orleans. (See Appendix, No. 17-b.) The army set out on the 9th of November, for fort Montgomery on the Alabama, whence the troops were marched to their respective destinations, and the general, after having made some dispositions at Mobile for the protection of that place, set out the 21st November, by land; and arrived at New Orleans the 2d of December, 1814.

The legislature of the state of Louisiana, which had convened by the governor's proclamation of the 5th of October, met on the 10th of November. The following day, the governor delivered to both houses, a speech, on which the limits of this work do not permit us to enlarge; we shall, therefore, merely observe, that after taking a cursory view of the military events that had taken place from the commencement of the war, and particularly during the last campaign, the governor informed the legislature of the well-founded apprehensions entertained of an attack on Louisiana by the British, with a force, as was presumed, of from twelve to fifteen thousand men. The governor next entered into minute details as to the forces we had to oppose to those of the enemy. He informed the legislature, that the troops which had already taken the field, were shortly to be joined by considerable reinforcements of Tennessee and Kentucky militia. He expressed his satisfaction at the zeal, patriotism, and military ardour, displayed by the inhabitants of the country, in this critical conjuncture; commended the alacrity with which the several militia officers had effected the levy of the quota of militia called out; and bestowed particular expressions of commendation, on the zeal of the inhabitants of Attakapas and Feliciana, who had already formed two companies of cavalry.

The governor finally recommended to the legislature to order the expenses to be incurred by the movements of the militia, in the event of the enemy's effecting a landing in any part of the state, to be advanced out of the state treasury, saving a claim on the general government for the reimbursement of the sums advanced.

On the 2d of December, general Jackson arrived at New Orleans, where he established his head-quarters. On the same day he reviewed the battalion of the uniform companies of New Orleans militia, commanded by major Daquin. The military appearance of those companies, completely equipped, and the precision of their manœuvres, gave the general great pleasure, and he testified his satisfaction to the officers. From that day the general foresaw what he might expect from that gallant battalion; and we shall see in the course of the campaign that it realized his expectations.

The situation of our country at that period, owing to the proximity of the enemy—the number of whose ships of war on our coast was daily increasing—was critical in the extreme: but the unbounded confidence which the nation in general had in the talents of general Jackson, made us all look up to that officer, as a commander destined to lead our troops to victory, and to save our country. It is hardly possible to form an idea of the change which his arrival produced on the minds of the people. Hitherto partial attempts had been made to adopt measures of defence; the legislature had appointed a joint committee of both houses, to concert with the governor, commodore Patterson, and the military commandant, such measures as they should deem most expedient; but nothing had been done. There was wanting that concentration of power, so necessary for the success of military operations. The citizens, having very little confidence in their civil or military authorities, for the defence of the country, were filled with distrust and gloomy apprehension. Miserable disputes on account of two different committees of defence; disputes, unfortunately countenanced by the presence and influence of several public officers, had driven the people to despondency; they complained, and not without cause, that the legislature wasted time, and consumed the money of the state, in idle discussions on empty formalities of election, while all their time, and all the wealth they squandered, might by profitably employed in the defence of the country. Credit was annihilated—already for several months had the banks suspended the payment of their notes; to supply the want of specie, one and three dollar notes had been issued, and dollars had been cut as a substitute for small change. On the banks' refusing specie, the monied men had drawn in their funds, which they no longer lent out, without an usurious interest of three or four per cent. per month. Every one was distressed; confidence had ceased; and with it, almost every species of business.

Our situation seemed desperate. In case of an attack, we could hope to be saved only by a miracle, or by the wisdom and genius of a commander-in-chief. Accordingly, on his arrival, he was immediately invested with the confidence of the public, and all hope centered in him. We shall, hereafter, see how amply he merited the confidence which he inspired.

With his usual activity, adhering to his constant practice of seeing every thing himself, as far as practicable, general Jackson, the second day after his arrival, set out to visit fort St. Philip, at Plaquemines, and to examine what parts of the river below New Orleans, it might be expedient to fortify. Previously to his departure, he had sent orders to governor Claiborne to cause all the bayous leading from the ocean into the interior of the country, to be obstructed. This measure had been ordered to be executed along the whole coast, from Attakapas to Chef-Menteur and Manchac.

On visiting fort St. Philip, the general ordered the demolition of the wooden barracks within the fort, several additional pieces of artillery to be mounted on the rampart, and a thirty-two pounder and a mortar in the covered way. He also ordered two batteries to be constructed, the one opposite the fort on the right bank, on the site of the former fort Bourbon, and the other half a mile above the fort, and on the same bank. These batteries were to be mounted with twenty-four pounders. The latter, in particular, was in a situation extremely advantageous for commanding the river, and could join its fire with that of fort St. Philip.

On his return to New Orleans, the general ordered me to draw out the necessary plans for those two batteries, which plans being drawn out and approved of by him, the necessary measures were taken for putting them into immediate execution. General Jackson proceeded to visit Chef-Menteur, and having gone as far as the confluence of the Bayou Sauvage and the river of Chef-Menteur, he ordered the erection of a battery at that point.

In the evening of the 13th of December, commodore Patterson received information that the naval forces of the enemy at anchor at Ship island, were increased to thirty sail, of which six were ships of the line; that others were every moment arriving, especially a number of light vessels, calculated for navigating on our coast where there is but little water, and that the enemy appeared to be sounding the passes.

The general wrote on the 10th to the governor of the state, and informed him of his return from visiting the posts down the river as far as fort St. Philip. In that letter he observes that the river is capable of being well defended, provided suitable batteries be raised on its banks; and that he has fixed on the points on which they ought to be erected. The general proposes to the governor to call on the patriotism of the members of the legislature, to assist him in the present conjuncture, with all the means in their power. As the works to be raised chiefly consist of earth thrown up, he is of opinion that it would be expedient to suggest to the planters the propriety of furnishing their gangs of negroes, to be employed for a certain time in those works. He thinks the importance of the subject worthy the immediate attention of the legislature, who, he hopes, will not delay a moment to furnish means for putting the country in a state of defence, by the erection of the fortifications contemplated. These, when completed, the general thinks, will secure the river against attacks of the enemy; but not a moment, says he, is to be lost in perfecting the defence of the Mississippi. With vigour, energy, and expedition, all is safe; delay may lose all.

The general concludes by requesting the governor to let him know, as soon as possible, what the legislature is disposed to do, to assist him in erecting the fortifications; he instances to him as a bright example, what had been done in New York. In case the legislature should not be able to realize the expectations he had conceived from their patriotism, the general wishes to know it, that he may make arrangements according to the means he possesses, for the defence of the country.

On the 14th of December, governor Claiborne addressed a circular letter to the inhabitants of the parishes of Plaquemines, St. Bernard, St. Charles, and St. John the Baptist, informing them of a resolution passed by the legislature, requiring the governor to call upon the inhabitants of such parishes as he might think proper, to send all such male negroes as they could dispose of to fort St. Charles or to the English Turn, to be thence sent to the different points that might be judged proper to be fortified, there to work on the fortifications. The governor in his circular letter, makes known to the inhabitants, that the state is in danger, that the enemy is in considerable force on our coast, and that his movements indicate a disposition to land. He concludes by expressing his reliance on the patriotism of the inhabitants, and his hopes that in the hour of peril, the voice of government will be listened to and respected by every good citizen.

CHAPTER 4

CAPTURE OF THE GUN-BOATS.

The arrival of a great number of the enemy's ships of various force on our eastern coast, sufficiently announced the intention of the British, soon to make an attack in this quarter. Commodore Daniel T. Patterson, commanding the New Orleans station, had received from Pensacola, a letter, dated the 5th of December, informing him of the arrival of sixty sail of British vessels, and of a still greater number being expected; that those vessels had on board a considerable number of troops destined to act against New Orleans. (See Appendix, No. 18.) On this information, the commodore had sent five gun-boats, one tender, and a despatch boat, towards the passes Mariana and Christiana, to watch the enemy's movements in that quarter. The command of this flotilla was given to Thomas ap Catesby Jones, who hoisted his flag on board gun-boat No. 156. Commodore Patterson's instructions directed that, if possible, it would be well to wait for the enemy's barges, launches, and pinnaces on the outside of the Rigolets; that perhaps the enemy would endeavour to cut off the gun-boats with his small craft and that if his forces were too considerable, it was not advisable to remain too long at the same anchoring ground, at that time between Ship and Cat islands, and that it was important to secure a retreat at the Rigolets, where they must wait for the enemy, and sink him or be sunk. The commodore particularly recommended the most vigilant attention in watching the enemy's movements, directing information thereof to be sent to him as frequently as possible.

Pursuant to his instructions, lieutenant Jones had detached gun-boats No. 23, lieutenant M'Keever, and No. 163, sailing-master Ulrick, to Dauphine island. On the 9th of December, these two vessels being at anchor within the island, espied two ships of war out at sea, steering westward. The two gun-boats immediately set sail, and accompanied them, keeping within the island till night; when the ships appeared to come to an anchor, the gun-boats continued on their course, and joined company, opposite Biloxi, with the three other gun-boats Nos. 5, 156 and 162, which composed the whole flotilla. They made sail the whole night, apprehending that if they remained at anchor, the enemy might send barges in the night to take them.

On the 10th, by break of day, they discovered an entire fleet of the enemy's vessels at anchor in the channel between Cat-island and Ship-island; on which the gun-boats made for pass Mariana, within which they anchored, and received provisions from the bay St. Louis.

On the 11th they remained at anchor the whole day, and put the gun-boats in the best condition to sustain an attack; and on the 12th they made sail towards the eastern point of Cat-island, whence they discovered the enemy's fleet so considerably increased, that it would have been imprudent to continue any longer where they then were.

On the 13th the gun-boats sailed for the bay St. Louis. At 4 o'clock in the afternoon were discovered a considerable number of the enemy's barges making for pass Christiana; upon which, agreeably to instructions, the gun-boats endeavoured to make for the Rigolets; but the wind having died away, and the current making strong towards the east, they could get no farther than the channel between the main land and Isle aux Malheureux, where they were obliged to come to an anchor about 2 after midnight.

Sailing-master Johnson, commanding the Seahorse tender, was then in the bay St. Louis for the purpose of protecting the public stores established on its western shore, when he was attacked that same day by several of the enemy's barges. He was supported in his defence by a battery of two six-pounders, and some of the enemy's barges were destroyed; but at last captain Johnson was forced to yield to numbers, and set fire to his vessel, as likewise to the public Stores, to prevent their falling into the hands of the enemy.

On the 14th, by break of day, were discovered, five miles to the eastward, a great number of barges formed in a line, which came to and laid on their graplings for about fifteen minutes, after which they advanced in a line of about forty-five barges and other craft in front, to attack the gun-boats. Lieutenant M'Keever's, No. 23, carrying a thirty-two pounder, tried immediately to fire on the barges, but the ball could not reach them. A small division of them made for the tender Alligator, which had been prevented by the calm from joining the gun-boats, and was at anchor two miles from them, to the southeast of Malheureux island. Having taken the Alligator, the division rejoined the flotilla, which continued to advance in line of battle, until they got so near that the fire from the gun-boats began to produce some confusion; on which they separated into three divisions. One of these consisting of fifteen barges, attacked commodore Jones's gun-boat, No. 156, at anchor half a cable's length from the others, in the centre towards the enemy. The others divided so as to attack all the gun-boats at once. By half after eleven in the forenoon, the attack became general, and after three quarters of an hour of a most vigorous resistance, made by one hundred and eighty-two men, including officers distributed in the different gun-boats, against about twelve hundred of the enemy in very large barges and other craft, carrying nine and twelve-pounders and twenty-four pound carronades, the gunboats were forced to strike, after having lost six men, and thirty-five being wounded, many of them severely. (See Atlas, plate No. 4.)

Lieutenant Jones who commanded the flotilla, was wounded in the left shoulder. Lieutenant R. Spidden [Spedden] was wounded in both his arms, one of which, it was necessary to amputate; and lieutenant M'Keever was also wounded, but slightly. The enemy having got possession of one of the gun-boats, fired several shot from her upon the others, without striking the American flag. The enemy's loss was very considerable, amounting, it is supposed, to upwards of three hundred men. Nor will this estimate appear exaggerated when it is considered that a great number of barges and lanches were sunk. One of the latter, with a crew of one hundred and eighty men, went down astern of No. 156.

In the report made by lieutenant Jones to commodore Patterson, (see Appendix No. 19) and transmitted by the latter to the secretary of war, may be seen all the particulars of the obstinate resistance made by the officers and crews of the gun-boats, notwithstanding the disadvantageous circumstances under which they were attacked. Amongst these was a very strong current running against them, while several of them were sunk eighteen inches in the mud, so that it was impossible to manœuvre against barges almost as large as the gun-boats themselves. It is presumable that had not the wind died away, the gun-boats under sail, would have destroyed the flotilla, though numerous and well armed. The British during the fight manœuvred very skilfully, and as soon as they became masters of any gun-boat, they directed her fire against such of the others as had not struck.

The observation, which a due regard to truth compelled me to make at the beginning of this work, respecting the defenceless state in which Louisiana was found at the time of its invasion, here forces itself again upon me. But it is far from my intention to impute any fault to those whose conduct exempted them from censure. Probably a concurrence of untoward circumstances, unknown to me, may have occasioned the apparent neglect of Louisiana. No one is more disposed than I am to render justice to the patriotism, activity and zeal displayed by the heads of the different departments of our administration during the whole course of the war, which is now so happily terminated: nor is any one more ready to acknowledge the firmness and wisdom that so strongly marked the line of conduct pursued by our worthy president. Twenty-five gun-boats, however, might at that time have saved Louisiana, by rendering it impossible for the British to land, and obliging them to abandon the project of attacking New Orleans by the lakes. In that case, the enemy would have been forced to take post at Mobile, in order to carry on the war by land in the Floridas. And fortunate it would have been for us, had he pursued this course, and much it is to be wished he may attempt it, should our country ever hereafter be at war with Great Britain. I predict that all the British troops that may attempt to march through the pine-barrens of Florida, will find their graves there; and for the accomplishment of my prediction, I would rely entirely on Tennessee riflemen.

Commodore Patterson, who had served several years on the New Orleans station, which he had commanded from nearly the commencement of the war, was perfectly acquainted with our coast, and consequently knew what means were necessary to defend it. On this subject he had written, at an early period, and several times since, to the secretary of the navy. At Tchifonte, on the eastern shore of lake Pontchartrain, a flat-bottomed frigate had been begun to be built, two years before, calculated for the navigation of the lakes of our coasts. She was to carry forty-two pieces of cannon, twenty-six of which were to be thirty-two pounders. The building of this frigate was suspended in consequence, I believe, of the representations of brigadier-general Flournoy, then commanding this district. From his first taking the command of the station, commodore Patterson had not ceased to solicit government to authorize him to have that frigate finished. Governor Claiborne's correspondence with the heads of the different departments was also to the same effect; but though much was promised, nothing was performed. It might have been thought, from the little regard that was paid to the representations of the superior officers of the district, and of our representatives in congress, that Louisiana was considered as a bastard child of the American family; or that to attack her was looked upon as an impossibility. Yet the attack made on us was within a hair's breadth of succeeding; for had the enemy appeared a few weeks sooner, before general Jackson arrived in New Orleans, he might have entered the city with little or no opposition, there being no means of resisting him; and however well inclined the citizens were to defend themselves, it would have been impossible to prevent the taking of the city. The capture of our gun-boats having left our coast defenceless, and permitted the enemy to choose whatever point he thought most convenient to land on, it became necessary to redouble our efforts in making preparations for defence.

General Jackson was returning from a tour of observation to the river of Chef-Menteur, when the intelligence of the loss of the gun-boats reached him. He immediately ordered the militia-battalion of men of colour, commanded by major Lacoste, and the dragoons of Feliciana, to proceed with two pieces of cannon and take post at the confluence of Bayou Sauvage and the river of Chef-Menteur, in order to cover the road to the city on that side, and watch the enemy's movements. Major Lacoste was also ordered to erect a close redoubt surrounded with a fosse, according to a plan which I drew agreeably to general Jackson's orders.

On his arrival in town, the general bent his attention to the fortifying of all assailable points, it being impossible to ascertain which the enemy would make choice of, the want of vessels on the lake depriving us of all means of obtaining any certain intelligence of his movements, before he could effect his landing.

Captain Newman of the artillery, who commanded the fort of Petites Coquilles, which stands at the inner entry of the pass of the Rigolets, towards lake Pontchartrain, was positively ordered to defend his post to the last extremity, and in case of his not being able to hold out, to spike the guns, blow up the fort, and evacuate on the post of Chef-Menteur.

Captain P. Jugeant was authorized to levy and form into companies all the Chactaw Indians he could collect. (See Appendix, No. 18-a.)

On the 15th the commander-in-chief informed generals Coffee, Carrol and Thomas of the taking of the gun-boats, by letters sent by express, urging them to use all possible speed in marching to New Orleans with the troops under their command.

General Winchester commanding at Mobile, was also informed of the loss of our naval force, and it was earnestly recommended to him to use the greatest vigilance in protecting the vicinity of that town, as the enemy might endeavour to make an attack in that quarter.

On the 16th general Jackson wrote to the secretary of war, apprizing him of the capture of the gun-boats; he expressed to him his concern for the consequences that might attend that event, which he apprehended might happen, when he wrote to government suggesting the propriety of giving the necessary orders for finishing the block-ship building at Tchifonte, and when he gave orders for supplying forts Strother, Williams, and Jackson, with six months provisions. The general apprehended lest the interruption of our communications by water with Mobile, might be attended with consequences fatal to the safety of the country. He however assured the secretary of war that, should the enemy effect a landing, he would, with the help of God, do all he could to repel him. He also informed the secretary that neither the Tennessee troops nor those of Kentucky had yet arrived, but that they were daily expected, and that in the meanwhile he was putting the river below the city in the best possible state of defence. He acquainted him with the taking of the post of the Balise, with all the pilots, and a detachment of troops that was there stationed, but he informed him at the same time of the establishment of martial law, and of the rising of the militia in mass. "The country," said the general, "shall be defended, if in the power of the physical force it contains, with the auxiliary force ordered. We have no arms here—will the government order a supply? If it will, let it be speedily. Without arms, a defence cannot be made."

During the summer, while yet among the Creeks, general Jackson had made a requisition of a quantity of arms, ammunition, heavy cannon, balls, bombs, &c. to be sent to New Orleans; but such was the fatality that appeared to be attached to all the measures adopted for our defence, that it was not till the middle of January, 1815, that a very small proportion of what had been ordered, arrived at New Orleans. (See Appendix, No. 18-b.)

A special law of the state had, some time before, authorized the formation of a battalion of free men of colour; and we have seen that it had already taken the field under the command of major Lacoste, and had been stationed at Chef-Menteur. Colonel Michael Fortier, senior, a respectable and worthy citizen of New Orleans, having the superior command of all the corps of men of colour, presided over the levying of a new battalion, of the same description, formed by the exertions and under the direction of the gallant captain Savary, who had acquired an honourable and distinguished reputation in the wars of St. Domingo. It was chiefly with refugees from that island, that colonel Savary formed that battalion, whose officers were immediately commissioned by the governor of the state; and its command was confided to major Daquin of the 2d regiment of militia. We shall hereafter see in the relation of the different engagements, that that brave corps realized, by a brilliant display of valour, the hopes that had been conceived of it.

The capture of the gun-boats was announced to the senate and house of representatives of the state, by a message from the governor: "I lay before you," said he, "a letter addressed to me by commodore Patterson, announcing the capture of five of the United States gun-boats of the New Orleans station, by a vastly superior force of the enemy. The length of the combat is a proof of the valour and firmness with which our gallant tars maintained the unequal contest, and leaves no doubt that, although compelled ultimately to strike, their conduct has been such as to reflect honour upon the American name and navy. The ascendancy which the enemy has now acquired on the coast of the lake, increases the necessity of enlarging our measures of defence."

Commodore Patterson addressed a second letter to the governor, in which he complained of the want of seamen to man the armed vessels then at New Orleans, and requested the support and assistance of the state authorities. This letter was laid by the governor before the legislature, who, on the ——— day of December, passed a resolution giving a bounty of twenty-four dollars to each seaman who would enter the service of the United States for three months, and to this end placed at the disposition of the governor six thousand dollars. The governor forthwith issued his proclamation (see Appendix No. 22.) Between seventy and eighty sailors received the bounty of the state, and were of the number of those brave tars who, by their incessant fire from the ship Louisiana and the schooner Carolina, so annoyed the enemy in all his movements, and so particularly harassed him on the night of the 23d of December, as will be seen hereafter.*

On the 18th of December, general Jackson reviewed the New Orleans militia, the first and second regiments, the battalion of uniform companies under the command of major Plauché, and part of the free men of colour. Addresses were read to them, and answered with acclamations of applause. My voice is too weak to speak of these addresses in adequate terms; I leave the reader to form an idea of the effect they must have produced on the minds of

*On a representation made by the governor on the 16th of December, the state legislature passed a law laying an embargo for three days, to facilitate to commodore Patterson the means of enlisting sailors.

the militia, from the impression that the mere perusal of them will make on himself. (See Appendix, No. 20.) These corps had two days before entered upon actual service, and did regular duty like troops of the line. On the 18th, Plauché's battalion was sent to Bayou St. John, and the major took the command of that post.

A general order of this day enjoined all officers commanding detachments, out-posts, and pickets, on the approach of the enemy, to remove out of his reach every kind of stock, horses, &c. and provisions; and directed them upon their responsibility to oppose the invaders at every point, and harass them by all possible means. It concluded with this animating sentence:

"The major-general anticipating that the enemy will penetrate into this district in a few days, requests of the people of Louisiana to do their duty cheerfully, and bear the fatigues incident to a state of war, as becomes a great people, anticipating from the ardour pervading, and the present help at hand, to make an easy conquest of them, and teach them in future to respect the rights of liberty and the property of freemen."

The garrison of fort St. John, on lake Pontchartrain, had been reinforced by the volunteer company of light artillery, under the command of lieutenant Wagner.

By an order of the day of the 19th, the commander-in-chief ordered several persons confined in the different military prisons, for having violated the laws of the country, to be set at liberty, on their offering to take up arms in defence of the country.

But that favour was restricted to such persons as were within two months of completing the term of imprisonment to which they had been condemned. These and all others not under sentence were, in pursuance of that order, set at liberty by the commanding officers at fort St. Charles, the barracks, and the powder magazine.

The country being now in imminent danger, it became necessary to adopt the most vigorous measures to prevent all communication with the enemy; and in order that such persons as might be apprehended for having given the British information as to the situation of the country, its means of defence in troops, artillery, fortifications, &c. might not escape punishment, general Jackson wrote to the governor, suggesting to him the propriety of his recommending to the legislature to suspend the writ of *habeas corpus*. As the danger was daily increasing, the general could not, without exposing the safety of the country, whose defence was committed to him, wait till the dilatory forms of deliberation should empower him to take the steps necessary for saving it.

Nor did it escape his penetration that the legislature was not disposed to second his views, by that energetic measure. The hour of combat grew near, that of discussing, deliberating, and referring to committees, had gone by. The time called for action and promptitude; and accordingly general Jackson proclaimed martial law, (see Appendix, No. 21.) and from that moment his means became more commensurate with the weight of responsibility he had to sustain. The object of his commission was to save the country; and this, he was sensible, could never be effected by half-measures. It was necessary that all the forces, all orders, all means of opposition to be directed against the enemy, should receive their impulse from the centre of the circumference they occupied. They ought to be radii, diverging from one and the same point, and not entangling chords intersecting that circumference and each other. From the moment martial law was proclaimed, every thing proceeded with order and regularity, nor did any of our means prove abortive. Every individual was stationed at his proper post. The guard of the city was committed to the corps of veterans and fire-engine men, who were to occupy the barracks, hospitals, and other posts, as soon as the troops of the line and the militia should be commanded on service out of town.

The privateers of Barataria, and all persons arrested for, or accused of, any infraction of the revenue laws, sent to tender their services to general Jackson. Mr. J. Lafitte, adhering to the line of conduct he had marked out for himself, and from which he had never deviated from the beginning of September, when the British officers made him proposals, waited on the commander-in-chief, who, in consideration of the eventful crisis, had obtained for him a safe conduct from judge Hall, and from the marshal of the district.

Mr. Lafitte solicited for himself and for all the Baratarians, the honour of serving under our banners, that they might have an opportunity of proving that if they had infringed the revenue laws, yet none were more ready than they to defend the country and combat its enemies.

Persuaded that the assistance of these men could not fail of being very useful, the general accepted their offers. Some days after, a certain number of them formed a corps under the command of captains Dominique and Beluche, and were employed during the whole campaign at the lines, where, with distinguished skill, they served two twenty-four pounders, batteries Nos. 3 and 4. Others enlisted in one or other of the three companies of mariners, raised by captains Songis, Lagaud, and Colson. The first of these companies was sent to the fort of Petites Coquilles, the second to that of St. Philip, and the third to bayou St. John.

All classes of society were now animated with the most ardent zeal. The young, the old, women, children, all breathed defiance to the enemy, firmly resolved to oppose to the utmost the threatened invasion. General Jackson had electrified all hearts; all were sensible of the approaching danger; but they waited its presence undismayed. They knew that, in a few days, they must come to action with the enemy; yet, calm and unalarmed, they pursued their usual occupations, interrupted only when they tranquilly left their homes to perform military duty at the posts assigned them. It was known that the enemy was on our coast, within a few hours sail of the city, with a presumed force of between nine and ten thousand men; whilst all the forces we had yet to oppose him amounted to no more than one thousand regulars, and from four to five thousand militia.

These circumstances were publicly known, nor could any one disguise to himself, or to others, the dangers with which we were threatened. Yet, such was the universal confidence; inspired by the activity and decision of the commander-in-chief, added to the detestation in which the enemy was held, and the desire to punish his audacity, should he presume to land, that not a single warehouse or shop was shut, nor were any goods or valuable effects removed from the city. At that period, New Orleans presented a very affecting picture to the eyes of the patriot, and of all those whose bosoms glow with the feelings of national honour, which raise the mind far above the vulgar apprehension of personal danger. The citizens were preparing for battle as cheerfully as if it had been a party of pleasure, each in his vernacular tongue singing songs of victory. The streets resounded with *Yankee Doodle, the Marseilles Hymn, the Chant du Depart*, and other martial airs, while those who had been long unaccustomed to military duty, were furbishing their arms and accoutrements. Beauty applauded valour, and promised with her smiles to reward the toils of the brave. Though inhabiting an open town, not above ten leagues from the enemy, and never till now exposed to war's alarms, the fair sex of New Orleans were animated with the ardour of their defenders, and with cheerful serenity at the sound of the drum, presented themselves at the windows and balconies, to applaud the troops going through their evolutions, and to encourage their husbands, sons, fathers, and brothers, to protect them from the insults of our ferocious enemies, and prevent a repetition of the horrors of Hampton.

The several corps of militia were constantly exercising from morning till evening, and at all hours was heard the sound of drums, and of military bands of music. New Orleans wore the appearance of a camp; and the greatest cheerfulness and concord prevailed amongst all ranks and conditions of people. All countenances expressed a wish to come to an engagement with the enemy, and announced a foretaste of victory.

Commodore Patterson sent gun-boat No. 65 to fort St. Philip. Lieutenant Cunningham who commanded it, had orders to send an armed boat to the Balise, for the purpose of bringing up the custom-house officer, and of ascertaining, if possible, the enemy's force. He was further directed to give to the commanding officer at Plaquemine all the assistance in his power. The commodore ordered captain M. B. Carrol, the officer who had the command of the navy-yard at Tchifonte, to cause the brig Aetna to ascend the bayou, and take a station opposite the unfinished block-ship, for the defence of the latter, in case of the approach of the enemy. Captain Carrol was further ordered not to suffer any boat to leave Tchifonte for the bayou St. John, without a passport, and in the event of the enemy's entering lake Pontchartrain, not to let the mail-boat pass.

Mr. T. Shields, purser, and doctor R. Morrell, surgeon of the navy, were sent, on the 15th December, at night, by commodore Patterson, with a flag of truce, to the British fleet, for the purpose of obtaining correct information as to the situation of the officers and crews made prisoners on board the gun-boats, and of endeavouring to obtain their being suffered to return to town on parole. Doctor Morrell was likewise sent to administer his professional assistance to the wounded. On the following day, near the eastern branch of Pearl river, they fell in with gun-boat No. 5, one of those taken. Shortly after they went on board the frigate Seahorse, captain Gordon, to whom they stated the object of their mission, and by whom they were sent in a tender to admiral Cochrane, who commanded the squadron. They met the admiral in his barge, who having read commodore Patterson's letter and the credentials he had given to those gentlemen, returned the letter without any observation, and ordered the tender to anchor at the mouth of Pearl river.

On the 18th, in the morning, the admiral sent for the gentlemen, who accordingly waited on him on shore on Isle-aux-Pois. He first inquired what rank they held in the American navy: and next observed that their visit was unseasonable under the existing circumstances; that he could not permit them to return, until the intended attack was made, and the fate of New Orleans decided. In support of his opinion, he instanced a similar case that had occurred at Baltimore, and concluded by observing, that prudence and policy obliged him to send them on board some vessel belonging to the fleet. On the gentlemen's expressing a wish to know in what light he thought proper to consider them, the admiral replied that it was his intention to respect the flag of truce, though he thought he should not be reprehensible, were he to treat them as prisoners of war.

The motive which induced these gentlemen to inquire of the British admiral in what light they were to be considered, was the just suspicion which they entertained from the previous conduct of the enemy towards them. Their boat had been moored astern of the tender, and plundered of all its rigging, and a guard had been stationed in her. It was with the greatest difficulty that a sail was obtained to shelter the men from the rain and intense cold during the night. Next morning, the tender was ordered to convey them on board the Gorgon, hospital ship, where were most of the wounded men of the crews of the gun-boats. Through the negligence of the officer commanding the tender, the boat which he had in tow, was sunk, and every thing on board of her was lost. But what particularly evinced the outrageous spirit of the British, was that the officer commanding the tender, forced the crew of the boat under a flag of truce, to work like his own sailors. To put a stop to this violation of the law of nations, it was necessary to come to an explanation with that officer, lieutenant Johnston; who, being irritated at the circumstance, refused to give the least assistance to some of our wounded men, who had been already twenty-eight hours on board the tender, whither they had been removed from on board the brig Anaconda, without having yet received any nourishment whatever. On board the Gorgon, the gentlemen found our wounded perfectly well treated by the British. As it is with reluctance that I have been under the necessity of reproaching them with their cruelty in a variety of instances, it is here particularly grateful to me, to have occasion to do justice to their humanity; for in describing the horrors of war, the feeling heart finds a most pleasing relief from his painful task, in dwelling upon instances of humane conduct.

Admiral Cochrane had promised Messrs. Shield and Morrell that they should be permitted to visit their countrymen, and yet, with duplicity unworthy his high rank, he gave a written order, "that on no pretence whatever were they to be permitted to leave the Gorgon, until further orders."

The loss of their boat having left these officers entirely without linen or any other clothes than those on their persons, and there appearing no rational ground to detain them as prisoners who had come under the sanction of a flag of truce, they several times, through the channel of different officers, applied to the admiral, claiming to be set at liberty, with their boat's crew. But all their applications were to no purpose, until the 12th of January, on which day they were released, and on the 18th they arrived in town. (See Appendix, No. 21-a.)

The defence of the country requiring the absence of a number of citizens from their homes, an interruption of business became unavoidable; and the obligation of performing military duty, precluded the possibility of fulfilling commercial engagements. This state of things induced the legislature to pass a law prolonging the term of payment on all contracts, till the 1st of May next ensuing, and providing various regulations on that subject. (See Appendix, No. 22.)

On the 21st of December, when the orders that had been given for obstructing the different canals of the bayous below Manchac were presumed to have been executed, a detachment of the 3d regiment of militia, consisting of eight white men and a serjeant, two mulattoes and one negro, with a single boat, was sent by major Villeré (the son) to the village of the Spanish fishermen, on the left bank of the bayou Bienvenu, a mile and a half from its entrance into lake Borgne, for the purpose of discovering whether the enemy might try to penetrate that way, and to give notice of such attempt.

The bayou Bienvenu has unfortunately become so remarkable from the British forces having penetrated through it, into Louisiana, that it deserves a particular description.

This bayou, formerly called the river St. Francis, under which designation it is laid down in some old maps, is the creek through which run all the waters of a large basin, of a triangular form, about eighty square miles in surface, bounded on the south by the Mississippi, on the west by New Orleans, by bayou Sauvage or Chef-Menteur on the northwest, and on the east by lake Borgne, into which it empties. It receives the waters of several other bayous, formed by those of the surrounding cypress swamps and prairies, and of innumerable little streams from the low grounds along the river. It commences behind the suburb Marigny, at New Orleans, divides the triangle nearly into two equal parts from the summit to the lake which forms its basis, and runs in a south-easterly direction. It is navigable for vessels of one hundred tons as far as the forks of the canal of Piernas' plantation, twelve miles from its mouth. Its breadth is from one hundred and ten to one hundred and fifty yards, and it has six feet water on the bar, at common tides, and nine feet at spring tides. Within the bar, there is for a considerable extent, sufficient water for vessels of from two to three hundred tons. Its principle branch is that which is called bayou Mazant, which runs towards the southwest, and receives the waters of the canals of the plantations of Villeré, Lacoste, and

Laronde, on which the enemy established his principle encampment. It was at the forks of the canal Villeré and bayou Mazant that the British ascended in their pinnances, and effected a landing.

Of the other branches of the bayou Bienvenu we shall take no particular notice; that called bayou Mazant being the only one connected with the British military movements. (See Atlas, plate No. 5.)

The level of the great basin, or the bank of the principal bayou, is usually twelve feet below the level of the banks of the Mississippi. The slope is usually one half of that height, or six feet, for the descent of the lands under culture, of from about one half to two-thirds of a mile in depth from the river, and the remaining six feet is the slope of cypress swamps and prairies, which are usually three or four times the depth, or extent of the high-lands susceptible of cultivation; so that one thousand yards, the usual depth of the lands under culture, have a slope of six feet, which gives less than 0,005 of a foot to each yard, whilst the prairies and cypress swamps together, commonly six thousand yards in depth, have but 0,001 of a foot to the yard in slope. The overflowing of the waters of all those bayous and canals, occasioned by the tide of the sea, or by the winds raising the waters in the lake, forms on all their banks deposits of slime, which are continually raising them above the rest of the soil, so that the interval between two bayous is, of course, below the level of their banks, and the soil is generally covered with water and mud, aquatic plants, or large-reeds, growing there in abundance to the height of from six to eight feet: it sometimes happens that the rains, or the filtrated waters collected in these intervals or basins, not finding any issue to flow off, form what are called *trembling prairies*, which are at all seasons impassable for men and domestic animals.

In times of great drought, and in low tides, the ordinary prairies are passable, and some of them are frequented by the cattle of the neighbouring plantations, which prefer the grass they find there to that which grows on the banks of the river, on account of the saline particles deposited among the former by the waters of the lakes overflowing into the bayous. Such is nearly the structure of those basins or prairies, which are very extensive in Louisiana, and what we have observed of those which are immediately connected with our subject, is applicable, more or less, to all the others in the country. From the high-lands of the Floridas, where the first hills begin, all the rest, as far as the sea, is alluvion land, gained from the water by the deposits from streams, particularly the Mississippi. This space is crossed in different directions by strips of high-land, between which there is invariably a river or bayou, more or less subject to periodical swells or tides; the surface of these waters is usually but little below the soil contiguous to their banks, and always higher than that which is at a certain distance. In a word, the land in Lower Louisiana slopes in the inverse direction of the soil of other countries, being most elevated on the sides of the rivers, and sinking as it recedes from them. The Mississippi swells annually and periodically at New Orleans fourteen or fifteen feet, and is then from three to four feet above the level of its banks. To contain its waters within its bed, dikes or ramparts, called in Louisiana *levees*, have been raised on its banks, from the high-lands towards its mouth, a little above the level of the highest swells; without which precaution the lands would be entirely overflowed from four to five months in the year. When, from accident, or negligence in keeping up these dikes, the river breaks through them, the rupture, called in this country a *crevasse*, occasions an extensive inundation, which lays the adjacent cypress swamps under ten and the prairies under twelve feet water. Such accidents unfortunately too common, usually destroy at once the crops of ten and sometimes of twenty plantations. It is hoped that the frequent recurrence of the evil, owing to a defective system of police for the levees, will determine the legislature to take effectual measures to prevent such disasters, by ceasing to confide to the respective landholders a care so important to the whole country as that of the levees, and imposing a tax on the lands where they run, for the purpose of keeping them always in repair.

This digression appeared to me necessary, to give a precise idea of the ground which was the theatre of the military operations I am about to relate, and which could not be perfectly understood without these preliminary observations.

The detachment, composed as I have observed, repaired in the night of the 21st December to the post assigned, the fishermen's village, consisting of twelve very large cabins, capable of containing from two hundred to three hundred men, and constructed with stakes, thatched and inclosed with palmetto leaves, on a tongue of land on the left bank of bayou Bienvenu. In these cabins lived about thirty or forty fishermen, almost all Spaniards or Portuguese. From lake Borgne, which being shallow and in their vicinity, afforded them an advantageous fishing ground, they used to convey their fish in pirogues (periaguas) to the extremity of the canal of La Ronde's and Villeré's plantations, from which place it was transported in wagons to town. The owners of those plantations Messrs. Villeré, Lacoste and La Ronde, permitted those fishermen to enjoy the gratuitous use of their canals, and constantly afforded relief to such of those wretches as happened to fall sick; and it will soon appear that in return for the beneficence of those gentlemen, the wretches sold the lives and fortunes of their benefactors.

I have not been able to discover the names of all those fishermen, to consign them to execration and infamy, as I here do the following few who have come to my knowledge.

Master Fishermen.

Maringuier	Francisco
Old Luiz	Graviella

Hireling Fishermen.

Antonio el Italiano	Manuelillo
El Campechano	Antonio El Mayorquin
Antonio El Portuguez	Garcia.

These are well known to have aided the British in disembarking their troops, serving as pilots on board their vessels and boats, and acting as spies for them from the period of their arrival on our coast. It was their practice, when they came to town to sell their fish, to get all the information they could, for the purpose of carrying it to the English, when they went out to fish in lake Borgne. On the 20th of December, the day preceding the arrival of the detachment at the village, the British captain Peddie had come disguised, accompanied by the three first named of these fishermen, as far as the bank of the Mississippi, and had even tasted its water. It was from his report, after having thus examined the country, that the enemy determined to penetrate by Villeré's canal, whose banks at the time afforded firm footing from the landing place in the prairie to the river.

When the detachment arrived at the village, they found only one fisherman, and him sick, all the others having gone the day before, under the pretence of fishing, to serve as pilots to the British barges. A few men were immediately sent into the lake to discover whether the enemy were already arrived, and on their return, a sentinel was posted at some distance in advance of the last cabin, for the rest of the night.

On the 22d by break of day a reconnoitring party of three men was again sent two miles into the lake, and during that whole day, fresh parties were sent out every two hours, to discover whether the enemy were approaching. Towards evening, three men in a pirogue arrived from Chef-Menteur, who had traversed part of the lake without seeing any enemy. That night a sentinel was again posted in advance of the cabins.

CHAPTER 5

AFFAIR OF THE 23d DECEMBER.

Some time after midnight, the sentinel having heard a noise, called his comrades, who all instantly seized their arms. By the last gleams of the setting moon, they perceived five barges full of men, with some pieces of artillery, ascending the bayou; on which, thinking it would be imprudent to fire, considering the great disproportion of numbers, they retired for concealment behind a cabin. As soon as the five barges had passed this cabin, a party determined to attempt to escape by the lake, and give information of the arrival of the enemy. With this view, seven men of the detachment had already got into the boat, when one of the barges having perceived them, gave the alarm to the four others, who all made for the boat and became masters of it, before it could be got ready to push off. Only four of those in the boat had time to land, and the remaining three were taken, as were two others on shore; so that of the whole detachment, only four escaped, who ran in different directions into the prairies; and of these four, three individuals, after having wandered a whole day in the prairies, where the height of the grass hindered them from seeing any way to get out of them, happened to fall into the hands of the enemy, at the very village from which they had fled. One alone, Mr. A. Rey, more persevering, or perhaps more fortunate, after three days of uncommon fatigue, hardships and perils, over trembling prairies, bayous, lagoons, and through cane brakes, arrived at the post of Bertoniere on the road leading from Gentilly to Chef-Menteur.

The enemy having made prisoners of all these men, shut them up in the cabin which they used as their quarters, and placed a guard at the door. What further corroborates the evidence of the communication of the fishermen with the British, is the precaution that had been taken by the only one of them that was at the village with the detachment on the arrival of the enemy, to shut up in a cabin, that same evening, all the dogs in the village, who had kept up an incessant barking, during all the preceding night. But this is not all: the British, through a mistake, shut up one of the fishermen with the detachment, on the morning of the 23d. This man seeing a British officer passing by the cabin, called to him, and on discovering himself to him as one of those whom he had frequently seen aboard British vessels, he was immediately set at liberty.

About an hour afterwards, Mr. Ducros, a native of Louisiana, was taken from among the prisoners in the cabin, and put on board a boat in which was captain Spencer of the navy, with a colonel of infantry. The boat proceeded to the lake, in which, when they had advanced about a mile, they met the rest of the first division, consisting of about three thousand men in eighty boats. That division was composed of the light brigade formed of the 85th and 95th regiments, captain Lane's rocketeers, one hundred men of the engineer corps, and the 4th regiment, all under the command of colonel Thornton.

Captain Spencer announced his prisoner to general Keane and admiral Cochrane, as one of those taken at the village. The admiral then inquired of Mr. Ducros, what might be the number of the American forces in the city and environs. The answer he received was, that there were from twelve to fifteen thousand men in the city, and from three to four at the English Turn. The admiral then ordered captain Spencer to proceed with all speed with the advanced guard, and to effect a landing at the point agreed on. The division proceeded accordingly, and when it arrived at the village, admiral Cochrane with several other officers, went on shore, and the division, under the command of general Keane, proceeded up the bayou. The admiral and the other officers put again to all the prisoners, the questions they had asked Mr. Ducros, and received from all nearly the same answer in consequence of a conversation the evening before, in which they had made the number of troops already arrived, or hourly expected at New Orleans, to amount to eighteen thousand men.

The division arrived at the extremity of Villeré's canal by four in the morning, and soon effected a landing, being almost wholly composed of light troops. After the troops had rested some hours, the British colours were displayed at the top of a tree, while the band played *God save the King*; and at about ten o'clock they commenced their march towards the banks of the Mississippi, cutting cane, as they went along, to facilitate their passage over the prairie and small bayous or *coulees*. From the mouth of the canal to the skirts of the wood, the distance is about a mile, and from thence to the bank of the river nearly two miles. At about half after eleven, the advance arrived at the side of the wood next to the river, and immediately extended along

Villeré's canal. They now surrounded the house of general Villeré, in which was stationed a company of the third regiment of militia, whom they made prisoners, and where they surprised major Villeré, his son, who, notwithstanding several pistols fired at him, made his escape through a window, and got to the river, where finding a pirogue, he crossed over to the right bank. Colonel Denis de la Ronde, who on that very night, the 23d, as indeed throughout the whole campaign, rendered essential services to his country, had also escaped from the enemy, and arrived in town by the opposite bank.

The rest of the troops of the division continued to arrive at general Villeré's house, and were on their march towards the higher boundary of the plantation, with intent to encamp there, when they were first discovered. Colonel Denis de la Ronde, who had stationed detachments of his regiment, the third of Louisiana militia, on general Villeré's and Jumonville's plantations, had, in the evening of the 22d sent, to inform general Jackson that several sails of vessels had been seen off the point of the three bayous, behind Terre aux Boeufs. The general ordered me to go, in company with major Tatum, topographical engineer, to ascertain whether this report were true; directing us to examine very particularly all the communications from Terre aux Boeufs to lake Borgne. We left town at eleven o'clock in the forenoon of the 23d, and when we arrived at the boundary of Bienvenu's and la Ronde's plantations, we met several persons flying towards town, who told us that the British had got to general Villeré's house by the canal, and had taken prisoner major Villeré, the general's son. It being of the utmost importance to inform general Jackson of an event no longer doubtful, major Tatum immediately returned to town, and I proceeded forward as far as over the boundary of Lacoste's and Villeré's plantations, whence I discovered British troops occupying the ground from the commencement of the angle made by the road in that place to the head of the canal. (See the plan of the affair of the 23d, Plate 6, in which that position is laid down.) I approached within rifle-shot of those troops, and judged that their number must amount to sixteen or eighteen hundred men. It was then half past one P.M., and within twenty five minutes after, general Jackson was informed of the enemy's position. On this the general, with that heroism and prompt decision which is characteristic of him, and of which he had exhibited such signal instances during the campaign, instantly said he would go to meet the British; and immediately issued orders to that effect. The alarm-gun was fired; the battalion of uniform volunteer companies, commanded by major Plauché, then stationed at the bayou St. John, was ordered to return and join the other corps with all possible speed, which order the battalion executed, running all the way.

By half after two in the afternoon, a detachment of artillery, two field pieces, commanded by lieutenant Spotts, and lieutenant-colonel McRae, the seventh of the line, the command of which regiment was given, for the present, to major Peire, on account of an accidental wound disabling major Nicks from active service, and a detachment of marines, commanded by lieutenant Bellevue, were all formed on the road, near Montreuil's plantation. Orders had likewise been sent to generals Coffee and Carroll, who were encamped four miles above the city, to march down with their commands, and these orders were executed in one hour's time.

General Coffee's command of mounted riflemen, and the volunteer dragoons of the Mississippi territory, formed the advance; the Orleans rifle company, commanded by captain Beale, followed on closely, and by four o'clock had taken a position on Rodriguez's canal; the battalion of men of colour, under major Daquin, the forty-fourth regiment, under captain Baker, and Plauché's battalion, which arrived about five o'clock from the bayou, marched with all expedition against the enemy. Commodore Patterson was requested to order such armed vessels as were ready, to drop down and take a station opposite the enemy. The schooner Carolina, captain Henley, was the only one in a condition to perform this service, as, there being no wind, the sloop of war Louisiana could not steer in the stream. Commodore Patterson went on board the Carolina, and there continued during the engagement. (See the commodore's letters to the secretary of the navy, Appendix, No. 23.)

Governor Claiborne was ordered, with the first, second, and fourth regiments of the Louisiana militia, and the volunteer company of horse, under captain Chauveau, to take a position between the Colson and Darcantel plantations, in the plain of Gentilly, in order to cover the city on the side of Chef-Menteur. About four o'clock, a piquet of five mounted riflemen, who had been sent to reconnoitre the road, was assailed by a discharge of musketry from a British out-post concealed behind the fence on the boundary of Laronde's and Lacoste's plantations, by which the reconnoitring party, too weak and too rash, lost a horse killed, and had two men wounded. Colonel Haines, inspector-general of the division, went forward, shortly after, with one hundred men, to reconnoitre the enemy; but he had no opportunity to form a correct estimate of their number, which he made to amount to no more than two hundred men; an error probably proceeding from his having taken the advance on the road for the troops drawn up in column some hours before, as reported by the officer who had first seen them.

A negro was apprehended, who had been sent by the British with printed copies of a proclamation, in French and Spanish, nearly in the following terms: "Louisianians! remain quiet in your houses; *your slaves shall be preserved to you*, and your property respected. We make war only against Americans." Signed by admiral Cochrane and major-general Keane.

We have seen, in the account of the offers made to Mr. Lafitte, what reliance was to be had on their promise to preserve slaves to their masters.

An hour before these papers were seized, the British had stuck up the same proclamation on the fences, all along the road below Laronde's plantation.

The troops now moved forward; general Coffee took the command of the left, composed of a part of his brigade, the Tennessee mounted riflemen, the Orleans company of riflemen, under captain Beale, forming the extremity of the left, a part of the Mississippi dragoons and mounted riflemen, amounting in all to seven hundred and thirty-two fighting men.

Colonel de la Ronde, the owner of the plantation on which the troops were formed, after having, about noon, escaped from the British at Villeré's, and crossed the river, had come to town and joined captain Beale's company as a volunteer; from his knowledge of the ground, he was now ordered by general Jackson to accompany general Coffee as a guide.

About nightfall, the left entered on La Ronde's plantation, and took a position in the back of it, on its boundary with Lacoste's.

The right formed on a line almost perpendicular to the river, stretching from the levée to the garden of La Ronde's plantation, and on its principal avenue. The artillery occupied the high road, supported by the detachment of marines. On the left of the artillery were stationed the seventh and forty-fourth of the line, Plauché's and Daquin's battalions, and eighteen Chactaw Indians, commanded by captains Jugeant and Allard, forming the extremity of the right wing towards the woods. The superior command of the battalions of militia was given to colonel Ross.

The boats that had landed the first division of the British troops returned down the bayou, and at eight o'clock passed the village on their way to take in the second division, which had been embarked in small vessels, and was already in the lake. By four in the afternoon, that division, consisting of the twenty-first, forty-fourth, and ninety-third regiments, with a division of artillery, in all two thousand five hundred men, arrived at the village. At half after seven in the evening, they were disembarking, when the firing was first heard from the schooner Carolina, which now opened on the division encamped on the river bank.

Admirals Cochrane and Malcolm, with several officers of the army and navy, had remained at the village to hasten the landing of the troops, and had there passed the whole day, during which time they frequently conversed with the prisoners, endeavouring to persuade them that the British army came with no hostile intent against the inhabitants of the country, who being mostly Frenchmen or Spaniards by birth or descent, must naturally (as these English gentlemen *naturally* supposed) prefer the British government to that of the United States. They told them that their intentions were to obtain and keep possession of the country, and to penetrate far up the Mississippi, to make the upper country the theatre of war; that to convince the inhabitants of their friendly intentions, they had brought with them three natives of Louisiana, serving in the troops of his catholic majesty in Pensacola; and accordingly those three persons alluded to, Messrs. Guillemard, Regio, and Grand Pré, were seen shortly after in company with the British officers; but fortunately were not able to give them any great assistance.

On the arrival of the second division at the village, the prisoners were embarked on board one of the boats, to be conveyed to their own homes. They landed at half past seven, with the second division, who, on hearing the report of the cannon, made all haste to repair to the scene of action, where they arrived in less than an hour, long before the action was over, so that several corps of that division were engaged in it.

The first division of British troops, having encamped, or rather bivouacked, as I have already observed, at the angle formed by the road, on the highest part of Villeré's plantation, in irregular order, some on the side of the levée, and others in the plain, out-posts had been stationed at different places, in an oblique line, extending from the boundary between La Ronde's and Lacoste's plantations, running along the negro huts of the latter, on the back of the dwelling house, as far as a cluster of live oaks, on Villeré's canal, near the wood. There was stationed a strong detachment to cover the communication with the rest of the army, by the road on the right bank of the canal. Through the plain ran a chain of out-sentries, very closely posted. A detachment of fifty men was stationed at Jumonville's bridge, on the border of the canal, on the road. One company had advanced as far as the bank of the river, behind the levée, and to the angle forming Mr. Villeré's inclosed batture, probably in order to prevent all surprise by the river. The detachment of the rocket brigade was stationed behind the levée, to use that diabolical invention against such vessels as might endeavour to annoy the camp. A few pieces of cannon had already arrived, and were mounted in the court near Villeré's sugar-works. A strong detachment of about five hundred men was stationed on the left bank of Villeré's canal, near the negro huts. General Keane and his officers, among whom was colonel Thornton, had established their head-quarters in Mr. Villeré's house.

The British general having thus, with little difficulty, succeeded in bringing his troops to the banks of the Mississippi, and there establishing his camp, in the belief that his arrival and position could not be known at New Orleans till late in the night, expected to meet with little or no resistance. Such was the security and confidence of the British army, that part of the troops had lain down in their bivouacs, and some picquets of the out-posts had lighted up large fires, at which the men were cooking their suppers, when they were surprised. It appears, indeed, not unlikely that the opinion they had of their superior military skill, the expectation with which they had been deluded, that the old population of the country would hail their arrival with joy, the cheering thoughts of their having arrived on the banks of the Mississippi, within nine miles of New Orleans, without having had occasion to fire a musket, contributed to make the British believe themselves in perfect security from any attack. (See the plan, Plate No. 6.)

About seven o'clock the Carolina came to anchor on the brink of Villeré's batture, opposite the centre of the British encampment, within musket-shot. Such was the security of the British, that taking that vessel for a common boat plying on the Mississippi, numbers of them went on the levée to examine her more closely. At half after seven the Carolina opened on them a dreadful fire, which continued for ten minutes before they could recover from the consternation with which they were struck by that sudden attack; so that they had not yet run to their arms, when the guns of the schooner had already killed or wounded upwards of a hundred of their men. The British at last extinguished the fires in their camp, and attempted to answer the schooner with a fire of musketry, from which the crew sustained no injury. Some Congreve rockets were tried with as little effect, and those who discharged them were forced to conceal themselves behind the levée. In less than half an hour the schooner drove the enemy from his camp. (See commodore Patterson's letter to the secretary of the navy, Appendix No. 24.)

At this moment a company of the seventh, commanded by lieutenant M'Klelland, under colonel Piatt, quarter-master-general, advanced from the gate of La Ronde's plantation, on the road, to the boundary of Lacoste's, at the distance of fifteen paces, where the detachment was received with a discharge of musketry, from one of the enemy's out-posts stationed on the road. Though this out-post consisted of a considerable number of men, that gallant company attacked them vigorously, and forced them to retire; and colonel Piatt, with a few men of the detachment, advanced to the ground from which they had just driven the enemy. The latter, having received a reinforcement of two hundred men, and being now about three hundred strong, returned to resume their former position, and kept up a brisk fire of musketry against the detachment, who as briskly returned it. In this affair colonel Piatt received a wound in the leg, lieutenant M'Klelland and a serjeant were killed, and a few men wounded.

Meantime the 7th regiment advanced by heads of companies parallel to the right, *appuye* on the high road, to the distance of 150 yards, where it formed in battalion before the enemy, with whom it instantly engaged with a very brisk and close fire. The 44th came up at the same time, formed on the left of the 7th, and commenced firing. The artillery having now arrived, the two pieces were put in battery on the road, the marines being drawn up on the right of the artillery on the river bank. The engagement now became general on both sides; the front of the British line greatly outflanked our line on the left, and the enemy seeing that he could not make our troops give way, caused some of his to file off on the old levée by a gate, three hundred yards from the river, with intent to turn our flank. The 44th had already been obliged to oblique on the left, to avoid being turned, when major Plauché's battalion, with that of major Daquin, with a very small number of Indians, advanced at the moment when their left was *appuye* on the angle of Laronde's garden, and the right a little in the rear of the 44th. The enemy's column advancing silently in the dark, to endeavour to turn the troops of the line, fell suddenly almost within pistol-shot of the extremity of Daquin's battalion, and instantly commenced a brisk firing. Plauché's battalion, now forming the centre, advanced in close column, and displayed under the enemy's fire, which was then kept up by his whole front, from the bank of the river to Laronde's garden, forming an angle, or curve, in the centre. Already had our troops, animated with martial ardour, forced the enemy to give way; and they continued to advance, keeping up an incessant fire; the cry of *charge! charge! push on with the bayonet!* ran from rank to rank on the left, when the enemy thought proper to retire, favoured by the darkness which was increased by the fog, and by the smoke which a light breeze from the south blew full in the faces of our men. The artillery had all this time been playing upon the enemy, who made an attempt to seize it; but the fire from the right of the 7th regiment, and from the marines, frustrated his intent. At last when the smoke dispersed, the enemy had already retired within the limits of Lacoste's plantation.

In the meantime, general Coffee's division had advanced towards the back of Laronde's plantation, in order to fall on the enemy's rear, according to the advice of colonel Laronde, the owner of the premises. General Coffee ordered his riflemen to dismount on the edge of the ditch separating the two plantations, where he left about one hundred men to take care of the horses, and have them ready when wanted. The division crossed the boundary line, and pushed forward in a direction perpendicular to that line. Captain Beale's company, which had advanced near the wood, within a short distance of one of the enemy's advanced guards, followed the movements of general Coffee, who drew up his division almost on the limits between the grounds of Lacoste and Villeré. The detachment of cavalry under the commend of major Hinds, not being able to manœuvre in fields cut up with ditches at very close intervals, remained drawn up on the edge of a ditch in the middle of the plantation. Colonel Coffee's division extended its front as much as possible, and the general ordered it to advance in silence, and fire without order, taking aim with their utmost skill. Long practice had enabled these riflemen to keep up a very brisk fire, the more destructive, as not a man discharged his piece without doing execution. The division continued to advance, driving the enemy before it, and took its second position in front of Lacoste's plantation, where was posted the 85th, which, on receiving the first discharge, fell back behind the old levée, towards the camp. Captain Beale's company advanced on the left within Villeré's plantation, almost in the midst of detachments of the enemy, incessantly coming up on that side. It was principally engaged with a corps of the enemy near the old levée, which it forced to fall back. About the same time Coffee's division discovered that several parties of the enemy were posted among Lacoste's negro huts. On this the general ordered his men to move forward to the right, to drive the enemy from that position, which was soon effected.

The negro huts of Mr. Lacoste's plantation still exhibit evident proofs of the unerring aim of the gallant Tennesseans of Coffee's division: in one spot particularly are seen half a dozen marks of their balls in a diameter of four inches, which were probably all fired at the same object.

Some British soldiers were killed or taken prisoners in endeavouring to escape towards the woods near the huts, in a direction opposite to that of their camp; so true it is that the British troops were struck with consternation on being attacked that night in so vigorous, judicious and unexpected a manner.

Captain Beale's company, after having penetrated into the very camp of the enemy, and made several prisoners, pushed forward to the right, following the movement of general Coffee; but unfortunately a party of those brave and most estimable men, through a mistake owing to the darkness, fell among a corps of one hundred and fifty of the British, who were moving on rapidly towards the camp, taking them for part of Coffee's division, and were made prisoners. The others followed the road to the right, and took several prisoners.

Coffee's division at last took a position in front of the old levée, near Laronde's boundary, where it continued to keep up a destructive fire on the troops that had been repulsed towards the right, as they were endeavouring to escape.

It was now about half after nine, when the enemy having learned by experience that he could not hope to obtain any advantage over our troops, and persuaded that he would greatly endanger his own safety by continuing the combat in which he had already suffered so much, fell back to his camp, where all the troops passed the night under arms and without fire.

During the engagement the second division arrived, and a considerable part of it was in the thickest of the fire. The fear of being cut off from the sole communication he had with the fleet, made the enemy take every precaution to prevent such a disaster. His posts were in continual alarm the whole night, and such were his apprehensions that he posted double lines of sentinels, so that as the one turned it was crossed by the other walking in a contrary direction.

General Jackson seeing that the darkness rendered it impossible for him to follow up victory any farther, was forced to content himself for the present with having convinced the British that Americans were not to be intimidated by the martial renown of the heroes of Wellington. He therefore led back his troops to their former position, from the principal entrance to the buildings of Laronde's plantation, where they remained until four in the morning. General Coffee took his position for the night in front of Laronde's garden, on the left of the other troops. About half after eleven a firing of musketry was heard in the direction of Jumonville's plantation.

The detachment of the Louisiana drafted militia, in cantonments at the

English Turn, under the commend of brigadier-general David Morgan, three hundred and fifty men strong, having learned, at about one o'clock in the afternoon, that the enemy was on Villeré's plantation, ran to their arms, and all the officers and privates desired to be led against him. General Morgan, not having received orders to that effect, did not think proper to yield to the earnest solicitations of the troops, whose impatience of inactivity increased every moment. At half after seven, when the report of the Carolina's guns struck their ears, it became almost impossible to hinder the men from marching against the enemy; and at last general Morgan, at the pressing request of the officers, gave orders to march, which diffused joy through the whole detachment.

Having instantly set out, it arrived at the entrance of the road to Terre-aux-Boeufs, during the hottest of the action, and continued to advance, preceded by two piquets, the one on the high road, the other in the fields near the woods. The picquet that followed the high road, being arrived within a short distance of the bridge over Jumonville's plantation, perceiving some of the enemy's troops, but not being able to ascertain their number, hailed them; but receiving no answer, the picquet fired on the enemy, who returned their fire, and instantly fell back behind the canal.

Some men were sent on reconnoitring, to endeavour to discover their strength, but without effect. Suspecting an ambush, the battalion took a position in a neighbouring field, where it remained until about three next morning, when it was thought advisable to return to the camp.

General Morgan, not thinking it expedient to quit his position before day-break, held a council of all his officers, in which it was resolved that, as they were ignorant of the position of the American army, it was advisable to march back to their station at the Turn, as soon as day appeared, which was executed accordingly.

The battalion arrived in its cantonments early in the morning, after much fatigue, having, from eight in the evening, marched fifteen miles in very muddy roads. Several soldiers belonging to the battalion, who had just left the hospital to march against the enemy, were obliged to remain behind, being exhausted with fatigue. These on their return, reported that in the same field in which the battalion had formed in the night, there was within a short distance a British corps of six hundred men, who, probably thinking the battalion stronger than it was, had not dared to attack it.

From the most accurate information that could be obtained, the enemy lost in this affair four hundred men. Their official report acknowledges three hundred and five killed, wounded or prisoners: the number of the latter was eighty-five, including officers.

The loss on our side was twenty-four killed, one hundred and fifteen wounded, officers included, and seventy-four prisoners, in all two hundred and thirteen men.

The loss of colonel Lauderdale, of general Coffee's brigade of mounted riflemen, was particularly regretted; he was a brave and accomplished officer; his death is lamented by all who knew him; and their only consolation is that he died at the post of honour; fighting in defence of his country.

Though the precise amount of the enemy's forces in this action cannot be exactly ascertained, it is well known that half of general Keane's division was encamped on the banks of the Mississippi, at the beginning of the attack; and that the remaining half of the division, which had embarked at the encampment on Isle-aux-Pois, in light vessels, several of which had run aground in the lake, had got on board of the barges that returned, after having landed the first half, and were disembarking when the cannon began to fire; that the greater part of these troops set out immediately from the landing place, two miles and a half from the Mississippi, and ran towards the field of battle, where their first platoons had already arrived, before Coffee's division began to fire, and where they all successively arrived long before the action was over, as it lasted till ten o'clock at night.

That division, composed of the regiments we have already mentioned, could not amount to less than four thousand five hundred men, as we know the strength of each regiment.

The first disembarkation consisted of the light brigade commanded by colonel Thornton, composed

of part of the 85th regiment, of	650	men
95th do. (rifle corps)	500	
A detachment of sappers and miners	100	
A detachment of the rocket brigade, commanded by captain Lane	80	
4th regiment	750	
Total	2080	

The 2d disembarkation consisted of the 21st regiment (royal North Britain) Fusileers	900	
44th do	750	
93rd do	1100	
A number of artillerists amounting, according to the best information, to	150	
In all	4980	men.

On the supposition that each regiment left a party on board the vessels, to take care of the baggage, as is sometimes the case, there would still remain four thousand five hundred effective men landed on the 23d before nine o'clock in the evening; and indeed several accounts from Jamaica, Providence and Bermuda, make the number amount to five thousand.

Let us now see with what number, and what kind of troops, the commander-in-chief, general Jackson, attacked this enemy, so powerful, so enured to warfare, preceded by a great reputation, and enjoying every possible advantage.

The right, commanded by general Jackson in person, was composed of a detachment of marines,

under the command of lieut. Bellevue	66 men strong	
A detachment of artillery with two six pounders, under the immediate command of colonel M'Rea and lieutenant Spot	22	
7th regiment, major Peire	465	
44th, commanded by captain Baker,	331	
		884
Major Plauché's battalion.		
Carabiniers, captain Roche	86	
Dismounted dragoons, major St. Geme	78	
Louisiana blues, captain White	31	
Francs, captain Hudry	33	
Chasseurs, captain Guibert	59	
		287

The battalion of St. Domingo men of colour, major Daquin	210	
Chactaws, capt. Pierre Jugeant	18	
		228
The left, commanded by general Coffee, was composed as follows:		
Tennessee volunteer mounted riflemen, forming general Coffee's brigade	563	
Orleans rifle company, capt. Beale	62	
Mississippi dragoons, major Hinds	107	
		732
In all		2131.

Of this number it is to be observed that the Mississippi dragoons were not in the action, but were, all the time it lasted, in the back ground of Lacoste's plantation. Two companies of Coffee's brigade had been left on the border of Laronde's plantation, to hold the horses whose riders had all dismounted; which reduces the number of fighting men to about one thousand eight hundred effective men. Plauché's battalion being composed of companies wearing each a distinct uniform, the enemy took those several companies for so many battalions, and represented them as such. I have thought proper to rectify this misrepresentation, by stating the number of each particular company.

This inconsiderable number of men,—strangers to the art of war, and of whom few had ever seen an engagement; but animated with that martial ardour which is soon excited in the breasts of men enjoying freedom, and indignant at seeing the soil of their country, the land of liberty, invaded by a mercenary soldiery, who came to renew in Louisiana the scenes of devastation and pillage recently exhibited on the banks of the Potomac and the shores of the Chesapeake,—advanced against the enemy with eager alacrity. Several of the corps, particularly Plauché's battalion, continued running as they advanced, till they arrived on the field of battle. All impatiently longed to be engaged and all were inspired with an auspicious presentiment of victory. In the heat of the action, the enemy was making towards the centre a movement which seemed to indicate that he designed to charge with bayonets. Instantly, the desire of anticipating him electrified our ranks, and they all expressed a wish to be ordered to charge. This impetuosity, however, the officers thought proper to restrain.

On the left of general Coffee's division, captain Beale's whole company of riflemen penetrated into the midst of the enemy, without bayonets or any other weapon of defence, except their rifles; supported by their courage, excited by their love for their country, and breathing rage and vengeance against its invaders, these brave men, almost all fathers of families, holding offices of honour and trust, or at the head of considerable commercial houses, regardless of all selfish or private considerations, advanced rashly into the centre of the hostile battalions, where they made a number of prisoners, and carried them almost all off; but, unfortunately, not without leaving several of their own companions prisoners to the foe.

General Coffee's Tennesseans, those modest and simple sons of nature, displayed that firm composure which accompanies and indicates true courage. In their expedition against Pensacola, and on their march to New Orleans, they had given abundant proofs of their bravery, good conduct and patience, in enduring hardships and privations. Instinctively valiant, disciplined without having passed through the formal training of reviews and garrison manœuvres, they evinced on this memorable night, that enthusiasm, patriotism, and a sense of a just cause, which were of far more avail than scientific tactics. The heroes of Wellington, who boasted of their military talents and disciplined valour, were often doomed, by woful experience, to appreciate the prowess of those warlike sons of the western country.

The gallant officer who commanded them, ever calm, ever active, without precipitation, tranquilly giving orders, which he well knew how to cause to be promptly obeyed; vigilant and provident to avoid unnecessarily exposing his men, for whose safety he was as anxious as a father for his son's, acquired by his conduct that night the strongest claim to the esteem and gratitude of his country. Sensible that in an incessant fire most of the discharges are ineffectual, general Coffee led on his men within a sure distance, and continually passing along the line, recommended to them to take deliberate aim, and never to fire at random.

Notwithstanding the darkness of the night, and the difficulty of manœuvring with two pieces of cannon in a road forty feet wide, bordered with ditches, the artillery took a position, and was served with the utmost promptitude. It several times forced the enemy to abandon the road, and to retire to the levée and behind gates and the ridges beside the ditches; in short, it contributed not a little to convince the enemy of our superiority.

The 7th regiment, commanded by major Peire, withstood and kept up a very brisk fire; having first come into action, and having been the longest engaged of all the corps that took part in it, that gallant regiment evinced that steadiness, precision in movements, regularity and promptitude in firing, implicit obedience to the orders of its commander, and, in short, proved that the discipline that constitutes troops of the line, do not exclusively belong to Europeans. The brave officers of that regiment, sacrificing to the exigency of the moment, and to the safety of the country, all particular attachment to their own corps, which is indeed natural and highly conducive to the united strength of an army, obeyed, without a murmur, the orders of major Peire, an officer drawn from another corps, whom general Jackson, in his discretion, had thought worthy to supply the place of their chief, major Nicks, who was prevented, by an accidental wound, from leading his men to victory.

The 44th regiment, which came into action soon after the seventh, though younger, and formed of more heterogeneous elements, fought with the steadiness and valour of veteran troops. Forced continually to oblique to the left, to avoid being turned by the enemy, this regiment showed that it was not intimidated by the enemy's manœuvre, and vigorously returned his fire. Captain Baker, who commanded it, and all the officers under him, though young in the art of war, and little acquainted with military evolutions, displayed great bravery, and were not deficient in the skill and judgment that the occasion called for.

Major Plauché's battalion of volunteers, coming into the line at the moment when the enemy was pressing hard upon the left of the 44th, and endeavouring to turn it, proved, by two or three brisk and well-directed fires, that it was worthy to be stationed by the side of veteran troops. This corps, though composed of several independent companies, has ever been exemplary for perfect union, harmony and subordination. Several of its officers, who had formerly followed the military profession, enjoyed the unlimited and well-deserved confidence of their men. These were ready to follow, wherever those might lead the way; and to speak to the former (all of whom were citizens of New Orleans) of marching against the enemy, was sufficient to exhilarate their spirits, and fill their hearts with exultation. Almost the whole of them were Frenchmen by birth or descent, and bore an inveterate hatred to Great Britain, from whose government most of them had suffered wrongs, which they wished to avenge. On this trying occasion they flew to the defence of the country which had kindly received them, and of which they were to become citizens, with the ardour and enthusiasm so characteristic of the French nation. Persuaded that musketry is often destructive, without producing any decided effect, the men of this battalion longed to charge with bayonets, and they expressed their wishes by loud acclamations. Already had the drums of the battalion began to beat in compliance with their desire, and the men waited only for the word of command to fall on the enemy with their national weapon, when colonel Ross, who had the superior command of the two battalions of volunteers, came up to restrain their ardour. Yet, had that manœuvre been made, had Plauché's battalion advanced to the charge, the enemy's retreat would have been cut off on his right, and he would have been completely surrounded by general Coffee's brigade, which was advancing in his rear, Planché's battalion on his left, Daquin's in front, and Laronde's great hedge of orange trees on the right; so that most of that column would have been forced to lay down their arms.

The above observations, as to Plauché's battalion, are almost wholly applicable to that commanded by major Daquin. The men composing it had the same motives of hatred towards the enemy, and of gratitude to this country; for they were almost all men who had long and bravely defended their native country, St. Domingo, against the British, and against the rebels, who at length subdued it, and who, choosing rather to go into exile than to become accomplices of the monsters who are desolating their native shores, came to this hospitable land to find repose in the peaceful exercise of their industry. At the call of general Jackson—at the cry of honour and of war against Britain, those brave men instantly united and joined our forces. In that memorable night they showed that they had not forgotten the exercise of arms; and almost in contact with the enemy on the left, they convinced him that in Louisiana, as formerly in St. Domingo, they should always experience from them a vigorous opposition.

It would not be proper for one whose name has appeared in general orders, to make particular mention of the several individuals who distinguished themselves on this occasion: he might expose himself to be taxed with partiality, or even to be reproached with injustice. I therefore refer the reader, for such details, to the general orders, and to the major-general's letters to the secretary of war. (See Appendix, No. 25.)

But I cannot decline paying the tribute of justice to general Jackson, to say that no man could possibly have shown more personal valour, more firmness and composure, than was exhibited by him through the whole of this engagement, on which depended, perhaps, the fate of Louisiana. I may say, without fearing to be taxed with adulation, that on the night of the 23d, general Jackson exposed himself rather too much. I saw him in advance of all who were near him, at a time when the enemy was making a charge on the artillery, within pistol shot, in the midst of a shower of bullets, and in that situation I observed him spiriting and urging on the marines, and the right of the seventh regiment, who, animated by the presence and voice of their gallant commander-in-chief, attacked the enemy so briskly, that they soon forced him to retire.

The result of the affair of the 23d was the saving of Louisiana; for it cannot be doubted but that the enemy, had he not been attacked with such impetuosity, when he had hardly effected his disembarkation, would, that very night, or early next morning, have marched against the city, which was not then covered by any fortification, and was defended by hardly five thousand men, mostly militia, who could not, in the open field, have withstood disciplined troops, accustomed to the use of the bayonet, a weapon with which most of the militia were unprovided.

Aware of this, the commander-in-chief was sensible of the necessity of immediately taking a position where he might throw up intrenchments; and accordingly, at four in the morning of the 24th, he ordered his little army to go and encamp on the left bank of Rodriguez's canal, about two miles behind the field of battle. The Mississippi mounted riflemen, and the Feliciana dragoons, with the 7th regiment, were left at Laronde's, in order to observe the enemy's movements.

Early next morning the enemy was seen drawn up at the distance of about three hundred yards from Laronde's boundary, occupying the space between the two levees. (See the plan of the affair of the 23d.) On the front boundary line was stationed a strong detachment. Towards eight o'clock, the British line broke, and the troops returned to their encampment. They occupied the whole of the front, and the greater part of the back of Lacoste's plantation. The whole extent of its principal ditch was lined with British troops, and there ran an oblique line of sentries from their advanced-posts on the road to the wood.

All this day our troops were employed in working on the intrenchments on Rodriguez's canal; the two six-pounders that had served on the preceding night were now mounted behind the line, on the bank of the river, to command the road. I received orders from the commander-in-chief, to cause the levée to be cut, on the fore-ground of Chalmette's plantation, for the purpose of overflowing the ground in front of our line; which was effected by several trenches, which let in a sufficient quantity of water to render the road impracticable for troops. But the temporary swell of the river having subsided, that measure proved at last ineffectual, for on the 28th the river was nearly on a level with the road.

Nothing of importance took place in the course of the three following days. Parties of our troops frequently went out to reconnoitre. Major Hinds, with his cavalry, several times displayed in sight of the enemy, who never ventured out of his position. In this interval he landed the rest of his troops, with his artillery, stores, and provisions.

The enemy, on this and the following day, cut up the road by an epaulment with a ditch, on the boundary line between Lacoste's and Laronde's, at the distance of one hundred yards towards his encampment, and at the back of the levée, opposite the sloop of war, the Louisiana, which was at anchor near the right bank. On the 26th, the enemy was employed day and night in preparing a battery on the most advanced angle of the levée, towards the west side of Villeré's plantation, for the purpose of firing on the schooner Carolina, which was at anchor near the right bank, opposite to it.

Major Nicks, who, by reason of an accidental wound, being incapable of active service, had been placed at the head of the arsenal and ordnance department, the duties of which station he performed with a zeal worthy of the highest praise, had been ordered the preceding day to remove the powder which was stored in great quantities in the magazine opposite the city, on board a vessel prepared to receive and convey it to Baton Rouge, reserving only such quantity as captain Humphreys should judge necessary for the daily service.

On the same day it was reported verbally to general Jackson, that the enemy had landed at Chef-Menteur, and that, in consequence of that event, major Lacoste, who commanded the post at the confluence of bayou Sauvage and Chef-Menteur river, had found himself under the necessity of abandoning it, and of removing his camp three miles back, on the principal plantation of Lafon. This report had alarmed all the troops stationed in the plain of Gentilly, insomuch that every officer and private apprehended an attack, though in that quarter the enemy could make no movement, from which danger could be apprehended, without undergoing the greatest fatigues and surmounting unheard-of difficulties. Major Lacoste informed the general-in-chief by letter, of the movement he had concluded to make, to avoid being intercepted in his rear. The prairies of Chef-Menteur were at that time very dry, and several bayous admitted of the enemy's approaching within a very short distance of Lafon's principal plantation. Some soldiers had even seen and pursued in a prairie some British sailors, who had landed to set fire to the dry grass. Such circumstances indicated an intention in the enemy to penetrate on that side; and hence the retrograde movement, made by major Lacoste, was proper and judicious. When he determined on retreating, he had the precaution to leave a piquet at the encampment he quitted, to give information of any movement the enemy might make by the river of Chef-Menteur.

General Jackson ordered me to repair with all speed to Chef-Menteur, with a re-enforcement of two hundred men from general Coffee's brigade, commanded by colonel N****, who was to take command of the post of Chef-Menteur, reoccupy the point of the confluence, finish the closed battery that bad been begun by major Lacoste's battalion, and to leave on the main plantation a detachment sufficient to cover the retreat, in the event of its becoming necessary, and keep open the communication with the city. As to the manner of executing these orders, that was left to the discretion of colonel N****, major Lacoste, and myself.

I must be allowed here to express the pleasure I felt on being ordered on such service. The perfect knowledge I had of the situation, which left on my mind no doubt of my being able, with three hundred riflemen, to rout ten times that number of the enemy, animated me with joyful assurance of success; and had the enemy dared to penetrate into the wood of Chef-Menteur, the opinion I had of the Louisianians composing major Lacoste's battalion, and of the gallant Tennesseans who accompanied me, made me fully confident of his complete discomfiture.

On arriving at the advanced post on Bertoniere's estate, we discovered that the report of the landing of the enemy was false. It was decided that the detachment should encamp on Dreux's plantation until further orders. The same day I repaired to major Lacoste's camp, which I found judiciously established, with the bivouacs close to the skirt of the wood, so that, in case of surprise, the men could instantly get among the trees, from behind which they might fire with the more advantage, as they were covered by very thick underwood.

On the same day general Morgan received orders to evacuate the post at the Turn, transporting the artillery to fort St. Leon, and leaving there a garrison of one hundred men, and to take a position on the right bank, opposite Camp Jackson; which was accordingly executed, and the troops encamped on Flood's plantation. The two six-pounders placed opposite the road, under the command of lieutenant Spotts, were replaced by the twelves commanded by captain Humphreys, and were established in the centre of the line.

Next day, the 26th, major Lacoste returned with me to head-quarters, where he requested and obtained permission for his battalion to take a station on the lines at Camp Jackson. Orders were given for his being relieved by the 4th regiment of Louisiana militia, colonel G. W. Morgan, one hundred and thirty strong, with two mounted companies of Tennesseans, a detachment of artillery of the line, commanded by lieutenant Bosque, with two field pieces, and about thirty Chactaw Indians. This force, commanded by colonel G. W. Morgan, occupied the former position on the river of Chef-Menteur until the 6th of January, when it returned to the camp of the main plantation.

The general-in-chief sent orders to general Morgan to cause the levée to be cut below the enemy, at Jumonville's, as near his posts as possible, in order to prevent his extending them. This operation was promptly and successfully executed, under the direction of major Lafon, the engineer attached to the division of the right bank, within musket-shot of the enemy's advanced sentries; but here, as before Jackson's lines, the river frustrated our views; and a measure which, had the river continued to rise, would have made an island of the enemy's encampment, and secured us from any attack, by forcing him to evacuate, produced a very different effect, as it introduced sufficient water into the canals and bayous, which till then were nearly dry, to enable the British to bring up their heavy artillery.

On the 27th, at 7 o'clock in the morning, the enemy opened on the Carolina the fire of a battery of several twelve and eighteen-pounders, and a howitzer, which he had been forty-eight hours erecting. In about fifteen minutes, the schooner was set on fire by the red-hot shot thrown into her, and in that condition the crew abandoned her. About an hour after, she blew up; and now the fire of the battery was directed against the Louisiana, whose preservation was the more important, as she was the only remaining armed vessel in the river, and as her powder magazine was above water. Lieutenant Thompson, who commanded her, endeavoured to take advantage of a light breeze from the east, to sail up the river, but the wind having died away whilst the sails were unfurling, there remained no other expedient than that of towing her up. Accordingly, one hundred men of his crew soon towed her without the range of the enemy's guns, and she was moored opposite to Flood's canal. In the evening, the 1st regiment of Louisiana militia, under colonel Dejan, was ordered from its position at Gentilly, and went to re-enforce the lines on the left.

CHAPTER 6

AFFAIR OF THE 28th DECEMBER, 1814.

In the evening of the 27th the enemy moved forward, and by the superiority of his force, obliged our advanced-guards to fall back. He occupied Bienvenu's and Chalmette's plantations; and during the night began to establish several batteries on the river. By break of day, he displayed in several columns, and drove in all our advanced-guards. Our posts had till this day occupied Laronde's plantation, and our reconnoitring parties were extended daily as far as his lines. Major Hinds, with the cavalry and the 7th regiment, had neglected no opportunity of harassing the enemy; and the advanced sentries and piquets had often exchanged with him a few shots. The 2d regiment of Louisiana militia now took a position on the left of the line.

At length the British, having begun to push forwards against our lines, all our out-posts fell back. The general-in-chief had ordered colonel MacKrea, the commander of the artillery, to fire and blow up all the buildings on Chalmette's plantation, which lay within five or six hundred yards of our lines, as they protected the enemy from our artillery. This order was accordingly executed, but its execution could not be extended to Bienvenu's plantation, as expedience required, and as the positive orders of the general-in-chief had directed.

The enemy advanced in columns on the road, preceded by several pieces of artillery, some of which played on the ship Louisiana, and the others, on our lines. The British, in this instance, gave a signal proof of their presumption; and while we do justice to the bravery of their troops, we cannot but pity the infatuation of their commanders, who thus brought up their army to lines which, though not completed, were yet proof against musket-shot, and had already five pieces of cannon in battery. They thought, no doubt, to intimidate us by their boldness, hoping that the sight of a deep column marching against our lines, would strike such terror as to make us abandon them, and retreat to the city; but they were greatly deceived. They did not yet know with what adversaries they had to contend, nor that they were destined to atone for their arrogance with streams of their blood. The Louisiana suffered the enemy's columns to advance a considerable space; and as soon as they had got as near to her as her commander wished, she opened on them a tremendous and well-directed fire. This was at first briskly answered by the enemy's artillery, which was soon silenced by the guns of the ship, and those of our lines. That very morning the engineer, H.S. Bonneval Latrobe, had established, under the fire of the enemy's artillery and a cloud of rockets, a twenty-four pounder on the left of the battery No. 1, on the line. This gun dismounted one of the field pieces which the enemy had placed in battery on the road. Captain Humphreys's battery had incessantly played upon and severely galled him from an early hour in the morning; but the guns of the *Louisiana*, from her position, were better calculated than any other to annoy him, as her broadside was in an oblique direction to his line of march. One single ball from her killed fifteen of his men. Her fire at last broke his columns, and forced them to disperse and fall back into the fields, where they took a position on Bienvenu's plantation, under cover of some buildings.

It is but justice to say, that the services rendered on this day by the Louisiana, were of the greatest importance. The cannonading lasted seven hours, during which she fired upwards of eight hundred shot. The spirited exertions of her commander, lieutenant Thompson, on that occasion, cannot be too highly commended. (See Appendix, No. 26.)

During this engagement the enemy abandoned several batteries he had established on the river the preceding night; and his loss, in other respects, was considerable.

Two days previous to this engagement, general Carroll's troops had taken post on the prolongation of Rodriguez's canal, and had worked without intermission at the breastwork of the lines, which, until the lst of January, had towards the left hardly more than sufficient thickness to protect the men from musketry. During the whole day, the enemy incessantly threw Congreve rockets, which wounded some of our men. By one of these, major Carmick, of the marines, had his horse killed, and was himself wounded in the hand. The British had great expectation from the effect of this weapon, against an enemy who had never seen it before. They hoped that its very noise would strike terror into us; but we soon grew accustomed to it, and thought it little formidable; for in the whole course of the campaign, the rockets only wounded ten men, and blew up two caissons. That weapon must doubtless be effectual to throw amongst squadrons of cavalry, and frighten the horses, or to set fire to houses; but from the impossibility of directing it with any certainty, it will ever be a very precarious weapon to use against troops drawn up in line of battle, or behind ramparts.

The twenty-four-pounder just mentioned, was served in the beginning of the action by a detachment of captain St. Gemes's dismounted dragoons, and afterwards by a part of the crew of the late Carolina, commanded by lieutenant Norris. About eight in the morning captain Dominique's artillery company, then about twenty men strong, returned from fort St. John, whither it had been sent on the 23d, and was stationed on the lines; to it was committed the service of a twenty-four-pounder, battery No. 3, which had been mounted the preceding evening. These mariners, all veteran gunners, served their piece with the steadiness and precision of men practised in the management of cannon, and inured to warfare; and the battery No. 3 was not the least destructive to the enemy during the campaign.

Lieutenant Crawley, with another part of the crew of the Carolina, repaired to the lines on the morning of the 28th, and during the whole of the action served a howitzer at the battery No. 1. In the evening, general Jackson having ordered a thirty-two-pounder to be mounted in the centre of the line, lieutenant Crawley caused the platform to be established, and had the piece mounted in the night.

The first regiment of Louisiana militia had taken a position on the right, the preceding evening, and remained on the line during the whole of the action of the 28th. On the morning of the same day, the 2d regiment received orders to re-enforce the extremity of the left, which was under the command of general Coffee.

We lost on that day seven men, and had ten wounded: amongst the former was colonel Henderson, of the Tennessee division, under general Carroll. The enemy's light troops having advanced along a ditch to a fence which ran in an oblique direction to our lines, its extremity being only at the distance of one hundred yards, opened an irregular fire on our outposts:—general Carroll ordered colonel Henderson to advance with a detachment of two hundred men along the wood, and then to make an oblique movement on the right, towards the river, and endeavour to turn the enemy, who, by this manœuvre, would have been cut off. Instead of executing this order, colonel Henderson advanced towards the right, leaving the fence between him and the wood: the enemy being thus covered by the fence, opened on our detachment a galling fire, which killed the colonel and five men, and forced the others to fall back. The enemy re-occupied the fence, where he maintained his position until our artillery once more dislodged him.

From the destruction that our artillery dealt in the enemy's ranks, and from the report of a prisoner and some deserters, the British must have lost from two to three hundred men on that day.

The Louisiana had but one man slightly wounded by the bursting of a shell, and the vessel was struck under her bowsprit by a red-hot shot, but without receiving any damage. (See Appendix, No. 27.)

It appears that this attack was but a feint, to try what effect would be produced on raw troops by the sight of columns marching, displaying, and forming in order of battle. But if after the night of the 23d the enemy could still have any doubt of our being firmly disposed to withstand him, the affair of the 28th must have convinced him that his manœuvres could no more intimidate us than his rockets, and that in whatever manner he might attack us, he would find men defending themselves with valour and intrepidity, and determined to sell their lives dearly. That attack served at least to convince the enemy that he must expect a most obstinate resistance, if he attempted to force our lines; and that perhaps, after having sacrificed numbers of his men, he might be once more obliged to retire within his camp, with the shame of having made a useless and disgraceful attempt. He had now witnessed the effect of our artillery, which was soon to prove to him, beyond all doubt, our superiority in skill, promptitude, and precision in firing.

It was ordered by general Jackson that fortified lines should be established on the right bank from the river to the Cypress swamp, behind general Morgan's encampment. For that purpose I made choice of Boisgervais' canal, three miles from the city. One hundred and fifty negroes, under the direction of Mr. Lefevre, in six days completed the parapet, the whole length of the canal, and levelled the earth to form a glacis on the opposite side. It will be seen in the sequel, that it was behind those lines, which we had not time to complete and secure with bastions and redoubts, that general Morgan's troops rallied after their flight, on the memorable 8th of January.

Captain Henley, of the late Carolina, came also next day to take command of a square redoubt, formed by a brick-kiln, opposite the city, on the very bank of the river. A fosse twenty-five feet wide was dug all round it, and the earth from it served to form a very steep glacis from the summit of the wall, serving as a parapet, to the brink of the fosse. A palisade extended along its whole length on the inside. The redoubt was furnished with a small powder magazine, and was mounted with two twenty-four-pounders. Its battery commanded at once the road and the river.

From all accounts it appears that at that time the British troops of the line amounted to between nine and ten thousand men. General Gibbs' division had landed, and sir Edward Packenham had taken the command of the army. The British head-quarters were at the house of general Villeré; their hospitals were established in the buildings of Jumonville's plantation, where their black troops were stationed. The British had taken all the horses belonging to the plantations, from Bienvenu's to Jumonville's inclusively; the finest were picked out for the officers of the staff, the others served to mount a squadron of dragoons, or to draw the artillery. Their reconnoitring parties advanced as far as Philipon's plantation, where they established a post of black troops, which continued there until their final evacuation. The meat served out to the troops was at first supplied by the cattle of the several plantations they occupied; and when this supply was exhausted, they had recourse to the cattle of the nearest plantations successively, as far as the end of Terre-aux-Boeufs, and even to Morgan's plantation at the Turn; the cattle of which they had almost entirely consumed at the period of their evacuation.

On the 29th lieutenant Spotts transported his two six-pounders to the extremity of the line, not far from the wood, and the detachment of the company of Francs, under the immediate command of lieutenant Bertel, established a platform for a twelve-pounder towards the left, between that of colonel Perry and that of lieutenant Spotts.

Commodore Patterson, on that day, caused to be landed from the Louisiana two twelve-pounders, which he placed in battery behind the levée, in front of Jourdan's plantation, on the right bank; and the following night he established a twenty-four-pounder beside the former. These pieces, with several others afterwards mounted, formed the marine battery, which rendered such important services during the remainder of the campaign. They were served entirely by sailors, mostly landed from the Louisiana, who had been enlisted or pressed in the streets of New Orleans, after the capture of the gun-boats. Those sailors were almost all of different nations, hardly one-third of them speaking English: but the care of lieutenant Thompson, in establishing excellent discipline among them, rendered eminent service; for it may justly be said that never were guns better served. The position commanded the left flank of the enemy, who was compelled to remove his camp to the back grounds of Laronde's and Bienvenu's plantations, and to abandon Chalmette's and Bienvenu's houses, where several corps and officers had already taken up their cantonments, in which the marine battery never suffered them to enjoy one moment's repose. All the buildings and fences of those plantations bear marks which attest how well the fire of that battery was directed. The enemy was even obliged to make several small epaulments, advanced one before the other, to cover the left of his camp, on the lower boundary of Bienvenu's plantation. The smallest group of British soldiers that was any where perceived, was instantly saluted with a discharge of cannon; so that this battery rendered it impossible for the enemy to attempt any reconnoissance on the river.

From the 28th of December to the 1st of January, the sloop of war every morning dropped down to the station which she occupied on the 28th, and returned every night opposite Cazelar's plantation.

In the evening, colonel Haines, inspector-general, accompanied by colonel Reuben Kemper, a volunteer in the Feliciana troop, went, by order of general Jackson, to reconnoitre in the Cypress swamp on the left, and ascertained that it was impossible for the enemy to penetrate by that way. It even appears that he was himself under great apprehension from that quarter; for, during the whole campaign, there was no instance of the enemy's having posted a single picket immediately on the skirt of the wood, so much did he fear lest our riflemen should come on him unawares, and shoot down the men; to avoid which he kept his out-posts beyond musket-shot of the wood. The Tennesseans, on account of their well-known skill at the rifle, were the terror of the British sentinels and advanced-posts. Their uniform, consisting of a brown hunting dress, rendered it difficult to perceive them among the underwood and dry grass through which they approached, to shoot down the British sentinels, whom they never missed. One single incident, which occurred about that time, will suffice to give an idea of the dread in which the British were of the Tennesseans, whom they denominated *dirty shirts*. An old inhabitant of Tennessee obtained from his officers leave to go on what they called a *hunting party*. He stole along through ditches and underwood, till he got near a British sentinel, whom he immediately killed; and having seized his arms and accoutrements, he laid them at some distance from that place, and went to post himself in a different direction. When it was time to relieve the sentinel, the corporal of the guard finding him dead, posted another in the same place, where the guard had hardly left him, when the Tennessean shot him down; and having conveyed his arms and accoutrements to the spot where he had left those of the man he had killed before, he again went to lie in wait in another place. The corporal, in his next round, had again to relieve a dead sentinel, and the man who took his place soon shared the fate of the two others; the Tennessean taking the same care to secure his arms and accoutrements, and then posting himself in another place. At last the corporal, amazed to see that in one night three sentinels had been killed at one post, determined to expose no more men in so dangerous a spot. Our Tennessean seeing this, returned to camp, with the spoils of the slain, and received the felicitations of his comrades.

The company of marines, commanded by lieutenant Bellevue, which, from the lines being first occupied, had been stationed in the centre, was removed to the left, near lieutenant Spott's battery, where it continued until the evacuation.

The 1st regiment of Louisiana militia, under colonel Dejan, was ordered to take a position in the wood on the bank of the canal of Piernas's plantation. An advanced-post had been stationed at the mouth of the canal, in the bayou Bienvenu, for the purpose of watching the manœuvres which the enemy might attempt by that canal, at the mouth of which it was possible he might ascend with schooners. The first regiment was ordered to furnish intermediate posts, and to support them all in case of an attack.

It was the more important to guard the Piernas canal, as it was the only point by which the enemy could have penetrated, on ascending the bayou Bienvenu.

General Jackson sent orders to the mayor of New Orleans, directing him to make domiciliary visits in town, for the purpose of ascertaining what arms were in the possession of private persons.

On the morning of the 30th, major-general Villeré, commanding the first division of Louisiana militia, arrived from the Acadian coast, whither he had gone to forward the arrival of the militia, of whom three hundred next day encamped behind the line Dupré.

General Villeré took also the command of the troops stationed on the Piernas canal. Major Hinds, at the head of the cavalry, went out on reconnoitring towards the enemy's advanced-posts on the right. His troop sustained the fire of all the outposts, and three dragoons were wounded. Our artillery, especially that of the centre batteries which was of heavy metal, galled the enemy without discontinuance. The thirty-two-pounder, commanded by lieutenant Crawley, and captain Dominique's twenty-four-pounder, were principally directed against the redoubt which the enemy was throwing up towards the wood. Notwithstanding its great distance, most of the balls struck the parapet, demolishing the work, and killing many men. Neither did the marine battery on the right bank neglect any opportunity of annoying the enemy in his camp, or in his posts. On that day the enemy began to establish in front of Bienvenu's house, a battery of hogsheads of sugar, ranged on the levée. In our camp, great efforts were making to complete the platforms of the batteries, strengthen the parapet, arrange the tents in proper order, and prolong the lines into the wood. The reports of deserters stated, that the enemy expected shortly to receive considerable re-enforcements, and was bringing up heavy artillery to batter our breastworks.

On the 31st, the enemy, who had already mounted a few guns on the redoubt erecting in front of our left, fired on our advanced-posts, which had some skirmishes with those of the enemy. The cannonading continued on both sides until two in the afternoon. The *Louisiana* supported our batteries with her fire, and contributed not a little to make the enemy take refuge behind some buildings. One of his officers of engineers, having advanced to reconnoitre our forces and our lines, was killed by the advanced-posts.

All these movements and reconnoitrings on the part of the enemy indicated an approaching attack. Meanwhile we learned the capture of a schooner with an officer and five men, made by our troops in the lake, near Chef-Menteur. That schooner served to transport provisions from the enemy's encampment on Pearl river, to his troops encamped on the bank of the Mississippi. In the night from the 31st December to the 1st of January, the enemy erected two batteries at the distance of about six hundred yards from our lines, on a ditch running along the side of Chalmette's plantation, the first being placed in advance of the buildings of the plantation, and at the distance of three hundred and fifty yards from the bank of the river; and the second about three hundred yards farther. During the whole night was heard the noise of the men working at the platforms and mounting the pieces of cannon.

CHAPTER 7

FIRST OF JANUARY, 1815.

The 1st of January was ushered in with a very thick fog, which did not begin to disperse until towards 8 o'clock. As soon as the horizon began to clear up, the enemy opened a very brisk fire from his three batteries, of which the left, established on the road, mounted two twelve-pounders; the centre, eight eighteen-pounders, and twenty-four-pound carronades, and that on the right towards the wood opposite our lines, mounted eight pieces of cannon and carronades. A cloud of Congreve rockets accompanied the balls, and for fifteen minutes the fire was kept up with unexampled celerity. The first discharges of the two batteries nearest the river, were principally directed against Macarty's house, where the head-quarters were established. In less than ten minutes, upwards of one hundred balls, rockets and shells struck the house, and rendered it impossible to remain there. The general-in-chief and all his staff were in the apartments when the firing began; but though bricks, splinters of wood and furniture, rockets and balls, were flying in all directions, not a single person was wounded. This fierce attack of the enemy's artillery, was answered by ours with a brisk, steady and well-directed fire, which in less than an hour made his slacken in a very perceptible degree. The cannonading however still continued to be kept up, vigorously on the part of the enemy, but with more precision and more effect on ours.

The enemy's object was to silence our artillery and make a breach in the breastwork of our lines, with a view to push on to the assault. For this purpose the troops were in readiness, drawn up in several parallel lines; but prudently waiting in the back ditches, and in the intervals between the batteries, for the favourable moment to advance to the attack of our lines. But on this occasion, as on the 28th of December, his expectations were frustrated; and instead of intimidating us by his artillery, he soon perceived the superiority of ours.

Yet every advantage was on the side of the enemy; his batteries presented but a narrow front, and very little elevation, on a spacious plain, the soil of which was from four to six feet below the level of our platforms; his gunners had for a target a line about one thousand yards long, the top of whose parapet was eight or nine feet higher than his platforms—whilst our batteries might be said to have only points to aim at, and our balls could not rebound on so soft a soil. Our batteries were the principal object against which the enemy's fire was directed; but we were not less intent on demolishing his; for in about an hour's time, our balls dismounted several of his guns; and when the firing ceased the greater part of his artillery was unfit for service. Justice obliges us to acknowledge that the fire of the British was for a long time vigorously kept up and well directed. We had the carriage of a twenty-four-pounder broken by one of their balls, at captain Dominique's battery, and that of the thirty-two-pounder, commanded by lieutenant Crawley of the navy, was also damaged by a ball; the fore-train of the twelve-pounder of general Garrigues was likewise broken by the balls of the enemy. The cheeks of the embrasures of our batteries were formed of bales of cotton, which the enemy's balls struck and made fly in all directions; the rockets blew up two artillery caissons, in one of which were a hundred rounds. When the enemy perceived this accident, he suspended his fire for some seconds, and the troops ranged in the ditches, with those at the batteries, gave three cheers, which were instantly answered by a general discharge of all the artillery of our lines. From that moment the enemy's fire began to slacken in a very perceptible degree, owing probably to his being convinced of the inutility of his attempt, and to the great number of his guns which our artillery had dismounted. About ten o'clock the enemy ordered some platoons of sharp-shooters to penetrate into the woods on the left of our line, with a view to ascertain whether it could be turned; but he soon perceived, from the brisk fire of our musketry, that on the left we were as well prepared to receive him as on the right. Part of general Coffee's brigade stationed in the fosse, two hundred yards behind the line, received orders to move forward towards the wood, in order to support, if necessary, the troops stationed immediately on the line; but Wellington's heroes discovered that they were ill qualified to contend with us in woods, where they must fight knee deep in water and mud, and that the various kinds of laurel which abound in Louisiana, in the cypress swamps and prairies, were not intended to grace their brows. Yet of these laurels there never was a fairer opportunity of making an ample provision; and the species called by botanists the laurel of conquerors, is found at every step in the woods and prairies of Louisiana. But on the other hand, cypress trees are still more common; the country presenting one continued forest of them on each bank of the river, for upwards of one hundred leagues in length; and such of the British troops as lived to return home, must have made known in England how provident nature has been in accumulating, as it were, on the banks of the Mississippi, the emblem of the disasters which will ever attend the invaders of that country.

The fire continued to slacken until noon, and at one o'clock the enemy's two batteries towards the right were abandoned. That on the road still continued to throw a few balls and rockets until three in the afternoon, by which time they were all silenced. His troops at last retired to their camp, persuaded that it was not practicable to make the assault, after having continued in the ditches from early in the morning. Our loss of men that day was very inconsiderable, in comparison with that of the enemy, and considering the long continuance of an intense fire; for it amounted to no more than thirty-four wounded or killed, eleven of the latter being persons going to or returning from camp, who were killed on the road behind the lines, by the enemy's shells or balls which were shot over the breastwork. About two hundred yards behind the line, on the river, near the bank, lay a boat laden with military stores, which was struck by several of the enemy's balls, and was on the point of sinking, when we succeeded in saving the greater part of the stores.

The batteries that the enemy had on the river in front of Chalmette's and Bienvenu's houses, continued likewise the whole day to exchange shots with those of commodore Patterson; and although the balls went through the breastwork, and the shells fell in great numbers in the batteries and on the road, the commodore lost not a single man, nor was his fire for a moment less intense than that of the enemy. It is presumable that in establishing batteries on the river, the enemy's object was not to command the passage of it, or to do any mischief on the other bank; but merely to destroy the *Louisiana*: and indeed several deserters reported that for that purpose he constantly kept red-hot balls ready to fire on her the moment she came within the range of his guns.—(See commodore Patterson's letter to the Secretary of the Navy, Appendix No. 28.)

Major-general Thomas, commanding the second division of Louisiana militia, arrived the same day with five hundred men from Baton Rouge, and encamped on Dupré's plantation. During the remainder of the day, the enemy was busily employed in working on the square redoubt he had begun, facing our left, nor did our heavy pieces of artillery one moment cease firing on his working parties, and they always fired with success. The officer commanding those parties stood upon the parapet, and as soon as he perceived the fire of our guns, he gave a signal to his men, who instantly stooped down behind the parapet.

The redoubt which stood on Bienvenu's plantation towards the wood, was of a quadrilateral form, its interior dimensions being eighty, sixty-two, one hundred and eight, and seventy feet. Two embrasures were made on the small front opposite our lines, but forming an angle with them. Each of the lateral fronts had likewise an embrasure in the middle, and that on the back had an opening twelve feet wide, serving as an entrance, and covered by a traverse within the fort. Along the intervals between the embrasures above the ground, ran banquettes raised three feet, for the musketry.

The parapet, which was fourteen feet thick at the base, and nine at the summit, had battlements for the musketry on three aspects; a fosse from twelve to fifteen feet wide and three deep surrounded the redoubt. That work had probably been made by the enemy in apprehension of an attack by the wood, with a view to protect the pickets posted on that side. Some days after, the enemy established another redoubt in advance of this, towards our lines, on the ditch separating the plantations of Bienvenu and Chalmette. This latter redoubt was smaller in its dimensions, and had an embrasure in each of the angles towards our lines. In erecting this redoubt, the enemy experienced the greatest difficulty, being constantly galled by our artillery, which mowed down the working parties. He again called in his outposts on the 1st of January, as he had done after the affair of the 28th of December. On all that space from Chalmette's old plantation in the direction of the furthest redoubt, there were no troops to be seen except near the river. The batteries had been dismantled during the night, and with much difficulty their guns were removed, by being dragged through the mud.

On the 2d, early in the morning, several parties went out to view the enemy's batteries, where they found some barrels of powder, a large quantity of cannon balls and implements of artillery, with broken gun-carriages belonging to the navy, and carronades which our balls had shattered.

General John Adair arrived at head-quarters, and announced the speedy arrival of the Kentucky militia, whom he had left the day before at Lafourche.

General Jackson, being desirous of ascertaining whether the enemy, by ascending the bayou Bienvenu, above the Piernas canal, could possibly penetrate either towards Chef-Menteur or towards the bank of the river, ordered colonel Reuben Kemper, a volunteer in the Feliciana troops, to go down with a detachment along Dupré's canal, cross the cypress swamps and prairies of the basin of Gentilly, and penetrate to the post of Bertonniere, on the Chef-Menteur road; which orders colonel Kemper executed, not without encountering numerous difficulties. The impossibility of the enemy's penetrating by that way, was thus fully ascertained, and all uneasiness on that score removed.

During the night of the 3d of January, word was brought to general Jackson that the enemy had ascended bayou Bienvenu as far as the forks of the Piernas canal, where he had landed in considerable force. This movement indicated a design to intercept us in the rear. The general instantly ordered major Davis, assistant inspector-general, to take with him two hundred men of general Coffee's brigade, and proceed to ascertain whether the report were true; and in case of the enemy's having really landed, to push on, and drive him into the bayou. Major Davis lost no time in executing these orders, and notwithstanding a heavy rain, and the badness of the road, in which the men sunk up to the knee in mud, the detachment reached the point indicated, where they did not find a single British soldier.

General Jackson, anxious to know whether there existed any possibility of the enemy's penetrating on that side, ordered colonel Kemper to choose out twenty volunteers from the different corps on the lines, and with them to descend the Piernas canal, as far as its junction with bayou Bienvenu, and this latter as far as its junction with bayou Mazant, if possible, and there reconnoitre the enemy's position. Owing to the difficulty of procuring boats, colonel Kemper was forced to undertake this service with only eleven men, whom he led that evening to the prairie, where they passed the night. Early next morning they proceeded on their way down the bayou, occasionally climbing up the trees on the bank, to see whether they could thence discover the enemy. At last they arrived sufficiently near the junction of the two bayous to perceive the fortified enclosure the enemy had there formed. Colonel Kemper, leaving the boats with some men to guard them, endeavoured to approach and reconnoitre the enemy from the prairie; but soon met with the obstruction of a bayou, which obliged him to return; when he was about half a mile from the point where he had left his boats, he perceived the enemy ascending the bayou in five small vessels, and distinctly saw sailors looking out from the mast head. When those vessels got near our boats, they fired two musket-shots on those who were left to guard them; on which four of them ran and escaped, and one was taken prisoner. The enemy proceeded up the bayou, setting fire to the prairie as he advanced, so that whoever happened to be in it, had to run from the flames rapidly gaining on the grass, which, as we have already seen, is of considerable height, and as thick as wheat in a field. At length, after great fatigues, the colonel, and part of his detachment, arrived in camp next day by nine o'clock; the others, who, having escaped from the boats, took another road, had reached camp the preceding day towards evening.

This reconnoitring discovered to us the enemy's position in the bayous, and on their banks. It was ascertained that at the forks of Villeré's canal, and bayou Mazant, where he effected his landing, he had thrown up a breastwork, within which he had built magazines for stores, which were guarded by a strong detachment; he had also an advanced sentinel constantly posted in a tree, which commanded a view of the whole prairie and of the bayous.

The precaution the enemy had taken to set fire to the prairie on the banks of bayou Bienvenu, leaves no room to doubt of his having apprehended an attack on that side. Had we indeed been stronger in troops, and better supplied with boats, we might, during the night, have descended bayou Bienvenu, as far as its junction with bayou Mazant, and thence reascending the latter, have surprised, or at least attacked their post at the mouth of Villeré's canal.

On the 4th of January the drafted militia from Kentucky, to the number of two thousand two hundred and fifty, arrived in town, and went to encamp on Prevost's plantation. On the following day seven hundred and fifty of them, but only five hundred and fifty being armed, repaired to the lines, and encamped at some distance in the rear. All these troops were under the command of major-general John Thomas, and brigadier-general John Adair, acting adjutant-general, took the command of the troops detached to the lines.*

*The deplorable condition of a great number of militiamen of this and the adjacent states, who were in want of clothing, in an inclement season, and obliged by the nature of the service to be constantly exposed in the open air, excited the sensibility of the citizens. Mr. Louaillier, the elder, a member of the house of representatives, obtained from the legislature the sum of six thousand dollars, which was put at the disposition of a committee formed for their relief. Subscriptions were also opened at New Orleans, for the same purpose, and another sum of six thousand dollars, was soon subscribed; and it is to be observed that the Orleans volunteers and militia, not satisfied with discharging their duty to their country, by their presence in the camp, sent for a subscription list, and filled it with their signatures. The county of the German coast subscribed about three thousand six hundred and that of Attakapas remitted to the committee five hundred dollars. The whole sum thus obtained, including what was voted by the legislature, amounted to sixteen thou-

In a letter of the 3d of January to the secretary of war, the general complains that the arms sent from Pittsburgh are not yet arrived, expressing his apprehensions as to the consequences with which this delay may be attended, and the effect these may have with regard to the issue of the war in this country. "Hardly," says he, "one third of the Kentucky troops, so long expected, are armed, and the arms they have are not fit for use." Justly does the general complain of the conduct of the agents of government, and presages that the defeat of our armies, and the dishonour not only of the officers commanding them, but of the nation, must inevitably be the consequence of so defective an administration. The general concludes by informing the secretary of war, that the enemy appears intent on fortifying his position; that it is doubtful whether he will renew his attacks, or change the seat of war; that in either case he has made the best disposition of the troops he commands (much inferior in number to those of the enemy) to act as circumstances may require.

Our artillery continued, in the meantime, to fire on the enemy, and whenever a group of four or five men showed themselves, they were instantly dispersed by our balls or shells. The advantage we derived from that almost incessant cannonading on both banks of the Mississippi, was that we exer-

---

sand one hundred dollars, and was laid out in purchasing blankets and woollens, which were distributed among the ladies of New Orleans, to be made into clothes. Within one week twelve hundred blanket cloaks, two hundred and seventy-five waistcoats, eleven hundred and twenty-seven pairs of pantaloons, eight hundred shirts, four hundred and ten pairs of shoes, and a great number of mattresses, were made up, or purchased ready made, and distributed among our brethren in arms, who stood in the greatest need of them. Though the gratitude of their fellow citizens, and the consciousness of their patriotic service, be, to Mr. Louaillier, and to Messrs. Dubuys and Soulié, who co-operated with him in his honourable exertions, a sufficient reward, yet I must be allowed to pay those gentlemen the tribute of applause so justly due to them.

In the course of the campaign several fathers, or men who were the support of families, among the volunteers and militia of the state, having been killed or wounded, those who depended on them for support were left in the greatest distress; wherefore the legislature, on the 6th of February, enacted that the pay of wounded men should be continued till the end of next session, and that the families of those slain in the service of the country, should receive pay for the deceased, until the same period. With pleasure I take this opportunity to do justice to the patriotic and highly praiseworthy conduct of the legislature, not only on this occasion, but during the whole session. The sole reproach that attaches to them, is their having, early in the session, spent, in unimportant discussions relative to elections, much more time than was consistent with a due regard to the exigencies of the critical circumstances in which we then were.

cised our gunners, annoyed the enemy to such a degree that he could not work at any fortification, nor, indeed, come within the reach of our cannon by day, and was deprived of all repose during the night.

From the report of some deserters, we learned that a re-enforcement of troops, under the command of major-general Lambert, had lately arrived in the British camp, and that the enemy intended shortly to make a general attack. For some days past, the communication between the fleet and bayou Bienvenu had been unusually active.

The 2d regiment of Louisiana militia was ordered to cross the river, to re-enforce general Morgan's camp. At the confluence of the Piernas canal and bayou Bienvenu, was established a post of cavalry, consisting of a detachment of captain Ogden's company of dragoons.

On the 6th of January, sailing-master Johnson left Chef-Menteur with three boats under his command, and succeeded in burning a British brig loaded with rum and biscuit, on her way to the fleet at bayou Bienvenu. On this occasion we took ten prisoners, and from them we learned that the enemy was digging out Villeré's canal, and extending it, in order to get his boats into the river.

On the 6th and 7th an unusual stir and bustle appeared to prevail amongst the enemy. Both banks of Villeré's canal were covered with soldiers and sailors, who seemed to be employed in dragging boats; troops were frequently observed exercising or reviewing, and every thing announced an approaching attack. Commodore Patterson had gone down on the right bank, to the point opposite the mouth of the canal, where he ascertained the movements of the enemy.

In the morning of the 6th we began to establish a small redoubt for two six-pounders, on that part of the bank of the river which joined the extremity of the right of our line, from which it was separated by the ditch, which in that part was very shallow, and without any water. This redoubt had two embrasures, which commanded the road and the river bank, and another which flanked the front of the line. A shallow fosse, which was also without water, in consequence of the river's having fallen, surrounded the redoubt, which was not yet completed on the morning of the 8th.

Before I proceed to relate the events of the 8th of January, a day of ever-glorious memory in the annals of America, and especially in those of Louisiana, I think it not unseasonable here to describe those lines, before which was performed the most important military exploit of the whole war, and, considering local circumstances and the respective forces contending, that which reflects on America the highest glory.

Jackson's lines, within five miles of the city of New Orleans, and running along the limits of Rodriguez's and Chalmette's plantations, formerly the property of the United States, were but one of those ancient mill-races, so common in Louisiana, extending from the bank of the river to the Cypress swamp. It has been already seen, from my description of the form of the soil in Lower Louisiana, and from its shelving from the river towards the swamps, that when the Mississippi is swelled to its greatest height, the level of the surface of its waters is some feet above that of the contiguous soil, and from twelve to fifteen above that of the prairies and bayous, which at those periods receive the waters flowing from the Mississippi. To add to the mass and the force of the water, the planters dig canals a few feet deep, throwing the earth on both sides, so as to afford a mass of water from eight to eleven feet deep; and at the head of these canals, which are commonly twenty-five feet wide, are constructed saw-mills. The canal on which Jackson's lines were formed, had long been abandoned, having no longer any mill to turn, so that its banks had fallen in and raised its bottom, which was covered with grass, presenting rather the appearance of an old draining ditch than of a canal. On the 24th of December, general Jackson had taken this position; and that it was well chosen, will sufficiently appear on an inspection of the map—(Plate No. 5.) I will only observe, that those lines leave the least possible space between the river and the wood, and that from the lines to Villeré's canal, the depth of the high-land continually increases, and is at Laronde's plantation nearly three times as great as at the lines. As soon as this position was chosen, the troops began to raise a parapet, leaving the ditch as it was except that by cutting the road it was laid underwater, as there was then a temporary rise of the river. Earth was fetched from the rear of the line and thrown carelessly on the left bank, where the earth had been thrown when the canal was originally dug. The bank on the right side being but little elevated above the soil, formed a kind of glacis. All the pales of the fences in the vicinity were taken to line the parapet, and prevent the earth from falling into the canal. All this was done at various intervals, and by different corps, owing to the frequent mutations in the disposition of the troops. This circumstance, added to the cold and to incessant rain, rendered it impossible to observe any regularity as to the thickness and height of the parapet, which in some places was as much as twenty feet thick at the top, though hardly five feet high; whilst in other places the enemy's balls went through it at the base. On the 1st of January there was but a very small proportion of the line able to withstand the balls; but on the 8th of January the whole extent, as far as the wood, was proof against the enemy's cannon. The length of the lines was eight hundred and fifteen toises, or about a mile, somewhat more than half of which ran from the river to the wood, the remainder extending into the depth, where the line took a direction towards the left, which rested on a cypress swamp almost impassable. On that part of the line which was in the wood, the breastwork was not thicker than was necessary to resist musketry; it was formed of a double row of logs, laid one over the other, leaving a space of two feet, which was filled up with earth. Along one part of the line ran a banquette; in some parts, the height of the breastwork above the soil was hardly sufficient to cover the men. The earth thrown up to form the breastwork, had been dug out at various intervals, and without any order, the rainy weather not admitting of the work's being carried on with regularity, as observed before.

The artillery was distributed on the lines in the following manner. On the soil of the road within the levée was battery No. 1, commanded by captain Humphreys, of the U.S. artillery. It consisted of two brass twelve-pounders, and a six-inch howitzer, on field carriages; these pieces enfiladed the road towards that side where the enemy was posted, and their fire grazed the parapet of the flank of the redoubt, towards the right. Battery No. 1, was seventy feet from the bank of the river. The two twelve-pounders were served by soldiers belonging to the regular artillery, and the howitzer by dragoons of major St. Geme's company.

Battery No. 2, which had a twenty-four-pounder, was commanded by lieutenant Norris, of the navy, and served by part of the crew of the late schooner Carolina; its distance from No. 1 was ninety yards. This battery was the most elevated above the soil.

Battery No. 3, commanded by captains Dominique and Beluche, commanders of privateers, had two twenty-four-pounders, which were served by French mariners; its distance from No. 2 was fifty yards.

Battery No. 4, commanded by lieutenant Crawley, of the navy, and served by part of the crew of the Carolina, had a thirty-two-pounder; its distance from No. 3 was twenty yards.

Battery No. 5, commanded by colonel Perry and lieutenant Kerr, of the artillery, had two six-pounders; its distance from No. 4 was one hundred and ninety yards.

Battery No. 6, commanded by general Garrigues Flaujeac, and served by a detachment of the company of Francs, under the immediate command of lieutenant Bertel, had a brass twelve-pounder; its distance from No. 5 was thirty-six yards.

Battery No. 7 had a long brass eighteen-pound culverine, and a six-pounder, commanded by lieutenants Spotts and Chauveau, and served by gunners of the U. S. artillery; its distance from No. 6 was one hundred and ninety yards.

The 8th battery had a small brass carronade, which rendered very little service, on account of the ill condition of its carriage; it was commanded by a corporal of artillery, and served by militia men of general Carroll's command; its distance from No. 7 was sixty yards.

Next to this piece the line formed a receding elbow, as laid down in the draught of the affair of the 8th—(See Atlas, Plate No. 7.)— enormous holes in the soil made impassable by their being full of water from the canal, rendered this bend in the line unavoidable.

From this bend, where the wood began, to the extremity of the line, the ground was so low, and so difficult to be drained, that the troops were literally encamped in the water, walking knee deep in mud; and the several tents were pitched on small isles or hillocks, surrounded with water or mud.

It was here that the brave troops of generals Carroll and Coffee, from the 24th of December, 1814, and part of those of Kentucky, from the 6th, until the 20th of January, 1815, gave an example of all the military virtues. Though constantly living, and even sleeping, in the mud, those worthy sons of Columbia never uttered a complaint, nor showed the lest symptom of discontent or impatience. Those who have not seen the ground, cannot form an idea of the deplorable condition of the troops encamped on the left of the line. But it was necessary to guard that quarter against the attacks of the enemy; it was necessary that troops should be stationed there, to repulse him on the edge of the breastwork, if, under cover of the bushes, he advanced to our intrenchments. Those brave men supported all their hardships with resignation, and even with alacrity. The safety of the country was at stake, and their desire to chastise insolent invaders, operated too strongly on hearts inflamed with patriotic ardour, to suffer them to perceive the uncomfortableness of their situation. Such conduct is so much superior to any eulogy I could bestow on it, that I must be content to admire it in silence.

In order to give a correct narrative of the affair of the 8th, I must previously make the reader acquainted with the respective position of the different corps stationed at the lines; that he may perceive, that if a considerable part of the troops exhibited no active valour, it was owing to the attack's not being made on their position; for had it been general, there can be no doubt but all would have equally vied in ardour and bravery.

The redoubt on the river, in front of the extremity of the line on the right, was guarded by a company of the 7th regiment, commanded by lieutenant Ross. The artillery was served by a detachment of the 44th, under the command of lieutenant Marant. Within the line, at the extremity of the right, between battery No. 1 and the river, was stationed the New Orleans volunteer company of riflemen, about thirty men strong.

The 7th regiment covered from that battery to battery No. 3, taking in the powder-magazine, built since the lst of January, as also battery No. 2, commanded by lieutenant Norris. This regiment, four hundred and thirty men strong, was commanded by major Peire.

The interval between that battery and No. 4, commanded by lieutenant Crawley, was occupied by major Plauché's battalion of volunteer uniform companies, and by major Lacoste's battalion of Louisiana men of colour. The former was two hundred and eighty-nine men strong, and the latter two hundred and eighty.

From battery No. 4, to colonel Perry's, No. 5, the line was defended by major Daquin's battalion of St. Domingo men of colour, one hundred and fifty men strong, and from that out by the 44th, two hundred and forty men strong, commanded by captain Baker. All the corps, from the 7th regiment to the 44th inclusively, were under the command of colonel Ross.

Two-thirds of the remaining length of the line, were guarded by the troops commanded by major-general Carroll. On the right of battery No. 7, commanded by lieutenants Spotts and Chauveau, were stationed fifty marines, under the command of lieutenant Bellevue.

On the preceding day, part of the Kentucky troops, under the command of general Adair, had gone to re-enforce that part of the line. The order in which they were ranged may be seen on the plan. All those troops formed a force of about sixteen hundred men.

The troops under the command of general Coffee occupied the rest of the length of the line, as also that part which turned off towards the left into the wood; their number was about five hundred men.

Captain Ogden's company of cavalry was stationed behind head-quarters, and a detachment of the Attakapas dragoons was posted within the court-yard, together about fifty men strong.

During the attack, captain Chauveau's company of horse volunteers, about thirty men strong, hasted from town and drew up in the same court-yard, to be ready for a sortie, should it be thought expedient.

The Mississippi cavalry, commanded by major Hinds, one hundred and fifty men strong, was encamped in the rear, on Delery's plantation. Our out-posts extended about five hundred yards in front of the line.

Different detachments, making an aggregate of two hundred and fifty men of colonel Young's regiment of Louisiana militia, were stationed at convenient intervals, on the skirts of the wood, behind the line, as far as the Piernas canal.

Four hundred yards behind the line, a guard was posted on the road, to prevent any one's going out of camp; and a line of sentinels extended from that post to the wood for the same purpose.

Although the above details show the number of our troops to have amounted to about four thousand men, including one hundred artillerists who did not belong to any corps, it is nevertheless true, that general Jackson's line was defended by only three thousand two hundred men, the remaining eight hundred having been distributed into various detachments, and posted behind to guard the camp, for the defence of the Piernas canal, and on the outskirts of the wood.—(See Atlas, plates Nos. 5 and 7.)

CHAPTER 8

BATTLE OF THE EIGHTH OF JANUARY.

I HAVE mentioned above, that on the 6th we were informed that the enemy intended shortly to attack our lines; every thing, indeed, announced such a determination; but we were in doubt whether the attack on the left bank would be feigned or real, or whether the enemy would not direct his principal force against general Morgan on the right bank. But in the afternoon of the 7th it became evident that the enemy's design was to attack Jackson's lines and attempt to storm them.

Though at so great a distance we could not distinctly see what was passing in the enemy's camp, we perceived that a great number of soldiers and sailors were at work, endeavouring to move something very unwieldy, which we concluded to be artillery. With the assistance of a telescope in the upper apartment of head-quarters, we perceived soldiers on Laronde's plantation, busy in making fascines, while others were working on pieces of wood, which we concluded must be scaling ladders. The picket-guards near the wood had moreover been increased and stationed nearer each other. Officers of the staff were seen riding about the fields of Laronde's, Bienvenu's and Chalmette's plantations, and stopping at the different posts to give orders. Finally, on the 7th, shortly after night-fall, we distinctly heard men at work in the enemy's different batteries; the strokes of hammers gave "note of preparation," and resounded even within our lines; and our out-posts informed us that the enemy was re-establishing his batteries: his guards were re-enforced about sunset, probably with a view to cover the movements of the troops. In our camp all was composure; the officers were ordered to direct their subalterns to be ready on the first signal. Half the troops passed the night behind the breastwork, relieving each other occasionally. Every one waited for day with anxiety and impatience, but with calm intrepidity, expecting to be vigorously attacked, and knowing that the enemy had then from twelve to fifteen thousand bayonets to bring into action, besides two thousand sailors and some marines.

A little before daybreak, our out-post came in without noise, having perceived the enemy moving forward in great force.

At last the dawn of day discovered to us the enemy occupying two-thirds of the space between the wood and the Mississippi. Immediately a Congreve rocket went off from the skirt of the wood, in the direction of the river. This was the signal for the attack. At the same instant, the twelve-pounder of battery No. 6, whose gunners had perceived the enemy's movement, discharged a shot. On this all his troops gave three cheers, formed in close column of about sixty men in front, in very good order, and advanced nearly in the direction of battery No. 7, the men shouldering their muskets, and all carrying fascines, and some with ladders. A cloud of rockets preceded them, and continued to fall in showers during the whole attack. Batteries Nos. 6, 7 and 8, now opened an incessant fire on the column, which continued to advance in pretty good order, until, in a few minutes, the musketry of the troops of Tennessee and Kentucky, joining their fire with that of the artillery, began to make an impression on it, which soon threw it into confusion. It was at that moment that was heard that constant rolling fire, whose tremendous noise resembled rattling peals of thunder. For some time the British officers succeeded in animating the courage of their troops, and making them advance, obliqueing to the left, to avoid the fire of battery No. 7, from which every discharge opened the column, and mowed down whole files, which were almost instantaneously replaced by new troops coming up close after the first: but these also shared the same fate, until at last, after twenty-five minutes continual firing, through which a few platoons advanced to the edge of the ditch, the column entirely broke, and part of the troops dispersed, and ran to take shelter among the bushes on the right. The rest retired to the ditch where they had been when first perceived, four hundred yards from our lines.

There the officers with some difficulty rallied their troops, and again drew them up for a second attack, the soldiers having laid down their knapsacks at the edge of the ditch, that they might be less incumbered.

And now, for the second time, the column, recruited with the troops that formed the rear, advanced. Again it was received with the same rolling fire of musketry and artillery, till, having advanced without much order very near our lines, it at last broke again, and retired in the utmost confusion. In vain did the officers now endeavour, as before, to revive the courage of their men; to no purpose did they strike them with the flat of their swords, to force them to advance: they were insensible to every thing but danger, and saw nothing but death which had struck so many of their comrades.

The attack on our lines had hardly begun, when the British commander-in-chief, the honourable sir Edward Packenham, fell a victim to his own intrepidity, while endeavouring to animate his troops with ardour for the assault. Soon after his fall, two other generals, Keane and Gibbs, were carried off the field of battle, dangerously wounded. A great number of officers of rank had fallen: the ground over which the column had marched, was strewed with the dead and the wounded. Such slaughter on their side, with no loss on ours, spread consternation through their ranks, as they were now convinced of the impossibility of carrying our lines, and saw that even to advance was certain death. In a word, notwithstanding the repeated efforts of some officers to make the troops form a third time, they would not advance, and all that could be obtained from them, was to draw them up in the ditch, where they passed the rest of the day.

Some of the enemy's troops had advanced into the wood towards the extremity of our line, to make a false attack, or to ascertain whether a real one were practicable. These the troops under general Coffee no sooner perceived, than they opened on them a brisk fire with their rifles, which quickly made them retire. The greater part of those who, on the column's being repulsed, had taken shelter in the thickets, only escaped our batteries to be killed by our musketry. During the whole hour that the attack lasted, our fire did not slacken for a single moment; and it seemed as though the artillery and musketry vied with each other in vivacity.

When the column first advanced to the attack, the troops partly moved forward along the skirt of the wood, which in that part forms a curve, and were by that means covered till they came within two hundred yards of our lines. After the attack on our left had commenced, the enemy made a column advance on the right by the road, and between the river and the levée. This column precipitately pushing forward, drove in our out-posts, following them so closely that it came up to the unfinished redoubt before we could fire on it more than two discharges of our cannon. A part of the column leaped into the ditch, and got into the redoubt through the embrasures, and over the parapet, overpowering with their numbers the few men they found there: others advancing along the brink of the river, killed the soldiers of the 7th, who bravely defended their post at the point of the bayonet, against a number much superior, and continually increasing.

To get into the redoubt was not a very arduous achievement: the difficulty was to maintain possession of it, and clear the breastwork of the entrenchment in the rear of the redoubt, which still remained to be attacked. Already several British officers, though wounded, were bravely advancing to encourage their men by their example.

Colonel Renee, followed by two other officers of high rank, had begun to mount the breastwork, when the gallant volunteer riflemen under captain Beale, who defended the head of the line, made them all find their graves in that redoubt which they had mastered with so much gallantry. Meanwhile, captain Humphreys' battery No. 1, lieutenant Norris's No. 2, and the 7th regiment, which was the only one within musket-shot, kept up a tremendous fire on that column, which, like that on the left, was obliged to fall back in disorder, leaving the road, the levée, and the brink of the river, strewed with its dead and wounded.

The enemy had opened the fire of the battery which he erected on the road on the 28th of December, as also of that erected on the 1st of January, behind the demolished buildings of Chalmette's plantation. The fire was at first very brisk, and was principally directed against Macarty's house, in hopes that the general and his staff might still be there: but to the enemy's disappointment, the general and all the officers had repaired to their post on the lines, long before daybreak. The only mischief done by that prodigious expense of balls and shells, was that major Chotard, assistant adjutant-general, received a contusion in his shoulder, and four or five pillars of the house were knocked down. Our batteries, Nos. 2, 3, and 4, principally directed their fire against those of the enemy, and dismounted several of the guns erected near Chalmette's buildings. Battery No. 1, after having poured a shower of grape-shot on the enemy's troops as they retreated, turned its fire against his battery which was opposite to it, and in less than two hours, forced the men to evacuate it. The marine battery on the right bank also fired on the enemy's column as it advanced along the brink of the river, until the troops which landed on the right bank, pushed forward, and obliged the seamen who served it to attend to their own defence.

By half after eight in the morning, the fire of the musketry had ceased. The whole plain on the left, as also the side of the river, from the road to the edge of the water, was covered with the British soldiers who had fallen. About four hundred wounded prisoners were taken, and at least double that number of wounded men escaped into the British camp; and, what might perhaps appear incredible, were there not many thousands ready to attest the fact, is that a space of ground, extending from the ditch of our lines to that on which the enemy drew up his troops, two hundred and fifty yards in length, by about two hundred in breadth, was literally covered with men, either dead or severely wounded. About forty men were killed in the ditch, up to which they had advanced, and about the same number were there made prisoners. The artillery of our lines kept up a fire against the enemy's batteries and troops until two o'clock in the afternoon. By the disposition of his troops, the enemy appeared to apprehend lest we should make a sortie, and attack him in his camp. The soldiers were drawn up in the ditches, in several parallel lines, and all those who had been slightly wounded, as soon as their wounds were dressed, were sent to join their corps, to make their number of effective men appear the greater, and show a firm countenance. The enemy's loss on the left bank, in the affair of the 8th January, was immense, considering the short duration of the contest, the ground, and the respective number of the contending forces. According to the most probable accounts, it cannot have amounted to less than three thousand men in killed, wounded, and prisoners. The number of officers who fell that day is a much greater loss in proportion, owing to the necessity they were under of exposing themselves in the brunt of the battle, to encourage the men, and lead them on to the desperate assault. Our loss was comparatively inconsiderable, amounting to no more than thirteen in killed and wounded, on the left bank of the Mississippi.

I deem it my indispensable duty to do justice to the intrepid bravery displayed in that attack by the British troops, especially by the officers. If any thing was wanting towards the attack's being conducted with judgment (speaking in a general and military point of view) it was, in my opinion, that they did not in the onset sacrifice the regularity of their movements to promptitude and celerity. The column marched on with the ordinary step, animating their courage with huzzas, instead of pushing on with fixed bayonets, *au pas de charge*. But it is well known that agility is not the distinctive quality of British troops. Their movement is in general sluggish and difficult, steady, but too precise, or at least more suitable for a pitched battle, or behind intrenchments, than for an assault. The British soldiers showed, on this occasion, that it is not without reason they are said to be deficient in agility. The enormous load they had to carry contributed indeed not a little to the difficulty of their movement. Besides their knapsacks, usually weighing nearly thirty pounds, and their musket, too heavy by at least one third, almost all of them had to carry a fascine from nine to ten inches in diameter, and four feet long, made of sugar canes perfectly ripe, and consequently very heavy, or a ladder from ten to twelve feet long.

The duty of impartiality, incumbent on him who relates military events, obliges me to observe that the attack made on Jackson's lines, by the British, on the 8th of January, must have been determined on by their generals, without any consideration of the ground, the weather, or the difficulties to be surmounted, before they could storm lines, defended by militia indeed, but by militia whose valour they had already witnessed, with soldiers bending under the weight of their load, when a man, unincumbered and unopposed, would that day have found it difficult to mount our breastwork at leisure and with circumspection, so extremely slippery was the soil. Yet those officers had had time and abundant opportunity to observe the ground on which the troops were to act. Since their arrival on the banks of the Mississippi, they had sufficiently seen the effects of rainy weather to form a just idea of the difficulty their troops must have experienced, in climbing up our intrenchments, even had the column been suffered to advance, without opposition, as far as the ditch. But they were blinded by their pride. The vain presumption of their superiority, and their belief that the raw militia of Kentucky and Tennessee, who now for the first time had issued from their fields, could not stand before the very sight of so numerous a body of regular troops advancing to attack them, made them disregard the admonition of sober reason. Had they at all calculated on the possibility of resistance, they would have adopted a different plan of attack, which, however, I am far from thinking would have been ultimately successful.

It has been repeated that division prevailed in a council of war, and that admiral Cochrane, combating the opinion of general Pakenham, who, with more judgment, was for making the main attack on the right bank, boasted that he would undertake to storm our lines with two thousand sailors, armed only with swords and pistols. I know not how far this report may deserve credit, but if the British commander-in-chief was so unmindful of what he owed his country, who had committed to his prudence the lives and honours of several thousands of her soldiers, as to yield to the ill-judged and rash advice of the admiral, his memory will be loaded with the heavy charge of having sacrificed reason in a moment of irritation, though he atoned with his life for having acted contrary to his own judgment.

But to return to the attack on our lines. I cannot forbear to mention a fact which fully proves the truth of my assertion in the beginning of this narrative, that the British had come to America to carry on war in the spirit of atrocity, determined to employ all means whatever to shed American blood, and glut their rage against us. (See Appendix, No. 28-a.)

As soon as the wrecks of the British column had disappeared, the fire of our musketry ceased, and our artillery only fired at intervals at the enemy's batteries, or at scattered platoons that were perceived in the wood. At this time, men from all our different corps, prompted merely by sentiments of humanity, went, of their own accord, to assist the wounded British, to give them drink, and carry them (as they did several on their backs) within our lines. All our troops unanimously applauded the humane sentiments of those brave men, whose dauntless hearts were grieved to behold the slaughter of the day, and in their wounded enemy saw but their suffering fellow creature.

But, with horror I record the atrocity! while they were in the very act of administering consolation—while they were carrying the wounded British—the troops that were in the ditch (in front of our lines) fired on them, and killed and wounded some men. Yet the others, regardless of the danger to which they exposed themselves, persevered in their laudable purpose. This instance of baseness may have proceeded from individuals; nor can it be presumed that the men were ordered to fire by any officer of rank. The known tenor of general Lambert's honourable and soldierly conduct, sets the commander-in-chief far above the suspicion of his being capable of such atrocity. But the officers who commanded the troops in the ditch, within musket-shot of the men fired on, cannot allege that they misconceived the intention of our men, most of them being unarmed, and assisting the wounded. They were near enough to see their actions, and seeing these, they could not possibly misconceive their motives. Upon a full view of this fact then, whatever reluctance we may feel, in branding with infamy military men whose actions should ever be directed by honour—men, amongst whom there were perhaps several who wore the honourable decorations of valour and good conduct, we cannot forbear to give them the appellation of barbarians. The private soldiers cannot be reproached with this atrocious act; the guilt of it rests solely with those who commanded them.—(See note No. 2, at the end of the volume.)

After having perused, with pleasing sensations, the recital of the brilliant defence made by our troops on the left bank, every American, whose bosom glows with the love of his country, must learn with pain the contrast exhibited in what took place on the right, the consequences of which were likely to have been so disastrous, that even now my mind shudders at the recollection of that moment, when, seeing our troops on the right bank fall back in disorder, while the enemy was rapidly advancing towards the city, all of us who were at Jackson's lines, were suddenly hurried from the transporting joy of victory to the fear of shortly seeing all its advantages wrested from our grasp. (For Monroe's view see Appendix, No. 28-b).

As the affair to which the course of my narrative has now brought me, is the only disaster we experienced during the campaign, the only fault committed on our defensive operations, I must request the indulgent attention of the reader, while I lay before him a minute, and perhaps irksome, detail of circumstances necessary to be known, in order that he may become perfectly acquainted with the causes of that unfortunate event.

At the period when the quota of Louisiana was levied, brigadier-general David Morgan, of the militia, was appointed to command it. We have seen that after the affair of the 23d of December, he was ordered to leave the cantonment at the English Turn, on the left bank, and cross the river to encamp on the right bank opposite Jackson's lines. (See plate No. 5) Agreeably to those orders, he made his troops take post near the saw-mill, on Flood's plantation. A few days after, those troops moved forward to Jourdan's plantation, next to that of Flood's, where they remained till the 7th of January, on which day they took a position along Raguet's old canal, near the lower boundary of the plantation. At this time the contingent amounted to no more than two hundred and sixty effective men.

We have already seen that in the morning of the 4th the second regiment of Louisiana militia, colonel Zenon Cavelier had crossed over to the right bank, and encamped on Cazelard's plantation. On the 7th, that regiment also took a position on Raguet's canal, on the left of the quota; its effective force being then only one hundred and seventy-six men armed.

The first regiment of militia, under colonel Dejean, quitted, in the evening of the 6th, the position it occupied on the Piernas canal, and that same day took a station on the left of the 2d regiment, and formed the extremity of the line on the bank of the river. To this regiment was annexed a detachment of the 6th Louisiana militia, forming together a force of one hundred and ten men, some ill armed, the rest without any arms.

General Morgan took the command of those troops, which, as I have already observed, he stationed along Raguet's old canal, where he had commenced lines of defence two hundred yards in length, which was but a very small portion of the whole length of the canal, this extending about two thousand yards to the wood. Thus all that part on the right of the space of two hundred yards, where a breastwork had been begun, was without any other defence than a ditch, and exposed to be turned; this, we shall see, is what actually happened.

Towards the beginning of January, while I was carrying on works at the line on Boisgervais' canal, general Jackson ordered me to assist general Morgan in choosing an advanced position, opposite Jackson's lines, for the purpose of establishing lines of defence, suitable to the number of troops on the right bank, and to the nature of the situation; and, on the choice being made, to draw a plan of the works, and immediately employ in their execution all the negroes that had till then been working at the battery, near the powder-magazine, and at Boisgervais' line, which then became a second line.

Agreeably to these orders I waited on general Morgan, whom I met accompanied by his staff, and by commodore Patterson, inspecting all the canals in the vicinity. I communicated to him my orders, observing that I was at his disposal. The general continued his inspection, and returned to his quarters, without having come to any determination, only that he appeared inclined to make choice of the position of the canal of Raguet; he then desired I would inspect the different situations myself, and make my report to him. My orders directed me to assist general Morgan, and my opinion was of course entirely subordinate to his decision. I beg the reader to excuse my appearing here in a conspicuous light, and to believe that it is with much reluctance I am forced to speak of myself, in investigating the cause of a disastrous event; my purpose being to show, by the simple recital of facts, that the disaster might perhaps have been avoided, had another point for defence been adopted.

I chose for the intended lines of defence, an intermediate position, nearly at equal distance from Raguet's and Jourdan's canals, in a place where the wood inclines towards the river, leaving only a space of about nine hundred yards of open ground. The adjoining wood being impassable, works occupying this whole space could not be turned. A rough draught, conformable to the plan in plate No. 5, under the title of *intended line*, was made, and immediately the overseer of the works set his men to execute this line. Having gone over to the left bank, I made my report to the commander-in-chief, who approved of the dispositions made, and was sensible of the advantage of the position that had been chosen. That it was a good position, may be seen on a view of the map. The small distance between the wood and the river, required but from a thousand to twelve hundred men to guard it, and half that number would have been sufficient, had pieces of cannon been mounted in the intended outworks. To attack that line, the enemy must have advanced in the open plain, which was commanded in every direction by the salient parts of the intrenchments. The wood, as I have before observed, was impassable towards the extremity of that line; the enemy's batteries on the left bank could not have infiladed its rear, as was the case with that established on Raguet's canal. The former, in short, united all advantages, and I dare affirm that, had the works been completed, the British would not have ventured to advance within cannon-shot. That line, defended only by the troops that were on the right bank, on the 8th amounting to about eight hundred men, might have defied the attempts of the British, had they come with three or four times the number that crossed the river, and might have given them a reception similar to that which they experienced on the left bank. But these dispositions had been changed, and the negroes ordered to be set to work on Raguet's canal.

This line, also marked in the Map, plate No. 5, had a kind of bastion on the bank of the river, and a small *redan* at some distance on the right. In the afternoon of the 7th, general Morgan caused one twelve-pounder and two six-pounders to be mounted on the line.

I have already observed, that on the 6th it was suspected that the enemy intended to cross over to the right bank; in the afternoon of the 7th there no longer remained any doubt of this intention. A little after sunset general Morgan was informed that the enemy was ready to cross the river, and that he might hourly expect to be attacked. On the 8th, before break of day, he received information of the landing of the enemy on the strand of Andry's plantation. Three miles in advance of the line, on Morin's estate, half a mile above the spot where the enemy landed, a detachment of one hundred men of the 6th of militia, under the command of major Arnaud, had been stationed, to oppose his landing. These men were very ill armed, most of them having only fowling-pieces, and musket-cartridges too large for them; several of them were even without any arms, and not one of them, I believe, excepting their commander, had ever been opposed to an enemy before. It is little strange, then, that they retreated. The enemy landed much lower than was his intention, having been carried down by the strength of the current. It was owing to this circumstance, that the attack on the right bank, which was to have been simultaneous with that on the left, did not commence until the later had completely failed, and our musketry, having routed the enemy, had ceased firing. Having landed his troops, the enemy ascended the river in his boats, carrying carronades and cannon, and keeping close to the bank, covered the flank of his troops, and discharged grape-shot against ours, who retired as he advanced.

In the evening of the 7th, general Jackson had ordered general Adair, on whom, in consequence of the sickness of general Thomas, had devolved the chief command of the Kentucky militia, to send a detachment of five hundred men, to re-enforce general Morgan's camp. The command of this re-enforcement was given to colonel Davis, and after much fatigue and difficulty in crossing the river, the detachment arrived, harassed and exhausted, at four o'clock in the morning, on Morgan's line, and there received orders to advance, to meet and repulse the enemy. What was the exact number of men under colonel Davis, has been a question of much contest. It appears pretty certain that, on leaving the camp of Prevost's plantation, he had five hundred men; that only one-fourth part of these had arms, mostly in an ill condition, and that about seventy of them received arms at the naval arsenal; that colonel Davis had not above two hundred and fifty armed men with him, when he arrived at Morgan's line, the rest having remained behind, spent with fatigue, and faint for want of food, having taken hardly any nourishment since the morning of the 7th. They had marched five miles, from the ferry near the powder magazine to the line, in bad roads, sometimes knee-deep in mud. It appears also that their arms were in an ill condition, their ammunition bad, and several of their muskets without flints, some having nothing but pebbles in their stead. What could be expected from men thus dispirited, ill armed and exhausted with inanition and fatigue?

Colonel Davis took his station on Mayhew's canal, about a mile in advance of Morgan's line, his left resting on the river bank. On the right of his detachment was stationed that of major Arnaud, consisting, as I have already observed, of one hundred men, of whom fifteen were without arms, and the others were armed with fowling-pieces. The enemy arrived in considerable force, and attacked that position with the troops that had landed, while his boats fired grape-shot at our flank. Colonel Davis made his troops fire two or three volleys, not without effect; but finding it impossible to maintain his ground any longer, as the enemy had already out-flanked him on the right, seeing himself abandoned by the detachment of major Arnaud, which, in spite of all the major's efforts to rally it, had taken to the wood, he determined to make his retreat on Morgan's lines, where he took a position on the right, along the canal, beyond the part that was fortified. It is to be observed, that owing to some cause to me unknown, there was a space unoccupied between the right of colonel Declouet, commanding the detachment of drafted militia, and colonel Davis's left. The troops under the latter's command, occupied a considerable front, the men were placed several feet from each other; and finally, on the same canal, but two hundred yards further to the right, was stationed lieutenant-colonel Caldwell, also of the drafted militia, with a detachment of sixteen men. The disposition of the troops on these lines, when colonel Davis took his station there, was therefore as follows. The first regiment of militia, on the river; on its right the second regiment; on the right of this last, the drafted militia of Louisiana. These corps occupied the whole length of the fortified line. Next to this was a space unguarded, extending to the left of colonel Davis, whose command occupied on the canal three hundred yards in front; and finally two hundred yards from his right was stationed colonel Caldwell with sixteen men; the whole forming a total of about six hundred men, one-third of whom, as before observed, were ill armed. There were mounted on those lines three pieces of cannon, one a twelve-pounder, commanded by midshipman Philibert, and two six-pounders, the one commanded by Mr. Batique, formerly a captain of a vessel, the other by Mr. Hosmer, both these gentlemen belonging to the first regiment of militia.

The enemy advancing rapidly by the road opposite the left of the line, the artillery played on him with effect, and as soon as he approached near enough, the musketry also began to fire; which having obliged him to fall back, he next directed his attack against our right, one column moving towards the wood, and the other towards the centre of the line. It was now that was felt the effect of the bad position that we occupied. One of the enemy's columns turned our troops, at the extremity of colonel Davis's detachment, while the other penetrated into the unguarded space between that detachment and the drafted militia. On this, the Kentucky militia gave way, nor was it possible from that moment to rally them, though their officers and general Morgan made every exertion for that purpose. Confidence had vanished, and with it all spirit of resistance. If, instead of extending over so considerable a space, those troops had been formed in close column, the confusion that took place might easily have been avoided; and in case of a retreat's becoming necessary, it might have been made in good order, our troops still keeping up their fire.

The enemy having turned our right, pushed on towards our left, which continued firing as long as possible; and at last the cannon was spiked, just as the enemy arrived on the bank of the canal.

Commodore Patterson, who, from break of day had, without intermission, kept up a fire from the guns of the marine battery, on the enemy's troops advancing up the road, wished now to turn his cannon, in order to fire on those who had forced the right of the line; but the Kentucky troops and the drafted militia, masked the guns, and it was impossible to fire without killing our own men. Seeing this, the commodore, enraged, I dare say, determined to spike his cannon, throw the ammunition into the river, and go on board the Louisiana.

The first and second regiments retreated by the road, and went to take a position on Boisgervais' line, where a considerable number of the flying troops rallied. Jourdan's mill and bridge, and successively those of Flood and Cazelard were set on fire.

A small detachment of the enemy advanced as far as the bridge of Cazelard's canal, and retired before evening; and in the course of the night all the enemy's troops recrossed to the left bank.

Let us now take a retrospective view of this affair, and let us examine the respective conduct of the corps of troops which defended the right bank. The task is painful indeed, but indispensable; for justice requires that it should be ascertained on which side lies the misconduct, that it may not be wrongfully imputed.

The principal charges brought against the Kentuckians are, that they fled before the enemy, when they ought to have waited for him at the point of the bayonet; that they retreated in disorder, instead of keeping up their fire as they retired. To these charges they answer, "We were very ill armed; we had been on our feet for twenty-four hours, during which time we had hardly tasted food; the cartridges we had were too large for our pieces; on our arrival before day, after a hard march of several leagues partly through the mud, without being allowed a moment's rest, we were ordered to advance a mile further; having obeyed without a murmur, we found ourselves within view of the enemy, on whom we fired several volleys, maintaining that position, which was none of the best, until being outflanked on our right, and cannonaded with grape-shot from the barges on our left, we were forced to retreat on Morgan's line, where we were ordered to take a position along a canal, uncovered and extended on a front of three hundred yards, our left separated from the other troops by an unguarded space of ground, and our right covered by a paltry detachment of sixteen men, stationed two hundred yards from us; a vast plain, affording no manner of shelter, lying in our rear. We were turned on the right, and cut off on the left. In so precarious a situation, how could we avoid giving way?" To this it may be answered, that the Kentuckians might have retreated without flying in disorder. While I acknowledge that observation to be just, I believe that veteran troops of the line, in a less perilous situation, have not unfrequently been seized with a panic, and given way; nor do I think that any military man of much experience will be surprised that militia troops, ill armed, drawn up, like Indians, on an immense front, seeing themselves turned and cut off by troops of the line, quitted their post, and retired in disorder.

What took place on the right bank, had made so much sensation in the immediate seat of war, and had been so variously reported abroad, to the disparagement of many brave men, that I thought it a duty incumbent on me to inquire into particulars, and trace the effect to its cause. I have stated facts from the best information. I have made observations and drawn inferences. The decision is left to the judgment of the reader.

The result of the attack made by the enemy on the right bank, was, on his part, the loss of one hundred and twenty men killed or wounded, and on ours that of one man killed and five wounded.—(See in Appendix general Jackson's and commodore Patterson's letters, No. 29.)

The commander-in-chief having received intelligence of the retreat of the troops on the right bank, ordered general Humbert, who had tendered his services as a volunteer, to cross over with a re-enforcement of four hundred men, take the command of the troops, and repulse the enemy, cost what it might. This general arriving on the ground, communicated to general Morgan the order he had received, which was only verbal, owing to the urgency of the occasion. The latter appeared inclined to furnish general Humbert with the means of justifying the confidence with which general

Jackson had honored him; but there arose disputes concerning military precedence. Other militia officers did not think it right that a French general, enjoying the confidence of a large proportion of the troops, known by a reputation which he had acquired, not on parades, or at reviews, but by his sword; holding a rank which he owed, not to the commission of the state governor and legislative assembly, but to which he had been raised, step by step, through all the inferior grades, and after having fought in a number of battles—those officers, I say, did not think it becoming, that the general to whom the French government had formerly confided the command of that expedition to Ireland, which will ever be recorded in the glorious pages of history, should be sent to remedy the faults of others, and repulse invaders, who, perhaps, would not, with impunity, have landed on that bank, had he there commanded. Happily, during this discussion, the enemy, as I have observed, thought it prudent to retreat, which they did that night and next morning. General Jackson made an address to the troops on the right bank, on the subject of the retreat they had made before the enemy. That document, breathing the most noble sentiments of patriotism and military ardor, cannot fail to be read with pleasure. (See Appendix, No. 30.)

In the course of the afternoon, the enemy sent a flag of truce, proposing a suspension of arms, for the purpose of burying the dead. General Jackson would grant a suspension for no longer than two hours, and only for the left bank; military operations being to continue on the right bank as usual. Flags of truce were reciprocally passing until near four in the afternoon. At that hour, our batteries again began to cannonade those of the enemy, and our heavy artillery fired on the buildings of Laronde's and Bienvenu's plantations, where some groups of soldiers were seen. From one of the deserters who came over in the evening of the 8th we learned, that the enemy's loss amounted to three thousand men, and that the commander-in-chief was killed, and generals Gibbs and Keane wounded. General Lambert, on whom, the command had devolved, was lately arrived, and was unknown to this deserter, who could not tell who commanded the British army.*

*In the evening of the 8th of January, the wounded prisoners were conveyed to New Orleans, and lodged in the barracks. The hospitals of the city being occupied by our sick and the few wounded amongst us, accommodations had not been prepared for so great a number of those of the enemy. Captain Dubuys, commander of all the veteran corps and of the city at that period, represented to the citizens the wants of those unfortunate victims of British ambition, and immediately one hundred and forty matresses, a great number of pillows, with a large quantity of lint and old linen for dressing their wounds, were procured

On the 9th, by break of day, the artillery again began to fire at intervals, which greatly annoyed the enemy, who about ten o'clock sent out another flag of truce. The letter addressed to general Jackson, signed "*Lambert,*" but without mentioning that he who bore that name was now commander-in-chief of the British forces; an avowal which he wished to avoid, to conceal from us, as long as possible, the death of general Packenham, of which we were informed on the evening of the 8th. General Jackson replied, that he was ready to treat with the commander-in-chief of the British army, and that it was to him a matter of surprise that the letter he had received was not directly from him. On this, general Lambert could not decline answering that he was commander-in-chief; and then general Jackson granted the suspension of arms required. The bodies of all the British who had died on our side, were delivered to the enemy, on the advanced line of our posts and his; they were received by British officers and buried. On beholding the remains of the three officers killed on the redoubt, and particularly those of colonel Renee, the British soldiers could not forbear to manifest strong emotions of admiration and grief, paying the tribute of their tears to the brave man whom they perhaps had often followed in the road to glory, to a father (for so they called him) who probably had often relieved their wants. He must have been an officer of no common merit, whose death excited such regret! If he did not live long enough to acquire great renown in arms, if the thread of his life was severed before he had time to run a glorious career, at least all of him is not inclosed in the tomb; his memory survives in the grateful hearts of those who experienced his benevolence.

On the 10th and 11th nothing occurred worthy of remark. Our troops on the right bank re-occupied their former position on Jourdan's plantations, where the engineer Lafon commenced a line of defence, which may be seen on the map, plate No. 5. In the night of the 11th there was heard the report of a very brisk cannonade, which was thought to come from fort St. Philip at Plaquemine, and the next evening we learned that the enemy was bombarding that fort. Our artillery continued to annoy the enemy to such a degree,

---

by contributions from all quarters, at a moment when such articles were extremely scarce in New Orleans, where not a truss of straw could be purchased.

Until the hospital directors could establish an hospital for those wounded men, whose number amounted to nearly four hundred, all kinds of refreshments and every attendance that their situation required, were liberally provided for them by a number of citizens. Several women of colour offered their services, and were employed in tending them, without any compensation but the pleasure of relieving suffering humanity.

that the deserters reported that the troops had no rest, and that all the out-posts had been doubled, as an attack was apprehended. On the 12th, fifty prisoners were brought in from Chef-Menteur. We every day continued to cannonade the enemy; the balls of our heavy pieces, as also of our shells, fell in his very camp, and greatly annoyed the men.

Several officers on our lines, who had long followed the military profession, perceived on the 15th some movements in the enemy's camp, which they thought indicated a retreat, and about the same time a deserter assured us that a retreat would shortly take place.

On the 17th of January, in consequence of proposals made by general Lambert to general Jackson, the latter appointed his aid-de-camp, colonel Edward Livingston, to confer with major Smith, military secretary to general Lambert, between the lines of the out-posts, for the purpose of drawing up a cartel of prisoners; and these officers concluded upon one which was mutually approved of by the commander-in-chief of each army. (See that document, Appendix, No. 31.)

Next day, towards noon, conformably to the articles of the cartel, the enemy delivered to us, on the line, sixty-three of our prisoners; the greater part of whom had been taken in the affair of the 23d of December. A guard of honour, composed of a detachment of the company of carabineers, of Plauché's battalion, commanded by captain Roche, with a detachment of captain Beale's riflemen, preceded by the music of the battalion, went to receive and escort them into camp. Several of them were not yet out of danger from their wounds. Their return to their friends and acquaintances was the more grateful to all, as, until that moment, it was feared that many of them were among the dead.

It recurred to Dr. R. Morrell and Mr. T. Shields, on their return from the British fleet, that a few well-armed boats could annoy the enemy on Lake Borgne. This suggestion was made to commodore Patterson on the morning of the 15th January, the period of their arrival in town. The commodore, after various inquiries concerning the description and force of the boats employed by the enemy on the lake, authorized those gentlemen to obtain volunteers for the expedition.* On the 19th they proceeded from the bayou

*I preserve in this narrative the form and nearly the words of the journal communicated to me by Dr. Morrell.

St. John in four boats (one of which carried a twelve pound carronade, the others being small) and thirty-four men, officers included. Next morning they were joined at fort Petites Coquilles by two small boats and nineteen men from captain Newman's command. This day they remained at the fort to fit masts and sails to the boats, and to distribute the men among the boats so as to give to each a few sailors; for it must be recollected the greater part of their number were soldiers and along-shore men. On the morning of the 20th they proceeded to pass Chef-Menteur, and arrived at the militia camp, situated about three miles from Lake Borgne, at 2 P.M. Here they reconnoitred the enemy's boats, passing and re-passing from their army to their fleet. At 9 P.M. they got under weigh with muffled oars: at 10 were in the lake, and took a course along the land towards the Rigolets. At about 11 P.M. a large boat was discovered at anchor; immediately all hands pulled up to her as fast as possible. She was boarded on the bow, stern and centre nearly at the same moment. She surrendered after very little resistance; and had on board thirty-eight dragoons, a lieutenant and cornet, and a master's mate and thirteen seamen. All returned to the encampment, where the prisoners were delivered to captain Collins, commanding officer. At 1 A.M. another sortie was made, and rowed about the lake till nearly day-light, but nothing could be found—21st, laid by. 22d, at 4 A.M. went out again, and steered towards the Rigolets: at 7 A.M. they captured a transport boat; at half past 8 captured a transport schooner of one hundred and ten tons, bound to the army, having only a few casks of rum on board, shaping her course for the Rigolets; soon after captured two launches. Before 10 A.M. captured three more boats; and at 11 reached the mouth of the Rigolets with some of the small boats. When unfortunately Mr. Shields was obliged to set fire to the schooner, then about two miles off the Rigolets, the bar of which would not permit her to pass. The wind came out strong against us, the tide was also running out rapidly—and in truth boats from the schooner had hardly reached the shore, when we perceived boats standing towards her from all directions. The smoke and blaze was very great. Our situation was now very alarming, having sixty-three prisoners and six prize-boats to guard, with a small force consisting of fifty-three men, inclusive, and this unhappily divided; for the wind and tide were so strong, that the largest boat, carrying the only piece of ordnance, was barely able to make the eastern shore of the Rigolets, whereas the others, as well as all the prizes except one, were on the western shore. The British boats, after vainly attempting to board the burning schooner, approached the shore, to ascertain the character of our men. When they discovered them to be Americans, they sent three boats laden with troops, on their way from the army to the fleet, to land about a mile and a half above them. A party of twenty men, led by Dr. Morrell, marched to meet them, and concealed themselves in the high grass, near where the first boat landed. As soon as the enemy began to land, a fire was commenced on them: the men being stationed a few yards apart, presented the appearance of a long line. The enemy continued to land, but not so rapidly; a second fire was given which they instantly returned—the other boats came up, but did not land. Our men fired a third round, and they embarked in great confusion, and rowed off. Our detachment returned to the body of our party, where they arrived just in time to beat off three other boats that came in, apparently to cut out two of the prizes. Soon after they saw two boats standing for the launch on the opposite side, and apprehended she must be taken from the appearance of the enemy's boats; but happily these fears were soon dispelled—sailing-master Daily throwing three shot so near them, that they hauled off without effecting a landing.

It was now nearly 4 P.M.—our men much fatigued, the prisoners troublesome, the wind and current so strong as to make it impossible to get through the Rigolets, and a gun-boat could be seen beating up for the expedition. It was determined that Dr. Morrell should go to fort Petites Coquilles (nine miles off) for a re-enforcement. Accordingly, he proceeded in a well-manned gig, and at 9 P.M. he reached the fort. Captain Newman promptly granted his request, and immediately embarked forty of his men; but before they could arrive, Mr. Shields thought proper to discharge, on parole,* all the prisoners on the western side. With the greatest exertion he was able to join the launch on the other side and reach the fort the next day at 2 o'clock, where twenty-one prisoners were delivered to captain Newman.

On the morning of the 19th, it was perceived that the enemy had evacuated, not a single man appearing. The commander-in-chief had already given orders to an officer to go out with a reconnoitring party, in order to ascertain whether the apparent evacuation were not a stratagem, when a doctor belonging to the British army arrived at our lines, with a letter from general Lambert, informing general Jackson that the army under his command had evacuated its position on the Mississippi, and had, for the present, relinquished every undertaking against New Orleans and its vicinity. Gen-

*The enemy refused to consider this parole as valid.

eral Lambert recommended to the humanity and generosity of general Jackson, eighty wounded men, of whom three were officers, whom he was obliged to leave behind, as their wounds did not admit of their being removed. One of these officers, lieutenant Darcy, had had his two legs carried off by a shell, at the moment when, after having been on guard for several days successively, while, as we have observed, the enemy hourly apprehended an attack, he was taking some repose, stretched on the ground, at the entrance of his bivouac.

Doctor Kerr, surgeon-general of our army, was immediately sent with the British doctor to Jumonville's plantation, where was the principal hospital of the British army, to visit the wounded, and make suitable arrangements for their accommodation.

Shortly after, general Jackson ordered colonel Hinds, commanding the cavalry, to repair with all speed to Villeré's canal, and proceed along it as far as possible, harassing the enemy on his retreat. Major Lacoste was ordered to form a detachment of the native Louisianians in his battalion as were expert hunters, to scour the woods in the vicinity of Villeré's canal, and pick up the stragglers of the enemy's army, as also such negroes as might have escaped from them; for, as might be expected, the British had carried off all the negroes of the plantations occupied by their troops.

General Jackson, accompanied by the officers of his staff, went to view the British camp. They had left in their different batteries fourteen pieces of cannon and carronades, the former spiked or with a trunnion broken off, and the latter with their pomiglions also broken off, so as to be no longer serviceable, and also a quantity of cannon balls. The general next proceeded to visit the wounded officers, whom he assured that they should receive every kind of assistance and attention that could tend to promote their cure. A few days after, all the wounded were conveyed in the steam-boat to New Orleans, where they were attended by the three surgeons who had been left by general Lambert for that purpose. All the buildings, as also the ground, of Chalmette's, Bienvenu's and Laronde's plantations, attested that our artillery must have been very destructive to the enemy. Chalmette's sugar-house, and the dwelling-house of Bienvenu, were perforated in numerous places, by the balls of the marine battery on the right bank.

Colonel Laronde, accompanied by colonel Kemper, and a detachment of major Hinds's cavalry, went in pursuit of the enemy through the prairie. They took four prisoners beyond the redoubt erected at the forks of bayou Mazant and Villeré's canal, and advanced within a mile of the forks of bayou

Bienvenu, where, concluding from the confused sound of voices they heard, that the enemy must be very numerous, and that it would be imprudent to advance any farther, they returned and made their report to general Jackson.

It appears that, immediately after the affair of the 8th of January, the enemy had determined to evacuate, and that he was desirous of proceeding as far as possible by land. For that purpose he threw bridges over all the small bayous and streams that fall into bayou Mazant by the right bank, and at the confluence of bayou Jumonville he had constructed a bridge of boats. The route still continued on the right bank, as far as the confluence of the bayous Mazant and Bienvenu, where another bridge of boats transferred it to the opposite bank, along which it continued as far as the beginning of a long elbow, where it took a direction in a straight line across the prairie, to the Catalonian village. (See plate No. 5.)

At the confluence of bayou Jumonville, on the right, the enemy in his retreat had thrown up an epaulement to cover the passage; the same had been done at the confluence of the bayous Bienvenu and Mazant; and at the Catalonian village he had commenced a large inclosure, capable of containing one thousand men, but had left it unfinished.

General Jackson received from major Overton, commanding at fort St. Philip, a letter dated the 18th in the morning, announcing to him that the enemy had discontinued to throw shells into the fort, and that his vessels had descended the river before day. General Jackson wrote on the same day to the secretary of war, informing him of the double retreat of the enemy. (See Appendix, No. 32.)

So early as the 17th, general Jackson had given to governor Claiborne the command on the right bank, and had ordered general Morgan to prepare to advance with six hundred men, in order to harass the enemy on his retreat, which was not then expected to be so prompt and clandestine.

The general requested the reverend abbé Dubourg, apostolical prefect for the state of Louisiana, to appoint a day of public prayer and thanksgiving, for the signal favour it had pleased the Supreme Being to show to our country, in delivering it from its enemies. (See the general's letter, No. 33.)

We will now proceed to the relation of the bombardment of fort St. Philip by the British; but it seems proper that it be preceded by a short description of the fort, and of the means that had been taken to put it in the best possible state of defence.

CHAPTER 9

BOMBARDMENT OF FORT ST. PHILIP, *AT PLAQUEMINES.*

Fort St. Philip is an irregular work, the body a parallelogram. Approaches to it are nearly impracticable, being surrounded by an impassable morass, a ditch, and in addition on the east by the bayou Mardi-Gras, forty-five yards wide. In the fort were mounted twenty-nine twenty-four-pounders, a thirteen-inch mortar, an eight and five-and-half-inch howitzer and a six-pounder, and in the covert-way two thirty-two pounders, mounted on a level with the water.

During the summer of 1814, every effort was made by the garrison of fort St. Philip, consisting of two incomplete companies of artillery, to place that post in the state of defence corresponding with its importance as the key of Louisiana, commanding the pass of the Mississippi. In October, the cannon having been remounted, the gun-carriages repaired, a signal station established three miles below the fort, alterations made in some of the batteries so as to afford security to the artillerists in case of an attack, and additional works erected to protect the rear of the fort, and the season approaching when an attack from the enemy might be expected, it was suggested that if a battery was placed on the opposite side of the river, thirty-two-pounders mounted in the covert-way and a thirteen-inch mortar fixed in the fort, the defence of the pass would be then complete, supposing the old buildings destroyed, and the requisite number of troops, and quantity of ordnance stores, &c. &c. to be furnished.

In the month of November, a company of infantry re-enforced the garrison, and about the last of that month the inspector-general descended the river to the Balize, and caused a guard to be stationed there.

Early in December, general Jackson visited the fort, and ordered the battery on the opposite side of the river to be immediately commenced, and that the thirty-two-pounders and thirteen-inch mortar should be mounted as before mentioned.

The mouth of the river was now more closely blockaded than before, and the guard stationed at the Balize was surprised and taken by the boats of the Herald sloop of war. The British at this time daily landed at the Balize, at which place a few of our pilots still remained. A re-enforcement arrived at the garrison of another company of the 7th infantry, and a company of volunteer free men of colour.

About the 15th December, major Overton of the rifle corps was placed in command, captain Wollstonecraft, of the artillery, who had charge of the post since the month of May, being ordered to New Orleans. On the 17th, the arrival of the enemy in our waters was ascertained, and a few days afterwards the fate of the gun-boats was known. From the 23d every effort was made to repel the attack which it was supposed would shortly be made. The interior was disencumbered of the rubbish of the barracks which had been torn down, the main magazine was disguised and secured by a covering of timber and earth, small magazines were erected, and covers made for the troops, as a security from the fragments of shells, should a bombardment take place, and the garrison were constantly on fatigue (under charge of captain Wollstonecraft, who had been ordered back from New Orleans,) for the above purpose, and in mounting the thirty-two-pounders in the covert-way, and the thirteen-inch mortar on the Spanish bastion, until the 3d of January. The 24th December, captain Lagau's company arrived. The battery on the opposite side, which was commenced on the 15th December, progressed but slowly, as many of the carpenters, negroes, and the superintendent of artificers, had ascended the river on the first notice of the arrival of the enemy. The cannon intended for that fort were taken over the river to fort St. Philip as a place of security, being useless in the then unfinished state of the works. The carpenters having been sent back from the 3d until the 8th January, the works on the new battery were carried on with unremitted exertion, and when our look-out boat returned with information on that day of the approach of the enemy, but a few days more labour were required for the completing of the gun-carriages and the work itself. On the 8th the gun-boat No. 65 warped into the bayou, and took post so as to flank the rear of the fort. To prevent the unfinished battery on the opposite side, which we were obliged to abandon, from being of any use to the enemy, every material capable of being removed was brought over the river. Our attention was solely occupied on our defence, and we anxiously awaited the approach of the enemy, which was announced to us by signal on the morning of the 9th. About 12 o'clock they hove in sight, when the furnace for hot shot was lighted, and the troops stationed at the posts before assigned to them in case of such an event taking place.

The signal station was abandoned about 1 o'clock, and, in the hurry to escape, the guard omitted to fire the buildings and lime-kiln, which they had been ordered to destroy, and at 2 o'clock that position was occupied by the enemy, by a force landed from their vessels.

The garrison was composed of the following companies, viz.

Field and Staff,	2
Captain Wollstonecraft's Artillery,	64
Murray's Artillery,	50
Detachment of captain Walsh's Artillery,	3
Captain Broutin's 7th regt. Infantry,	78
Waides's 7th Infantry,	85
Lagau's Louisiana Volunteers,	54
Listeau's Free men of Colour,	30
	366

making, with the crew of gun-boat No. 65, four hundred and six effective men. A detachment of lieutenant Cunningham's sailors, under the direction of that officer, had charge of two thirty-two-pounders mounted in the covert-way. Captain Walsh commanded the right bastion: the centre bastion, on which an eight-inch howitzer and a thirteen-inch mortar were mounted, was commanded by captain Wollstonecraft; and the left battery was commanded by captain Murray. The infantry and volunteers not attached to the cannon, were stationed in the rear of the curtain, and otherwise posted under the command of captain Broutin, so as to be able to support the troops on the batteries, and to act as occasion might require. Captain Lagau's two lieutenants and a party of his company of Louisiana volunteers were attached to the artillerists on the centre and left batteries. At 3 o'clock the enemy advanced several boats to sound opposite a point about one mile and a half from the fort, which had been cleared of its timber some time before, by order of the general. The guns of the left battery and those of the water batteries were opened on them, and they retreated. Having ascertained the distance to which our shot reached their vessels, consisting of a sloop of war, a gun-brig, a schooner and two bomb-vessels, they came to anchor out of the range of our shot, at the distance of 3960 yards; the bomb-vessels formed broadside to the fort, behind the point of land, a little in advance of the men of war, hoisted their colours, and commenced the action. The first shell from the enemy fell short, but the next burst over the interior of the fort. All that day and night the firing continued, with only short intervals, generally a shell every two minutes. No injury was done to the men or works, as the shells, from the nature of the soil, sunk in the ground, without bursting, or burst under the ground, at so great a depth as to produce no other effect than a tremulous motion. In the night several boats approached near the fort, and came so close as to allow us almost distinctly to hear their crews conversing. They fired several rounds of grape and round-shot over and into the fort. The wind blowing fair up the river, and in gusts during the night, this approach of the enemy was only considered as an effort to divert our attention from their vessels, which might attempt to pass under our smoke. Their attack was therefore received in silence, and our attention directed to the vessels alone. Finding we were not to be moved by this stratagem, they retired, and during the rest of the night fired a few shells from their boats stationed on both sides of the river. On the 10th the bombardment was continued with the same vivacity as on the former day, except that a cessation occurred of about two hours at noon and at sundown, which respite was daily granted us during the remainder of the siege. Occasionally on these two days a fire was opened from the batteries of the fort, but the shot fell short. On the third day of the bombardment several pieces of shells struck the flag-staff and in one instance nailed the halyards to the mast, in another severed them in the midst of the fire; the topmast was lowered down, and it took nearly an hour to have the flag replaced on the mast. This was done by a sailor who had the courage to stand on the cross-trees, exposed as a mark; and though the fire from the enemy was very brisk and well-directed, and several shells burst over his head, he escaped unhurt. The evening of this day the enemy directed their fire with great exactness at the contractor's store, supposing it to be the main magazine. Several whole shells passed through this building, and two burst in it, killing one man and wounding another; but as their spies had only described the magazine in the state in which it was a few days before the attack commenced, they were deceived; and by making every effort to lodge shells in the before-mentioned building, which had the appearance of the powder-magazine in its former state, the magazine itself escaped, having only been struck two or three times by fragments of shells.

At four this evening the garrison opened an animated fire for a quarter of an hour on the bomb vessels from all the guns that could bear on them, but apparently without any other effect than deranging their fire; it served however, to animate our men, showed the quickness and precision with which our guns were pointed and served, and gave a fortaste of what might be expected should the enemy attempt to pass up.

On the 12th, 13th and 14th the firing continued with the usual intervals, doing comparatively little injury: the enemy, probably aware of the inefficacy of their shells when discharged so as to alight whole in the interior of the works, now arranged their fuses, so that the shells burst in the air over the works, and scattered fragments therein in every direction. The evening of the 14th a man was killed on the right battery, another slightly wounded, a man on the centre battery lost his leg, and several of the gun-carriages were materially injured; on the right and centre batteries, the thirty-two-pounder in the covert-way, in the angle of the Spanish bastion, was struck five times, and for upwards of an hour was rendered unserviceable. Several shells entered the blacksmith's shop; one burst near the main magazine, and another passed into the ditch through the magazine in the covert way.

This evening we were employed in carrying into the fort all the timber that we could collect, and in forming covers between the guns, so as effectually to secure the men on the batteries from the fragments of shells, and to shelter them from the rain, which had fallen, with little intermission, from the commencement of the siege. This work was finished on the evening of the 15th, and it is almost incredible that during all this time, though the men were more exposed than before, passing in and out of the fort in parties, after materials, no one was hurt. At this time the interior of the fort was nearly a pond of water; the tents stood, many of them, torn by shells, but unoccupied. The small magazines were also strengthened, and an additional quantity of earth thrown on them. This evening several boats arrived, with ammunition from New Orleans, fuses for the thirteen-inch mortars, &c. &c. The 16th was occupied in conveying the powder and ordnance stores from about a mile above the fort into the magazine; and the weather being fair, we were comparatively comfortable, and in high spirits, having now the means of annoying the enemy. On the morning of the 17th, the fire from the enemy was not as animated as usual; in the evening we returned their fire from our mortar with considerable effect, as far as we were able to judge, and for several hours they threw shells more frequently than before. At night one of our shells struck one of their bomb vessels; we distinctly heard the shock, and for near five minutes the fire from one of the vessels was discontinued. The firing continued during the night of the 17th; several shells were lodged in the parapet; one burst passing through the ditch into the angle of the centre bastion. This was the last shot we received: a little before day the enemy got under way, and at daylight we could perceive the sternmost vessel descending the river.

From three o'clock on the 9th until daylight on the 18th the bombardment continued with very little intermission. During that time the enemy threw more than one thousand shells and carcases, expended upwards of seventy tons of shells, and more than twenty thousand pounds of powder, besides small shells, and round and grape-shot from their boats. During the whole of this bombardment, we lost no more than two men, one of whom was killed on the right battery, and the other in the contractor's store. Our wounded were two men on the right, and three on the centre battery, one in the store, and one in the interior of the garrison.

The troops were on the battery nine days, five days without cover; and exposed to the rain and weather which was extremely cold. They cannot be denied praise for the unremitted exertion they made to receive the enemy, the fatigues they underwent during the bombardment, which was almost incessant, and the patience they exercised thus exposed. Perhaps the duration of the siege would not have been so long, had the fuses, sent from the northward, been of a good quality; for several days the mortar, with which only there was any probability of reaching the enemy, was entirely or nearly useless. From the effect produced after good fuses arrived (for there was no materials in the garrison to make any) it may perhaps be surmised that the enemy's vessels would have found it unsafe to have remained for so long a time in the station they occupied within the range of our shells.

From the day the attack commenced until it concluded, we were constantly employed in preparing grape and canister-shot from bar lead, making up fixed ammunition, repairing gun-carriages, making implements, &c. &c. and we were, in fact, in a much better state of defence, and better provided when it terminated, than at its commencement.

After the enemy left us we had time to examine the interior, and the ground in the neighbourhood of the fort; upwards of one hundred shells had fallen and buried themselves within the fort; the surrounding buildings, workshops, stores, and the hospital, were almost in ruins, and the ground for half a mile around, was literally torn up in every direction. (See Appendix, No. 34.)

On the 20th of January the general made the necessary dispositions for the protection of the most vulnerable parts of the country, in case the enemy should attempt a new attack. The 2d regiment of militia was ordered to encamp on Villeré's plantation, while a detachment of the Kentucky troops encamped on that of Lacoste; and on the 21st, all the troops stationed on Jackson's lines, except the 7th regiment, which was left to guard them, returned to town. Their arrival was a triumph; the non-combatant part of the population of New Orleans, that is, the aged, the infirm, the matrons, daughters and children, all went out to meet their deliverers, to receive with felicitations the saviours of their country. Every countenance was expressive of gratitude—joy sparkled in every feature, on beholding fathers, brothers, husbands, sons, who had so recently saved the lives, fortunes, and honour of their families, by repelling an enemy come to conquer and subjugate the country. Nor were the sensations of the brave soldiers less lively, on seeing themselves about to be compensated for all their sufferings by the enjoyment of domestic felicity. They once more embraced the objects of their tenderest affections, were hailed by them as their saviours and deliverers, and felt conscious that they had deserved the honourable title. How light, how trifling, how inconsiderable did their past toils and dangers appear to them at this glorious moment! All was forgotten, all painful recollections gave way to the most exquisite sensations of inexpressible joy.

On the 22d, general Jackson gave orders for erecting a strong battery at the forks of the bayous Bienvenu and Mazant. For that purpose, colonel Laronde was ordered to take the command of two hundred Kentuckians from camp Dupré, where general Thomas's division had been stationed some days before, and proceed to reconnoitre the enemy. Colonel Laronde came up with the British advanced-posts at the forks of the bayous Jumonville and Mazant, where they had thrown up intrenchments, and had a strong detachment. Two large barges, and four small ones, were stationed opposite the intrenchments in the bayou; these barges fired twenty discharges of cannon, loaded with grape-shot, against colonel Laronde's detachment, as soon as it approached within cannon-shot; but without any effect. After having reconnoitred the enemy, finding it impossible to cross over for want of boats, bayou Jumonville being in that place sixty yards wide, colonel Laronde retired.

The 23d of January having been appointed as a day of thanksgiving, for the interposition of Providence, on which Te Deum was to be sung; every preparation was made to render the festival worthy the occasion. A temporary triumphal arch was erected in the middle of the grand square, opposite the principal entrance of the cathedral. The different uniform companies of Plauché's battalion lined both sides of the way, from the entrance of the square towards the river, to the church. The balconies and windows of the city hall, the parsonage house, and all the adjacent buildings, were filled with spectators. The whole square, and the streets leading to it, were thronged with people. The triumphal arch was supported by six columns. Amongst those on the right was a young lady representing Justice, and on the left another representing Liberty. Under the arch were two young children, each on a pedestal, holding a crown of laurel. From the arch, in the middle of the square to the church, at proper intervals, were ranged young ladies, representing the different states and territories composing the American union, all dressed in white, covered with transparent veils, and wearing a silver star on their foreheads. Each of these young ladies held in her right hand a flag, inscribed with the name of the state she represented, and in her left a basket trimmed with blue ribands, and full of flowers. Behind each was a shield suspended on a lance stuck in the ground, inscribed with the name of a state or territory. The intervals had been so calculated, that the shields, linked together with verdant festoons, occupied the distance from the triumphal arch to the church.

General Jackson, accompanied by the officers of his staff, arrived at the entrance of the square, where he was requested to proceed to the church by the walk prepared for him. As he passed under the arch, he received the crowns of laurel from the two children, and was congratulated in an address spoken by miss Kerr, who represented the state of Louisiana. The general then proceeded to the church, amidst the salutations of the young ladies representing the different states, who strewed his passage with flowers. At the entrance of the church he was received by the abbé Dubourg, who addressed him in a speech suitable to the occasion, and conducted him to a seat prepared for him near the altar. Te Deum was chanted with impressive solemnity, and soon after a guard of honour attended the general to his quarters, and in the evening the town, with its suburbs, was splendidly illuminated. (See the abbé Dubourg's speech, and the general's reply, in the Appendix, No. 35.)

Thus, in the space of a little less than one month, was terminated a campaign, ever memorable in the annals of America. On the 23d of December the enemy succeeded so far as to take a position on the Mississippi, and on the 19th of January he had already disappeared, leaving behind him the dead bodies of some thousands of private soldiers, and of many officers of distinction, and carrying with him the shame of having miscarried in an undertaking, so easy to accomplish, as he at first believed; but, as he was taught by thirty day's experience, really too arduous to be attempted with any prospect of success.

The British troops found that, notwithstanding the appalling renown which they thought had preceded their expedition to Louisiana, and the striking effect they expected would be produced by the very title of *heroes of Wellington*, which several regiments had vauntingly assumed, they could make no impression, even with a great superiority of numbers, on undisciplined militia, not one-fourth of whom had ever before seen a camp, or had any idea of the art of war. The whole success, indeed, of this boasted expedition, was the occupation of a tongue of land, beyond which the British army never durst advance, and which it left drenched with its bravest blood.

During their stay on the banks of the Mississippi, the British made several excursions into the settlement of Terre-aux-Boeufs, and even as far as Mr. Benjamin Morgan's plantation, two miles below the junction of the road on the Mississippi, with that of Terre-aux-Boeufs. They carried off the cattle of all the plantations, giving to the planters, in payment, one-half or two-thirds of their value, and that seldom in money, but generally in draughts on the commissary-general of their army. The youngest son of general Villeré, a youth about the age of fourteen, had been detained by them on his father's plantation, from their first arrival. On the eve of their evacuation, which he did not perceive till pretty late next day, he received in payment of about eighty head of cattle consumed on the plantation, the sum of five hundred dollars in specie, which he returned, instead of three thousand dollars, which was their value at a low price. They also, as I have already observed, carried off all the negroes of the plantations they had occupied. There were doubtless some amongst these, who were very willing to follow them; but by far the greater part, particularly the women, were decoyed, or carried off by force.

It is an undeniable fact, that during the whole campaign, the negroes were employed by the British in working for the army in general, or as servants to officers. I will not speak of the pillage of the different houses they occupied, that being an evil inseparable from the presence of an army in all countries; but here, as in Virginia, and on the shores of the Chesapeake, the conduct of the British with respect to negroes cannot be palliated. After having repeatedly declared their intention to restore them to their owners, on their coming to claim them; after having gained time by specious pretences, the result was that they carried almost all the negroes off with them. Yet those negroes were private property, and without them their masters could not cultivate their plantations. Thus, several planters are ruined by the loss of their slaves, taken from them by the British, and are obliged to let their lands lie fallow.

During the night of the 25th of January, colonel Hinds with his troop of horse, general Humbert and the engineer Latrobe, went once more to reconnoitre the enemy's position, which they found he had not changed. Colonel Hinds had one man killed and two wounded, by the cannon of the enemy; and finding it impossible to execute, for the present, the object he had in view, which was to erect a battery on bayou Bienvenu, in the place best calculated to oppose the enemy, should he be disposed to revisit the Mississippi, he returned with his detachment. General Jackson, aware that the enemy was still master of bayou Bienvenu, on which he had fortified himself, as also of Lake Borgne, which enabled him still to attack many parts of the country, and it being impossible to discover against what quarter he might direct his forces, had several days before, ordered a redoubt to be constructed on Philippon's canal, another on Regio's, at Terre-aux-Boeufs, and a third on bayou Boeuf at the cut of lake Lery, the communication of which with the sea, by the river aux Chenes, though very long and difficult, might still admit of flat boats. Lieutenant Bosquez of the artillery, had likewise been ordered to continue the construction of the redoubt begun on the river of Chef-Menteur, at the confluence of bayou Sauvage; the number of troops encamped on Lafon's plantation, had been augmented with colonel Nelson's regiment of volunteers, from the Mississippi territory, four hundred and fifty men strong.

Major Reynolds occupied the post of the Temple, at Barataria, and a strong detachment was stationed down the river la Fourche, and another post established at Tigouyon could give notice of the approach of the enemy in time to oppose his landing, which he could not attempt, until he had first penetrated into lake Pontchartrain, by forcing the passage of Chef-Menteur, or that of the Rigolets, defended by the fort of Petites Coquilles. The troops were distributed agreeably to these arrangements: those of generals Coffee and Carrol, had returned to their encampment on Avart's plantation, four miles above New Orleans; the Kentuckians were encamped on Dupré's line; Plauché's battalion, the 44th regiment, and major Daquin's battalion of men of colour, had returned to town; that of major Lacoste furnished detachments for Chef-Menteur; Jackson's lines were guarded by the 7th regiment; the 1st and 2nd of militia, a detachment of Kentuckians, and another of the militia of Red river, commanded by colonel Plauché, occupied Villeré's plantation, and furnished a strong advanced-guard, posted in the place where the enemy had thrown up fortifications when he landed at the junction of bayou Mazant and Villeré's canal.

The right bank was guarded by the drafted militia, general Hopkins's brigade, and colonel Johnson's regiment, which had arrived from Rapides on the 14th. The levy-en-masse of the militia had been arriving by companies every day from the 8th of the month. Every thing was in readiness vigorously to repulse the enemy, on whatever point he might make an attempt. All the damaged arms had been repaired, and a barge had arrived from Pittsburgh with muskets, cannon, and balls. Louisiana had been defended and saved with means much inferior to those of the enemy; and towards the end of January she was in condition to defy double the force that had at first attacked her.

About this time the remaining prisoners comprised in the cartel, agreed to on the 18th of January, who being on board the British fleet could not be sooner returned, were delivered up at Petites Coquilles, and arrived in town.

During the course of the campaign the mayor of New Orleans, Mr. Nicholas Girod, and all those employed under him, manifested the greatest zeal in assisting the troops to repel the invaders.

The ladies of New Orleans were constantly employed in making up clothes for the militia of Tennessee, whom so long an absence from their homes had reduced to extreme want in that particular, as most of them had served in the campaign against the Creek Indians, and in the expedition against Pensacola, in which they had made many long and difficult marches.

General Jackson, in a letter to the mayor, expressed his sense of the assistance he had received from that magistrate, and the citizens of New Orleans. The perusal of that letter cannot fail to interest the reader. (See Appendix, No. 36.)

By a resolution of the 2d of February the legislature voted thanks to the troops of Tennessee, Kentucky, and the Mississippi Territory; to their commanders, generals Carroll, Coffee, Thomas, and Adair, and also to colonel Hinds, for their services in the defence of the state. Those of general Jackson they thought proper to pass over in silence: but that silence produced a greater effect in his favour in the public mind than the most laboured panegyric would have done. It was in vain to attempt to throw into the shade services so eminent, and so fresh in the remembrance of a grateful people; they were present to every imagination, and, in the language of the Roman historian, shone with superior lustre for the very reason that they were not displayed. *Præfulgebant Cassius et Brutus, eo ipso quod effigies eorum non visebantur.**

The governor, in compliance with the assembly's resolution, wrote a letter to each of the officers mentioned in it, to which they severally replied. (See Appendix, No. 37.) General Coffee's answer is particularly worthy of observation. At the same time that he expresses his grateful sense of the high value which the legislature are pleased to set on his services, he cannot forbear to hint what it would become them to have done in justice to the great man under whose guidance those laurels were earned, which they had distributed with such an unequal hand.

This act of flagrant injustice is attributed to the discontent of some of the leading members of the legislative body. History will search into their motives, and hold up to the animadversion of posterity those unworthy intrigues, which produced an instance of ingratitude unparalleled in the annals of mankind.

Let me not be understood as reflecting on all the members; several of them there are, who evinced, by their conduct, both in the camp and in the house, that they were proof against the machinations of party spirit, and far above being influenced by petty considerations of private interest. But ingratitude is supposed to be characteristic of republics. It is well known that the very individuals, who extolled with enthusiasm, the measures adopted by general Jackson, early in the campaign, while the enemy was hovering on our coast, became his malignant traducers, when the danger was over, and they could enjoy the fruits of his foresight and energy, to which the country owes its safety.

On the 4th of February, Col. Edward Livingston was sent by general Jackson with a flag of truce, for the purpose of negociating a cartel for the general exchange of prisoners (those of the navy not being yet exchanged) and of endeavouring at the same time to obtain the restitution of the negroes carried off by the British, at the time of their evacuation. To understand this matter, it is necessary to peruse the correspondence that took place on that subject, between general Lambert, admiral Cochrane, and general Jackson. (See Appendix, No. 38.)

The exchange of prisoners was agreed on and arranged to the satisfaction of both parties. As to the negroes, general Lambert and admiral Cochrane inflexibly adhered to the principle they had laid down, that they could not be restored, without their own consent. (See Appendix, No. 38.)

*Tacit. Annal. l. 3.

CHAPTER 10

SECOND ATTACK OF FORT BOWYER.

THE British army having entirely abandoned the banks of the Mississippi, and those of the bayou Bienvenu, proceeded towards Mobile point. The officers who commanded the expedition had conceived hopes of taking fort Bowyer, situated at the extremity of that point, in an advantageous position, as I have already observed, for commanding the entrance of Mobile; but incapable, in its present condition, of defending the point, or preventing the enemy's becoming master of the peninsula.

After having suffered such signal and unforeseen reverses, the honour of the British arms seemed to require that their troops should achieve some exploit that might compensate, at least, for what could not be retrieved, and afford some consolation to the wounded pride of Britain. Every disposition, therefore, was made that could tend to insure the success of an attack on fort Bowyer. The enemy had learned by experience, in his former attack, that that fort possessed on the sea-side means of defence, which rendered it formidable to ships; and though the naval force that could then be brought against it was sufficient for its speedy reduction, it was not improbable but the attempt would cost the enemy the loss of part of his squadron. He therefore prudently determined to attack the fort by land.

It has already appeared, from the account of the attack made on it on the 15th of September, that fort Bowyer was so weak on the land-side, as to be incapable of defence against any considerable force.

On the 6th of February the British fleet was descried off Dauphine island. On the 7th, at nine o'clock in the morning, it separated into several divisions. Twenty-five vessels anchored about five miles from the fort, in a circular position, extending from Dauphine island towards the peninsula of the Mobile. Thirteen ships of the line, or frigates, came to anchor about one mile from the land, in a line parallel with the coast, and at the distance of about two miles and a half from the back of the fort. In the afternoon several barges were perceived on the look out, near Dauphine island. They returned to their several ships towards sunset. A few boats however still continued, during that night, to keep up an incessant communication with the different ships of the fleet.

Early in the morning of the 8th the enemy landed his troops, to the number of five thousand men, opposite the anchoring ground. They encamped at nearly an equal distance from both shores of the peninsula, which in that part is only about half a mile in breadth. Their camp was covered, on the side adjoining the continent, by two batteries erected half a mile from the encampment. The battery on the north side (marked B on the Map, plate No. 9.) mounted two field pieces, and was protected by two hundred men; the pieces were mounted behind a simple parapet, in front of which was a ditch that communicated with a lagoon, extending over two thirds of the breadth of the isthmus. The remaining space, as far as the shore of the ocean, was cut by a trench, and covered with an epaulment, behind which were mounted four pieces of cannon, (marked A on the Map) and protected by a detachment of three hundred men. By the erection of these two batteries, fort Bowyer was completely cut off from receiving any succours by land; and even could they have been taken, it would still have been necessary to force the camp, in order to arrive at the fort. Four gun-boats, which the enemy had taken from us at Malheureux island, were at anchor close to the shore, and covered the two extremities of the camp on the side of the gulf. On the opposite shore, within the bay, several barges and boats served to keep up a constant communication with Dauphine island. On the east point of that island, opposite the fort, was stationed general Kean's division, for the purpose of re-enforcing the principal camp, or of acting on any other point, as occasion might require. Towards noon the enemy caused a number of riflemen, and some other detachments, to advance towards the fort to a considerable distance from his camp. A few discharges of cannon stopped their progress, and forced them to seek shelter behind sand hillocks, or in ditches. Our riflemen fired on several of the British sentinels, of whom one was killed. About nine in the evening a body of troops was seen advancing towards the fort, and was likewise forced to retire by a few discharges of our cannon.

On the 9th, at break of day, it was discovered that the enemy had begun to cut a trench parallel to the curtain on the north side; and shortly after a brisk fire of artillery was directed against his works, which he had already advanced to the length of one hundred and fifty yards. The extremity of the trench was perpendicular to the shore of the bay, and joined the downs, that skirted the whole compass of the peninsula, so that the enemy, in following the shore between the downs and the sea, had a communication from his camp to the trench, secure from all danger. He had stationed in the trench 750 riflemen, who, during the whole time of the siege, kept up, day and night, a fire of musketry, directed chiefly against our artillery-men, who could not show themselves at the embrasure without being immediately assailed with a shower of bullets. Notwithstanding the constant fire from our cannon, the enemy succeeded in erecting batteries on the sandy mound that commands the fort. At noon some shells were thrown into the trench, which partly dispersed the soldiers stationed there; after which our riflemen dislodged almost all the others. Two ships now anchored between Mobile point and Dauphine island, and several boats full of men were passing and repassing the whole day between Dauphine island and Navy cove, lying at the distance of three miles from the back of fort Bowyer, behind the British camp. About two in the afternoon the enemy was employed in cutting down and levelling the summit of the great mound; a few discharges from the battery of the right flank dispersed them, and in the course of the afternoon, the other parties at work were much incommoded by our bombs and shells. Two barges having approached the fort, were received with several discharges of cannon, which obliged them to return towards Dauphine island. The fire of our artillery and musketry was incessant the whole day until sunset.

During the 10th, the enemy continued his works, notwithstanding the fire from the artillery of the fort. His riflemen were also engaged with ours, while his barges were employed in transporting troops from Dauphine island to Navy cove. Another trench had been commenced on the south shore, at the distance of three hundred yards, so as to be made, without much difficulty, to unite with that on the north side. Had the siege been protracted, these two trenches would have completely invested the fort. On the 11th, by break of day, it was discovered that during the night the enemy had advanced his works to within forty yards of the ditch of the fort, which was now completely hemmed in on its two sides behind. He had also completed the establishment of his batteries, erected at the distance of from three hundred yards to five hundred yards from the fort, whose rear batteries began to play. We hoped to have dislodged him from the advantageous position he had taken; but after having for some time kept up a very brisk fire, we found our expectations frustrated by the parapets of his batteries, which were from fifteen to eighteen feet thick. By this time he had mounted on his battery, eight howitzers, two mortars, four eighteen pounders, with other pieces of inferior calibre.

About 10 o'clock, a white flag was seen flying on the back of the trench; it was answered from the fort, and a suspension of hostilities took place. Lieutenant-colonel Lawrence then received from major-general Lambert, a summons to capitulate; on which he desired all the officers of the garrison to repair to his quarters, where he laid before them the articles of capitulation proposed, and for an answer to which only half an hour was allowed. That term was indeed prolonged until noon; but the enemy required the surrender of the fort that very evening; which article being rejected, it was finally agreed that the garrison should march out next day at noon. (For articles of capitulation, see Appendix, No. 39.)

Next day, 12th of February, the garrison evacuated the fort, agreeably to the capitulation, and the evacuation was completely effected by two o'clock in the afternoon. The troops were embarked on board three ships of the line, where the officers and soldiers were treated with all the civilities due to brave men, forced to comply with the resistless exigency of circumstances.

The loss sustained by the garrison during the siege, amounted only to one man killed, and ten wounded, among the latter was the brave commander. The besiegers had about forty men killed or wounded.

From this circumstantial account of the taking of fort Bowyer, the impartial reader will see that the brave garrison who defended it, being left to their own resources, deprived of all communication, and cut off from all hope of receiving relief, exerted all the means in their power to defend the fort intrusted to them; never failing to annoy the enemy, when he came within the range of their guns. What could they do more? What useful purpose could it have answered to expose themselves to a bombardment in a fort entirely constructed of timber, so combustible that a single shell falling within the parapet, would have sufficed to set the whole fort on fire? Attacked on the land side, what defence could they make against sixteen pieces of artillery, within so short a distance, behind strong intrenchments, that in less than half an hour would have battered down the parapets of the fort, on that side not more than three feet thick, above the platforms?

As no part of the fort was bomb proof, the ammunition was exposed, nor could even the wounded be sheltered; so that they with the whole garrison might have been destroyed by an explosion. The ground did not here present the advantages enjoyed by fort Plaquemine. A firm soil mixed with shells, that resisted the pressure of cannon without platforms, not yielding to the bombs, dreadful must have been the effects of their explosion; for all military men will agree that without casemates, no garrison can hold out against a regular bombardment. But it may be asked, why was no attempt made to dismount the enemy's batteries, as soon as they were successively erected? It has already been seen, that nothing had been neglected to that effect by the garrison, but that all their efforts were vain. Besides, the enemy had worked chiefly by night, and it was also during the night that he had mounted his artillery. It has been seen that the parapets of his batteries were from fifteen to eighteen feet thick, of hard sand, as firm as any kind of earth; and the inside was formed of sacks laid on one another. Could the slightest doubt still remain on this subject, I think it would be sufficient to remove it, to know that the mortars were established as is usual, on the most solid ground. Seven pieces of cannon, of which three were nine-pounders, three twelves and one twenty-four, were all the garrison had to oppose to the enemy on the side where the attack was directed. It may be said that the garrison might, during the night, have made sorties, have carried the enemy's cannon, and have destroyed his works. All this may indeed be effected with adequate forces; but this garrison's effective force amounted to no more than three hundred and twenty men fit for service. It was surely impossible with so small a force to cross a trench which already commanded the gate of the fort, and was guarded by about one thousand men, through which our troops must have cut their way, before they could arrive at batteries well manned, with powerful succours ready to re-enforce them. Any attempt of that kind, by a garrison of three hundred and twenty men, against an army of five thousand, which would within a few hours receive a re-enforcement of three thousand men, would certainly have been rather a culpable act of folly, than a laudable instance of valour. The brave garrison of fort Bowyer did, upon the whole, their duty, and all that could have been expected of them under such circumstances. Major-general Lambert testified to colonel Livingston, then on mission at his head-quarters, his warm approbation of the conduct of colonel Lawrence, adding, that under similar circumstances, he should not think it derogatory to his honour to act as that officer had done.

On the arrival of colonel Lawrence at New Orleans, it was directed in general orders of March 25th, that a court of inquiry should be held for the purpose of examining into his conduct, during the defence, and in the surrender of fort Bowyer. The court having heard several witnesses, after mature deliberation, declared the conduct of colonel Lawrence, and that of the garrison under his command, no way reprehensible. (See Appendix, No. 40.)

I have been more minute in relating the particulars of this affair, and have the more freely given way to my own reflections on it, as in the whole course of this glorious campaign, the surrender of fort Bowyer, is the only instance in which the efforts of the enemy obtained any advantage. Whoever considers the disproportion of the forces, and the desperate situation of the garrison, left to itself, beyond the reach of succours; whoever asks himself the question, whether, under such circumstances, he should have acted differently, must acknowledge that the glory acquired in this instance, by the troops of his Britannic majesty, amounts to a very inconsiderable advantage.

CONCLUSION.

The news of the success obtained over the enemy on the 8th of January, diffused the greatest joy throughout the union, particularly in Kentucky, the governor of which state transmitted a message to the legislature, recommending to them to vote a levy of ten thousand militia, to march to the assistance of Louisiana.

While colonel Livingston was on board the British fleet, the Brazen sloop of war, arrived with intelligence of the preliminaries of peace between the United States and Great Britain having been signed. On the 10th of February, that officer returned with the gladsome tidings, which was received with universal joy.

On this occasion, general Jackson published an address to the army and citizens, exhorting them not to let themselves be so far led away by the hopes of peace founded on vague rumours, as to relax in their duty; observing that, even were it certain that peace had been concluded, and the treaty signed in Europe, it could not be considered as putting an end to the war, until ratified by the president of the United States. (See the address in the Appendix, No. 41.)

After the affair of the 8th of January, some of our men found on the scene of action, an elegant sword, which was at first supposed merely to belong to some officer; but some prisoners chancing to see it, declared it to be the sword of general Packenham, the commander-in-chief. In this persuasion we were confirmed, by the silence of the British officers on that subject, when general Keane caused application to be made to general Jackson, requesting his sword found on the field, to be restored to him, as he set a fond value on it, being the present of a friend. General Jackson accordingly gave the sword in charge to colonel Livingston, who went with the flag of truce; and the colonel in person delivered it into the hands of general Keane, who in return wrote to general Jackson the letter of thanks inserted in the Appendix, No. 42.

In his letter of the 17th of February, to the secretary of war, general Jackson takes notice of this incident, with several others, as may be seen in the Appendix, No. 43.

Notwithstanding the assertion of general Keane, there are still some individuals inclined to think that that sword belonged to the general-in-chief, from this circumstance, amongst others, that the British officers who happened to be present at the delivery of it to general Keane, betrayed some surprise, and appeared not to have known that he had lost his sword; and hence they infer that the mystery in this affair, arose from a persuasion that, had it been known to us that the sword belonged to the commander-in-chief, it would have been retained as a trophy.

About this period, the exchange of prisoners, and the claiming of the negroes carried off by the British, gave rise to a very animated correspondence between general Jackson, admiral Cochrane, and general Lambert. (See these letters in the Appendix, No. 44.)

On the 24th of February, general Jackson announced to the secretary of war, the surrender of fort Bowyer. (See Appendix, No. 45.) The opinion which the general expresses in his letter, as to the conduct of the garrison, was founded on misinformation; and he afterwards rendered justice to those brave men, as soon as he was correctly informed of the circumstances which had obliged them to capitulate. It has already been seen, in the account of the second attack on fort Bowyer, that a court martial honourably acquitted colonel Lawrence and the garrison he commanded, declaring their conduct irreproachable.

Four hundred prisoners had set out from New Orleans for the Balize, agreeably to the arrangements entered into by admiral Cochrane with colonel Livingston: the remaining prisoners, daily expected from Natchez, were to be sent immediately on their arrival. Of this, the general informed general Lambert, by a letter of the 26th. (See Appendix, No. 46.)

On the 6th of March, general Jackson informed general Lambert, that he had reason to believe that the treaty of peace had been ratified by the president and senate of the United States; but that, owing to some mistake committed in the postmaster-general's office, the packet addressed to him on that subject, had not come to his hands.

The British commanders having promised to afford to the owners of the negroes who had followed them, every facility towards their prevailing on them to return, general Jackson made known to general Lambert, on the 7th of March, that he had given permission to a certain number of the owners of those negroes, to go to the British fleet with a flag of truce; and his letter concludes with a request to the British general, to restore the negroes. (See Appendix, No. 47.)

On the 8th of March, general orders were published, discharging the levy in mass, from all further service. (See Appendix, No. 48.)

At length general Jackson received the official confirmation of the ratification of the treaty of peace, and immediately communicated the intelligence to the commander of the British forces, by a letter of the 13th of March, which he transmitted by major Woodruff of the 3d regiment of infantry, who was appointed to receive the restitution of fort Bowyer, and such other posts and property of the United States, as might be in the possession of the British. (See that letter and major Woodruff's instructions in the Appendix, No. 49.)

In general orders of the same day, the commander-in-chief announced to the army, the ratification of the treaty of peace, revoking the general orders relative to martial law, ordering a final cessation of hostilities against Great Britain, and proclaiming a general pardon for all military offences, and the enlargement of all persons confined for the same. (See Appendix No. 50.)

By general orders of the following day, all the militia sent by the different states to the assistance of Louisiana, as also the militia of this latter state, were discharged. (See Appendix, No. 51.)

The treaty of peace concluded at Ghent, on the 14th of December, between the plenipotentiaries of the United States and those of Great Britain, is inserted at large in the Appendix, No. 52. Its construction having been a subject of discussion between general Jackson and the British commander-in-chief, I have thought that its insertion here would not be considered out of place.

I have likewise deemed proper to insert an address presented to general Jackson, by the different volunteer companies composing Plauché's battalion, with the general's answer. The sentiments expressed in these documents do honour to those from whom they proceed. The address was presented to the general, immediately after a review which took place on the 16th of March on the lines. About to bid farewell to his brethren in arms, he wished once more to behold those brave men drawn up on the very ground that had so often been witness of their valour, and of the patience with which they endured extreme hardship. The time, the place, the crowd of spectators, all conspired to present an interesting spectacle, and to awaken affecting recollections. On that very ground where, two months before, those brave troops had given such signal proofs of courage and of love for their country, they were now assembled to bid farewell to one another, and seal with assurances of lasting attachment a friendship contracted in the midst of alarms. General Gaines, who was about to assume the immediate command of that part of the district, commanded the evolutions, which were executed by the 3d, the 7th, and the 44th regiments of infantry, and by major Plauché's battalion of volunteers. (See Appendix, No. 53.)

General Jackson wrote to the secretary of war, acknowledging the receipt of his letter of the 16th of the preceding month, by which he had announced to him the ratification of the preliminaries of peace, and informing the secretary that he had discharged all the militia. (See the general's letter in the Appendix, No. 54.)

Major Woodruff having returned from the mission on which he had been sent to the commander of the British forces, made his report to general Jackson, which will be found in the Appendix, No. 55. It appears from that report, that, as to the long agitated question of slaves, the British constantly refused to consider them as personal property, and seemed inclined to leave them at their own disposal. Hence it follows, that they took upon themselves to give them their freedom. Surely such maxims can find no support in the law of nations. It is evident from the report, that general Lambert refused to execute that part of the treaty of peace entered into by the two nations, which extended to the restitution of slaves, under the general description of property. He pretended to construe it otherwise, but how could a British commander-in-chief take upon himself to explain away the plain and obvious meaning of a solemn treaty?

The truth is, that though a portion of the negroes carried off, enjoy amongst the British a condition nearly equivalent to freedom, yet it is well known that a great number of them were prevailed upon to enlist in their black regiments, and a still greater number were sent to the island of Trinidad and New Providence. Though the importation of foreign negroes into

Jamaica is prohibited, yet it is notorious that they are imported thither clandestinely; and it has been asserted, not without some appearance of foundation, that numbers of the negroes, carried off from Georgia and Louisiana, found their way to that island through the means of fraudulent practices.

In his letter of the 18th general Lambert uses this pitiful subterfuge—that he considers the negroes either as deserters, having come over of their own accord, or as property taken and carried of in the course of the war.

He observes that he cannot abandon to the severity of their masters, slaves who had come over to the army during the existence of hostilities, and had thus become criminal in the eye of the law of the country. (See that letter in the Appendix, No. 56.)

This pretext is the more specious, as it appears to be founded on a humane and generous principle. But the reader must know that general Jackson had obtained from the masters of the slaves their word of honour, that they would grant them a full and entire pardon; and that the known honour of those planters leaving him no room to doubt of the strict performance of their promise, he had pledged himself to general Lambert that the slaves should suffer no manner of ill treatment on their return.

The importance of the services rendered to the union by the army under the command of major-general Jackson, in Louisiana, was duly appreciated by the whole people of the United States, and the successes obtained at New Orleans were celebrated with public rejoicings in every town. The spirit of the nation exulted in the glorious achievement of her defenders. The newspapers were, for some months, filled with addresses presented, and speeches delivered on the occasion. The legislatures of most of the states voted their thanks to general Jackson, and the army under his command, for the service they had rendered to the union. Those votes have appeared in so many of the public prints, that it is not necessary to annex them to this work. But I have thought proper to insert in the Appendix some resolutions of congress, relative to the campaign of Louisiana, as being the collective expression of the sentiments of the several states. (See Appendix, No. 57.)

In one of these resolutions, the congress tenders its thanks to the army and its general, and requests the president to cause a medal to be struck, ornamented with suitable devices, commemorative of the victories over the English, in Louisiana, and to present it to general Jackson.

If ever, at any important period, the representatives of the people were faithful interpreters of the public feeling, it was at this moment. The nation had already appreciated the services of its defenders, and had distinctly expressed its sentiments; the congress did nothing more than give them body and shape, and convey them to posterity in all authentic and permanent form. (See Appendix, No. 57-a.)

These resolutions were communicated to the army, and received by the different corps with the most lively emotions of joy and gratitude. These brave men were about to return to their fire-sides and the objects of their affection. They bore with them a conviction highly flattering to freemen—that of having contributed to strengthen the independence of their country, to procure for it an honourable peace, and to establish its military glory on an imperishable basis:—they had surpassed the expectations of the nation, and this day received its thanks through its representatives:—they could desire nothing more.

I have above remarked that immediately after the departure of the English troops from the shores of the Mississippi, a body of Kentucky militia was encamped on the plantation of Dupré, and the remainder on the right bank of the river. Those from Tennessee, under the orders of generals Carrol and Coffee, resumed their former encampment, on the plantation of Avart. The commanding general had thus wisely disposed them, that in case of need he might easily transfer them to such points of the coast as the enemy should invade. The troops occupied those posts until the disbanding of the army, which took place, as we have seen above, when general Jackson received the ratification of the treaty of peace by our government: they then took up the line of march for their respective states. The loss they had sustained during the campaign was very inconsiderable; and we should thank providence that our triumphs were achieved, at the expense of so small a portion of the usual afflictions of war: yet, these undaunted soldiers, who were able to overwhelm the enemy with so destructive a fire, and to bear the incessant fatigues of the campaign, were obliged to pay a severe tribute to the climate of Louisiana. The hardships they were obliged to undergo, in the duties of a camp, within Jackson's lines, added to the unhealthiness of the constantly wet soil, caused them to contract pernicious fevers and dysenteries, which soon became epidemical. The effect of these disorders were speedily seen and terribly felt:—in the space of one month five hundred men perished in this way! Let us drop a tear to the memory of these noble fellows! May their virtues ever live in our memory. They lived long enough to glory and their country, which they freed from its enemies; but they did not live long enough to receive the recompense of their toils, to enjoy, in the midst of domestic enjoyments, that felicity, which they had secured to others, and had thus acquired a right to expect for themselves.

After the capitulation of fort Bowyer, the English army preserved its encampments on Dauphine island and at Mobile point. General Lambert and admiral Cochrane, waiting an official communication of the ratification of the treaty of peace, by the president of the United States, made the necessary preparations for the embarkation of their troops:—but, the exchange of prisoners, and the difficulty of procuring a sufficiency of water, for a long voyage, occupied much time, and rendered the embarkation tedious and painful. Want of provisions obliged the commissaries of the English army to purchase them at New Orleans, where they were obliged to put them in-boats, which carried them to the fleet, where they were distributed among the transports.

These dispositions occupied much time, during which the mortality among their troops, and especially the black regiments was very great. The number of sick and wounded in the fleet is estimated at two thousand; but it is impossible to ascertain correctly the number of the victims of disease, from the 19th of January until the end of March, the time of evacuation by the army. Judging from the number of graves around their camps, it certainly was considerable. We cannot but regret the lot of these unfortunate victims of the ambition of the British government. Those poor creatures, whose bodies are entombed on the shores of Louisiana, were but passive instruments which were broken in the hands of those who used them. They died in a foreign land, but they have, doubtless, left somewhere friends and relations to whom they were dear; and who will never have even the sad consolation of shedding a mournful tear on their graves.

During the stay of the English prisoners at New Orleans, a fact occurred, which I shall detail circumstantially, in order to counteract the effect of any statement that may be made, unfavourable to the American nation. General Jackson, presuming that, after their departure from the waters of the Mississippi, the English would attempt to carry Mobile, and establish themselves on the Dauphine and Ship islands, made the proper dispositions to repel them. Among other measures to this end, he authorized general Humbert to form a legion, and permitted him to enroll in it all the English deserters who were willing to enter the service. Prudence requiring that they should be carefully watched, it became necessary, for want of a proper place, to confine some of them among the prisoners of war. When the *hero of Castlebar* issued a proclamation, addressed principally to the Irish, inviting the deserters to enter his legion, some prisoners of that nation requested to be also admitted; and unfortunately, the officer charged with the recruiting service, from ignorance or mistake enlisted some of them. General Jackson, as soon as this circumstance was made known to him, ordered that the prisoners should be remitted to prison, with their companions, and when an exchange took place, they were, to their great regret, delivered up with the others. Fearing, however, lest these men, on their arrival, should be severely punished, general Jackson interceded in their behalf, with general Lambert, (see Appendix, No. 58,) who answered, that in respect to him, the conduct of those prisoners should not be noticed in any manner. (See his letter, dated February 27, Appendix, No. 44.)

The legislature of Louisiana passed a resolution expressive of their sense of the good conduct of certain individuals, as well as of the patriotic zeal displayed by the citizens of certain parts of the state, at the time of invasion by the enemy. (See Appendix, No. 59.) This article needs no comment. It is sufficient for me to recommend it to the attention of the reader, who will here have occasion to remark what I have, in the course of this work, had the pleasure of announcing—that, at this memorable crisis, all the inhabitants of Louisiana, without distinction of birth, colour, age, or sex, vied in zeal for the service of their country, and strained every nerve to repulse the enemy. I pass no encomium on the conduct of the people of this state, while the enemy occupied a portion of their territory. I am convinced that they attach to their actions no merit but that of doing their duty; and that the satisfaction they derived from this source was an ample reward; but these citizens have been calumniated; they were considered, for a long time, as suspicious members of the American family, and as persons who could not be relied on; disposed, in fact, to receive, if not with joy, at least with indifference, such other form of government as the fate of war, or the train of political events might subject them to. It was not by words, that those meritorious citizens vindicated their character; but by the best proofs of devotion to their country, by defending it faithfully, and by valiantly repelling the invading enemy. Their conduct throughout this campaign is the most emphatic refutation of the unjust charges of their calumniators.

Mention is made, in this resolution, of the assistance received from the council of the city of Orleans, by those families, whose principals, being employed in the service of their country could not minister to their wants. I shall merely add, that more than thirty-four thousand rations of bread, and nearly thirteen thousand of meat, were distributed, to the most necessitous, in the space of about a month.

The artillery and engineering service received very important assistance from the officers of the mayoralty. I have frequently witnessed their zeal in availing themselves of immediate resources, and even creating new ones, to hasten the transportation of materials, munitions, and provisions.

I must be permitted to add to the enumeration of acts of zeal and devotion, noticed in this resolution, an example of patriotism, worthy to be compared with the most brilliant instances of the same kind recorded in ancient histories. Madame Devance Bienvenu, a respectable widow, and rich inhabitant of Atakapas, after sending her four sons to the defence of their country, in captain Dubuclay's company of dragoons, wrote to governor Claiborne that she sincerely regretted having no other sons to offer to her country, but that, if her own services, in the duty of taking care of the wounded, should be thought useful, notwithstanding her advanced age, and the great distance of her residence, she would hasten to New Orleans for that purpose.

General Jackson, in his correspondence with the secretary at war, did not fail to notice the conduct of the "corsairs of Barataria," who were, as we have already seen, employed in the artillery service. In the course of the campaign they proved, in an unequivocal manner, that they had been misjudged by the enemy, who, a short time previous to the invasion of Louisiana had hoped to enlist them in his cause. Many of them were killed or wounded in defence of the country. Their zeal, their courage, and their skill, were remarked by the whole army, who could no longer consider such brave men as criminals, or avoid wishing their permanent return to duty and the favour of the government. These favourable sentiments were expressed by the legislature of the state, in a memorial to the president, and general Jackson added his and those of the army. The chief magistrate of our government yielded to these intercessions, and issued a proclamation, by which he granted a full and complete pardon to all those who, having formerly violated the laws of the United States, by smuggling at Barataria, had aided, during the campaign, in repulsing the enemy, and should produce a certificate, to this effect, from the governor of Louisiana. He likewise ordered a suspension of all proceedings against their persons and property, as well as the restitution of whatever might have been sequestrated. This proclamation, written in a noble and dignified style, is fraught with the true principles of philanthropy: a perusal of it cannot fail to afford pleasure. (It will be found in the Appendix, No. 60.)

On the 23d of December, 1814, when the enemy approached the banks of the Mississippi, near the plantation of major-general Villeré, after having taken prisoners the men who composed the detachment sent to the village of the Catalans, major Villeré, his son, of the third regiment of Louisiana militia, had the immediate command of the post, formed at his father's plantation; and it was he who sent the detachment to the village, two days previous to the arrival of the enemy. Although it is to be regretted, that he had not placed some intermediate posts between this village and the Mississippi, which might have discovered the enemy, and given notice of his approach, by the discharge of small arms or rockets, we must, in justice to major Villeré affirm, that he does not deserve the reproaches inserted by some malignant or inconsiderate persons, in the different gazettes of the union. In his correspondence with the secretary at war, general Jackson has borne testimony to the good conduct of this officer, and the legislature, in the resolution, inserted in the Appendix, No. 59, notices the presence of mind, the address, and the courage, which he displayed in escaping the enemy, in a manner, almost miraculous, and returned to give intelligence of their approach. The decision of the court-martial held to examine the conduct of major Villeré, who produced, however, no testimony in his own favour, will be found in the Appendix, No. 61.

If it were not presumptuous to form a conjecture as to the unfortunate circumstance of the arrival of the enemy on the shores of the Mississippi, unperceived by us, I should be inclined to attribute it to the capture of our gun-boats, by which we were deprived of the means of following his movements, and observing the point to which his attack was directed. If, as I have before remarked, in the narration of this affair, the number of our vessels on the lakes had been proportioned to the extent of coast we had to defend, the commander of the station, commodore Patterson, possessing an accurate knowledge of local circumstances, could have so disposed them, as to give timely notice of the approach of the enemy.

The momentary success of the English, on the 8th of January, on the right bank of the river, required an examination of the conduct of many officers of the Louisiana and of the Kentucky militia under the command of colonel Davis. In my narrative of the events of that day, I have endeavoured to remove unfavourable impressions, as to these troops, as well as to free the Kentuckians from the charges advanced against them, I take the liberty of saying, with unjustifiable precipitation. If a shadow of doubt remain in the mind of the reader, on this subject, the decision of the court of inquiry, will, I think, remove it entirely. (See Appendix, No. 62.)

By order of commodore Patterson, a court of inquiry was convened at New Orleans, for the purpose of hearing several testimonies relative to the conduct of lieutenant Jones, commanding the division of gun-boats, captured on the 14th December, by a flotilla of English barges. The report of this court, containing minute details of the conduct of the officers and of the crews of the gun-boats, as well as an account of the manner in which the attack was made cannot fail to interest the reader. (See Appendix, No. 63.)

So many various estimates have been made of the force of the British army which came to Louisiana, that it would be very difficult to ascertain which is the most correct; I have, however, procured a very circumstantial one, including the names of the different corps with those of their commanders, and the amount of their respective force, which I have inserted in the Appendix, No. 64.

This document is supported by a letter from Dr. Morrell of the navy, who, having been detained several weeks on board the British fleet, had many opportunities to converse with British officers, on the subject of the force of their army. The circumstances related by Dr. Morrell cannot fail to be interesting to my readers.

Under the same number of the Appendix will also be found a list of the officers, composing the staff of the British army at the time of its landing.

Arrived at the close of my narration of the important events of the memorable campaign in Louisiana, I consider myself bound, as a faithful historian, to insert the official reports of the commanders of the British fleet and army relative to the operations of the forces confided to their charge. These will be found at length and in the order of their dates, in the Appendix, No. 66.

No. 1 of these documents is a despatch of admiral Cochrane, addressed to the board of admiralty, in England, dated on board the Armide, off the Isle au Chat, 16th December, 1814, and accompanied by a report of captain Lockyer, relative to the capture of our gun-boats, off Isle aux Malheureux, on the 14th of the same month. No. 2 is a report of major-general Keane, addressed to the commanding general Packenham, dated 26th December, in which he mentions the disembarkation of his troops and their arrival on the banks of the Mississippi: it contains also an account of the affair of the 23d December at night. No. 3 is an extract of a journal kept by major Forrest, in the quarter-master-general's department, giving a succinct account of all the transactions, from the arrival of general Packenham, on the banks of the Mississippi, on the 25th of December 1814, until the 31st of the same month. No. 4 is a letter from major-general Lambert, addressed to lord Bathurst, secretary of state of his Britannic majesty, dated 10th January, 1815, giving an account of the operations of the English army up to this period, and particularly of the unfortunate result of their attack on our line on the 8th of January. No. 5 contains a report of colonel Thornton, commanding the expedition on the right bank of the river, dated January 8, and addressed to general Packenham (now dead) detailing the operations of the troops confided to his charge, on that side. No. 6 is a despatch of admiral Cochrane, dated 18th January 1815, addressed to the admiralty office, relating principally to the service of the marines and sailor up to this date. No. 7 is a despatch of general Lambert, dated 28th January 1815, addressed to lord Bathurst, in which he sets forth the events posterior to the 10th January; and No. 8 is another despatch from the same officer to the same minister, dated head-quarters, Isle Dauphine, 14th February 1815, containing an account of the capture of fort Bowyer on Mobile point.

The same impartiality which induces me to insert these official reports demands some observations on the facts and circumstances comprised in them. I shall follow the order in which I have placed them.

In No. 1, admiral Cochrane, giving an account of the capture of the gun-boats, vaunts the valour and skill of his force, and augments, according to custom, the difficulties surmounted. To establish a fair scale of comparison between the attack and the defence, and to appreciate justly the respective merits of the conquerors and the conquered, it will be sufficient, in my opinion, to compare the disproportion of our forces with the strength of the enemy.

Five gun-boats, some of which were planted in the mud, and, of course, unable from this circumstance, in addition to that of a strong current, to change their position, defended by one hundred and eighty-two men, were attacked by forty-two barges and launches, some of which were as large as our gun boats, (one of those, which was sunk, carrying one hundred and eighty men,) and three gigs;—the whole having a complement of twelve hundred men!—Notwithstanding this monstrous disparity of force, the Americans defended themselves for an hour and a half, and did not strike their flag until they had destroyed more than a third of the force of the enemy, who now occupied the decks of these same vessels, where the victory had been disputed, blow for blow. Such is the plain fact, which the English admiral endeavours to involve in useless details, in order to divert the attention from the principal point. He says also that his barges advanced to the attack with the greatest resolution, in defiance of our vessels, which he calls *formidable, having the advantage of a chosen position,* &c. Unfortunately for sir Alexander, captain Lockyer, who commanded, and was wounded in this attack, and who, consequently, must have been better acquainted with all that passed, expresses himself thus, in his letter, above mentioned: "*Fortunately, for the English flotilla, the wind failing (the American vessels,) after a chase of thirty-six hours, they were obliged to come to off Isle St. Joseph.*" In another part of the same letter he accords perfectly with the report of captain Jones, as to the velocity of the current.

The admiral acknowledges that the victory cost them dear; and when we consider the price, we readily pardon some little inaccuracies. He was doubtless, too much occupied with his preparations for the establishment, at Orleans, of his judges, custom-house officers, and others brought over for the purpose of extending the blessings of *regular government* to recolonized Louisiana; or in preparatory arrangements for the transportation of all the cotton and sugar which he expected in a few minutes to possess, to give to his despatch the attention one would suppose it required. I shall make but one more remark on this report. The American sloop represented as carrying one six-pounder and two twelve-pound carronades, and twenty men, had only one four-pounder and eight men; and it is a fact, that this boat, which we should suppose, according to the reports of these gentlemen, to be of a size capable of defending herself against an imposing force, was built five years previous, in the navy-yard, at New Orleans, to serve as a gig, for commodore Porter, then commanding on that station, who caused her to be transported, on a wagon, to Bayou St. John, a distance of two miles, where she was used for short excursions on the lakes.

Captain Lockyer has also made a mistake in his account of the captured gun-boats. He estimates the men at two hundred and forty-five, whereas their number was really but one hundred and eighty-two effective men—that is to say, the English force was to ours rather more than six to one.

No. 2 is the report of the general Keane, after the affair of the 23d of December. It is worthy of remark, that this paper is dated the 26th, three days after the battle. The general had then, at least, two whole days to collect positive facts, and consequently, time to prepare an accurate report. Let us see how far he has made his conformable to truth. He says,

"*When the men, much fatigued by the length of time they had been in the boats, were asleep in their bivouac, a heavy flanking fire of round and grape-shot was opened upon them, by a large schooner and two gun-vessels, which had dropped down the river from the town, and anchored abreast our fires, &c.*" As to the schooner, the general is literally correct. The fire was very lively, and well kept up. Commodore Patterson, who was on board, and captain Henley, who commanded the vessel, with his brave crew, knew too well what was due to such distinguished guests, to fail in paying them due honours; I hope they do not complain of this—if they do, they are certainly much to blame; for, before colonel Thornton had made those *judicious dispositions*, of which the report speaks, to place his brigade in safety behind the levee, more than one hundred of his men were killed or wounded by the fire of the Carolina. But what were those gun-vessels of which general Keane speaks? Whence came they, and who saw them? There were, it is true, at that time on the waters of the Mississippi, a great many very large floating trees; its surface was sometimes covered with them, and I can find no other cause for this mistake of the general, than in some of those drifted logs, which, in the darkness of the night, he may have taken for vessels! This is not absolutely impossible;—but the gun-vessels that fired in company with the schooner—it is indeed too much. The reader must be struck with the similarity that there is between this little affair and the celebrated battle of the kegs at Philadelphia during the revolutionary war! If general Keane's optic nerves were so affected on this memorable night of the attack of the schooner *and two gun-boats*, the reader may well expect to find his sense of hearing more acute, for it is said that nature always turns the loss of one sense to the profit of the others. It appears, however, from the report of the general, that he was, at this time, as unfortunate in his hearing, as we have just shown him to have been in his sight. He says that, "*the enemy, favoured by the darkness of the night, concealed themselves under a high fence, and calling to his men, under the pretence of being a part of their own force, offered to assist them in getting over,*" &c. The general or some of his officers, certainly dreamt this; for I can affirm that no such thing occurred. The only circumstance which bore the least particle of resemblance to this romance, is that which I am about to relate. I leave the reader to trace the similitude, and draw his inference.

It has been seen, in the narration of the affair of the 23d December, that colonel Piatt, quarter-master-general, advanced at the head of a detachment of the 7th regiment, towards the enemy, for the purpose of reconnoitring and repulsing him.—On reaching the boundary lines of Laronde's and Lacoste's plantations, the detachment was saluted by a discharge of musketry, from an advanced-guard of the enemy, which had not yet been discovered, although at a very short distance; this was owing to the soldiers being placed behind the fence, along both sides of the road, with one knee on the ground, and in this position they fired. The colonel advanced towards them, at a full gallop, and called to them to turn out and fight like brave men, instead of firing crouched on the ground like cowardly Indians. This is the only occurrence which has any relation to a *fence*. If this be the origin of the story given us by the general, he deserves great credit, for his admirable talent in dressing up a report.—But let us proceed. The general places under the head of simple *casualty*, the loss which he sustained from the fire of the schooner, and which we know positively to have been more than one hundred men. After supposing that the 85th regiment advanced in consequence of a pretended *ruse de guerre* on our part, he found himself, says the report, *"surrounded by a superior number the enemy, who ordered him to surrender"—"the answer,"* continues he, *"was an instantaneous attack. A more extraordinary conflict has, perhaps, never occurred; absolutely hand to hand, both officers and men."* This *"superior number of the enemy,"* was simply captain Beale's company of volunteer riflemen, amounting in all to sixty-two; they penetrated, as I have before mentioned, into the midst of the enemy's camp without a bayonet, and nevertheless, disarmed and took prisoners a considerable number of his men. This took place within the enclosure of Lacoste's plantation, near the houses. I also refer the reader to my narrative of this affair to correct the mistake, which makes half of the company fall into the hands of the enemy, and which the general would fain attribute to the bravery of his 85th regiment.

In another part of the same report, general Keane makes his 93d regiment advance to charge with the bayonet, keeping the 4th *"as his reserve."* Here there is only one single mistake, that of taking an American for a British corps; it certainly was Plauché's battalion, instead of his 93d regiment, of which the general meant to speak; for as soon as, throughout this part of our line, that is to say, from the left of our right division, which was directly in front of the *centre*, of which general Keane speaks, the general shout *"a la bayonnette"* was given, this famous centre, after making a single discharge of musketry, gave way precipitately. The general may have heard the word *"bayonet,"* and supposed it proceeded from his own mouth! Let us pass over this mistake. I must, however, remark, that general Keane's watch was probably regulated for another meridian than that of Louisiana, since it was only half past eight o'clock, when this took place, and the report says it happened at half past ten. But the general proceeds: *"The enemy now determined to make a last effort, and collecting the whole of his force, formed an extensive line, and moved,"* &c. *"The line drove in all advanced posts,"* &c.

Who would not suppose, from the preceding sentence, that our little band had made a desperate and general attack! The report certainly conveys this idea, but it is very wide from the truth. The enemy retired before our right, and the firing had ceased on both sides, when general Coffee, who commanded the left division, advanced and drove them before him. I refer the reader again to my narrative of this affair, and to the Atlas, (plate No. 6) I would have too much to do if I were obliged to correct all the errors in point of fact, and all the perversions of circumstances, contained in general Keane's report. I shall content myself with remarking, that he states our force at five thousand men, whereas it consisted of but nineteen hundred effective; and that the engagement terminated, not at half past twelve, as he pretends, but at half past nine. The remainder of the report consists of eulogies on the officers who distinguished themselves in this affair. I do not pretend to say that they have not merited this distinction, but I venture to affirm, that if the reports of general Keane are correctly made up from those handed him by the different commanders of corps, these gentlemen must have been under great agitation during the engagement, to commit such gross blunders. They had better have honestly confessed that they were unprepared for the scene, and that the firmness and promptitude of our attack astonished and disconcerted them. But it belongs only to superior minds to make such acknowledgments, and besides, an official report, composed of such materials, would not have the desired effect, and could not have been submitted to the inspection of the most thinking people of England, as one of their writers affects to call them.

No. 3 contains an extract from major Forrest's journal, beforementioned. This extract dates the loss of the schooner Carolina on the 26th, whereas she blew up on the 27th: and again, the first attack on our line, said to have taken place on the 27th, was made on the 28th. The report of this last day is given in a very succinct form. I request the reader to compare it with my account. That of the 1st January, 1815, is equally concise, and makes no mention of the effect of our artillery upon the enemy's batteries, nor of the number of men destroyed by our fire. As to the rest, this journal breathes a tone of moderation honourable to its author; if it does not contain the whole truth, it at least contains no direct assertions in opposition to it.

No. 4 contains a despatch of major-general Lambert, on whom devolved the command of the British army, after the death of general Packenham, as being the next in rank, generals Gibbs and Keane having been carried off the field of battle, severely wounded, on the 8th of January. General Lambert assumed the command at a critical moment, and under very unfavourable auspices, and I doubt not, under circumstances very painful to his feelings. He had a melancholy duty to perform, in announcing the result of the attack of the 8th January. His was the painful task to render an account of a complete defeat, to a minister of his government, to a member of the same cabinet who, with the sang froid of politicians, had prepared this formidable armament, whose success had not even been questioned and who instead of the recital of a brilliant victory, announced in anticipation, in their gazettes, as a certain event, to express a doubt of which would have been an insult to the English nation, and of which, they said they awaited only the particulars—this general was obliged to detail a disaster the most complete, and reverse the most poignant that the British arms had ever sustained in the new hemisphere. This task, it must be confessed, was hard to perform, especially as to the recital of an attack which had miscarried so entirely, though made by numerous and experienced troops, this officer must necessarily subjoin the enormous loss of his nation, in officers and men. It is well known that general Lambert felt and understood all that was disagreeable and embarrassing in his situation, much better than he expressed it; but upon the whole, he gives a correct account of the localities and the respective positions of the troops.

Our triumph was so distinguished, that I cannot, in honour, indulge in any reflections on this report. If general Lambert does not give all the details of an affair so disastrous to his army, if he passes slightly over many circumstances of this memorable day, the body of facts that he does present, is nevertheless generally correct. I shall take the liberty, however, of rectifying two mistakes in his report. The first is, where he mentions the death of the commander-in-chief, general Packenham. It was not this officer, but brigade-major Wilkinson who fell, on the glacis of our line. The former was killed by grape-shot, from the twelve pounder in battery No. 8, while in the act of encouraging the troops, at the point marked in the plan of the affair of the 8th January. (See Atlas, plate 7.)

The second and more important error, is in the passage, where general Lambert says.—"*As they* (the British troops,) *advanced, a continued and most galling fire was opened from every part of the line,*" &c. In my plan of this affair, I have distinguished, by lines, and I venture to say, with the greatest exactness, both the extent and the direction of our fire. The battalions of Plauché, Daquin, Lacoste, with three-fourths of the 44th regiment, that is to say, our whole centre, did not fire a single shot! Two companies of this last corps had fired two or three rounds, when the officers, observing that their shot did not reach the enemy, ordered them to cease firing. The majority of the troops under general Coffee did not fire at all, so that but one half of our line was engaged. This is a fact for the truth of which I appeal to the individual testimony of every man in our army, and even to all those of the enemy who have candour enough to acknowledge an unpleasant truth.

In my account of the affair of the 8th January, which I beg the reader to compare with the report of general Lambert, I have forgotten to mention a circumstance that reflects the highest honour on our troops. I shall insert it here; and it cannot fail to afford pleasure to the feeling mind.

At the time of the preceding attacks, those of the 28th of December, and first of January, after our artillery had silenced that of the enemy, and forced his troops to retire, repeated huzzas from the whole of our line rent the air; the most lively demonstrations of joy were everywhere exhibited by our soldiers, a presage of the fate of the enemy, in a general attack. On the 8th of January, on the contrary, no sooner was the battle over than the roar of artillery, and musketry gave place to the most profound silence. Flushed with victory, having just repulsed an enemy who had advanced to scatter death in their ranks, our soldiers saw, in the numerous corpses that strewed the plain, only the unfortunate victims of war; in the wounded and prisoners, whom they hastened to attend, only suffering and unhappy men, and in their vanquished enemies, brave men, worthy a better cause. Elated with their success, but overpowered by the feelings of a generous sympathy for those unfortunate victims of the ambition of their masters, they disdained to insult the unfortunate by an untimely exultation, and cautiously avoided any expression of joy, lest they should wound the feelings of those whom the chance of battle had placed in their hands. In the midst of the horrors of war, humanity dwells with delightful complacency, on the recital of such noble traits; they sooth the heart under the pressure of adversity, and divert the mind from the contemplation of ills which we can neither avoid nor entirely remedy.

I have said, that the English troops advanced on our line, with the greatest firmness, and I willingly seize the present opportunity of adding my feeble testimony of this fact to that of general Lambert. In the list of killed and wounded, which is subjoined to his report, it will be remarked that the proportion of officers is enormous. From this circumstance may be formed a correct idea of the vigour of the attack, on the part of the enemy, and of the valour with which it was sustained. Independently of three general officers who succumbed, on this day a great many of the most distinguished families of England have to deplore the loss of some of their relatives, who died like heroes on the bed of honour; with such men it is always glorious to be connected.

The report of general Lambert is written in the same liberal and dignified style which has always been remarked in his communications with general Jackson and his officers.

No. 5 is the report of colonel Thornton, commander of the English troops, in the attack on the right bank of the river, on the 8th of January. It is addressed to general Packenham, of whose death he was unadvised. The colonel in one part of this report says: *"we met with no obstacle, until we reached picket a posted behind a bridge,"* &c. *"and secured by a small work, apparently just thrown up."* The bridge, of which he here speaks, is that over Mayhew's mill-race, but as for the "small work" apparently just thrown up, I really cannot conceive what he means. There existed nothing of this nature, or which he could consider as such, but the embankment of the canal, raised several years ago, with the earth dug out of it. If colonel Thornton should ever travel along the banks of the Mississippi, especially below New Orleans, he will meet with many such fortifications.

In the 5th plate of the Atlas, will be found a correct view of that position, which, to colonel Thornton, seemed to be *"a very formidable redoubt, on the bank of the river, with the right flank secured by an entrenchment, extending back to a thick wood, and its line protected by an incessant fire of grape."* This pretended *redoubt*, with its *entrenched flank*, extended but two hundred yards from the bank of the river, and not to a wood, as the colonel asserts. Beyond these two hundred yards, and in front of the troops under colonel Davis, there was only an extension of the old canal Raguet, two-thirds filled, and affording no sort of shelter. I refer the reader to what I have said, in this work, of the above line, and the disposition of the troops, &c.

According to this officer's account, our troops on the right bank of the river, amounted to fifteen hundred; while in fact the number of our effective men did not exceed eight hundred. He takes care not to say, that the greater part of our pieces of artillery were spiked—and their ammunition thrown into the river: it would seem, on the contrary, that he took a considerable quantity of it, which cannot be the case, as commodore Patterson had taken care to destroy them, and all that he got possession of were a few rounds for the pieces mounted on the line, and some musket cartridges.

I renew my invitation to the reader, to compare every document of the enemy, with my narrative, and to trace the movements on the map, as the only means to arrive at the truth.

No. 6 is a despatch of admiral Cochrane, to the secretary of the admiralty, which gives an account of the operations reported by his generals Keane and Lambert, with those mentioned by major Forrest, but in a more succinct manner. His letter is devoted principally to the operations of the marines and sailors landed from the fleet, to aid the land service;—and the mention of the marine officers who had distinguished themselves. Accompanying his letter is one of captain Thomas Trowbridge, who commanded the sailors that were disembarked, reporting favourably the names of some of his officers whose good conduct he had occasion to notice.

Admiral Cochrane also announces the bombardment of fort Plaquemine, which he fears, has not yet produced all the effect he no doubt had expected from it. More than one thousand bombs had been thrown at the fort—but in vain. It appears, that the admiral had not sufficiently studied the quality of the soil of Louisiana, when he despatched this little squadron into the Mississippi, to make, as he says, a diversion; but in fact, to force a passage; unfortunately, however, for his expectations, the bravery and vigilance of the garrison of fort St. Philip defeated his scheme.

No. 7 contains a long letter from general Lambert, addressed to lord Bathurst, detailing the movements of the British army, from the affair of the 8th of January until the 28th of the same month, the day after the total evacuation by their forces. In this letter, he says what is not altogether correct, viz. that the army was not at all harassed, in its retreat. I have given an account of the movements ordered by general Jackson, to annoy the enemy, who certainly feared being harassed, as is proved by his placing, in the bayous, barges armed with artillery, to cover his retreat, and fire on the troops sent in pursuit, which they did, as I have related in this work, in its proper place. The enemy also raised breastworks, in several places, on the borders of the bayous. (See Atlas, plate No. 5.)

Effectually to annoy the enemy, in his retreat, we had need of boats, to descend the Bayou Bienvenu, sufficiently large to carry artillery. These, as I have already said, we did not possess. General Jackson, with men and muskets could make soldiers; but he could not fabricate arms, nor supply the want of a naval force.

In support of what I have advanced, as to the intention of the British government, to carry on a war of pillage and devastation against the United States, I insert several letters which establish this fact, beyond all possibility of doubt. (See Appendix, No. 67.) Some of these letters were written by superior officers, to others of similar grade; all of whom would have cautiously avoided the expression of such sentiments, had they not been assured beforehand, that they corresponded with those of their government. I shall abstain from all reflection on these letters—they speak for themselves. Comment upon them might subject me to the charge of wishing to influence the opinion of my readers respecting documents which are alone sufficient to give finish to the picture of the enemy with whom we had to contend.

In the above review of the British official reports, I have been guided by that strict regard to truth and that severe impartiality, to which an historian is ever bound to adhere and should never lose sight of. The reader may compare for himself and form his own opinion. He will also observe, that these reports are written in a style of decorum and modesty, by no means usual with the enemy, previous to this period. It appears to have been reserved for the British officers, to be taught on the shores of the Mississippi, to know a nation, who, neither in the course nor at the commencement of this struggle, had ever any cause for self reproach, but who, on the contrary, had given many proofs of her patience in enduring the repeated and long-continued injustice of the English, and was, at length obliged to redress her grievances by the sword.

Far from me be the wish of recriminating further on the conduct of the British in the war which is now happily closed by a peace, honourable to both nations. I shall terminate this work, by offering up, in common with all good citizens, my prayer to heaven that it may long endure, and the effusions of my gratitude to divine Providence, for the protection, which has encouraged and supported us through the glorious struggle. The unexampled prosperity, to which America has attained, notwithstanding the obstacles inseparable from a state of warfare, is a new proof of the divine favour; and a sure pledge of our future safety. While the names of Bridgewater, Chippewa, fort Erie, Stonington, Plattsburg, Baltimore and New Orleans, will ever excite, in the hearts of Americans the most lively sensations of joy and of national pride, it is to be hoped they will teach the English this important lesson, that none can insult with impunity a nation, which is firmly determined to maintain itself in the enjoyment of FREEDOM and INDEPENDENCE.

NOTES.

1. After what I have said in the text of this work, relative to the Barratarians, had been prepared for the press, other particulars came to my knowledge, which I have thought proper to insert here.

In the month of September, 1814, commodore Patterson had received instructions from the secretary of the navy, to disperse the Barratarian association, and the schooner Carolina had been ordered to New Orleans, for that purpose—he was accordingly making preparations, jointly with colonel Ross, of the 44th regiment, then military commandant at New Orleans, but previous to the completion of his arrangements, communications of considerable importance were received by the governor, from Barrataria, which rendered doubtful the course which prudence required to be taken. These communications furnished the particulars of an overture which had been made by certain British officers, then at Pensacola, to Mr. Lafitte, as the officer commanding at Barrataria, to join the British, in an attack on New Orleans. The letters and propositions of the English were sent by Mr. Lafitte, under cover to Mr. Blanque, a distinguished and influential member of the legislature. This gentleman deeming the disclosure by Mr. Lafitte, of great importance to the safety of the state, hastened to lay the same before the governor. Copies of these letters are inserted in the appendix.

The governor of Louisiana thought proper to invite, on the occasion, the opinions and counsel of some of the principal officers of the army, navy, and militia, then in New Orleans, and to whom, after communicating the letters of the English officers, the manner in which they had come to his hands, or his reasons for believing them genuine, he submitted two questions.—1st, whether the letters were genuine, and 2d, whether it was proper that the governor should hold intercourse, or enter into any correspondence with Mr. Lafitte and his associates. To each of those questions, an answer in the negative was returned; major-general Villeré alone dissenting—this officer being, as well as the governor, who presiding in the council could not give his opinion, not only satisfied as to the authenticity of the letters, but believing that the Barratarians might be employed at the present crisis, in such manner as greatly to contribute to the safety of the state and the annoyance of the enemy. The preparations for the expedition, under captain Patterson and colonel Ross, were continued, the former acting under the orders of the secretary of the navy, and the latter co-operating, as is understood, at the request of the governor of Louisiana. The result of the expedition was fully communicated in a letter from captain Patterson to the secretary of the navy, which has been published in several of the newspapers.

Many of the fugitives having reached New Orleans, and several being committed to jail, it was evident that the Barratarian association was extensive, and many good citizens seemed to think, that in the perilous condition of Louisiana, it was good policy to avail themselves of the services of men, most of whom had been accustomed to war, and who, from the perfect knowledge of our coast, and the various points of approach to New Orleans, might be particularly useful to the enemy, by whom it was now well ascertained, they had so earnestly been entreated to repair to his standard. But as a preliminary and indispensable step, a pardon for all real or supposed offences was necessary, and this could be granted only by the president. The governor was one of those, who thought that the Barratarians might be advantageously employed against the enemy, and as early as the—day of October 1814, in a letter to the attorney-general of the United States, he recommended them to the favour of the executive. "It is greatly to be regretted (says the governor) that the general or state government had not sooner put them down—the length of time they were permitted to continue their practices, added much to their strength, and led the people here to view their course as less vitious. Measures tending to the prevention of crimes, can alone relieve us from the distress of punishing them; had such measures in regard to the offences in question, been earlier taken, we should not now have to lament the frequency of their commission. Justice may require the punishment of some of the more culpable, but I see no good end to be attained by making the penalties of the law to fall extensively and heavily—the example is not the less imposing, by circumscribing the numbers of its victims, and the mercy which should dictate it seldom fails to make a salutary and lasting impression." After the capture of our gun-boats, the invasion of the state was inevitable, and the expediency of inviting the Barratarians to our standard was generally admitted. The governor conferred on the subject with major-general Jackson; and with his approbation issued, on the 17th of December, 1814, the following general orders:

"The governor of Louisiana, informed that many individuals, who may be or who are supposed to be, implicated in the offences heretofore committed against the United States at Barrataria, and who have some time past concealed themselves on account of their inability to procure bail in case of arrest; at the present crisis express a willingness to enrol themselves and march against the enemy.—He does hereby invite them to join the standard of the United States, and is authorized to say, should their conduct in the field meet the approbation of major-general Jackson, that that officer will unite with the governor in a request to the president of the United States to extend to each and every individual as aforesaid so marching and acting a free and full pardon."

(Signed) William C. C. Claiborne.
Governor commanding the militia.

These orders were sent in every direction, and tended to bring to our standard many brave men and excellent artillerists, whose services contributed greatly to the safety of Louisiana, and received the highest approbation of the commanding general. The legislature of the state, previous to their adjournment, recommended the Barratarians as proper objects for the clemency of the president, who, by his proclamation upon the subject bearing date the 6th of February 1815, and transmitted officially to the governor, by the secretary of state of the United States, granted to them a full and entire pardon.

NOTE 2. It has been asserted from the concurrent report of a great number of the British prisoners and deserters, that on the memorable 8th of February, the parole and countersign of the enemy's army were *beauty and booty*. Although this report is generally believed in the United States, particularly as it never has been formally denied by those whom it most concerns, I have not thought it sufficiently authenticated to record it as an historical fact. It is indeed a most heinous charge, and if untrue, requires not only a clear and positive denial, but also the proof of the genuine parole and countersign, which may be easily obtained, as it is well known that it is consigned in the orderly books of every corps in the army. It has been said that the British government considers it below its dignity to condescend to refute a calumny which has been only circulated through the medium of newspapers and other periodical publications in the United States. But this will not do; the almost unanimous assertion of the deserters and prisoners on which this report is founded, is a fact too serious to be looked over, and it is but too much supported by the positive and repeated threats of admiral Cochrane in his letters of the 18th August and 19th September 1814, (See Appendix, No. 8,) by the letters of other officers intercepted on board the St. Lawrence, (See also Appendix No. 67) and the conduct of the British at Hampton, Alexandria, and other places. It cannot be considered derogatory to the dignity of any government to undeceive a great nation, among whom every individual exercises a portion of the sovereignty. The voice of that nation will be heard, and its historians, if the British government persists in its unjustifiable silence, will at last no longer be swayed by the motives of delicacy and respect to a vanquished enemy which have actuated the author of these memoirs. The fame of general Packenham and his officers, the moral character of the British military, strongly implicated by a charge of this nature, and the honour of the British government all imperiously demand that it be refuted, if capable of refutation, which may be easily done, if general Lambert, whose honourable conduct in the course of this campaign does not permit the least doubt to be entertained of his veracity, will only come forward and state the real state of the fact—otherwise, and if proof, such as this, cannot be obtained, the report must be considered as true, and, I leave to future historians the unpleasant task of animadverting upon a conduct so shocking to humanity.

APPENDIX.

TABLE OF CONTENTS.

NO. I.

NO. I-a.

NO. I-b.

NO. II.

NO. III.

NO. IV.

NO. V.

NO. VI.

NO. VII.

NO. VIII.

NO. IX.

NO. X.

NO. XI.

NO. XII.

NO. XIII.

NO. XIV.

NO. XIV-a.

NO. XV.

NO. XVI.

NO. XVII.

NO. XVII-a.

NO. XVII-b.

NO. XVIII.

NO. XVIII-a.

NO. XVIII-b.

NO. XIX.

NO. XX.

NO. XXI.

NO. XXI-a.

NO. XXII.

NOS. XXII–XXIV.

NO. XXV.

NOS. XXVI–XXVII.

NO. XXVIII.

NO. XXVIII-a.

NO. XXVIII-b.

NO. XXIX.

NO. XXX.

NO. LXII.

NO. LXIII.

NO. LXIV.

NO. LXVI.

NO. LXVII.

NO. LXVIII.

NO. LXIX.

APPENDIX

NO. I.

Copy of a letter from vice-admiral Cochrane to Mr. Monroe.

His Britannic majesty's ship the Tonnant,
in the Patuxent river, 18th August, 1814.

SIR—Having been called upon by the governor-general of the Canadas to aid him in carrying into effect measures of retaliation against the inhabitants of the United States, for the wanton destruction committed by their army in Upper Canada, it has become imperiously my duty, conformably with the nature of the governor-general's application, to issue to the naval force under my command, an order to destroy and lay waste such towns and districts upon the coast, as may be found assailable.

I had hoped that this contest would have terminated, without my being obliged to resort to severities, which are contrary to the usage of civilized warfare, and as it has been with extreme reluctance and concern that I have found myself compelled to adopt this system of devastation, I shall be equally gratified if the conduct of the executive of the United States will authorize my staying such proceedings, by making reparation to the suffering inhabitants of Upper Canada: thereby manifesting that if the destructive measures pursued by their army were never sanctioned, they will no longer be permitted by the government.

I have the honour to be, sir, with much consideration, your most obedient humble servant,

(Signed) ALEX. COCHRANE.

Copy of a letter from Mr. Monroe to sir Alexander Cochrane, vice-admiral, &c. &c.

Department of state, September 6, 1814.

SIR—I have had the honour to receive your letter of the 18th of August, stating, that having been called on by the governor-general of the Canadas, to aid him in carrying into effect measures of retaliation against the inhabitants of the United States, for the wanton desolation committed by their army in Upper Canada, it has become your duty, conformably with the nature of the governor-general's application, to issue to the naval force under your command, an order to destroy and lay waste such towns and districts upon the coast as may be found assailable.

It is seen with the greatest surprise, that this system of devastation which has been practiced by the British forces, so manifestly contrary to the usage of civilized warfare, is placed by you on the ground of retaliation. No sooner were the United States compelled to resort to war against Great Britain, than they resolved to wage it in a manner most consonant to the principles of humanity, and to those friendly relations which it was desirable to preserve between the two nations, after the restoration of peace. They perceived however with the deepest regret, that a spirit alike just and humane was neither cherished nor acted on by your government. Such an assertion would not be hazarded, if it was not supported by facts, the proof of which has perhaps already carried the same conviction to other nations that it has to the people of these states. Without dwelling on the deplorable cruelties committed by the savages in the British ranks, and in British pay, on American prisoners at the river Raisin, which to this day have never been disavowed or atoned, I refer, as more immediately connected with the subject of your letter, to the wanton desolation that was committed, at Havre-de-Grace, and at Georgetown, early in the Spring 1813. These villages were burnt and ravaged by the naval forces of Great Britain, to the ruin of their unarmed inhabitants, who saw with astonishment that they derived no protection to their property from the laws of war. During the same season, scenes of invasion and pillage, carried on under the same authority, were witnessed all along the waters of the Chesapeake, to an extent inflicting the most serious private distress, and under circumstances that justified the suspicion, that revenge and cupidity, rather than the manly motives that should dictate the hostility of the high-minded foe, led to their perpetration. The late destruction of the houses of the government in this city is another act which comes necessarily in view. In the wars of modern Europe, no examples of the kind, even among nations the most hostile to each other, can be traced. In the course of ten years past, the capitals of the principal powers of the continent of Europe have been conquered, and occupied alternately by the victorious armies of each other, and no instance of such wanton and unjustifiable destruction has been seen. We must go back to distant and barbarous ages, to find a parallel for the acts of which I complain.

Although these acts of desolation invited, if they did not impose on the government the necessity of retaliation, yet in no instance has it been authorized. The burning of the village of Newark in Upper Canada, posterior to the early outrages above enumerated, was not executed on that principle. The village of Newark adjoined fort George, and its destruction was justified by the officer who ordered it, on the ground that it became necessary in the military operations there. The act however was disavowed by the government. The burning which took place at Long Point was unauthorized by the government, and the conduct of the officer subjected to the investigation of a military tribunal. For the burning at St. David's, committed by stragglers, the officer who commanded in that quarter was dismissed without a trial, for not preventing it.

I am commanded by the president distinctly to state, that it as little comports with any orders which have been issued to the military and naval commanders of the United States, as it does with the established and known humanity of the American nation, to pursue a system which it appears you have adopted. This government owes it to itself, to the principles which it has ever held sacred, to disavow, as justly chargeable to it, and such wanton, cruel and unjustifiable warfare.

Whatever unauthorized irregularity may have been committed by any of its troops, it would have been ready, acting on these principles of sacred and eternal obligation, to disavow, and as far as might be practicable, to repair. But in the plan of desolating warfare which your letter so explicitly makes known, and which is attempted to be excused on a plea so utterly groundless, the president perceives a spirit of deep-rooted hostility, which, without the evidence of such facts, he could not have believed existed, or could have been carried to such an extremity.

For the reparation of injuries, of whatever nature they may be, not sanctioned by the law of nations, which the military or naval force of either power may have committed, against the other, this government will always be ready to enter into reciprocal arrangements. It is presumed that your government will neither expect nor propose any which are not reciprocal.

Should your government adhere to a system of desolation, so contrary to the views and practice of the United States, so revolting to humanity, and repugnant to the sentiment and usages of the civilized world, whilst it will be seen with the deepest regret, it must and will be met with a determination and constancy becoming a free people, contending in a just cause for their essential rights, and their dearest interests.

I have the honour to be, with great consideration, sir, your most obedient humble servant

(Signed) JAMES MONROE.

From the National Intelligencer.

We observe it mentioned in some prints, that the late letter of admiral Cochrane to the secretary of state was received before the enemy entered Washington. This is not so. We state the fact, on the most unquestionable authority, that it did not arrive in Washington until late in the night of the 30th of August, and that it was not received by the secretary of state until the morning of the 31st.

The letter was dated on the 18th, probably the very day the Tonnant arrived in the Patuxent. It affects to give previous notice of an intention to destroy and lay waste our towns, and yet is not even *sent off* (although antedated) until *after* this purpose has been accomplished at Washington. This is a very pretty little *trick* played off by the vice-admiral in his first essay at diplomatic correspondence, and we doubt not has been matter of pleasant chuckling between himself and friend, that accomplished and high-bred gentleman admiral George Cockburn. It is worthy of remark, that a near blood relation of the vice-admiral's has lately been convicted in England and sentenced to the pillory for a deception practiced upon the public there. The vice appears to run through the family.

Vice-admiral Cochrane to the secretary of state.

His B.M. ship Tonnant, in the Chesapeake, Sept. 19, 1814.

SIR—I had the honour to receive your letter of the 6th inst. this morning, in reply to the one which I addressed to you from the Patuxent.

As I have no authority from my government to enter upon any kind of discussion relative to the points contained in your letter, I have only to regret that there does not appear to be any hope that I shall be authorized to recall my general order; which has been further sanctioned by a subsequent request from lieutenant-general sir George Provost.

A copy of your letter will this day be forwarded by me to England, and until I receive instructions from my government the measures which I have adopted must be persisted in: unless remuneration be made to the inhabitants of the Canadas for the injuries they have sustained from the outrages committed by the troops of the United States.

I have the honour to be, &c.
ALEX. COCHRANE.

NO. I-a.

Copy of a letter from the secretary of war to the governor of Tennessee

Department of War,
September 25th, 1814.

His Excellency The Governor of Tennessee,
Sir,

Intelligence has been received that the enemy contemplate an expedition against the State of Louisiana, thro' the Mobile, with intention to occupy all the country from Cape Florida to the provinces of Spain, westward of the Mississippi. The desolating spirit with which the British Government now wages war against the United States, looking to conquest and subjugation with the enlarged means which their successes on the continent have given them entitle this intelligence to full credit, indeed recent accounts state, that they have landed a considerable force at Pensacola, which if true, leaves no doubt of the object.

Should the enemy take possession of Louisiana, I need not describe to you its pernicious effect, not on the interests of that growing state only, but of all that portion of the United States, lying westward of the Allegheny Mountains. Its whole commerce would be in the hands of an inveterate foe. It is therefore indispensably necessary to repel this invasion at once, and for that purpose to put forward an adequate force to meet it.

On full consideration of this important subject, the President desires that you will immediately detach five thousand troops of your state, in addition to those already detailed, which it is presumed have been called for by General Jackson, and that you will hasten them to him by such routes as with the intelligence you may possess, may appear best calculated to afford the necessary aid in repelling the expected invasions. As soon as you receive this letter, I have to request that you will transmit a copy of it to General Jackson, informing him of the time the troops called for, will begin their march, and of the routes they intend taking, that he may give any advice which appears to him to be practical on either point. It may happen that the force already under his command [MS torn] may be adequate to the objects or that he may wish this additional force to proceed in some other direction than that contemplated. If so, by giving him prompt notice of what is intended, he may advise you of the actual danger, and of the necessity there may be of the aid intended for him. Viewing the danger of the crisis and its possible consequences, to so vast and important a portion of our country, in the light I have placed it, the President has considered it his duty to take this measure to avert it, aware that too prompt and effectual a remedy cannot be afforded should the intelligence received be well founded. It is proper, however, in taking this step to guard against the unnecessary exposure of our citizens and unnecessary expense, should General Jackson, on a nearer view and a more correct knowledge of the actual state of things, think the force already under his command adequate to the defence of the country against any force the enemy may bring against him.

For the arriving, equipping, and supplying of these, we must rely, in the first instance, on the local resources and the arrangements of your Excellency. The staff which have heretofore been employed for the Tennessee militia, are probably well qualified for this expedition. Herewith enclosed you will receive copies of the contracts for supplying rations, and I must request your excellency to make such further adjustments as may be found necessary. It is impossible at this time to furnish the funds for this object.

The proper agents must be authorized to draw on this Department at sixty and ninety days, until money can be remitted to meet the expenditures.

To guard against any misconceptions of the views of the President, I wish it to be distinctly understood that the march of these 5000 men is not to be delayed till you hear from Gen. Jackson, but is to commence without a moments delay after the receipt of this letter.

I have the honor to be
JAMES MONROE.

Copy of a letter from the secretary of war to the governor of Georgia

Department of War,
September 25, 1814.

His Excellency The Governor of Georgia,

Sir,

Intelligence has been received that the enemy contemplate an expedition against the State of Louisiana, thro' the Mobile, with intention to occupy all the country from Cape Florida to the provinces of Spain, westward of the Mississippi. The desolating spirit with which the British Government now wages war against the United

States, looking to conquest and subjugation with the enlarged means which their successes on the continent have given them entitle this intelligence to full credit, indeed recent accounts state, that they have landed a considerable force at Pensacola, which if true, leaves no doubt of the object.

On full consideration of this important subject, the President has determined to put forward an adequate force to meet and repel any invasion which may be attempted in that quarter. In addition to the force already in service under General Jackson, the governor of Tennessee has been required to detach, organize, and march to his support, five thousand militia of that state, and the President desires that your Excellency will immediately organize, arm, and equip two thousand five hundred of the militia of Georgia, detached conformably to the orders of this department of the 4th July last. This detachment will be held in readiness to join General Jackson as soon as circumstances shall require.

I have to request your Excellency to state the time necessary for accomplishing this object, and the place designated for the rendezvous of the troops.

I have the honor to be
JAMES MONROE.

NO. I-b.

Copy of a letter from the secretary of state to general Jackson

Department of War
September 27, 1814

Major General Andrew Jackson
Sir,

I have had the honor to receive your letter of the 10th August by Mr. Cassida, and subsequent letters of August 23, 24, 25, & 27th by mail.

By these communications which are strongly supported by others from various quarters, there is great cause to believe that the enemy have set on foot an expedition against Louisiana, thro' the Mobile, in the expectation that while so strong a pressure was made from Canada, and in this quarter, whereby the force of the country and attention of the government would be much engaged, a favorable opportunity would be afforded them to take possession of the lower parts of that state, and of all the country along the Mobile. In this, as well in all their other, disorganizing and visionary projects, they will be defeated by the virtue and gallantry of our people. The European Governments reasoning from examples of their own, are always led into false conclusions of the consequences to be expected from attacks on our union, and from the distress of our citizens. This war will give them useful lessons, in every quarter of the United States, where the experiment may be made.

By your last letter it seems probable that a considerable British force had been landed at Pensacola, with the connivance of the Spanish authorities there, and at Havannah; and by other intelligence it may be presumed that a pressure, or at least, a menace will be made on the western side of the Mississippi by Nacagdoches and

Natchitoches, which latter will probably be by Spanish troops and for the purpose of menace only.

You have had at your command all the regular force in the district with the detached militia in Louisiana, the Mississippi territory, and Tennessee, and you have also had authority to engage on our side the warriors of the Choctaw, Chickasaw, and Creek Nations, or so many of them you might think proper to employ, having it in view at the same time to secure the affection and neutrality of all the members of those tribes. It is known that the regular troops are distributed into many posts, and that the militia of Louisiana will be less efficient for general purposes, from the dread of domestic insurrections, so that on the militia of Tennessee your principal reliance must be.

The President taking all circumstances in consideration, has thought proper to order five thousand additional troops from Tennessee to march to your aid as soon as possible, in the most direct and convenient routes, unless, before they set out on their march, they should receive countermanding orders from you. He has likewise requested the Governor of Georgia, to hold in readiness, subject to your orders twenty five hundred men on the presumption that a cooperating force from that quarter may possibly be necessary. I send you a copy of my letter to the Governor of Tennessee to whom you will hasten to communicate your views and wishes. Full confidence is entertained in your judgement in the discharge of this discretionary power.

Measures are taken for procuring in the neighbouring towns and forwarding to your order, blankets and some other presents for the Creeks, Choctaws, and other friendly Indians. These will be sent by wagons direct to —.

Apprehending much difficulty in the prosecution of your campaign, which it may not be in your power to remove without money, I have transmitted to Governor Blount, one hundred thousand dollars in Treasury notes, to be applied to the necessary expenses of the campaign in discharging Indian claims, and supplying their wants; an object to be attended to at this time, equally from motives of policy and humanity. You will therefore draw on him for the necessary funds. Of these expenditures you will keep a regular account should it be found more convenient you are authorized to draw on this Department for such necessary expenditure as sixty and thirty days sight.

I have the honor to be
JAMES MONROE.

Copy of a letter from the secretary of war to the governor of Tennessee

Department of War,
October 10, 1814.

His Excellency The Governor of Tennessee,
Sir,

There is strong reason to presume, from intelligence just received from our ministers at Ghent, that a British force consisting of twelve or fifteen thousand men, would sail from Ireland, early in September for New Orleans and the Mobile with intention to take possession of the city and the country through which the great rivers, on which the whole of the states westward of the Allegheny Mountains so essentially depends. This invasion must be met with firmness and repelled with promptitude.

I have therefore to request that your Excellency will hasten the march down the river subject to the orders of Major General Jackson, all the troops required by my letter of September 17th without regard to the force from Kentucky, of which I advised you on the 3rd instant, making a militia force from Tennessee of seven thousand five hundred.

The governor of Kentucky will be required to march the detachment from that state in addition to these and the whole will be put under the orders of General Jackson and I have to request your excellency to communicate with him relative to their movements and disposition.

I have the honor to be
JAMES MONROE.

NO II.

ANONYMOUS.

Havanna, August 8, 1814.

Dear Sir,

I Embrace an opportunity offered for Pensacola, to inform you, that an expedition has sailed from Bermuda for Mobile, who touched and left this on the 11th instant, under the command of colonel Nicholls of the artillery, a brave officer well known in the European wars.

They touched here for aid in gun-boats, small vessels, &c. and for leave to land at Pensacola, all of which were refused by the captain-general. However, I learn that they are determined to land at Pensacola, with or without leave, where they will disembark their park of artillery. The colonel was conveyed with his troops in two sloops of war, the Hermes, commanded by the hon. W. H. Percy, and the Caron, commanded by the hon. P. Spencer, who, with such vessels as may be on the station, will co-operate with the land forces.

The brig Orpheus, some time past, landed arms and some officers at Apalachicola, to arrange with the Creek nation for future operations against Mobile, New Orleans and that district of the country, which they effected, and caused the breaking off the treaty.

The whole nation are ready to join the British troops under colonel Nicholls, who will immediately on his arrival issue his proclamation, declaring all slaves who will join their standard free and liberated forever from their masters. He will also issue another to the Indians, promising all the tribes who will join him, to reinstate them in all their lands taken from them by the United States, and to guarantee the same to them forever. Having thus prepared the minds of the negroes and Indians, he will, on the arrival of two or three black regiments, from Nassau, &c. of fine troops, calculated for that climate (who may pass by this next week) push for New Orleans—first having secured and fortified Mobile point, and taken Mobile, as well as placed a force at every point on the lakes, of any importance, as well as Plaquemines, in order to cut off all trade of the Mississippi.

This force with him is small, but he will soon be re-enforced from Bermuda, &c.— the flying artillery appears well calculated for his operations in that country.

When I have stated these facts, it will become your duty, and the duty of every citizen in the state, who has property or a family to protect and defend, to rise in mass, and defeat this most damnable and infamous plan of burning and carnage, the most horrible and atrocious ever before projected by a civilized nation.

You have not a moment to lose; because if they get a footing, it will be very difficult to get clear of them. The commander of the sea-forces, the hon. W.H. Percy, is a very young man, a Scotchman, and mild and gentlemanly, the son of lord Beverly; but the colonel is an impatient blustering Irishman, who was governor of Andant, in the German seas, and apparently brave and cruel.

I have only a moment to insist upon you again to save the state and the property of the planters at this awful crisis.

NO. III.

PROCLAMATION,

By lieutenant-colonel Edward Nicholls, commanding his Britannic majesty's forces in the Floridas.

Natives of Louisiana! on you the first call is made to assist in liberating from a faithless, imbecile government, your paternal soil: Spaniards, Frenchmen, Italians, and British, whether settled or residing for a time, in Louisiana, on you, also, I call to aid me in this just cause: the American usurpation in this country must be abolished, and the lawful owners of the soil put in possession. I am at the head of a large body of Indians, well armed, disciplined, and commanded by British officers—a good train of artillery with every requisite, seconded by the powerful aid of a numerous British and Spanish squadron of ships and vessels of war. Be not alarmed, inhabitants of the country, at our approach; the same good faith and disinterestedness which has distinguished the conduct of Britons in Europe, accompanies them here; you will have no fear of litigious taxes imposed on you for the purpose of carrying on an unnatural and unjust war; your property, your laws, the peace and tranquillity of your country, will be guaranteed to you by men who will suffer no infringement of theirs; rest assured that these brave red men only burn with an ardent desire of satisfaction, for the wrongs they have suffered from the Americans, to join you in liberating these southern provinces from their yoke, and drive them into those limits formerly prescribed by my sovereign. The Indians have pledged themselves, in the most solemn manner, not to injure, in the slightest degree, the persons or properties of any but enemies; to their Spanish or English fathers, a flag over any door, whether Spanish, French, or British, will be a certain protection, nor dare any Indian put his foot on the threshold thereof, under penalty of death from his own countrymen; not even an enemy will an Indian put to death, except resisting in arms, and as for injuring helpless women and children, the red men, by their good conduct and treatment to them, will (if it be possible) make the Americans blush for their more inhuman conduct lately on the Escambia, and within a neutral territory.

Inhabitants of Kentucky, you have too long borne with grievous impositions—the whole brunt of the war has fallen on your brave sons; be imposed on no longer, but either range yourselves under the standard of your forefathers, or observe a strict neutrality; if you comply with either of these offers, whatever provisions you send down, will be paid for in dollars, and the safety of the persons bringing it, as well as the free navigation of the Mississippi, guaranteed to you.

Men of Kentucky, let me call to your view (and I trust to your abhorrence) the conduct of those factions, which hurried you into this civil, unjust, and unnatural war, at a time when Great Britain was straining every nerve in defence of her own and the liberties of the world—when the bravest of her sons were fighting and bleeding in so sacred a cause—when she was spending millions of her treasure in endeavouring to pull down one of the most formidable and dangerous tyrants that ever disgraced the form of man—when groaning Europe was almost in her last gasp—when Britons alone showed an undaunted front—basely did those assassins endeavour to stab her from the rear; she has turned on them, renovated from the bloody but successful struggle—Europe is happy and free, and she now hastens justly to avenge the unprovoked insult. Show them that you are not collectively unjust; leave that contemptible few to shift for themselves; let those slaves of the tyrant send an embassy to Elba, and implore his aid; but let every honest, upright American, spurn them with united contempt. After the experience of twenty-one years, can you any longer support those brawlers for liberty, who call it freedom, when themselves are free; be no longer their dupes—accept of my offers—every thing I have promised in this paper I guarantee to you, on the sacred honour of a British officer.

Given under my hand at my *head-quarters*,
Pensacola, this 29th day of August, 1814.
EDWARD NICHOLLS.

Edward Nicholls to Mr. Laffite, or the commandant at Barataria.

Head-quarters, Pensacola, August 31, 1814.

Sir,

I have arrived in the Floridas for the purpose of annoying the only enemy Great Britain has in the world, as France and England are now friends. I call on you, with your brave followers, to enter into the service of Great Britain, in which you shall have the rank of a captain; lands will be given to you all, in proportion to your respective ranks, on a peace taking place, and I invite you on the following terms. Your property shall be guaranteed to you, and your persons protected: in return for which I ask you to cease all hostilities against Spain, or the allies of Great Britain.—Your ships and vessels to be placed under the orders of the commanding officer on this station, until the commander-in-chief's pleasure is known; but I guarantee their fair value at all events. I herewith inclose you a copy of my proclamation to the inhabitants of Louisiana, which will, I trust, point out to you the honourable intentions of my government. You may be an useful assistant to me, in forwarding them; therefore, if you determine, lose no time. The bearer of this, captain M'Williams, will satisfy you on any other point you may be anxious to learn, as will captain Lockyer of the Sophia, who brings him to you. We have a powerful re-enforcement on its way here, and I hope to cut out some other work for the Americans than oppressing the inhabitants of Louisiana. Be expeditious in your resolves, and rely on the verity of

Your very humble servant,
EDWARD NICHOLLS.

By the hon. William Henry Percy, captain of his majesty's ship Hermes, and senior officer in the gulf of Mexico.

Having understood that some British merchantmen have been detained, taken into, and sold by the inhabitants of Barataria; I have directed captain Lockyer, of his majesty's sloop Sophia, to proceed to that place, and inquire into the circumstances, with positive orders to demand instant restitution, and in case of refusal to destroy to his utmost every vessel there, as well as to carry destruction over the whole place, and at the same time to assure him of the co-operation of all his majesty's naval forces on this station. I trust at the same time, that the inhabitants of Barataria, consulting their own interest, will not make it necessary to proceed to such extremities—I hold out at the same time, a war instantly destructive to them; and on the other hand, should they be inclined to assist Great Britain in her just and unprovoked war against the United States, the security of their property, the blessings of the British constitution—and should they be inclined to settle on this continent, lands will, at the conclusion of the war, be allotted to them in his majesty's colonies in America. In return for all these concessions on the part of Great Britain, I expect that the directions of their armed vessels will be put into my hands (for which they will be renumerated,) the instant cessation of hostilities against the Spanish government, and the restitution of any undisposed property of that nation.

Should any inhabitants be inclined to volunteer their services into his majesty's forces, either naval or military, for limited service, they will be received; and if any British subject, being at Barataria, wishes to return to his native country, he will, on joining his majesty's service, receive a free pardon.

Given under my hand on board H.M. ship Hermes,
Pensacola, this 1st day of September, 1814.
W.H. Percy,
Captain and senior officer.

Letter from the hon. W.H. Percy, captain of his majesty's ship Hermes, and senior officer in the gulf of Mexico, to Nicholas Lockyer, esq. commander of H.M. sloop Sophia.

Sir,

You are hereby required and directed, after having received on board an officer belonging to the first battalion of Royal colonial marines, to proceed in his majesty's sloop under your command, without a moment's loss of time, for Barataria.

On your arrival at that place, you will communicate with the chief persons there—you will urge them to throw themselves under the protection of Great Britain—and should you find them inclined to pursue such a step, you will hold out to them that their property shall be secured to them, that they shall be considered British subjects, and at the conclusion of the war, lands within his majesty's colonies in America, will be allotted to them in return for these concessions. You will insist on an immediate cessation of hostilities against Spain, and in case they should have any Spanish property not disposed of, that it be restored, and that they put their naval force into the hands of the senior officer here, until the commander-in-chief's pleasure is known. In the event of their not being inclined to act offensively against the United States, you will do all in your power to persuade them to a strict neutrality, and still endeavour to put a stop to their hostilities against Spain. Should you succeed completely in the object for which you are sent, you will concert such measures for the annoyance of the enemy as you judge best from circumstances;—having an eye to the junction of their small armed vessels with me for the capture of Mobile, &c. You will at all events yourself join me with the utmost despatch at this post, with the accounts of your success.

Given under my hand on board his majesty's ship Hermes, at Pensacola, this 30th day of August, 1814.

W. H. Percy, capt.

NO. IV.

Letter from Mr. Laffite to Captain Lockyer.

Barataria, 4th September, 1814.

SIR,

The confusion which prevailed in our camp yesterday and this morning, and of which you have a complete knowledge, has prevented me from answering in a precise manner to the object of your mission; nor even at this moment can I give you all the satisfaction that you desire; however, if you could grant me a fortnight, I would be entirely at your disposal at the end of that time—this delay is indispensable to send away the three persons who have alone occasioned all the disturbance—the two who were the most troublesome are to leave this place in eight days, and the other is to go to town—the remainder of the time is necessary to enable me to put my affairs in order—you may communicate with me, in sending a boat to the eastern point of the pass, where I will be found. You have inspired me with more confidence than the admiral, your superior officer, could have done himself; with you alone I wish to deal, and from you also I will claim, in due time, the reward of the services which I may render to you.

Be so good, sir, as to favour me with an answer, and believe me yours, &c.

LAFFITE.

NO. V.

Letter from Mr. Laffite to Mr. Blanque.

Barataria, 4th September, 1814.

SIR,

Though proscribed by my adoptive country, I will never let slip any occasion of serving her, or of proving that she has never ceased to be dear to me. Of this you will here see a convincing proof. Yesterday, the 3d of September, there appeared here, under a flag of truce, a boat coming from an English brig, at anchor about two leagues from the pass. Mr. Nicholas Lockyer, a British officer of high rank, delivered me the following papers, two directed to me, a proclamation, and the admiral's instructions to that officer, all herewith enclosed. You will see from their contents the advantages I might have derived from that kind of association. I may have evaded the payment of duties to the custom house; but I have never ceased to be a good citizen; and all the offence I have committed, I was forced to by certain vices in our laws. In short, sir, I make you the depository of the secret on which perhaps depends the tranquillity of our country; please to make such use of it as your judgment may direct. I might expatiate on this proof of patriotism, but I let the fact speak for itself. I presume, however, to hope that such proceedings may obtain amelioration of the situation of my unhappy brother, with which view I recommend him particularly to your influence. It is in the bosom of a just man, of a true American, endowed with all other qualities that are honoured in society, that I think I am depositing the interests of our common country, and what particularly concerns myself.

Our enemies have endeavoured to work on me by a motive which few men would have resisted. They represented to me a brother in irons, a brother who is to me very dear! whose deliverer I might become, and I declined the proposal. Well persuaded of this innocence, I am free from apprehension as to the issue of a trial; but he is sick and not in a place where he can receive the assistance his state requires. I recommend him to you, in the name of humanity.

As to the flag of truce, I have done with regard to it every thing that prudence suggested to me at the time. I have asked fifteen days to determine, assigning such plausible pretexts, that I hope the term will be granted. I am waiting for the British officer's answer, and for yours to this. Be so good as to assist me with your judicious counsel in so weighty an affair.

I have the honour to salute you,

J. LAFFITE.

Letter from Mr. Laffite to Mr. Blanque.

Grande Terre, 7th September, 1814.

SIR,

You will always find me eager to evince my devotedness to the good of the country, of which I endeavoured to give some proof in my letter of the 4th, which I make no doubt you received. Amongst other papers that have fallen into my hands, I send you a scrap which appears to me of sufficient importance to merit your attention.*

Since the departure of the officer who came with the flag of truce, his ship, with two other ships of war have remained on the coast, within sight. Doubtless this point is considered as important. We have hitherto kept on a respectable defensive; if, however, the British attach to the possession of this place, the importance they give us room to suspect they do, they may employ means above our strength. I know not whether, in that case, proposals of intelligence with government would be out of season. It is always from my high opinion of your enlightened mind, that I request you to advise me in this affair.

I have the honour to salute you,
J. LAFFITE.

Copy of the Declaration of Jean Blanque

Towards the end of the month of August or at the beginning of September last year, an individual I do not know came to me and handed me a sealed packet from M. Lafitte. I opened this packet addressed to Jean Blanque, Senator from the State of Louisiana. It contained a letter from Jean Lafitte in which he informed me that he had made up his mind to send me various documents that had fallen into his power and that would prove he was not his country's enemy. In the letter Lafitte added that he wanted me to make whatever uses I considered necessary and most appropriate to the interests of Louisiana. This packet contained moreover a letter by an English officer, named Nicholl's and dated from Pensacola, a letter of orders by Commodore Perry, and two other documents the contents of which I do not recall. After reflecting a moment about the nature of this odd communication, I decided it was my duty to notify high-level state authority. Consequently, the same day I turned all these documents over to Gov. Claiborne, asking him to make whatever use of him he thought proper and to name the person he got them from if he thought it necessary. I only asked the governor to return Lafitte's letter to me after making a copy because I thought I detected in it a piece of evidence against him. Not many days later, I received a second letter also signed Lafitte, with a letter in English, with no address, shedding some light on the position of the English insofar as he can remember it.

Since the amnesty granted the Barataria delinquents by the President of the

*This piece is numbered II in this Appendix.

United States, I returned to one of the Lafittes, at his request, the letters that had remained in my hands.

J[EA]N BLANQUE.

Let me add that, in asking me for the letters mentioned above, M. Lafitte told me he was doing so on the advice of a friend of Gen. Jackson, who wanted to do him a favor and who would use these documents with the general so as to get his property [returned:], and I affirm that the letters that were [handed:] back to me are the same.

J[EA]N BLANQUE.

Letter from Mr. Laffite to his excellency W.C.C. Claiborne.

SIR,

In the firm persuasion that the choice made of you to fill the office of first magistrate of this state, was dictated by the esteem of your fellow-citizens, and was conferred on merit, I confidently address you on an affair on which may depend the safety of this country.

I offer to you to restore to this state several citizens, who perhaps in your eyes have lost that sacred title. I offer you them, however, such as you could wish to find them, ready to exert their utmost efforts in defence of the country. This point of Louisiana, which I occupy, is of great importance in the present crisis. I tender my services to defend it; and the only reward I ask is that a stop be put to the proscription against me and my adherents, by an act of oblivion for all that has been done hitherto. I am the stray sheep, wishing to return to the sheepfold. If you were thoroughly acquainted with the nature of my offences, I should appear to you much less guilty, and still worthy to discharge the duties of a good citizen. I have never sailed under any flag but that of the republic of Carthagena, and my vessels are perfectly regular in that respect. If I could have brought my lawful prizes into the ports of this state, I should not have employed the illicit means that have caused me to be proscribed. I decline saying more on the subject, until I have the honour of your excellency's answer, which I am persuaded can be dictated only by wisdom. Should your answer not be favourable to my ardent desires, I declare to you that I will instantly leave the country, to avoid the imputation of having co-operated towards an invasion on this point, which cannot fail to take place, and to rest secure in the acquittal of my own conscience.

I have the honour to be
Your excellency's, &c.
J. LAFFITE.

Copy of a Sworn statement by William C. C. Claiborne

William C. C. Claiborne being duly sworn says—that early in the month of September 1814, Wm. C. Lacey a member of the legislature of Louisiana, handed to the witness a packet covering a letter from John Lafitte to Mr. Blanque, and enclosing sundry letters, papers and documents (the original of which are now in possession of the court) purporting to be propositions made by certain British officers to Lafitte and his Baratarian associates to join the British in an attack at New Orleans.

Among these paper was an address to the Louisianians signed Edward Nicolls and dated at Pensacola 29th of August 1814; a letter of instructions, signed W. H. Percy, Capt. dated on board of his Majesty's ship Hermes at Pensacola 30th of August 1814. And directed to Nicolas Lockyer Esqr. commander of his Majesty's sloop Sophia. A letter signed Edward Nicolls Lt. colonel commanding his Britannic Majesty's forces in the floridas, dated Pensacola August 31, 1814, and directed to Mr. Lafitte, or the commandant at Barataria, and a letter directed to Monsseiur Lafitte, signed W. H. Percy capt & senior officer, and dated on board his Majesty's ship Hermes the 1st of September 1814. Mr. Blanque expressed at that time to the witness his surprise at the packets being addressed to him, saying that he had no acquaintance with Lafitte, but the contents of the papers, left him, in doubt as the disposition to be made of them; he had esteemed it his duty to lay them without delay before the governor of the state, and to recommend their contents to his seniors considerations.

The letter of Lafitte after the witness had perused it, was returned to Mr. Blanque at his request. The witness recollects that in the letter of Mr. Blanque, Lafitte said that he had required time, or rather a delay of some days to return an answer to the English propositions, but declared in effect at the same time, in his letter to Mr. Blanque, a determination to take no part with the English.

(Signed) WILLIAM C. C. CLAIBORNE.

NO. VI.

Letter from Mr. Laffite, the elder, to Mr. Blanque,

Grande Terre, 10th September, 1814

SIR,

On my arrival here, I was informed of all the occurrences that have taken place; I think I may justly commend my brother's conduct under such difficult circumstances. I am persuaded he could not have made a better choice, than in making you the depositary of the papers that were sent to us, and which may be of great importance to the state. Being fully determined to follow the plan that may reconcile us with the government, I herewith send you a letter directed to his excellency the governor, which I submit to your discretion, to deliver or not, as you may think proper. I have not yet been honoured with an answer from you. The moments are precious; pray send me an answer that may serve to direct my measures in the circumstances in which I find myself.

[I] have the honor to be, &c.
P. LAFFITE.

P.S. I join with this the letter for Mr. Claiborne, which I submit to your judgment. Should you think, from its contents, that it may be delivered or communicated to him, you will do either, as you think proper. I send it to you under cover; after having read it, I request you to seal it.

NO. VII.

Circular letter to the governors of the several states.

"War department, July 4th, 1814.

"SIR,

"The late pacification in Europe, offers to the enemy a large disposable force, both naval and military, and with it the means of giving to the war here a character of new and increased activity and extent—without knowing with certainty, that such will be its application, and still less that any particular point or points will become objects of attack, the president has deemed it advisable, as a measure of precaution, to strengthen ourselves on the line of the Atlantic, and (as the principal means of doing this will be found in the militia) to invite the executives of certain states, to organize and hold in readiness for immediate service, a corps of ninety-three thousand, five hundred men, under the laws of the 28th of February 1795, and the 18th of April 1814.

"The enclosed detail, will show your excellency, what, under this requisition, will be the quota of your state.

"As far as the volunteer uniform corps can be formed, they will be preferred.

"The expediency of regarding (as well in the designation of the militia, as of their places of rendezvous) the points, the importance or exposure of which, will be most likely to attract the views of the enemy, need not be suggested.

"A report of the organization of your quota, when completed, and of the place or places of rendezvous will be acceptable.

I have the honour to be, &c.

(Signed) JOHN ARMSTRONG."

Of the force thus required to be holden in readiness, the quota assigned to Georgia, was three regiments, and one battalion—viz. three hundred and fifty artillery, three thousand one hundred and fifty infantry, total, three thousand five hundred. To Kentucky five regiments, and one battalion, viz. five thousand five hundred infantry. To Tennessee, two regiments, and one battalion—viz. two thousand five hundred infantry. To Mississippi territory one battalion, viz. five hundred infantry;—and Louisiana, was required to furnish one regiment, viz. one thousand infantry.

The letter of the secretary at war reached governor Claiborne early in August, and by him promptly attended to. On the 6th of March, he apportioned the quota assigned to Louisiana, between the first and second division of militia of the state.

Extract of a letter from major-general Jackson to governor Claiborne,

dated head-quarters, 7th military district, fort Jackson 21st July, 1814.

This morning I was presented with a new British musket given to a friendly Indian by those at Apalachicola bay. Information has been received by this fellow tending to confirm the rumour of a considerable force having landed there with large quantity of arms and other munitions of war, and with intentions to strike a decisive blow against the lower country. Mobile and Orleans are of such importance as to hold out strong inducements to them, at such a crisis: I must look to the constitutional authorities of the state of Louisiana for such support as will be effective in any emergency, and I trust this support will be afforded with promptitude whenever required.

NO. VIII.

Militia general orders,

head-quarters, New Orleans, August 6th, 1814.

In a letter from the honourable the secretary at war, under date of the 4th ultimo, the governor of Louisiana has received the orders of the president of the United States, to organize and hold in readiness for immediate service, a corps of a thousand militia infantry, being the quota assigned to this state, of a requisition for ninety-three thousand five hundred men, made on the executives of the several states, under the laws of the 28th February 1795, and 18th of April 1814, the governor and commander-in-chief in consequence directs, that one complete regiment a thousand strong, to be composed of two battalions 1st and 2nd be organized and equipped for service, with the least possible delay. The first division of militia will furnish four full companies, each company to consist of one captain, one first lieutenant, two second lieutenants, four serjeants, four corporals, one drummer, one fifer, and ninety privates—the whole to be apportioned among the several brigades or regiments attached to the first division by the major-general commanding the same; and under his orders to be organized on or before the 4th of September next, and due returns made to the adjutant-general.

The second division of militia will furnish five full companies—each company to consist as aforesaid of one captain, one first lieutenant, two second lieutenants, four serjeants, four corporals, one drummer, one fifer, and ninety privates—the whole to be apportioned among the several brigades or regiments attached to the second division by the major-general commanding the same, and under his orders to be completely organized on or before the 15th September next, and due returns made of the same.

In all cases volunteer uniform companies of the strength required will be preferred, and a tender of service from all such promptly accepted in assigning the quota of the first and second division. The commander-in-chief, as was his duty, has taken into view the exposure of particular points, and the amount and description of population; like considerations will influence the major-generals in making apportionment among the several brigades and regiments. The returns to the adjutant-general will give the names of the officers, non-commissioned officers and privates, and particularly state the number and condition of the arms, in order that provision may be made for the supply of deficiencies. Each non-commissioned officer and private to furnish himself with a knapsack and blanket. The colonel-commandant of the regiment, and the medical staff will be named by the commander-in-chief; the major of the first battalion to be selected by the major-general of the second division; the major of the second battalion by the major-general of the first division, and the paymaster, adjutant, and quartermaster of the regiment by the colonel-commandant.

The corps thus to be organized and kept in readiness for active duty, will on the further commands of the president, or on the requisition of any officer acting under his authority, be ordered into the service of the United States, for a term not exceeding six months after their arrival at the point of rendezvous unless sooner discharged. The point of rendezvous for the detachment drawn from the first division, will be the city of New Orleans, and from the detachment drawn from the second division, the town of Baton Rouge.

"The late pacification in Europe (says the secretary at war) offers to the enemy a large disposable force, both naval and military, and with it the means of giving to the war here a character of new and increased activity and extent.

"Without knowing with certainty, that such will be its application, and still less that any particular point or points, will become objects of attack, the president has deemed advisable, as a measure of precaution, to strengthen ourselves on the line of the Atlantic." To these just reflections, the commander-in-chief will only add his firm reliance, that Louisiana will cheerfully participate with the sister states in whatever toils or dangers, the safety of our common country shall advise.

The desire manifested by the United States to sheathe the sword, on terms alike honourable to both parties, may indeed be met with a correspondent disposition. It is not easy to believe, that a nation should be so wholly regardless of duty to herself, as always to reject the claims of justice—but let us not be so far deluded with a hope of peace, as to leave our country uncovered and unprotected. If the latest reports from Europe are to be accredited, the enemy had determined on the most vigorous prosecution of the war—it is added, that this section of the union was to be attacked with design "of wresting Louisiana from the hands of the United States and restoring it to Spain."

A project so chimerical illy comports with that character for wisdom, to which the English government aspires, nor is it believed to be seriously contemplated. That the bare rumour, however, of such a design should awaken some anxiety, is cause of no surprise. But if there be individuals so much deceived, as to suppose its accomplishment possible, they are cautioned against being instrumental in deceiving others. The principles of the American government, no less than the interest and honour of the American people forbid the relinquishment of one tenth of the American territory. Whilst the western rivers flow, no foreign power can hold or detach Louisiana from the United States. She may indeed be temporarily exposed to an invading foe, but until by some convulsion of nature that numerous, gallant, and hardy race of men, inhabiting the vast tract of country watered by the tributary streams of the Mississippi, shall become extinct, the political destiny of Louisiana is placed beyond the possibility of change. Her connexion, interest and government must remain American. We however do not solely rely for security on our northern and western brethren. We shall not be wanting in duty to ourselves. The commander-in-chief therefore avails himself of this occasion, to invite the officers throughout the state, and particularly colonels of regiments, and commandants of separate corps, to be faithful and diligent in the discharge of their respective duties. He orders the several regimental, battalion and company musters, as prescribed by law to be regularly holden, and every effort made to introduce order and discipline. If the war continues, we cannot hope for exemption from its calamities.

In case of invasion, the whole militia will be ordered to front the enemy—if our homes and fire-sides are menaced, union, zeal, and mutual confidence should warm every heart and strengthen every arm.

By order of his excellency William C.C. Claiborne, governor and commander-in-chief.

(Signed) A. LANEUVILLE.

NO. IX.

Extract of a letter from major-general Jackson to governor Claiborne,

dated fort Jackson, August 15th, 1815.

Information this moment received by express from Alabama Heights, bringing me a letter from Pensacola, added to the intelligence received by captain Gordon, who was the bearer of a letter from me to the governor of Pensacola, makes it necessary, that all the forces allotted for the 7th military district, should be held in a state of preparation to march to any point required at a moment's warning.

NO. X.

Militia general orders

head-quarters, New Orleans, September 5th 1814.

Major-General Jackson acting under the authority of the president, having demanded the immediate service in the field of the whole corps of Louisiana militia, directed to be holden in readiness for service, under the general orders of the 6th ult. the governor and commander-in-chief directs that the officers, non-commissioned officers and privates, drawn from the first, second, third, fourth, and fifth regiments under the orders aforesaid, rendezvous in New Orleans, on Saturday the 10th instant, at 10 o'clock, A.M. in the enclosure in front of the barracks, where, being organized into companies under the orders of major-general Villeré, in manner heretofore directed, they will be inspected by major Hughes, inspector-general of the seventh military district, and mustered into the service of the United States, and quartered in or near New Orleans, until further orders.

Every individual will be punctual in his attendance: those, if any there be, who may be prevented by severe indisposition, will send well-attested certificates of the fact, or they will be reported as delinquents. Those who may claim exemption on the ground of bodily infirmity (and some few have exhibited such claims) will attend at the rendezvous, where they will be examined by a surgeon, upon whose report they will be rejected or passed by the inspector as justice shall dictate. Privates, wishing to serve by substitutes, will attend with the same, being previously instructed that no substitute will be received but an able-bodied man.

The time of rendezvous for detachments drawn from the more distant counties, will be fixed in after orders.

(Signed) W.C.C. CLAIBORNE.

AFTER GENERAL ORDERS.

H.Q. New Orleans, September 5th, 1814.

Major-General Jackson, acting under the authority of the president, having required the service in the field of the whole corps of Louisiana militia, holden in readiness for active service under the orders of the 6th ult. the governor and commander-in-chief directs that the detachment drawn from the second division of militia, rendezvous at the post of Baton Rouge, on or before the 1st day of October next, where after being organized into companies, under the order of major-general Thomas, in manner as heretofore directed, they will be inspected and mustered into the service of the United States.

The commander-in-chief, confiding in the patriotism of the several corps attached to the second division, assures himself that at this moment of peril, they will deserve well of their country. Louisiana is openly menaced, and it is believed that the force destined to invade her is at this time assembled at Apalachicola and Pensacola. Major-general Jackson, commanding the seventh military district, who has often led the western warriors to victory, invites me to lose no time in preparing for the defence of the state. This gallant commander is now at or near Mobile watching the movements of the enemy, and making the necessary preparations to cover and defend this section of the union. He will in due time receive re-enforcements from the other states on the Mississippi: he calculates also, on the zealous support of the Louisianians, and must not be disappointed. The time has come when every man must do his duty, when no faithful American will be found absent from his post.

By order of his excellency W.C.C. Claiborne.
(Signed) A. LANEUVILLE,
Adjutant-general.

By another general order the detachment drawn from the sixth, seventh, eighth, and ninth regiments, are ordered to rendezvous at the Magasin barracks opposite New Orleans, on Saturday the 4th instant.

NO. XI.

Militia general orders,

head-quarters, New Orleans, September 8th, 1814.

The governor and commander-in-chief directs that the several companies of militia, within the city and suburbs of New Orleans, muster for inspection and exercise twice, and those in the interior counties of the state, once in each and every week, at such times and places as the captains or officers commanding companies shall designate. He recommends also to all fathers of families and others who, by their stations or age, are exempted from militia service, to afford at this eventful crisis a laudable example; he invites them to the formation of military associations; to choose their officers; to procure arms, and to assemble occasionally for military exercise.

The commander-in-chief would be sorry unnecessarily to draw his fellow citizens from their private pursuits and subject them to useless fatigues, but in his judgment their safety demands that they be trained to the use of arms, and holden in readiness to turn out at a moment's warning in defence of their families and homes; he does not wish to excite alarm, and trusts none will exist; but it is his duty to declare that the state is menaced with dangers which require all our union, zeal, and activity to avert. A hope is still cherished that the pending negociation between the United States and Great Britain may eventuate in a peace honourable to both parties; but there is too much reason to apprehend that the enemy feeling power may forget right. Indeed from the information before us, we shall act wisely in preparing for the worst. At this moment a fleet of the enemy is hovering on our coast, and he is assembling a force at Apalachicola, Pensacola, and elsewhere, avowedly for the invasion of Louisiana. We must be prepared to meet him; to dispute every inch of ground; harass him on his march; make a stand at every favourable position, and finally to triumph or lose with our country, our lives. Every individual, therefore, attached to the militia will be in constant readiness for active service—officers of every grade at all times be prepared to repair to their posts, and assume the command which may be assigned them—non-commissioned officers and privates will put their arms, whether muskets, rifles, or shot-guns in the best possible condition, furnish themselves with six flints each, as much powder and ball as can conveniently be carried, and pack in their knapsacks one blanket, one shirt, and one pair of shoes, being the necessary clothing on a march. The greatest vigilance will be observed, and every precaution taken to guard against surprise. Captains and subalterns will keep their field officers advised of every occurrence which interests the public safety, and colonels or officers commanding regiments will communicate the same to the generals of their respective brigades and division, and the general officers to the commander-in-chief. Strong patroles will be ordered on every night, particularly within the city and suburbs of New Orleans and the adjacent counties. The strictest discipline will be maintained among the slaves, and every person of suspicious conduct or character, will be arrested and carried before a judge, or justice of the peace, for examination. If the enemy should enter the state, the several colonels of militia nearest the point of attack, will immediately order into the field their respective regiments, and (after detailing a suitable guard for the protection of the women and children, and the maintenance of a proper police on the plantations) will advance without waiting for further orders to the scene of danger. Of the skill and courage of the regular troops of the United States in our vicinity, we are fully assured; we will unite our efforts with theirs against the common enemy, and if called to act with our gallant countrymen of the western states, vie with them also in deeds of valour.

The commander-in-chief persuades himself that no efforts which have or may be made to divide us, will prove successful. The intrigues, the means of corruption by which in other countries our enemy has so much profited, will doubtless be attempted here. But his character is well understood, and it is hoped, that his arts will not avail him. In defence of our homes and families there surely will be but one opinion—one sentiment. The American citizen, on contrasting his situation with that of the citizen or subject of any other country on earth, will see abundant cause to be content with his destiny. He must be aware how little he can gain, and how much he must lose by a revolution, or change of government.

If there be a citizen who believes that his rights and property would be respected by an invading foe, the weakness of his head should excite pity. If there be an individual who supposes the kind of force with which we are menaced could be restrained from acts of violence, he knows little of the character of those allies of Great Britain, who committed the massacre at fort Mims.

In these evil days, small indeed is the portion of affliction which has hitherto befallen Louisiana: when a hostile army breaks into the territory of a nation, its course is marked with scenes of desolation, which centuries of industry cannot repair. With what union, with what zeal, should all our energies be exerted to defend our country against like misfortunes!

(Signed) Wm. C. C. CLAIBORNE.

NO. XII.

Head-quarters, Pensacola, August 26, 1814.

Order of the day for the first colonial battalion of the royal corps of marines.

You are called upon to discharge a duty of the utmost danger, of the utmost peril. You will have to perform long and tedious marches through wildernesses, swamps and water-courses; your enemy from long habit inured to the climate, will have great advantages over you. But remember the twenty-one years of toil and glory of your country, and resolve to follow the example of your glorious companions, who have fought and spilt their blood in her service. Be equally faithful and strict in your moral discipline, and this, the last and most perfidious of your enemies, will not long maintain himself before you. A cause so sacred as that which has led you to draw your swords in Europe, will make you unsheath them in America, and I trust you will use them with equal credit and advantage. In Europe, your arms were not employed in defence of your country only, but of all those who groaned in the chains of oppression, and in America they are to have the same direction. The people whom you are now to aid and assist have suffered robberies and murders committed on them by the Americans.

The noble Spanish nation has grieved to see her territories insulted; having been robbed and despoiled of a portion of them while she was overwhelmed with distress and held down by the chains which a tyrant had imposed on her gloriously struggling for the greatest of all possible blessings (true liberty.) The treacherous Americans, who call themselves free, have attacked her, like assassins, while she was fallen. But the day of retribution is fast approaching. These atrocities will excite horror in the heart of a British soldier, they will stimulate you to avenge them, and you will avenge them like British soldiers. Valour, then, and humanity!

As to the Indians, you are to exhibit to them the most exact discipline, being a pattern to those children of nature. You will have to teach and instruct them; in doing which you will manifest the utmost patience, and you will correct them when they deserve it. But you will regard their affections and *antipathies, and never give them just cause of offence*. Sobriety, above all things, should be your greatest care—a single instance of drunkenness may be our ruin; and I declare to you, in the most solemn manner, that no consideration whatsoever shall induce me to forgive a drunkard. Apprised of this declaration, if any of you break my orders in this respect, he will consider himself as the just cause of his own chastisement. Sobriety is your first duty; I ask of you the observance of it among your brethren. Vigilance is our next duty. Nothing is so disgraceful to our army as surprise.—Nothing so destructive to our cause.

EDWARD NICHOLLS.

NO. XIII.

At a very numerous and respectable meeting of the citizens of New Orleans and its vicinity, assembled pursuant to public notice at Tremoulet's coffee-house, on the 15th day of September, 1814, to consider of the propriety of naming a committee to co-operate with the constituted authorities of the state and general government, in suggesting measures of defence, and calling out the force of the country in the present emergency,

Edward Livingston, Esq. was called to the chair, and Richard Relf, Esq. appointed secretary of the meeting.

The chairman opened the meeting by a speech analogous to the occasion, in which he showed the propriety and necessity of the meeting, and the good effects that would probably result from an expression of public opinion in the present posture of our affairs, and took occasion, from the English assertion of disaffection in this state, to show, that we owed it to ourselves to disavow such unfounded and calumnious insinuations, and by a prompt and cheerful offer of support, to show to the rest of the United States that we are not unworthy of a place among them. After a strong and eloquent invitation to union, he proposed the following resolutions, which were unanimously adopted:

Resolved, That on all important national questions, it is proper, and in urgent emergencies it is necessary, for the citizens of a free government to aid their magistrates and officers by a proffer of their support in the performance of their functions.

Resolved, That in this state such an expression of public opinion is peculiarly proper, because the enemy has dared to allege that we are disaffected to our government, and ready to assist him in his attempts on our independence, an allegation which we declare to be false and insidious, tending to create doubts of our fidelity to the union of which we are a member, and which we repel with the indignation they are calculated to inspire.

Resolved, That an union with the other states is necessary to the prosperity of this, and that while we rely upon them for assistance and protection, we will not be wanting in every exertion proportionate to our strength, in order to maintain internal tranquillity, repel invasion, and preserve to the United States this important accession to its commerce and security.

Resolved, As the sense of this assembly, that the good people of this state are attached to the government of the United States, and that they will repel with indignation every attempt to create disaffection and weaken the force of the country, by exciting dissentions and jealousies at a moment when union is most necessary.

Resolved, That we consider the present as a crisis serious but not alarming—that our country is capable of defence—that we do not despair of the republic, and that we will at the risk of our lives and fortunes defend it.

Resolved, That a committee of nine members be appointed to co-operate with the constituted civil and military authorities, in suggesting means of defence, and calling forth the energies of the country to repel invasion and preserve domestic tranquillity, and that the said committee consist of the following persons: Edward Livingston, Pierre Foucher, Dussuau de la Croix, Benjamin Morgan, George M. Ogden, Dominique Bouligny, J. Noel Destrehan, John Blanque, Augustin Macarty.

(Signed) EDWARD LIVINGSTON, *chairman*.

(Signed) RICHARD RELF, *secretary*.

NO. XIV.

Address from the committee of public defence, to their fellow citizens.

FELLOW CITIZENS,

Named by a numerous assembly of the citizens of New Orleans, to aid the constituted authorities in devising the most certain means of guarding against the dangers which threatened you, our first duty is to apprize you of the extent of those dangers—your open enemy is preparing to attack you from without, and by means of his vile agents dispersed through the country, endeavours to excite to insurrection a more cruel and dangerous one in the midst of you.

Fellow citizens! the most perfect union is necessary among all the individuals which compose our community; all have an equal interest in yielding a free and full obedience to their magistrates and officers, and in forwarding their views for the public good—all have not only their property, but their very existence at stake; you have, through your representatives in the convention, contracted the solemn obligation of becoming an integral part of the United States of America; by this measure you secured your own sovereignty and acquired the invaluable blessing of independence. God forbid that we should believe there are any among us disposed to fail in the sacred duties required by fidelity and honour. A just idea of the geographical situation of your country will convince you that your safety, and in a greater degree your prosperity, depends on your being irrevocably and faithfully attached to an union with the other states; but if there exist among you men base or mad enough to undervalue their duties and their true interest—let them tremble on considering the dreadful evils they will bring down upon themselves and upon us, if by their criminal indifference they favour the enterprises of the enemy against our beloved country.

Fellow citizens! the navigation of the Mississippi is as necessary to two millions of our western brethren, as the blood is to the pulsation of the heart—those brave men, closely attached to the union, will never suffer, whatever seducing offers maybe made to them—they will never suffer the state of Louisiana to be subject to a foreign power, and should the events of war enable the enemy to occupy it, they will make every sacrifice to recover a country so necessary to their existence. A war ruinous to you would be the consequence, the enemy, to whom you would have had the weakness to yield, would subject you to a military despotism, of all others the most dreadful; your estates, your slaves, your persons would be put in requisition, and you would be forced at the point of the bayonet to fight against those very men whom you have voluntarily chosen for fellow citizens and brethren. Beloved countrymen, listen to the men honoured by your confidence, and who will endeavour to merit it; listen to the voice of honour, of duty, and of nature! unite! form but one body, one soul, and defend to the last extremity your sovereignty, your property—defend your own lives, and the dearer existence of your wives and children.

(Signed)

PIERRE FOUCHER,
DESTREHAN,
BENJAMIN MORGAN,
EDWARD LIVINGSTON,
DUSUAU DE LA CROIX,
AUGUSTUS MACARTY,
GEORGE M. OGDEN,
D. BOULIGNY.

NO. XIV-a.

Copy of a letter from the secretary of war to general Jackson.

Department of War,
October 21, 1814.

Major General Andrew Jackson,
Sir,

Your letter of the 9th ultimo, covering your correspondence with the governor of Pensacola, is received. I hasten to communicate to you the directions of the President, that you should, at present, take no measures, which would involve this Government in a contest with Spain.

A minister having lately been appointed on our part to that Government, and our relations with it being amicable, it is deemed more proper that a representation of the insolent and unjustifiable conduct of the Governor of Pensacola, should be made to that Government, through the ordinary channels of communication, than that you should resent it by an attack on Pensacola.

The President approves the manly tone with which you have asserted the rights of your country, in your correspondence with the governor of that province.

Very important interests are committed to you, and great confidence is entertained, that you will meet the expectations of the government in the discharge of your duties.

It is thought very probable that the British forces expected from Europe under Lord Hill, will be directed against Louisiana. To enable you to meet this pressure 7,500 men have been ordered from Tennessee, 2,500 from Kentucky and a like number from Georgia, and it is expected that the warriors of all the friendly tribes of Indians, will be secured by you on our side. One hundred thousand dollars have been placed subject to your orders, in the hands of the governor of Tennessee, for the public service, and blankets and other articles will be forwarded without delay for the use of the Indians.

I have the honor to be
JAMES MONROE.

NO. XV.

At a meeting of the committee of public defence on the 21st September, 1814,

On motion, resolved, that a *sabre*, with a suitable inscription and proper emblems, be presented to major W. Lawrence, as a testimonial of the sense which is entertained of his skill and gallantry in the defence of fort Bowyer, and in the repulse of the enemy's squadron and forces before that place.

Ordered that the chairman communicate a copy of this resolution to major Lawrence, with a request that he will convey to the brave officers and men under his command, the expression of gratitude which is felt for the important service they have rendered to this state, as well as to the United States.

(Signed) EDWARD LIVINGSTON, *chairman.*

NO. XVI.

PROCLAMATION.

Head-quarters, seventh military district,
Mobile, September 21st, 1814.

LOUISIANIANS!

The base, the perfidious Britons have attempted to invade your country—they had the temerity to attack fort Bowyer with their incongruous horde of Indians and negro assassins—they seemed to have forgotten that this fort was defended by freemen—they were not long indulged in their error—the gallant Lawrence, with his little spartan band, has given them a lecture that will last for ages; he has taught them what men can do when fighting for their liberty, when contending against slaves. He has convinced sir W.H. Percy that his companions in arms are not to be conquered by proclamations; that the strongest British bark is not invulnerable to the force of American artillery, directed by the steady nervous arm of a freeman.

Louisianians!—The proud Briton, the natural and sworn enemies of all Frenchmen, has called upon you, by proclamation, to aid him in his tyranny, and to prostrate the holy temple of our liberty. Can Louisianians, can Frenchmen, can Americans, ever stoop to be the slaves or allies of Britain.

The proud, vain-glorious boaster colonel Nicholls, when he addressed you, Louisianians and Kentuckians, had forgotten that you were the votaries of freedom, or he would never have pledged the honour of a British officer for the faithful performance of his promise, to lure you from your fidelity to the government of your choice. I ask you, Louisianans, can we place any confidence in the honour of men who have courted an alliance with pirates and robbers? Have not these noble Britons, these honourable men, colonel Nicholls and the honourable captain W.H. Percy, the true representatives of their royal master, done this? Have they not made offers to the pirates of Barataria to join them, and their holy cause? And have they not dared to insult you by calling on you to associate, as brethren with them, and this hellish banditti.

Louisianians!—The government of your choice are engaged in a just and honourable contest for the security of your individual and her national rights—on you, a part of America, the only country on earth where every man enjoys freedom, where its blessings are alike extended to the poor and the rich, calls to protect these rights from the invading usurpation of Britain; and she calls not in vain. I well know that every man whose soul beats high at the proud title of freeman; that every Louisianan, either by birth or adoption, will promptly obey the voice of his country; will rally round the eagle of Columbia, secure it from the pending danger, or nobly die in the last ditch in its defence.

The individual who refuses to defend his rights, when called upon by his government, deserves to be a slave, and must be punished as an enemy to his country, and a friend to her foe.

The undersigned has been intrusted with the defence of your country—on you he relies to aid him in this important duty; in this reliance he hopes not to be mistaken. He trusts in the justice of his cause and the patriotism of his countrymen—confident that any future attempt to invade our soil will be repelled as the last, he calls not upon either pirates or robbers to join him in the glorious cause.

Your governor has been fully authorized by me to organize any volunteer company, battalion, or regiment which may proffer its services under this call, and is informed of their probable destination.

(Signed) ANDREW JACKSON.

NO. XVII.

PROCLAMATION.

Head-quarters, 7th military district, Mobile, September 21, 1814.

To the free coloured inhabitants of Louisiana.

Through a mistaken policy you have heretofore been deprived of a participation in the glorious struggle for national rights in which our country is engaged. This no longer shall exist.

As sons of freedom, you are now called upon to defend our most inestimable blessing. As Americans, your country looks with confidence to her adopted children, for a valorous support, as a faithful return for the advantages enjoyed under her mild and equitable government. As fathers, husbands, and brothers, you are summoned to rally round the standard of the eagle, to defend all which is dear in existence.

Your country, although calling for your exertions, does not wish you to engage in her cause, without amply remunerating you for the services rendered. Your intelligent minds are not to be led away by false representations.—Your love of honour would cause you to despise the man who should attempt to deceive you. In the sincerity of a soldier, and the language of truth I address you.

To every noble-hearted, generous freeman of colour, volunteering to serve during the present contest with Great Britain, and no longer, there will be paid the same bounty in money and lands, now received by the white soldiers of the United States, viz. one hundred and twenty-four dollars in money, and one hundred and sixty acres of land. The non-commissioned officers and privates will also be entitled to the same monthly pay and daily rations, and clothes furnished to any American soldier.

On enrolling yourselves in companies, the major-general commanding will select officers for your government, from your white fellow citizens. Your non-commissioned officers will be appointed from among yourselves.

Due regard will be paid to the feelings of freemen and soldiers. You will not, by being associated with white men in the same corps, be exposed to improper comparisons or unjust sarcasm. As a distinct, independent battalion or regiment, pursuing the path of glory, you will, undivided, receive the applause and gratitude of your countrymen.

To assure you of the sincerity of my intentions and my anxiety to engage your invaluable services to our country, I have communicated my wishes to the governor of Louisiana, who is fully informed as to the manner of enrolment, and will give you every necessary information on the subject of this address.

ANDREW JACKSON,
Major-general commanding.

NO. XVII-a.

Copy of a letter from the secretary of war to the governor of Tennessee.

Department of War,
October 3, 1814.

His Excellency The Governor of Tennessee,

Sir,

I have this day written to the Governor of Kentucky to call out twenty five hundred militia, and order them to join General Jackson without delay in lieu of that number of the militia which have been ordered from your state. He has been requested to inform you whether that number can be sent from Kentucky, and if so, the requisition on your state to join General Jackson, will be reduced to five thousand.

I have the honor to be
JAMES MONROE.

Copy of a letter from the secretary of war to the governor of Kentucky.

Department of War,
October 3, 1814.

His Excellency The Governor of Kentucky,

Sir,

General Jackson having called to his aid two thousand five hundred men from Tennessee, and this department having ordered five thousand from that state to join General Jackson, making a total of seven thousand five hundred men; which number upon further reflection being thought to be too great, to call at one time from that state. You are therefore requested to furnish from the state of Kentucky two thousand five hundred men in lieu of that number called from the State of Tennessee, and to advise the governor of that state, whether you can or not; for should any unforseen circumstances occur to prevent your furnishing them, they must go from Tennessee. You will take the necessary measures to forward these men to General Jackson, with all possible dispatch.

I have the honor to be
JAMES MONROE.

Copy of a letter from the secretary of war to the governor of Georgia.

Department of War,
October 10, 1814.

His Excellency The Governor of Georgia,
Sir,

There is strong reason to presume, from intelligence just received from our ministers at Ghent, that a British force, consisting of twelve or fifteen thousand men, sailed from Ireland early in September for New Orleans and the Mobile with intention to take possession of that city and the country thro' which the great rivers, on which the whole of the United States westward of the Allegheny Mountains so essentially depend. This invasion must be met with firmness and repelled with promptitude. I have therefore to request that your Excellency to put in march as soon as practicable, the two thousand five hundred detached militia, required by my letter of September 25th.

These troops will move in a direction to support General Jackson, subject to his disposition, when they shall receive his orders. He is advised of this measure and will lose no time in communicating with your Excellency on the subject, in the mean time he should be advised of such arrangements as you may adopt to meet the object.

I have the honor to be
JAMES MONROE.

Copy of a letter from the secretary of war to the governor of Kentucky.

Department of War,
October 25, 1814.

His Excellency The Governor of Kentucky,
Sir,

General McArthur and Governor Cass in his absence have been authorized to call upon you for any number of the detailed militia from the state of Kentucky, which circumstances may require. It is hoped you will be prepared promptly to answer any such call. You will have the men called for, armed and equipped, and the officers apportioned to the men, agreeably to the regulations of the United States.

I trust that the twenty five hundred men, you were requested to send to General Jackson, moved on, and that they are armed and equipped. If you are not able to supply the necessary arms and equipments to all the militia you may be called on for, you must have recourse to the deposits which the United States have at Newport; they are however, inconsiderable.

Should your state laws make any assurances from the Department necessary, with respect to the state arms that may be taken without the limits of the state by the militia that are in the service of the United States, you may rest assured they will be complied with by this Department.

I have the honor to be
JAMES MONROE.

NO. XVII-b.

Copy of a letter from the secretary of war to general Jackson.

Department of War,
December 7, 1814.

Major General Andrew Jackson,

Sir,

I had the honor to receive your letter of the 26th & 31st October, two days past.

I hope that my letter of the 21st October reached you in time, to prevent the attack, which you then contemplated, making, on the British at Pensacola.

Altho' the conduct of the Spanish authorities, there, may justify the measure, the President nevertheless desires that it may be avoided, in the hopes that the new efforts, which he is now making, to obtain justice and preserve amity with that power, may be successful. Should you have made the proposed attack, you will on the receipt of this letter, withdraw your troops from the Spanish Territory, declaring that you had entered it for the sole purpose of freeing it from British violation.

General Gaines is ordered to join and act under you, in the defence of New Orleans, and of the district under your command. Full confidence is entertained that this appointment of an officer of his merit, will afford to you a very acceptable aid, in the discharge of your highly important duties.

Recent intelligence tends to confirm the opinion before entertained that the enemy have already or will soon make an attack on New Orleans. A strong force from Europe connected with that, which lately infested this bay, and with the troops released from Guadelupe & Martinique, were said to be making preparations to assail you. I need not assure you of the entire confidence which exists, that you and the troops under you will all do your duty.

Much anxiety is felt, lest you should remain too long on the Mobile, or at other points East of New Orleans. The city, it is presumed, is a principal object with the enemy and it cannot be defended, on either of the passes by which it may be approached, one by the river Mississippi itself, another by La Fourche, the third by Lake Pontchartrain, without occupying the ground bearing on these passes.

The Indian goods will have reached you, I presume, before you receive this letter.

You shall want for nothing necessary to your comfort, and to that of our fellow citizens, acting under you, which your country can supply.

I have the honor to be
JAMES MONROE.

NO. XVIII.

ANONYMOUS.

To commodore Daniel T. Patterson, New Orleans.

Pensacola, 5th December, 1814.

Sir,

I feel it a duty to apprize you of a very large force of the enemy off this port, and it is generally understood New Orleans is the object of attack. It amounts at present to about eighty vessels, and more than double that number are momentarily looked for, to form a junction, when an immediate commencement of their operations will take place. I am not able to learn, how, when, or where the attack will be made; but I heard that they have vessels of all descriptions, and a large body of troops. Admiral Cochrane commands, and his ship, the Tonnant, lies at this moment just outside the bar; they certainly appear to have swept the West Indies of troops, and probably no means will be left untried to obtain their object.—The admiral arrived only yesterday noon.

I am yours, &c.
N***.

NO. XVIII-a.

Copies of letters from the secretary of war to general Jackson.

Department of War,
September 5, 1814.

Major General Andrew Jackson,

Sir,

Your letter of the 10th August has been received. The avowed objects of the enemy, and their recent outrage of all the principles of civilized warfare, warrant a belief, that they will make their devastations as extensive as their means will enable them.

The writer of the enclosed copy of a communication without signature, is known and entitled to credit.

Your prompt attention and vigorous operations, will be required in the lower country. All the friendly Indians should be organized, and prepared to cooperate with your other forces. There appears to be some disatisfaction among the Choctaws.

Their friendship and services should be secured without delay. The friendly Indians must be fed and paid, and made to fight when and where their services may be required.

It is desirable that you should repair to New Orleans as soon as your arrangements can be accomplished in other parts of the district, unless circumstances should render another point more eligible.

I have the honor to be
JAMES MONROE.

Department of War,
October 10, 1814.

Major General Andrew Jackson,
Sir,

There is strong reason to presume, from intelligence just received from our ministers at Ghent, that a British force consisting of twelve or fifteen thousand men, sailed from Ireland, early in September, for New Orleans and the Mobile with intention to take possession of the city and of the country through which the great rivers, on which the whole of the United States westward of the Allegheny Mountains so essentially depend. This invasion must be met with firmness and repelled with promptitude.

I have required the governors of Tennessee, Kentucky and Georgia, to communicate with you relative to the march of the troops detached from those states, to meet the occasion, viz. seven thousand five hundred from Tennessee, two thousand five hundred from Kentucky, and two thousand five hundred from Georgia. The whole will be subject to your orders and disposition.

I have the honor to be
JAMES MONROE.

P.S. You will not fail to secure the friendship and cooperation of the Creeks and Choctaws and other tribes in our favor, should the menaced invasion take effect.

To enable you to do this, blankets etc. will be forwarded without delay, to our agents with those tribes. You may, however, calculate on the supply in your communications with them.

NO. XVIII-b.

Copy of a letter from the secretary of war to the governor of Kentucky.

Department of War,
November 3, 1814.

His Excellency The Governor of Kentucky,
Sir,

I have the honor to acknowledge the receipt of your Excellency's letter of the 19th and 22nd of October. Five thousand stands of arms have been ordered and will immediately leave Pittsburgh, directed to the commanding officer of the United States troops at Baton Rouge, for the use of the militia, ordered into service from Kentucky & Tennessee. The deputy Commissary of Purchases at Pittsburgh will be directed to send as far as may be practicable, tents, camp kettles, etc, for five thousand men.

The existing necessary for occasioning our army, incurs me to request your Excellency to furnish and put into the hands of the militia (detached) as many arms as can be procured before they march, as part of those ordered must be issued to the Tennessee troops and no further supply can be immediately sent down the Mississippi.

In case volunteers offer, it will be proper on your part to accept them in lieu of the militia. This Government cannot object to the substitution of one for the other.

I have the honor to be
JAMES MONROE.

Copy of a letter from the secretary of war to the governor of Georgia.

Department of War,
October 20, 1814.

His Excellency The Governor of Georgia,

Sir,

I have had the honor to receive your Excellency's letter of the 10th instant.

The contractor for Georgia is bound to supply rations to the militia, or will as the regulars when in the service of the United States.

I enclose a copy of the contract and request your Excellency to make requisitions on Mr. Carter accordingly.

General Pinckney will be requested to order Major Fannin or some other officer of the Quarter Masters Department to join the detachment of militia now on their march from Georgia.

I have the honor to be
JAMES MONROE.

Copies of letters from the secretary of war to the governor of Tennessee.

Department of War,
November 3, 1814.

His Excellency The Governor of Tennessee,

Sir,

I have had the honor to receive your Excellency's letter of the 14th of October.

There is no law authorizing the President to accept volunteers, but there can be no objection and it will be perfectly agreeable to have a part or the whole of the detachment required, composed of volunteers accepted by your Excellency in lieu of such number of detached militia. Such troops must be considered the same as other militia called into actual service.

Five thousand stands of arms, with ammunition to, and as many tents & camp equippage as can be spared immediately, have been ordered from Pittsburgh to the commanding officer of the U.S. army at Baton Rouge for the use of the detached militia of Tennessee and Kentucky. I must however request your Excellency to have all the troops armed and equipped if practicable, before they march as this supply will be very limited even for a deposit in reserve at that point.

I have the honor to be
JAMES MONROE.

Department of War,
November 4, 1814.

His Excellency The Governor of Tennessee,

Sir,

Your Excellency's letter of October 13th has been received. In my letter of yesterday I had the honor to inform you that all the arms, equipments and camp equippage which could be spared would be immediately sent down the Ohio for the accommodation of the detached militia from Tennessee and Kentucky. All the troops which have been required from your state must be marched to reinforce General Jackson. Louisiana being still, it is believed the object of Lord Hill's expedition.

The Accountant of this Department has communicated your unwillingness to receive the money which has been remitted, to meet those engagements when you had interceded, yourself, to procure funds, for General Jackson. This Government acknowledges with great pleasure and satisfaction the uniform and uneasing exertions which have been made by you to promote the interests of the service since the commencement of the war and it is my intention to give you as little trouble as possible in future. At the time that money was ordered, your Quarter Master William B. Lewis was in this city and no other agent was recognized to whom the remittance could be made. It will be perfectly satisfactory to have your Excellency deliver over the money to him or such other officer as you may appoint in the Quarter Master Department with instructions to make the necessary arrangements for supplying General Jackson and the troops ordered into service for his command.

I have the honor to be
JAMES MONROE.

NO. XIX.

Copy of a letter from commodore Patterson to the secretary of the navy, dated

New Orleans 17th March, 1815.

Sir,

Inclosed I have the honour to transmit for your information a copy of a letter from lieutenant Thomas Ap Catesby Jones, giving a detailed account of the action between the gun-vessels under his command, and a flotilla of the enemy's launches and barges, on the 14th December, 1814, which, after a most gallant resistance, terminated, as stated in my letter of the 17th December, in the capture of our squadron.

The courage and skill which was displayed in the defence of the gun-vessels and tender, for such a length of time, against such an overwhelming force as they had to contend with, reflects additional splendour on our naval glory, and will, I trust, diminish the regret occasioned by their loss.

I have the honour to be, &c.
DANIEL T. PATTERSON.

New Orleans, 12th March, 1815.

Sir,

Having sufficiently recovered my strength, I do myself the honour of reporting to you the particulars of the capture of the division of United States' gun-boats late under my command.

On the 12th December, 1814, the enemy's fleet off Ship island increased to such a force as to render it no longer safe or prudent for me to continue on that part of the lakes with the small force which I commanded. I therefore determined to gain a station near the Malhereux islands as soon as possible, which situation would better enable me to oppose a further penetration of the enemy up the lakes, and at the same time afford me an opportunity of retreating to the Petite Coquilles if necessary.

At 10, A.M. on the 13th I discovered a large flotilla of barges had left the fleet, (shaping their course towards the Pass Christian) which I supposed to be a disembarkation of troops intended to land at that place. About 2, P.M. the enemy's flotilla having gained the Pass Christian, and continuing their course to the westward, convinced me that an attack on the gun-boats was designed. At this time the water in the lakes was uncommonly low, owing to the westerly wind which had prevailed for a number of days previous, and which still continued from the same quarter. Nos. 156, 162 and 163, although in the best channel, were in 12 or 18 inches less water than their draught. Every effort was made to get them afloat by throwing overboard all articles of weight that could be dispensed with. At 3:30, the flood-tide had commenced; got under weigh, making the best of my way towards the Petite Coquilles. At 3:45, the enemy despatched three boats to cut out the schooner Seahorse, which had been sent into the bay St. Louis that morning to assist in the removal of the public stores, which I had previously ordered. There finding a removal impracticable, I ordered preparations to be made for their destruction; least they should fall into the enemy's hands. A few discharges of grape-shot from the Seahorse compelled the three boats, which had attacked her, to retire out of reach of her gun, until they were joined by four others, when the attack was recommenced by the seven boats. Mr. Johnson having chosen an advantageous position near the two six-pounders mounted on the bank, maintained a sharp action for near 30 minutes, when the enemy hauled off, having one boat apparently much injured, and with the loss of several men killed and wounded. At 7:30, an explosion at the bay, and soon after a large fire, induced me to believe the Seahorse was blown up and the public storehouse set on fire, which has proved to be the fact.

About 1 A. M. on the 14th, the wind having entirely died away, and our vessels become unmanageable, came to anchor in the west end of Malheureux island's passage. At daylight next morning, still a perfect calm, the enemy's flotilla was about nine miles from us at anchor, but soon got in motion and rapidly advanced on us. The want of wind, and the strong ebb-tide which was setting through the pass, left me but one alternative; which was, to put myself in the most advantageous position, to give the enemy as warm a reception as possible. The commanders were all called on board and made acquainted with my intentions, and the position which each vessel was to take, the whole to form a close line abreast across the channel, anchored by the stern with springs on the cable' &c. &c. Thus we remained anxiously awaiting an attack from the advancing foe, whose force I now clearly distinguished to be composed of forty-two heavy launches and gun-barges, with three light gigs, manned with upwards of one thousand men and officers. About 9:30, the Alligator (tender) which was to the southward and eastward, and endeavouring to join the division, was captured by several of the enemy's barges, when the whole flotilla came to, with their grampnels a little out of reach of our shot, apparently making arrangements for the attack—At 10:30, the enemy weighed, forming a line abreast in open order, and steering direct for our line, which was unfortunately in some degree broken by the force of the current, driving Nos. 156 and 163 about one hundred yards in advance. As soon as the enemy came within reach of our shot, a deliberate fire from our long guns was opened upon him, but without much effect, the objects being of so small a size. At 10 minutes before 11, the enemy opened a fire from the whole of his line, when the action became general and destructive on both sides. About 11:49, the advance boats of the enemy, three in number, attempted to board No. 156, but were repulsed with the loss of nearly every officer killed or wounded, and two boats sunk.—A second attempt to board was then made by four other boats, which shared almost a similar fate. At this moment I received a severe wound in my left shoulder, which compelled me to quit the deck, leaving it in charge of Mr. George Parker, master's-mate, who gallantly defended the vessel until he was severely wounded, when the enemy, by his superior number, succeeded in gaining possession of the deck about 10 minutes past 12 o'clock. The enemy immediately turned the guns of his prize on the other gun-boats, and fired several shot previous to striking the American colours. The action continued with unabating severity until 40 minutes past 12 o'clock, when it terminated with the surrender of No. 23, all the other vessels having previously fallen into the hands of the enemy.

In this unequal contest our loss in killed and wounded has been trifling, compared to that of the enemy.

Enclosed you will receive a list of the killed and wounded, and a correct statement of the force which I had the honour to command at the commencement of the action, together with an estimate of the force I had to contend against, as acknowledged by the enemy, which will enable you to decide how far the honour of our country's flag has been supported in this conflict.

I have the honour to be, &c.

(Signed) THOMAS AP CATESBY JONES.

Statement of the effective forces of a division of the United States' gun-boats under the command of lieutenant-commanding Thomas Ap Catesby Jones, at the commencement of the action, with a flotilla of English boats, on the 14th December, 1814.

Gun-boat No. 5, 5 guns, 36 men, sailing-master John D. Ferris; gun-boat 23, 5 guns, 39 men, lieutenant Isaac M'Keeve [McKeever] gun-boat No. 156, 5 guns, 41 men, lieutenant-commandant Thomas A.C. Jones; gun-boat 162, 5 guns, 35 men, lieutenant Robert Spedden; gun-boat 163, 3 guns, 31 men, sailing-master George Ulrick—Total, 23 guns, 182 men.

N.B. The schooner Seahorse, had one six pounder, and 14 men, sailing-master William Johnson, commander; none killed or wounded.

The sloop Alligator (tender) had one four-pounder and 8 men, sailing-master Richard S. Shepperd, commander.

(Signed) THOMAS AP CATESBY JONES.

The following is a correct statement of the British forces which were engaged in the capture of the late United States' gun-boats, Nos. 23, 156, 5, 162 and 163, near the Malhereux islands, lake Borgne, 14th December, 1814.

Forty launches and barges, mounting one carronade, each of 12, 18, and 24 calibre.

One launch mounting one long brass twelve-pounder.

One launch mounting one long brass nine-pounder.

Three gigs, with small arms only.

Total number of boats 45

Total number of cannon 43

The above flotilla was manned with one thousand two hundred men and officers, commanded by captain Lockyer, who received three severe wounds in the action. The enemy, as usual, will not acknowledge his loss on this occasion in boats or men; but from the nature of the action, and the observations made by our officers, while prisoners in their fleet, his loss in killed and wounded may be justly estimated to exceed three hundred, among whom are an unusual proportion of offlcers.

NO. XX.

On Sunday, the 18th December, general Jackson reviewed the militia of the city, the battalion commanded by major Plauche, and a part of the regiment of men of colour. Being drawn up on their respective parades, the following addresses were read to them by Mr. Livingston, one of his aids:

TO THE EMBODIED MILITIA.

Fellow citizens and soldiers!

The general commanding in chief would not do justice to the noble ardour that has animated you in the hour of danger, he would not do justice to his own feeling, if he suffered the example you have shown to pass without public notice. Inhabitants of an opulent and commercial town, you have, by a spontaneous effort, shaken off the habits which are created by wealth, and shown that you are resolved to deserve the blessings of fortune by bravely defending them. Long strangers to the perils of war, you have embodied yourselves to face them with the cool countenance of veterans—and with motives of disunion that might operate on weak minds, you have forgotten the difference of language and the prejudices of national pride, and united with a cordiality that does honour to your understandings as well as to your patriotism. Natives of the United States! They are the oppressors of your infant political existence, with whom you are to contend—they are the men your fathers conquered whom you are to oppose. Descendants of Frenchmen! natives of France! they are English, the hereditary, the eternal enemies of your ancient country, the invaders of that you have adopted, who are your foes. Spaniards! remember the conduct of your allies at St. Sebastians, and recently at Pensacola, and rejoice that you have an opportunity of avenging the brutal injuries inflicted by men who dishonour the human race.

Fellow citizens, of every description, remember for what and against whom you contend. For all that can render life desirable—for a country blessed with every gift of nature—for property, for life—for those dearer than either, your wives and children—and for liberty, without which, country, life, property, are no longer worth possessing; as even the embraces of wives and children become a reproach to the wretch who would deprive them by his cowardice of those invaluable blessings. You are to contend for all this against an enemy whose continued effort is to deprive you of the least of these blessings—who avows a war of vengeance and desolation, carried on and marked by cruelty, lust, and horrors unknown to civilized nations.

Citizens of Louisiana! the general commanding in chief, rejoices to see the spirit that animates you, not only for your honour but for your safety; for whatever had been your conduct or wishes, his duty would have led, and will now lead him to confound the citizen unmindful of his rights, with the enemy he ceases to oppose. Now, leading men who know their rights, who are determined to defend them, he salutes you, brave Louisianians, as brethren in arms, and has now a new motive to exert all his faculties which shall be strained to the utmost in your defence. Continue with the energy you have begun, and he promises you not only safety, but victory over the insolent enemy who insulted you by an affected doubt of your attachment to the constitution of your country.

TO THE BATTALION OF UNIFORM COMPANIES.

When I first looked at you on the day of my arrival, I was satisfied with your appearance, and every day's inspection since has confirmed the opinion I then formed. Your numbers have increased with the increase of danger, and your ardour has augmented since it was known that your post would be one of peril and honour. This is the true love of country! You have added to it an exact discipline, and a skill in evolutions rarely attained by veterans; the state of your corps does equal honour to the skill of the officers and the attention of the men. With such defenders our country has nothing to fear. Every thing I have said to the body of militia, applies equally to you—you have made the same sacrifices—you have the same country to defend, the same motive for exertion—but I should have been unjust had I not noticed, as it deserved, the excellence of your discipline and the martial appearance of your corps.

TO THE MEN OF COLOUR.

SOLDIERS—From the shores of Mobile I collected you to arms—I invited you to share in the perils and to divide the glory of your white countrymen. I expected much from you, for I was not uninformed of those qualities which must render you so formidable to an invading foe—I knew that you could endure hunger and thirst and all the hardships of war—I knew that you loved the land of your nativity, and that, like ourselves, you had to defend all that is most dear to man—but you surpass my hopes. I have found in you, united to those qualities, that noble enthusiasm which impels to great deeds.

Soldiers—The president of the United States shall be informed of your conduct on the present occasion, and the voice of the representatives of the American nation shall applaud your valour, as your general now praises your ardour. The enemy is near; his "sails cover the lakes;" but the brave are united; and if he finds us contending among ourselves, it will be for the prize of valour and fame, its noblest reward.

(By command) THOMAS L. BUTLER, Aid-de-camp.

NO. XXI.

The following spirited order gives a sufficient account of the motives which induced general Jackson to resort to the measure of proclaiming martial law. At the same time that it served to convince the emissaries, whom the enemy might have sent among us, of the inutility of their mission, it convinced also the people of Louisiana, that the man who had come to take command of the forces, was decidedly determined to save the country, and to make use of all the means in his power to obtain that desirable end.

New Orleans, December 15, 1814.

TO THE CITIZENS OF NEW ORLEANS,

The major-general commanding, has, with astonishment and regret, learned that great consternation and alarm pervade your city. It is true the enemy is on our coast and threatens an invasion of our territory, but it is equally true, with union, energy, and the approbation of Heaven, we will beat him at every point his temerity may induce him to set foot upon our soil. The general, with still greater astonishment, has heard that British emissaries have been permitted to propagate seditious reports among you, that the threatened invasion is with a view of restoring the country to Spain, from a supposition that some of you would be willing to return to your ancient government. Believe not such incredible tales—your government is at peace with Spain—it is the vital enemy of your country, the common enemy of mankind, the highway robber of the world that threatens you, and has sent his hirelings amongst you with this false report, to put you off your guard, that you may fall an easy prey to him;—then look to your liberties, your property, the chastity of your wives and daughters—take a retrospect of the conduct of the British army at Hampton and other places, where it has entered our country, and every bosom which glows with patriotism and virtue, will be inspired with indignation, and pant for the arrival of the hour when we shall meet and revenge those outrages against the laws of civilization and humanity.

The general calls upon the inhabitants of the city to trace this unfounded report to its source, and bring the propagator to condign punishment. The rules and articles of war annex the punishment of death to any person holding secret correspondence with the enemy, creating false alarm, or supplying him with provision; and the general announces his unalterable determination rigidly to execute the martial law in all cases which may come within his province.

The safety of the district entrusted to the protection of the general, must and will be maintained with the best blood of the country; and he is confident all good citizens will be found at their posts, with their arms in their hands, determined to dispute every inch of ground with the enemy: that unanimity will pervade the country generally: but should the general be disappointed in this expectation, he will separate our enemies from our friends—those who are not for us are against us, and will be dealt with accordingly.

(By command) THOMAS L. BUTLER, *aid-de-camp,*

NO. XXI-a

Copy of a letter and enclosures from Thomas Shields and Robert Morrell to Daniel T. Patterson.

New Orleans, 14th Jan. 1815.

Master Commandant Daniel T. Patterson,

Sir,

In obedience to your orders of the 15th ult. we have the honor to report to you that we proceeded toward the British fleet under a "Flag of Truce" on the evening of the same day and at 2 P.M. on the 16th we boarded the late U.S. Gun Vessel No. 5 off the eastern mouth of the Pearl River, under British colours. In an interview with Capt. Gordon of the British frigate Sea Horse, the senior officer present, we explained our business; he proposed sending our flag down to the Commander in Chief who we then understood to be Sir Alex. Cochrane, as we were exceedingly anxious to perform immediately our mission and to learn the fate of our countrymen we urged our departure and were sent on board a tender under command of a Lieut. in the British Navy. On the morning of the 17th we met the admiral in his barge. When we presented our letter, together with the authority you had invested in us, your letter was read and returned to us without comment and the tender was ordered to her anchorage off the Pearl River. At 10 o'clock on the morning of the 18th the adm. sent for us on shore, when after asking our rank in the Navy of the U.S. he observed that our visit was an improper one, and ought not to have been made, that as we had been in the heart of his army then moving against N. Orleans he could not possibly think of permitting us to return until the battle was over & the fate of the town determined; he cited a similar case which he said occurred at Baltimore, and that motives of policy & prudence induced him to send us down to the fleet. We then asked him to say in what light he viewed us, as we insisted to know distinctly our character in his estimation. He replied he intended to respect the flag, although he might be justified in considering us prisoners of war.

One reason, sir, for asking the admiral this question are these, the evening before our boat was ordered astern of the tender, her tackle and apparel taken out, and a guard placed over her; the night being wet & excessively cold we were allowed to retain our sails to make an awning for the protection of our men from the weather, we believed also, from the precautioning measures of the admiral that we were regarded rather as spies than otherwise & that we were only watching an opportunity to escape. In no other way can we account for this mortifying and contemptuous treatment. On Monday 19th we were required to go on board his tender the Tender, the commander of whom was instructed to convey us to the Gorgon, Hospital ship, on board of which vessel we were informed the most of our wounded country men lay. On the same evening our boat owing to the negligence of the lieut. commandg. the tender, was towed under and lost with every thing in her. Doct. Barnwell with several of the wounded of gun vessel No. 156 came on board the tender from the Anaconda Brig of War, where he had been detained since the action on the 14th. On the evening of that day we anchored in Pass Marian and the next morning the Tender grounded on the shoal; some time after we observed our boat's crew at work and upon enquiry learned from them that they had been ordered by the Commg. officer, which he took the liberty of doing without our consent or knowledge, we immediately ordered them to desist with instructions to obey no person without our approbation.

This produced an explanation on the part of the commg. officer, who was much irritated, tho' we cannot say his language was indecent to us. We mention this trivial circumstance, sir, this minutely because Lieut. Johnston (the commander's name) refused to let our wounded have anything to eat when asked, altho' they had been on board the Tender 28 hours & had sent to us begging for food, which we had not to give them.

Doctr. Barnwell who had taken some bread for them out of the cabin without Lieut. Johnston's knowledge, was on asking his permission to give it to them, told by him "they had no bread to spare they wanted it themselves" it was consequently returned to the cabin where he got it & our men had to go without; on the same day our wounded were sent on board the Brig Sophia & the next day we followed them—the tender being still aground. On the 22nd she floated and we again joined her, the wounded having been sent to the hospital ship the day before, on the 23rd we got on board the Gorgon, where we were happy to find our loss in killed was not so severe as you apprehended. Lieut. Commg. Jones severely wounded in the left shoulder, Lieut. Spedden severely in both arms, his left was afterward amputated he is doing well. Mids. Reynolds in the thigh the bone badly fractured, some time after the boat struck, it is said unintentionally, since dead. We had five killed & between 25 and 30 wounded, three only have died since the action.

We remarked, Sir, that our wounded officers and men were treated with the same attention as their own. Were we to say any thing of our treatment *personally* we should simply state that we were generally received with politeness—but we cannot help believing that Admiral Cochrane in every instance shewed his jealousy of our character; on leaving kind he said we should be permitted to visit our countrymen, they being on board of different vessels. We applied to Capt. Bowden of the Gordon for a conveyance to another frigate for the above purpose, he replied by shewing us the Admiral's orders to him in which it is stated that "on no pretence whatever were we to be permitted to leave the Gordon until further orders!!!" We were consequently disappointed tho' Lieut. McKeever was permitted to visit us twice, the other officers having we believe been sent to the Line of Battle Ship laying outside Ship Island.

On the 20th we wrote the note No.1 to Capt. Bowden and same evening received his reply marked No.2. On the 28th we wrote the Note No. 3 and received for answer verbally that Sir Thos. Hardy would see us at 8 o'clock next morning on board the Hydra frigate. We stated to Capt. Hardy very concisely our situation; he expressed his opinion with us that the cause which produced our detention had ceased to exist; he seemed to intimate that it was possible or probable the admiral had forgotten us; he said he was going up to the admiral that morning, that he would mention the subject of our conversation and our expectation to him and that he had no doubt we should immediately be liberated. He returned from the Headquarters of the British Army three days afterward, but passed on to his ship without letting us hear from him, and as the admiral continued silent. We wrote to him on the 3rd the letter marked No. 4 and on the 11th inst. had the inexpressible pleasure to receive his answer No. 5 dated the 6th!!!—permitting our return. We left the fleet on the morning of the 12th and arrived at this place at midnight on the 18th. We would just observe that on our arrival at the Coquille Fort the wind being fair, Mr. Shields borrowed of Capt. Newman his sail boat for the sake of greater expedition leaving yr. Gig that had no sails until his return. Mr. Shield pledged himself personally to Capt. Newman to make good her value should any accident happen, or the boat lost. Capt. Newman estimates her at $300.

Very respectfully we have the honor to be Sir, yr. most obedt. servants

(Signed) Tho. Shields—purser
Robt. Morrell M.D.

No. 1

H. M. Ship Gorgon, 26 December 1814

Capt. Bowden,

The undersigned having visited the adm. Sir Alexr. Cochrane, commander of his Majesties naval force on the Bermuda Station under the sacred character of a "Flag of Truce," which they hoped and believed would have been respected & conceiving themselves to be treated with more rigour than is usually exercised toward "*prisoners of war*" being confined to this ship solely without permission to visit any other, wish to ask of Capt. Bowden if in his power to grant (and if not, his interest or influence to obtain it) permission for the following officers late in the service of the U. States to visit this ship.

Lieut. Isaac McKeever com.ing No. 23
Sail.g Master Jon. an D. Ferris No. 5
ditto. George Ulrick No. 163

Doctor Barnewell & Doctor Marshall, Surgeons, the latter of whom came down under a flag of truce on the 15th inst. & has not since been heard of.

Adm. Cochrane assured the undersigned that so soon as the fate of the Battle pending between his forces and that of the U. States was determined, liberty free and unrestrain'd should be granted the flag to return.

The undersigned presume the Adm. would not have thought of a siege as a few days only was mentioned as necessary to decide the contest.

Should the request of the undersigned be inadmissible in the opinion of Capt. B., we only ask in the event of our being "*contrary to law*" considered as prisoners of war, Capt. B. to the admiral that we are without stores of clothing of any kind—calculating on not being from home more than a week & let us add we hope this state of suspence will be terminated as soon as possible.

We have the honor to be yr obedt Servnt

Signed Ths. Shields
U.S.N.
Robt. Morrell

No. 2

To. Mess. Shields & Morrell,
U. States Navy.

H.M. Ship Gorgon, 26th December 1814.

Gentlemen,

I have received your note of this day requiring more than I have power to grant, but I shall forward to the senior officer your wishes for my guidance. I cannot help remarking that the conclusion of your note is not fairly stated. I examined carefully the lieut. commg. the admiral's tender and by his evidence it appeared to me impossible to save your boat.

I remain gentlemen your most obt. servt.
(signed) B. Bowden

No. 3

To Captain Bowden, His B.M. Ship Gorgon.
28th December 1814.

Having understood that Sir Thos. Hardy is the senior commanding officer present, the undersigned bearer of a flag of truce, will feel themselves obliged in being permitted to have half an hour conversation with him tomorrow, at such time and place as may be most convenient to him.

(Signed) Ths. Shields &
Robt. Morrell

No. 4

His M. Ship Gorgon on 3rd January 1815.

To the Vice Adm. Sir A. Cochrane,

The undersigned bearer of the Flag of Truce from N. Orleans, who visited your fleet for a specific and clearly expressed object in the full belief it saved character—would be respected by you as it is by every other civil power in Christendom and who consequently approach you with perfect confidence address you in the present instance for the purpose of remonstrating and solemnly protesting against this, their unwarrantable and outrageous detention.

To be distinctly considered a prisoner of war & *openly* not *covertly* treated as such would be regarded by the undersigned as honorable in Adm. Cochrane when compared to the mode of conduct adopted & pursued toward them. They left New Orleans on the 13th ulto not expecting to be absent more than a week. Consequently they brought but a change or two of linen with them, their boat's crew had but the cloths on their backs, one of them has already perished and the others suffer much.

The surgeon, one of the officers under the flag whose health has been much impaired for a length of time is now seriously indisposed.

Individual oppression when no public good can possibly result, the undersigned did think would not have been inflicted or even tolerated by a man of Sir Alex. Cochrane's high standing in society; and they have only to lament that in their persons without cause, it is so pertaneciously adhered to & persevered in. They communicated with Sir Th. Hardy of H.M. Ship Ramilles on the 29 ulto. who pledged himself to represent their situation to you, he has however returned from your neighbourhood and has given us no satisfaction or information whatever.

The undersigned cannot help expressing their belief that the cause of their detention as state by you, must long since have ceased to exist, tis the case with all the armies more or less, to experience desertion, and no doubt something of this kind has occured in yours and men of this class are surely better able to give intelligence than a flag of truce possibly could be who have no intercourse except among your own officers and who would not divulge any thing that might prove disadvantageous to themselves. They have therefore only to request of Sir A. Cochrane, if he intends to respect the Flag a he said he would do, to order their immediate release. They further deemed necessary to state that their boat with every thing in her was towed under and lost through the negligence of the Lieut. commanding the tender on their way down to the fleet, & they hope some kind of boat will be furnished them to return in.

In expecting of an answer as soon as it may be convenient to the admiral,

We have the honor to be very respectfully His obedient servants

---

No. 5

Headquarters of the British force, near, N. Orleans, 6th January 1815.

Gentlemen,

I have received a letter of the 3rd inst. and I am concerned to find that you should consider your detention as a harsh measure. You must be aware that it cannot be personal.

The nature of your mission requiring your visiting the hospital ship, and it happening upon your arrival the forces were moving against N. Orleans, it would not have been prudent, or consistent with the Rule of War, to have permitted your immediate return. I trust however that you have individually been made as comfortable as circumstances would admit of and that you have found the wounded prisoners receiving the same treatment as our own People. Directions have been sent to the fleet for your being conveyed with a Flag of Truce to Coquille and I have acquainted Commodore Patteson of the accidental loss of your boat and requested I may be permitted to make good her value.

I am gentleman yr, obt. servant

Messr. Shields and Morell
on board the Gorgon

(Signed) Alex. Cochrane
Vice Adm. and Commander
in chief of the Naval forces

Copy of a letter from Daniel T. Patterson to Alexander Cochrane, with Cochrane's remarks.
Copy

Sir,

I have delayed until the return of the officers sent with my Flag to reply to that part of your letter which I had the honor to receive from you under date of the 8th inst. informing me that my Flag of Truce—sent for the purpose of obtaining my wounded officers and seamen met you with British forces while on your passage up the Bay and that prudential reason did not admit of its immediate return. Policy, Sir, may excuse the detention of my flag even in violation of the law of war but I know not how you can justify the want of respect which it, my letter, and officers experienced from you personally and thro' many of your officers. It would also have been more noble, more consistent with the character of magnanimity with which the British Nation wish to impress foreign nations for you to have sent a boat to meet my Flag at a distance from your force to say they could not be received, or if they were, they must be detained, prudence certainly would not have forbid a measure so much more honourable than that which was pursued, was it worthy an officer of your standing and command first to take my officers into the heart of your army, an act of compulsion, not of choice, then to use as a pretext for their detention their being there.

The measure pursued towards my officers from the time my Flag first met you till their departure from your fleet was infinitely more rigourous than was shewed towards your prisoners of war, the former were confined to one single vessel, the latter permitted to pass from one to another, for such disregard of the Sacred Character in which a Flag of Truce is considered by all civilized nations, there can be no palliation.

[Cochrane's comments:] I know of no perceived insult offered to these officers. The situation in which I was myself placed, bivouacking on swampy ground in a rainy night, would not allow of my shewing them any particular attention further than that of offering them any supplies they wanted, which was done.

They occupied the cabin of the vessel I had intended for myself and slept dry while I was drenching with rain.

The flag of truce was met by me between the advanced position of our army at the entrance of the Pearl River and Bay St. Louis. It was necessary I should confer with the officers who sent it on before determining whether to admit the Flag to proceed, these officers accordingly went back with me to the advance, and from thence were forwarded to the Hospital ship by the earliest opportunity that offered. They would not have fulfilled the declared object of the Flag without passing through our army and fleet, it cannot be supposed therefore, that advancing to the attack of N. Orleans we could admit of their immediate return.

The wounded prisoners being in the hospital ship, I know not of any occasion for their visiting other ships; nor am I aware that any prisoner went from our ship to another excepting for a change of residence, until my return to the fleet.

The humane purposes which had brought Mess. Shields and Morrell to the squadron, seemed to have escaped them the moment they were met by my boat, for instead of being desirous of being sent on to where they could see the wounded and administer to their comfort, the service upon which it is stated they were employed; they had no sooner delivered Capt. Patterson's letter than their job attention appeared to be directed to then return to N. Orleans and I must confess that their manner created a general suspicion of what their subsequent conduct has fully verified.

Since these officers were permitted to return they have thrown aside their non-combattant character, and have returned at the head of a predatory expedition to take advantage of the information which our regard to the wounded suffered them to obtain, by their passing under a flag of truce thru the ground our vessels occupied.

I have now to regret that I placed so much reliance upon their honor and the character they had approached us under, as to allow them to return until the operations had ceased in that quarter.

I have questioned Lt. Johnson on this subject and he acquaints me that having brought up troops unexpectedly his bread & other provisions were entirely out, excepting two or three pounds of bread, which he had reserved in his cabin, & divided equally with the officers of the Flag of Truce, and others who were on board, this statement is corroborated by another officer who was on board, as well as the American officer expressing themselves satisfied upon their leaving the vessel at the treatment they had experienced on board.

I have certainly no reason to doubt Mr Johnson's account, as he is an officer on whom I have at all time place much dependence.

Vice Admiral Sir Alexander Cochrane
Comdg. H.B.M. Forces in North America
and Jamaica Stations

New Orleans 23rd January 1815

Motives of humanity and a reliance upon the honor and magnanimity which I had been led to believed I should find in a British officer, induced me alone to send a flag, the result has proven to me how very fallacious were those impressions I had received.

You inform me of the loss of the boat which bore my Flag of truce and offer renumeration. This, sir, I cannot receive, altho' from the statement of my officers I feel convinced it occurred from the willful neglect of Lieut. Johnson, the commander of your tender the same who refused with savage sternness when earnestly solicited by my surgeon a mouth full of bread for my wounded men who had then fasted twenty eight hours (and emplored my officers to give them food but on which they had not to give) and whose reply was that he wanted it himself and had no "Bread to Spare" the treatment they recd. after their arrival on board the Gorgon Hospital ship I am satisfied with it was as you correctly informed me such as was paid to your own and I could expect no more, for this, sir, I beg you to receive my thanks, but when you received your wounded ask them if by the inhumanity of any subaltern officer any petty tyrant they were kept twenty eight hours without food, and when they implored it were refused a little bread, I should blush sir, with shame for the American character could any of your prisoners wounded or in health with truth so assert.

I am willing to believe that your discontenance such inhuman unmanly conduct in any officer under your command and that you only require it to be made known to you to notice it in the manner it deserves.

Very Respectfully
Sir,
I have the honor to be your most obt. servt.
Sig. Daniel T. Patterson Comd the U.S.
Naval forces , New Orleans Station

NO. XXII

AN ACT.

To grant a delay in the cases therein mentioned.

WHEREAS the present crisis will oblige a great number of citizens to take up arms in defence of this state, and compel them to quit their homes, and thus leave their private affairs in a state of abandonment, which may expose them to great distress, if the legislature should not, by measures adapted to the circumstances, come to their relief,

Sec. 1. *Be it enacted by the senate and house of representatives of the state of Louisiana in general assembly convened,* That no protest on any note or bill of exchange, payable to order or bearer, or on any note, bill of exchange, or obligation for the payment of money, shall or can be legally made, until one hundred and twenty days after the promulgation of the present act.

Sec. 2. *And be it further enacted,* That no property, either moveable or immoveable, belonging to successions or bankrupts, or any property seized by virtue of any execution issued by the courts of justice, or justices of the peace of this state, shall be sold within one hundred and twenty days after the promulgation of the present act; *Provided however,* that the delay aforesaid shall not prejudice the holders or proprietors of the said notes, bills; obligations, or judgments, from demanding the interests which they would or might have legally demanded, if the said delay did not exist.

Sec. 3. *And be it further enacted,* That from and after the promulgation of this act, no civil suit or action shall be commenced or prosecuted before any court of record or other tribunal of this state, nor shall any execution issue or be proceeded upon; and all proceedings in civil suits or actions, now pending before any such court or tribunal, shall henceforth cease and be suspended during the time this act shall remain in force.

Sec. 4. *And be it further enacted,* That no state of lands or slaves which may be passed during the time this act remains in force, shall have any effect to the prejudice of the rights of the creditor or creditors, of the persons making such sale. *Provided however,* that such creditor or creditors who may have no existing lien on such property, shall, before the first day of June next, make known to the person possessing the same, the claim or demand he or they may have against the person who shall have sold the same.

Sec. 5. *And be it further enacted,* That for the purpose of preserving the securities of creditors under the said suspension of judicial proceedings, the several judges and justices of the peace of this state, having original jurisdiction, shall have the power of granting writs of sequestration, in case any debtor or debtors, during such suspension, shall remove or attempt to remove their personal estate and slaves; or either of them without the jurisdiction of the courts; which may be detained under sequestration on petition filed by the creditor, the allegations contained in which petition shall be supported by the oath of the petitioner, his agent or attorney, *Provided however*, that the debtor may replevy his estate so sequestered, on giving bond and security for the payment of any judgment against him, or any debt to be liquidated by judgment or otherwise by the debtor and creditor.

Sec. 6. *And be it further enacted*, That this act, within the parish of Orleans, shall be considered as being legally promulgated, on the day it shall have been approved by the governor, and within the other parishes of this state, on the day of its promulgation, agreeably to the now existing laws. This act shall continue and be in force until the first day of May next and no longer.

MAGLOIRE GUICHARD,
Speaker of the house of representatives
FULWAR SKIPWITH, *President of the Senate.*

Approved December 18, 1814.

WILLIAM C. CLAIBORNE.
Governor of the state of Louisiana.

NO. XXIII–XXIV.

Letter from commodore Patterson to the hon. Secretary at War,

U.S. ship Louisiana, December 28, 1814.

Sir,

I have the honour to inform you that on the 23d instant, while at the bayou St. John; examining the batteries erecting there by the navy, under the superintendence of captain Henley of the Carolina, I learnt that information had been received by general Jackson that the enemy had penetrated through bayou Bienvenu with a large force, and had effected a landing at general Villere's plantation on the banks of the Mississippi, which upon application to the general proved to be true. The alarm was immediately given in town, and the troops put in motion; I repaired on board the United States' schooner Carolina, with captain Henley, and after ordering the Louisiana, commanded by lieutenant-commandant C.B. Thompson, to follow me, at 4 P.M. weighed, and it being calm, dropped down with the current; at about half past six I received a request from general Jackson, through Mr. Edward Livingston, his aid-de-camp, to anchor abreast of the enemy's camp, which he pointed out, and open a fire upon them. It continuing calm, got out sweeps, and a few minutes after, having been frequently hailed by the enemys' sentinels, anchored, veered out a long scope of cable, sheered close in shore abreast of their camp, and commenced a heavy (and as I have since learned most destructive) fire from our starboard batter, and small arms, which was returned most spiritedly by the enemy with congreve rockets and musketry from their whole force, when after about forty minutes of most incessant fire, the enemy was silenced; the fire from our battery was continued till nine o'clock upon the enemy's flank while engaged in the field with our army, at which hour ceased firing, supposing from the distance of the enemy's fire (for it was too dark to see any thing on shore) that they had retreated beyond the range of our guns—weighed and swept across the river, in hopes of a breeze the next morning to enable me to renew the attack upon the enemy, should they be returned to their encampment; but was disappointed on the 24th by a light air from north-northwest, which towards the evening, hauled toward northwest, and blew a heavy gale, compelling me to remain during the 24th, 25th, and 26th at anchor in a position abreast of the enemy, although every possible exertion was made by captain Henley to warp the schooner up, without success, from the extreme rapidity of the current occasioned by the very uncommon rise of the river. On the afternoon of the 26th, at the request of general Jackson, I visited him at his head-quarters, and went from thence to town to equip and arm with two thirty-two-pounders, such merchant vessels in port, as I might find capable of supporting them. During the 24th, 25th, and 26th, fired at the enemy whenever they could be seen. Owing to the calmness of the night of the 23d, the Louisiana could not join me till the morning of the 24th, when she fortunately anchored about one mile above the Carolina. By the fire from the enemy on the night of the 23d, one man only was wounded, and very little injury done to the hull, sails, and rigging; in her bulwarks were a great number of musket balls, several in her masts and topmasts, and through her mainsail. Nothing could exceed the incessant fire from the Carolina, which alone can be attributed to the high state of discipline to which captain Henley has brought her crew. Of him, lieutenants Norris and Crawley, and sailing-master Haller, I cannot speak in too high terms; the petty officers and crew behaved with that cool determined courage and zeal which has so strongly characterized the American tars in the present war.

I have the honour to be, &c.
D.T. PATTERSON.

NO. XXV.

Copy of a letter from general Andrew Jackson to the secretary of war

dated Camp near New Orleans, 26th December, 1814.

THE enemy having, by the capture of our gun-boats, obtained command of the lakes, were enabled to erect a passage to the Mississippi at a point on the side of New Orleans, and about nine miles below it. The moment I received the intelligence, I hastened to attack him in his first position. It was brought on in the night and resulted very honourably to our arms. The heavy smoke, occasioned by an excessive fire, rendered it necessary that I should draw off my troops, after a severe conflict of upwards of an hour.

The attack was made on the night of the 23d. Since then both armies have remained near the battle-ground, making preparations for something more decisive.

The enemy's force exceeded ours by double, and their loss was proportionately greater. The moment I can spare the time, I will forward you a detailed account. In the meantime I expect something far more important will take place. I hope to be able to sustain the honour of our arms and to secure the safety of this country.

I have the honour to be, &c.
ANDREW JACKSON

Major-general Jackson to the secretary of war.

Head-quarters, 7th military district, camp below New Orleans, 27th December, A.M.

Sir,

The loss of our gun-boats near the pass of the Rigolets, having given the enemy command of lake Borgne, he was enabled to choose his point of attack. It became therefore an object of importance to obstruct the numerous bayous and canals leading from that lake to the highlands on the Mississippi. This important service was committed, in the first instance, to a detachment from the 7th regiment, afterwards to colonel Delaronde of the Louisiana militia, and lastly, to make all sure, to major-general Villeré, commanding the district between the river and the lakes, and who, being a native of the country, was presumed to be best acquainted with all those passes. Unfortunately, however, a picquet which the general had established at the mouth of the bayou Bienvenu, and which, notwithstanding my orders, had been left unobstructed, was completely surprised, and the enemy penetrated through a canal leading to his farm about two leagues below the city, and succeeded in cutting off a company of militia stationed there. The intelligence was communicated to me about 2 o'clock of the 23d. My force, at this time, consisted of parts of the 7th and 44th regiments, not exceeding six hundred together, the city militia, a part of general Coffee's brigade of mounted gun-men, and the detached militia from the western division of Tennessee, under the command of major-general Carrol—these two last corps were stationed four miles above the city. Apprehending a double attack by the way of Chef-Menteur, I left general Carroll's force, and the militia of the city, posted on the Gentilly road; and at 5 o'clock P.M. marched to meet the enemy, whom I was resolved to attack in his first position, with major Hind's dragoons, general Coffee's brigade, parts of the 7th and 44th regiments, the uniform companies of militia under the command of major Plauche, two hundred men of colour (chiefly from St. Domingo) raised by colonel Savary and acting under the command of major Daquin, and a detachment of artillery under the direction of colonel M'Rea, with two six-pounders under the command of lieut. Spots—not exceeding in all fifteen hundred. I arrived near the enemy's encampment about 7, and immediately made my dispositions for the attack. His forces amounting at that time on land to about three thousand, extended half a mile on the river, and in the rear nearly to the wood. General Coffee was ordered to turn their right, while, with the residue of the force, I attacked his strongest position on the left, near the river. Commodore Patterson having dropped down the river in the schooner Carolina, was directed to open a fire upon their camp, which he executed at about half after 7. This being the signal of attack, general Coffee's men, with their usual impetuosity, rushed on the enemy's right, and entered their camp, while our right advanced with equal ardour. There can be but little doubt that we should have succeeded on that occasion, with our inferior force, in destroying or capturing the enemy, had not a thick fog, which arose about 8 o'clock, occasioned some confusion among the different corps. Fearing the consequences, under this circumstance, of the further prosecution of a night attack with troops then acting together for the first time, I contented myself with lying on the field that night; and at 4 in the morning assumed a stronger position about two miles nearer to the city. At this position I remain encamped, waiting the arrival of the Kentucky militia and other re-enforcements. As the safety of the city will depend on the fate of this army, it must not be incautiously exposed.

In this affair the whole corps under my command deserve the greatest credit. The best compliment I can pay to general Coffee and his brigade, is to say they behaved as they have always done while under my command. The 7th, led by major Peire, and the 44th, commanded by colonel Ross, distinguished themselves. The battalion of city militia, commanded by major Plauche, realized my anticipations, and behaved like veterans—Savary's volunteers manifested great bravery—and the company of city riflemen, having penetrated into the midst of the enemy's camp, were surrounded, and fought their way out with the greatest heroism, bringing with them a number of prisoners. The two field pieces were well served by the officer commanding them.

All my officers in the line did their duty, and I have every reason to be satisfied with the whole of my field and staff.—Colonels Butler and Piatt, and major Chotard, by their intrepidity, saved the artillery. Colonel Haynes was every where that duty or danger called. I was deprived of the services of one of my aids, captain Butler, whom I was obliged to station, to his great regret in town. Captain Reid, my other aid, and Messrs. Livingston, Duplessis and Davezac, who had volunteered their services, faced danger wherever it was to be met, and carried my orders with the utmost promptitude.

We made one major, two subalterns, and sixty-three privates prisoners; and the enemy's loss in killed and wounded must have been at least—. My own loss I have not as yet been able to ascertain with exactness, but suppose it to amount to one hundred in killed, wounded and missing. Among the former I have to lament the loss of colonel Lauderdale of general Coffee's brigade, who fell while bravely fighting. Colonels Dyer and Gibson, of the same corps, were wounded, and major Kavenaugh taken prisoner.

Colonel Delaronde, major Villeré of the Louisiana militia, major Latour of engineers, having no command, volunteered their services, as did Drs. Kerr and Flood, and were of great assistance to me.

I have the honour to be, &c.
ANDREW JACKSON.

NO. XXVI–XXVII.

Copy of a letter from captain Henley, commanding late United States' schooner Carolina, to commodore Patterson,

dated New Orleans, December 28, 1814.

Sir,

I have the honour to inform you, that after you left here on the 26th instant, in pursuance to your order, every possible exertion was made to move the schooner Carolina higher up the river and near general Jackson's camp, without success; the wind being at N.N.W. and blowing fresh and too scant to get under way, and the current too rapid to move her by warping, which I had endeavoured to do with my crew.

At daylight, on the morning of the 27th, the enemy opened upon the Carolina a battery of five guns, from which they threw shells and hot shot; returned their fire with the long twelve-pounder, the only gun on board which could reach across the river, the remainder of her battery being light twelve-pound carronades.

The air being light and at north, rendered it impossible to get under way; the second shot fired by the enemy lodged in the schooner's main-hold under her cables, and in such a situation as not to be come at, and fired her, which rapidly progressed; finding that hot shot were passing through her cabin and filling room, which contained a considerable quantity of powder; her bulwarks all knocked down by the enemy's shot, the vessel in a sinking situation, and the fire increasing, and expecting every moment that she would blow up, at a little after sunrise I reluctantly gave orders for the crew to abandon her, which was effected, with the loss of one killed and six wounded; a short time after I had succeeded in getting the crew on shore, I had the extreme mortification of seeing her blow up.

It affords me great pleasure to acknowledge the able assistance I received from lieutenants Norris and Crawley, and sailing-master Haller, and to say that my officers and crew behaved on this occasion, as well as on the 23d when under your own eye, in most gallant manner.

Almost every article of clothing belonging to the officers and crew, from the rapid progress of the fire, was involved in the destruction of the vessel.

I have the honour to be, &c.

(Signed) JOHN D. HENLEY.

P.S. I have not made out a detailed account of the action on the night of the 23d, as you were on board during the whole action.

Letter from major-general Jackson, to the secretary of war, dated

Head-quarters, seventh military district, Camp below New Orleans, December 29, 1814.

Sir,

The enemy succeeded on the 27th in blowing up the Carolina (she being becalmed) by means of hot shot from a land battery which he had erected in the night.

Emboldened by this event, he marched his whole force the next day up the levee, in the hope of driving us from our position, and with this view, opened upon us, at the distance of about half mile, his bombs and rockets. He was repulsed, however, with considerable loss; not less, it is believed, than one hundred and twenty in killed. Ours was inconsiderable; not exceeding half a dozen killed and a dozen wounded.

Since then he has not ventured to repeat his attempt, though lying close together. There has been frequent skirmishing between our picquets.

I lament that I have not the means of carrying on more offensive operations. The Kentucky troops have not arrived, and my effective force at this point, does not exceed three thousand. Theirs must be at least double; both prisoners and deserters agreeing in the statement that seven thousand landed from their boats.

ANDREW JACKSON.

Copy of a letter from commodore Patterson, commanding our naval force on the Orleans station, to the secretary of the navy, dated

U.S. ship Louisiana, 4 miles below New Orleans,
29th December, 1814.

Sir,

I have the honour to inform you, that on the morning of the 28th instant, at about half past seven, perceived our advanced-guard retreating towards our lines—the enemy pursuing; fired shot, shells, and rockets, from field artillery, with which they advanced on the road behind the levee; sprung the ship to bring the starboard gun to bear upon the enemy; at 25 minutes past 8 A.M. the enemy opened their fire upon the ship, with shells, hot shot, and rockets, which was instantly returned with great spirit and much apparent effect, and continued without intermission till one P. M. when the enemy slackened their fire, and retreated with a part of their artillery from each of their batteries, evidently with great loss. Two attempts were made to screen one heavy piece of ordnance mounted behind the levee, with which they threw hot shot at the ship, and which had been a long time abandoned before they succeeded in recovering it, and then it must have been with very great loss, as I distinctly saw, with the aid of my glass, several shot strike in the midst of the men (seamen) who were employed dragging it away. At 3 P.M. the enemy were silenced; at 4 P.M. ceased firing from the ship, the enemy having retired beyond the range of her guns. Many of their shot passed over the ship, and their shells burst over her decks, which were strewed with their fragments; yet, after an incessant cannonading of upwards of seven hours; during which time eight hundred shot were fired from the ship, one man only was wounded slightly, by the piece of a shell, and one shot passed between the bowsprit and heel of the jib-boom.

The enemy drew up his whole force, evidently with an intention of assaulting general Jackson's lines, under cover of his heavy cannon; but his cannonading being so warmly returned from the lines and ship Louisiana, caused him, I presume, to abandon his project, as he retired without making the attempt. You will have learned by my former letters, that the crew of the Louisiana is composed of men of all nations, (English excepted) taken from the streets of New Orleans not a fortnight before the battle; yet I never knew guns better served, or a more animated fire, than was supported from her.

Lieutenant C.C.B. Thompson deserves great credit for the discipline to which in so short a time he had brought such men, two-thirds of whom do not understand English.

General Jackson having applied for officers and seamen to work the heavy cannon on his lines furnished by me, lieutenants Norris and Crawley, of the late schooner Carolina, instantly volunteered, and with the greater part of her crew were sent to those cannon, which they served during the action herein detailed. The enemy must have suffered a great loss in that day's action, by the heavy fire from this ship and general Jackson's lines, where the cannon was of heavy calibre, and served with great spirit.

I have the honour to be, with great consideration and respect, your obedient servant,

DANIEL T. PATTERSON.

NO. XXVIII.

Letter from commodore Patterson to the secretary of the navy.

Marine Batteries, 5 miles below New Orleans, January 2, 1815,

Sir,

Finding the advantageous effect which resulted from the flanking-fire upon the enemy from the Louisiana, as detailed in my letter of the 29th ultimo, I that night had brought down from the navy yard, and mounted in silence, a twenty-four pounder on shore, in a position where it could most annoy the enemy when throwing up works on the levee or in the field. On the 30th opened upon the enemy with the twenty-four pounder, which drove them from their works, the ship firing at the same time upon their advance, which retired from the levee and sheltered itself behind houses, &c. The great effect produced by the gun on shore, induced me on the 31st to land from the Louisiana two twelve-pounders, which I mounted behind the levee in the most advantageous position, to harass the flank of the enemy in his approaches to our lines, and to aid our right. At four A.M. the enemy opened a fire upon the left of our line with artillery and musketry, which was returned most spiritly with artillery and musketry. At two P.M. the enemy having retired, the firing ceased.

On the first instant, at ten A.M. after a very thick fog, the enemy commenced a heavy cannonading upon general Jackson's lines and my battery, from batteries they had thrown up during the preceding night on the levee; which was returned from our lines and my battery, and terminated, after a most incessant fire from both parties of nearly five hours, in the enemy being silenced and driven from their works; many of their shells went immediately over my battery, and their shot passed through my breast-work and embrazures, without injuring a man. On this, as on the 28th, I am happy to say, that my officers and men behaved to my entire satisfaction; but I beg leave particularly to name acting lieutenant Campbell, acting sailing-master John Gates, acting midshipman Philip Philibert, of the Louisiana, and sailing-master Haller, of the late schooner Carolina. I did not drop the Louisiana down within the range of their shot, having learnt from deserters that a furnace of shot was kept in constant readiness at each of their batteries to burn her; and the guns being of much greater effect on shore, her men were drawn to man them, and I was particularly desirous to preserve her from the hot shot, as I deemed her of incalculable service to cover the army in the event of general Jackson retiring from his present line to those which he had thrown up in his rear.

I have the honour to be, &c.
DANIEL T. PATTERSON.

NO. XXVIII-a.

Copy of a letter from the secretary of war of general Jackson.

Department of War,
December 10, 1814.

Major General Andrew Jackson,
Sir,

Intelligence was received yesterday from Cuba of the 9th ultimo, that the British force from this Bay under Admiral Cochrane, had united at Jamaica with other troops, and had sailed or were on the point of sailing to make an attack on New Orleans. It is hoped that you will have long since taken a suitable position on the river to afford complete protection to that city. Mobile is comparatively a trifling object with the British Government. Your presence at such a point, on the river, with the main body of your troops, will be of vital importance. It will inspire the inhabitants with confidence, and animate them to vigorous exertions. It will enable you to direct your whole force to the proper points, and to make the necessary preparations to meet the enemy on either pass, and to overwhelm him wherever he presents himself. All the boasted preparations which the British Government has been making through the year, with veteran troops from France & Spain; after having been gloriously foiled in attacks on other parts of our union, is about to terminate in a single blow against New Orleans. It will, I hope, close there, its inglorious career in such a repulse as will reflect new honor on the American army.

I have already written to you by Major Fannin, a copy of which letter is enclosed in this, which is committed to Doctor Cozins. I shall also send copies of x x x x x x x x x x x x x x x x x x x x x x by the route of Tennessee.

I have the honor to be
JAMES MONROE.

Copy of a letter from the secretary of war to the governor of Georgia.

Department of War,
December 10, 1814.

His Excellency The Governor of Georgia,

Sir,

By intelligence lately received it is rendered highly probable that the contemplated expedition of our enemy at New Orleans, of which I had the honor to advise your Excellency in my letter of the 10th of October, is on the point of sailing, if it has not sailed already to its place of destination. It would be gratifying to me to learn that the troops lately required from your state to reinforce General Jackson are well on their way and that your Excellency would adopt such measures as might hasten their march.

I have the honor to be
JAMES MONROE.

NO. XXVIII-b.

Copy of a letter from the secretary of war to the governor of Kentucky.

January 30, 1815.

His Excellency
The Governor of Kentucky,

Sir,

The result of the conflict which is so gallantly sustained by our troops at New Orleans, under the command of Major General Jackson, is still doubtful. The enemy seems to have directed their whole disposable force there, in the hopes of getting possession of that city, and the command of the Mississippi, that important outlet to all the productivity of the Western country. I trust that the justice of our cause indeed by the bravery of our troops, under the favor of a gracious Providence, will finally prevail over these invaders, and completely overwhelm them.

As the result, is however, uncertain, and the enemy may receive reinforcements, we ought not to be less attentive to the succour of our brave countrymen, who have so nobly submitted to every degree of privation and encountered every danger. An army must be formed and sent to their aid, without delay. If our troops should be repulsed, which we cannot believe, this army will unite with their brethren, renew the attack, and repel the intruders. If the contest should still be undecided, this reinforcement will turn the scale. The President requests that you will immediately detach 4,000 of the militia of your state for this service, preferring volunteers if they can be obtained, and hasten them down the river, with the greatest dispatch possible. Arrangements will be made by this department for their transportation, of which you shall be advised. Every thing will be in readiness to take the troops down by the time they are collected. Let every man bring his rifle or musket with him. 150,000$ in Treasury notes will be remitted to you to pay for the expenses of transportation already incurred for the troops, now at New Orleans, and for the contingent expenses of those now required, which you are hereby authorized to distribute to such agents of the Government as may be employed in paying, subsisting, transporting, and providing forage for the troops. Enclosed you will receive a copy of a letter from the Secretary of the Treasury to me, of this date, giving assurance that the Treasury notes will be soon forwarded on the authority of which, I trust that your Excellency will be enabled to obtain of the Banks, without difficulty, on loan, by anticipation, any sum that will be necessary for those purposes.

It may be gratifying to your Excellency to know, that a strong force is also ordered from Tennessee, for this service.

I need not observe that should you understand that the enemy have been vanquished and either made prisoners or driven out, that the march of these troops will be suspended. Let not this expectation, however, prevent their collection as soon as prepared for it.

I have the honor to be
JAMES MONROE.

Copy of a letter from the secretary of war to the governor of Tennessee.

Department of War
January 30, 1815.

His Excellency
The Governor of Tennessee,
Sir,

In calling on the freemen of Kentucky and Tennessee to repair to New Orleans in defense of their rights. I did not appeal to a base and sordid spirit. I know that the call was made on gallant men, who would submit to every privation, and encounter every danger in support of the great cause in which we are engaged.

The result of the conflict is still uncertain. Our brave countrymen are contending against superior numbers, aided by vessels which give them the command of the river and lakes. There is cause also to apprehend that the enemy will soon be reinforced. The highest interests of the nation require that succour be sent to General Jackson without delay. The President, therefore, requests that you will immediately detach 2,500 men. Volunteers, if to be obtained, and hasten them down to New Orleans. I shall remit to you in a few days 150,000 dollars in Treasury notes to meet the expenses of this service. You will distribute among the agents of the government employed in providing transportation, subsistence and forage, and in the payment of the troops, as much of this money as circumstances my require. I enclose you a copy of a letter from the Secretary of the Treasury to me, giving assurances that these notes shall be forwarded immediately, on which your Excellency may obtain by loan from the banks, in anticipation, any sum that may be necessary for these purposes.

Let the men take their rifles & muskets with them as it is doubtful whether a full supply of arms can be furnished in time, tho' every effort will be made for that purpose.

Should your Excellency receive satisfactory intelligence that our troops have been victorious, and have either made prisoners of the enemy or expelled them from the country, you will suspend the march of this detachment until further orders; but let not the probability of this result, however great, prevent their collection or march as soon as collected.

It will be satisfactory to your Excellency to know that a strong force is also ordered from Kentucky for this service.

I have the honor to be
JAMES MONROE.

NO. XXIX.

Copy of a letter from major-general Jackson to the secretary of war dated

Camp, four miles below Orleans, 9th January, 1815.

Sir,

During the days of the 6th and 7th, the enemy had been actively employed in making preparations for an attack on my lines. With infinite labour they had succeeded on the night of the 7th in getting their boats across from the lake to the river, by widening and deepening the canal on which they had effected their disembarkation. It had not been in my power to impede these operations by a general attack—added to other reasons, the nature of the troops under my command, mostly militia; rendered it too hazardous to attempt extensive offensive movements in an open country, against a numerous and well-disciplined army. Although my forces, as to number, had been increased by the arrival of the Kentucky division, my strength had received very little addition; a small portion only of that detachment being provided with arms. Compelled thus to wait the attack of the enemy, I took every measure to repel it when it should be made, and to defeat the object he had in view. General Morgan with the Orleans contingent, the Louisiana militia, and a strong detachment of the Kentucky troops, occupied an intrenched camp on the opposite side of the river, protected by strong batteries on the bank, erected and superintended by commodore Patterson.

In *my* encampment every thing was ready for action, early on the morning of the 8th the enemy, after throwing a shower of bombs and congreve rockets, advanced their columns on my right and left, to storm my intrenchments. I cannot speak sufficiently in praise of the firmness and deliberation with which my whole line received their approach. MORE could not have been expected from veterans inured to war.—For an hour the fire of the small arms was as incessant and severe as can be imagined. The artillery, too, directed by officers who displayed equal skill and courage, did great execution. Yet the columns of the enemy continued to advance with a firmness which reflects upon them the greatest credit. Twice the column which approached me on my left, was repulsed by the troops of general Carroll, those of general Coffee and a division of the Kentucky militia, and twice they formed again and renewed the assault. At length, however, cut to pieces, they fled in confusion from the field, leaving it covered with their dead and wounded. The loss which the enemy sustained on this occasion, cannot be estimated at less than fifteen hundred in killed, wounded, and prisoners. Upwards of three hundred have already been delivered over for burial; and my men are still engaged in picking them up within my lines, and carrying them to the point where the enemy are to receive them. This is in addition to the dead and wounded whom the enemy have been enabled to carry from the field during and since the action, and to those who have since died of the wounds they received. We have taken about five hundred prisoners, upwards of three hundred of whom are wounded, and a great part of them mortally. My loss has not exceeded, and I believe has not amounted to ten killed and as many wounded. The entire destruction of the enemy's army was now inevitable, had it not been for an unfortunate occurrence, which at this moment took place on the other side of the river. Simultaneously with his advance upon my lines, he had thrown over in his boats a considerable force to the other side of the river. These having landed, were hardy enough to advance against the works of general Morgan; and, what is strange and difficult to account for, at the very moment when their entire discomfiture was looked for with a confidence approaching to certainty, the Kentucky re-enforcements, in whom so much reliance had been placed, ingloriously fled, drawing after them, by their example, the remainder of the forces; and thus yielding to the enemy that most formidable position. The batteries which had rendered me, for many days, the most important service, though bravely defended, were, of course, now abandoned; not however until the guns had been spiked.

This unfortunate rout had totally changed the aspect of affairs. The enemy now occupied a position from which they might annoy us without hazard, and by means of which they might have been able to defeat, in a great measure, the effects of our success on this side the river. It became therefore an object of the first consequence to dislodge him as soon as possible. For this object, all the means in my power, which I could with any safety use, were immediately put in preparation. Perhaps, however, it was owing somewhat to another cause that I succeeded even beyond my expectations. In negociating the terms of a temporary suspension of hostilities, to enable the enemy to bury their dead and provide for their wounded, I had required certain propositions to be acceded to as a basis, among which this was one—that, although hostilities should cease on *this* side the river until twelve o'clock of this day, yet it was not to be understood that they should cease on the *other* side; but that no re-enforcements should be sent across by *either* army until the expiration of that day. His excellency major-general Lambert begged time to consider of those propositions until ten o'clock of to-day, and in the meantime re-crossed his troops. I need not tell you with how much eagerness I immediately regained possession of the position he had thus happily quitted.

The enemy having concentrated his forces, may again attempt to drive me from my position by storm. Whenever he does, I have no doubt my men will act with their usual firmness, and sustain a character now become dear to them.

I have the honour to be, &c.
ANDREW JACKSON.

Copy of a letter from major-general Jackson to the secretary of war, dated

Camp, four miles below New Orleans, January 13, 1815.

Sir,

At such a crisis I conceive it my duty to keep you constantly advised of my situation.

On the 10th instant I forwarded you an account of the bold attempt made by the enemy on the morning of the 8th, to take possession of my works by storm, and of the severe repulse which he met with. That report having been sent by the mail which crosses the lake, may possibly have miscarried; for which reason I think it the more necessary briefly to repeat the substance of it.

Early on the morning of the 8th, the enemy having been actively employed the two preceding days in making preparations for a storm, advanced in two strong columns on my right and left. They were received however, with a firmness which it seems they little expected, and which defeated all their hopes. My men, undisturbed by their approach, which indeed they had long anxiously wished for, opened upon them a fire so deliberate and certain, as rendered their scaling ladders and fascines, as their more direct implements of warfare, perfectly useless. For upwards of an hour it was continued with a briskness of which there has been but few instances, perhaps, in any country. In justice to the enemy it must be said, they withstood it as long as could have been expected from the most determined bravery. At length, however, when all prospects of success became hopeless, they fled in confusion from the field—leaving it covered with their dead and wounded. Their loss was immense. I had first computed it at fifteen hundred; it is since ascertained to have been much greater. Upon information which is believed to be correct, colonel Hayne, the inspector-general, reports it to be in the total two thousand six hundred. His report I enclose you. My loss was inconsiderable being only seven killed and six wounded.* Such a disproportion in loss, when we consider the number and the kind of troops engaged, must, I know, excite astonishment, and may not every where, be fully credited; yet I am perfectly satisfied that the account is not exaggerated on the one part, nor underrated on the other.

The enemy having hastily quitted a post which they had gained possession of on the other side of the river, and we having immediately returned to it, both armies at present occupy their former positions. Whether, after the severe loss he has sustained, he is preparing to return to his shipping or to make still mightier efforts to

*This was in the action on the line—afterwards skirmishing was kept up, in which a few more of our men were lost.

attain his first object, I do not pretend to determine—it becomes me to act as though the latter were his intention. One thing, however, seems certain, that if he still calculates on effecting what he has hitherto been unable to accomplish, he must expect considerable re-enforcements; as the force with which he landed must undoubtedly be diminished by at least three thousand. Besides the loss which he sustained on the night of the 23d ult. which is estimated at four hundred, he cannot have suffered less between that period and the morning of the 8th inst. than three hundred—having, within that time, been repulsed in two general attempts to drive us from our position, and there having been continual cannonading and skirmishing during the whole of it. Yet he is still able to show a very formidable force.

There is little doubt that the commanding general, sir Edward Packenham, was killed in the action of the 8th, and that major-generals Kean and Gibbs were badly wounded.

Whenever a more leisure moment shall occur, I will take the liberty to make out and forward you a more circumstantial account of the several actions, and particularly that of the 8th; in doing which my chief motive will be to render justice to those brave men I have the honour to command, and who have so remarkably distinguished themselves.

I have the honour to be, &c.
ANDREW JACKSON.

P.S. A correct list of my killed and wounded will be forwarded you by the adjutant-general.

Letter from A.P. Hayne, to major-general Jackson, dated

Head-quarters, left bank of the Mississippi,
five miles below New Orleans, January 13, 1815.

Sir,

I have the honour to make the following report of the killed, wounded, and prisoners taken at the battle of Macrardie's plantation on the left bank of the Mississippi, on the morning of the 8th January, 1815, and five miles below the city of New Orleans.

Killed,	700
Wounded,	1400
Prisoners taken; one major, four captains, eleven lieutenants, one ensign, four hundred and eighty-three non-commissioned officers and	500
Making a grand total of	2600

I have the honour to be, &c.
A.P. HAYNE.

Copy of a letter from major-general Jackson to the secretary of war, dated

Camp, four miles below New Orleans, January 19, 1815.

Last night, at twelve o'clock, the enemy precipitately de-camped and returned to his boats, leaving behind him, under medical attendance, eighty of his wounded including two officers, fourteen pieces of his heavy artillery, and a quantity of shot, having destroyed much of his powder. Such was the situation of the ground which he abandoned, and of that through which he retired, protected by canals, redoubts, intrenchments, and swamps on his right, and the river on his left, that I could not without encountering a risk, which true policy did not seem to require or to authorize, attempt to annoy him much on his retreat. We took only eight prisoners.

Whether it is the purpose of the enemy to abandon the expedition altogether, or renew his efforts at some other point, I do not pretend to determine with positiveness. In my own mind, however, there is but little doubt that his last exertions have been made in this quarter, at any rate for the present season, and by the next I hope we shall be fully prepared for him. In this belief I am strengthened not only by the prodigious loss he has sustained at the position he has just quitted, but by the failure of his fleet to pass fort St. Philip.

His loss on this ground, since the debarkation of his troops, as stated by the last prisoners and deserters, and as confirmed by many additional circumstances, must have exceeded four thousand; and was greater in the action of the 8th than was estimated, from the most correct data then in his possession, by the inspector-general, whose report has been forwarded to you. We succeeded, on the 8th, in getting from the enemy about one thousand stand of arms of various descriptions.

Since the action of the 8th, the enemy have been allowed very little respite—my artillery from both sides of the river being constantly employed till the night, and indeed until the hour of their retreat, in annoying them. No doubt they thought it quite time to quit a position in which so little rest could be found.

I am advised by major Overton, who commands at fort St. Philip, in a letter of the 18th, that the enemy having bombarded his fort for eight or nine days, from thirteen-inch mortars without effect, had on the morning of that day retired. I have little doubt that he would have been able to have sunk their vessels had they attempted to run by.

Giving the proper weight to all these considerations, I believe you will not think me too sanguine in the belief that Louisiana is now clear of its enemy. I hope, however, I need not assure you, that wherever I command, such a belief shall never occasion any relaxation in the measures for resistance. I am but too sensible that the moment when the enemy is opposing us, is not the most proper to provide for them.

I have the honour to be, &c.

ANDREW JACKSON.

P.S. On the 18th our prisoners on shore were delivered to us, an exchange having been previously agreed to. Those who are on board the fleet will be delivered at Petit Coquille—after which I shall still have in my hands an excess of several hundred.

20th—Mr. Shields, purser in the navy, has to-day taken fifty-four prisoners; among them are four officers.

A.J.

Letter from adjutant-general Robert Butler, to brigadier-general Parker, dated

Head-quarter, 7th Military district, Adjutant-general's office, Jackson's Lines, below Orleans, Jan. 16, 1815.

Sir,

I have the honour herewith to enclose for the information of the war department, a report of the killed, wounded, and missing of the army under the command of major-general Jackson, in the different actions with the enemy since their landing.

I have the honour to be, &c.
ROBERT BUTLER.

Report of the killed, wounded, and missing, of the army under the command major-general Andrew Jackson, in the action of the 23d and 28th of December 1814, and 1st and 8th of January, 1815, with the enemy.

ACTION OF DECEMBER 23d, 1814.

Killed—Artillerymen, l; 7th United States' infantry, 1 lieutenant (McClellan), 1 sergeant, 1 corporal, 4 privates; 44th do. 7 privates; general Coffee's brigade volunteer mounted gun-men, 1 lieutenant-colonel (Lauderdale), 1 captain (Pace), 1 lieutenant (Samuel Brooks), 2 sergeants, 4 privates.—Total 24.

Wounded—General staff, 1 colonel (col. Piatt)—7th United States' infantry, 1 captain (A. A. White), l ensign, 1 sergeant, 2 corporals, 23 privates; 44th do. 2 lieutenants, 3 sergeants, 2 corporals, 19 privates; general Coffee's brigade, 1 colonel, 2 lieutenant-colonels, l captain, 2 lieutenants, l quarter-master sergeant, 3 sergeants, 2 corporals, 1 musician, 30 privates; New Orleans volunteer corps, 1 captain, 2 sergeants, 7 privates; volunteers of colour, 1 adjutant and 6 privates.—Total wounded, 115.

Missing—General Coffee's brigade; 1 major, 2 captains, 3 lieutenants, 1 quarter-master, 3 ensigns or cornets, 4 sergeants, 1 corporal, 2 musicians, 57 privates.—Total missing 74.

Total killed, wounded, and missing on the 23d—213.

ACTION OF DECEMBER 28th, 1814.

Killed—General Coffee's brigade, 1 private; New Orleans volunteer company, 1 private; general Carroll's division of Tennessee militia, 1 colonel (Henderson), 1 sergeant, 5 privates—Total 9.

Wounded—Marines, 1 major (Carmick); New Orleans volunteer company, 3 privates; general Carroll's division, 1 lieutenant, 3 privates.—Total wounded, 8.

Missing—None.

Total killed, wounded, and missing on this day, 17.

ACTION OF 1st JANUARY, 1815.

Killed—Artillery, navy, and volunteers at batteries, 8 privates; 44th ditto, 1 private; general Coffee's brigade, 1 sergeant; general Carroll's division, 1 private.—Total 11.

Wounded—Artillery, navy, and volunteers at batteries, 8; 7th United States' infantry, 1 private; 44th do. 3; general Coffee's brigade, 2; New Orleans volunteers, 3 privates; general Carroll's division, 1 sergeant, 2 privates; volunteers of colour, 1 lieutenant, 1 sergeant, l private—Total 23.

Missing—None

Total of killed, wounded, and missing this day, 34.

ACTION ON BOTH SIDES THE RIVER, 8th JANUARY, 1815.

Killed—Artillery, navy, and volunteers at batteries, 3 privates; 7th United States' infantry, 1 sergeant, 1 corporal; general Coffee's brigade, 1 private; Carroll's division, l sergeant, 3 privates; Kentucky militia 1 private; majors Lacoste's and Dacquin's volunteers of colour, 1 private; general Morgan's militia, 1 private. Total killed, 13.

Wounded—Artillery, &c. one private; 7th United States' infantry, one private; general Carroll's division, one ensign, one sergeant, six privates; Kentucky militia, one adjutant, one corporal, and ten privates; volunteers of colour, one ensign, three sergeants, one corporal, eight privates; general Morgan's militia, two sergeants, two privates.—Total wounded, thirty-nine.

Missing—Kentucky militia, four privates; Morgan's militia, fifteen privates—Total nineteen.

Total killed, wounded and missing this day, seventy-one.

Note—Of the killed, wounded and missing on this day, but six killed and seven wounded in the action on the east bank of the river, the residue in a sortie after the action, and in the action on the west bank.

RECAPITULATION.

Total killed,	55
Total wounded,	185
Total missing	,93
Grand Total.	333

Truly reported from those on file in this office.

ROBERT BUTLER.

Letter from Commodore Patterson to the Secretary of the Navy.

Marine battery, five miles below New Orleans, 13th January, 1815.

Sir,

I have the honour to inform you, that during the 2d and 3d instant, I landed from the ship and mounted, as the former ones, on the banks of the river, four more twelve-pounders, and erected a furnace for heating shot, to destroy a number of buildings which intervened between general Jackson's lines and the camp of the enemy and occupied by him. On the evening of the 4th I succeeded in firing a number of them, and some rice stacks by my hot shot, which the enemy attempted to extinguish, notwithstanding the heavy fire I kept up, but which at length compelled them to desist. On the 6th and 7th I erected another furnace, and mounted on the banks of the river two more twenty-four pounders, which had been brought up from the English Turn, by the exertions of colonel Caldwell, of the drafted militia of this state, and brought within and mounted on the intrenchments on this side the river, one twelve-pounder; in addition to which, general Morgan, commanding the militia on this side, planted two brass six-pound field pieces in his lines, which were incomplete, having been commenced only on the 4th; these three pieces were the only cannon on the lines, all the others being mounted on the bank of the river, with a view to aid the right of general Jackson's lines on the opposite shore, and to flank the enemy should they attempt to march up the road leading along the levee, or erect batteries on the same, of course could render no aid in defence of general Morgan's lines. My battery was manned in part from the crew of the ship, and in part by militia detailed for that service by general Morgan, as I had not seamen enough to fully man them.

During greater part of the 7th, reconnoitred the enemy at Villeré's plantation, whose canal, I was informed, they were deepening and opening to the river, for the purpose of getting their launches in, which upon examination with my glass I found to be true, and informed general Jackson of my observations by letters, copies of which I enclose herewith; a re-enforcement to general Morgan's militia was made in consequence, consisting of about four hundred militia from Kentucky, very badly armed or equipped, the general not having arms to furnish them, who arrived on this side on the morning of the 8th much fatigued. At 1 A.M. finding that the enemy had succeeded in launching their barges into the river, I despatched my aid-de-camp, Mr. R.D. Shepherd, to inform general Jackson of the circumstance, and that a very uncommon stir was observed in the enemy's camp and batteries on the banks of the river, and stating again the extreme weakness of this side the river, and urging a re-enforcement. I would have immediately dropped down with the Louisiana upon their barges; but to do so I must have withdrawn all the men from the battery on shore, which I deemed of the greatest importance, and exposed the vessel to fire by hot shot from the enemy's batteries, mounting six long eighteen-pounders, which protected their barges; and at this time she had on board a large quantity of powder, for the supply of her own guns, and those on shore, most of which was above the surface of the water, consequently exposed to their hot shot.

General Morgan despatched the Kentuckians immediately on their arrival, about 5 A.M. to re-enforce a party which had been sent out early on the night of the 7th, to watch and oppose the landing of the enemy, but who retreated after a few shot from the enemy within the lines, where they were immediately posted in their station on the extreme right. At daylight, the enemy opened a heavy cannonade upon general Jackson's lines and my battery, leading their troops under cover of their cannon to the assault of the lines, which they attempted on the right and left, but principally on the latter wing; they were met by a most tremendous and incessant fire of artillery and musketry, which compelled them to retreat with precipitation; leaving the ditch filled, and the field strewed with their dead and wounded. My battery was opened upon them simultaneously with those from our lines, flanking the enemy both in his advance and retreat with round, grape and canister, which must have proved extremely destructive, as in their haste and confusion to retreat they crowded the top of the levee, affording us a most advantageous opportunity for the use of grape and canister, which I used to the greatest advantage. While thus engaged with the enemy on the opposite shore, I was informed that they had effected their landing on this side and were advancing to general Morgan's breastwork. I immediately ordered the officers in command of my guns to turn then in their embrazures, and point them to protect general Morgan's right wing, whose lines not extending to the swamp, and those weakly manned, I apprehended the enemy's outflanking him on that wing; which order was promptly executed by captain Henley and the officers stationed at the battery, under a heavy and well directed fire of shot and shells from the enemy on the opposite bank of the river. At this time the enemy's force had approached general Morgan's lines, under the cover of a shower of rockets, and charged in despite of the fire from the twelve-pounder and field-pieces mounted on the lines as before stated; when in a few minutes I had the extreme mortification and chagrin to observe general Morgan's right wing, composed as herein mentioned of the Kentucky militia, commanded by major Davis, abandon their breastwork and flying in a most shameful and dastardly manner, almost without a shot; which disgraceful example, after firing a few rounds, was soon followed by the whole of general Morgan's command, notwithstanding every exertion was made by him, his staff and several officers of the city militia, to keep them to their posts. By the great exertions of those officers a short stand was effected on the field, when a discharge of rockets from the enemy, caused them again to retreat in such a manner that no efforts could stop them.

Finding myself thus abandoned by the force I relied upon to protect my battery, I was most reluctantly and with inexpressible pain, after destroying my powder and spiking my cannon, compelled to abandon them, having only thirty officers and seamen with me. A part of the militia were rallied at a saw-mill canal, about two miles above the lines from which they had fled, and there encamped. I ordered the Louisiana to be warped up for the purpose of procuring a supply of ammunition, and mounting other cannon, remaining myself to aid general Morgan. A large re-enforcement of militia having been immediately despatched by general Jackson to this side, every arrangement was made by general Morgan to dislodge the enemy from his position, when he precipitately retreated, carrying with him the two field pieces and a brass howitzer, after having first set fire to the platforms and gun-carriages on my battery, two saw-mills, and all the bridges between him and general Morgan's troops, and recrossed the river, and secured his boats by hauling them into his canal. On the 9th we re-occupied our former ground, and recovered all the cannon in my battery, which I immediately commenced drilling and remounting; and on the evening of the 10th had two twenty-four-pounders mounted and ready for service, on the left flank of a new and more advantageous position. From the 10th to the present date I have been much engaged in mounting my twelve-pounders along the breastwork erected by general Morgan on this new position, having three twenty-four pounders (with a furnace) to front the river, and flank general Jackson's lines on the opposite bank, from which we fired upon the enemy wherever he appeared. Our present position is now so strong that there is nothing to apprehend should the enemy make another attempt on this side.

To captain Henley, who has been with me since the destruction of his schooner, and who was wounded on the 8th, I am much indebted for his aid on every occasion, and to the officers commanding the different guns in my battery, for their great exertions at all times, but particularly on the trying event of the 8th. The exertions of general Morgan, his staff, and several of the officers of the city militia, excited my highest respect, and I deem it my duty to say that had the drafted and city militia been alone on that day, that I believe they would have done much better; but the flight of the Kentuckians paralized their exertions and produced a retreat, which could not be checked. The two brass field pieces, manned entirely by militia of the city, were admirably served, nor were they abandoned till deserted by their comrades, one of which was commanded by Mr. Hosmer, of captain Simpson's company, the other by a Frenchman, whose name I know not. The twelve-pounder under the direction of acting midshipman Philibert, was served till the last moment, did great execution, and is highly extolled by general Morgan. The force of the enemy on this side amounted to one thousand men, and from the best authority I can obtain, their loss on this side, I have since learned, was ninety-seven killed and wounded; among the latter is colonel Thornton who commanded; of the former five or six have been discovered buried, and lying upon the field; our loss was one man killed and several wounded.

I have the honour to be, &c.
DANIEL T. PATTERSON.

NO. XXX.

Address of the major-general commanding the 7th military district, to the troops stationed on the right bank of the Mississippi.

January 8, 1815.

While by the blessing of Heaven directing the valour of the troops under my command, one of the most brilliant victories in the annals of the war, was obtained by my immediate command; no words can express the mortification I felt at witnessing the scene exhibited on the opposite bank. I will spare your feelings and my own by entering into no detail on the subject; to all who reflect, it must be a source of eternal regret, that a few moments exertion of that courage you certainly possess, was alone wanting to leave rendered your success more complete than that of your fellow citizens in this camp, by the defeat of the detachment which was rash enough to cross the river to attack you. To what cause was the abandonment of your lines owing? To fear? No! You are the countrymen, the friends, the brothers of those who have secured to themselves by their courage, the gratitude of their country; who have been prodigal of their blood in its defence, and who are strangers to any other fear than that of disgrace—to disaffection to our glorious cause! No, my countrymen, your general does justice to the pure sentiments by which you are inspired. How then could brave men, firm in the cause in which they were enrolled, neglect their first duty, and abandon the post committed to their care? The want of discipline, the want of order, a total disregard to obedience, and a spirit of insubordination, not less destructive than cowardice itself, this appears to be the cause which led to the disaster, and the causes must be eradicated, or I must cease to command; and I desire to be distinctly understood, that every breach of orders, all want of discipline, every inattention of duty will be seriously and promptly punished, that the attentive officers, and good soldiers may not be mentioned in the disgrace and danger which the negligence of a few may produce. Soldiers! you want only the will, in order to emulate the glory of your fellow citizens on this bank of the river—you have the same motives for action; the same interest; the same country to protect, and you have an additional interest from past events, to wipe off the stain and show, what, no doubt, is the fact, that you will not be inferior in the day of trial to any of your countrymen.

But remember, that without obedience, without order, without discipline, all your efforts are vain, and the brave man, inattentive to his duty, is worth little more to his country than the coward who deserts her in the hour of danger. Private opinions, as to the competency of officers, must not be indulged and still less expressed; it is impossible that the measure of those who command should satisfy all who are bound to obey, and one of the most dangerous faults in a soldier is a disposition to criticise and blame the orders and characters of his superiors. Soldiers! I know that many of you have done your duty; and I trust in my next address, I shall have no reason to make any exception. Officers! I have the fullest confidence that you will enforce obedience to your commands, and above all, that by subordination in your different grades, you will set the example of it to your men; and that hereafter the army of the right will yield to none in the essential qualities which characterize good soldiers; and that they will earn their share of those honours and rewards, which their country will prepare for its deliverers.

ANDREW JACKSON.

NO. XXXI.

Provisional articles agreed on between major Smith, authorized by major-general Lambert, and Edward Livingston, an aid-de-camp to major-general Jackson, authorized by him for that purpose, subject to the ratification of the respective commanders of the two armies between the lines.

January 17, 1815.

Article 1st. It being understood that admiral sir Alexander Cochrane has sent, or will immediately send the American prisoners, as well of the army as of the navy, now on board the British fleet, to the mouth of the Rigolets, it is agreed that a nominal and descriptive receipt shall be given for the same upon honour, and that on the receipt of the said prisoners a number of British prisoners equal in rank and number to those so sent to the Rigolets, together with those confined in the British camp, shall be sent to the mouth of the river and be received by ships appointed for that purpose by the admiral.

Art. 2d. At the same time all the prisoners now in the British camp, shall be sent to the American lines, and receipted for as above, not to serve until an equal number of English prisoners shall be delivered.

Art. 3rd. Officers of equal rank shall be exchanged for equal rank, and wounded for wounded, as far as circumstances will permit.

EDWARD LIVINGSTON.
H. SMITH, Major.

I approve and ratify the above arrangement.

ANDREW JACKSON.

NO. XXXII.

Letter from major-general Jackson to the secretary at war, dated

H.Q. camp, four miles below N. Orleans, January 19, 1815.

Sir,

Last night at twelve o'clock the enemy precipitately decamped, leaving behind him, under medical attendance, eighty of his wounded, including two officers, fourteen pieces of artillery, and a considerable quantity of shot, having destroyed much of his powder.

Such was the situation of the ground which he abandoned, and that through which he retired, protected by canals, redoubts, and intrenchments on his right, and the river on his left, that I could not, without encountering a risk which true policy did not seem to require or authorize, annoy him much on his retreat. We took only eight prisoners.

Whether it is the purpose of the enemy to abandon the expedition altogether, or renew his efforts at some other point, I shall not pretend to decide with positiveness; in my own mind, however, there is very little doubt but his last exertions have been made in this quarter, at any rate for the present season, and by the next, if he shall choose to revisit us, I hope we shall be fully prepared for him. In this belief I am strengthened, not only by the prodigious loss he sustained at the position he has just quitted, but by the failure of his fleet to pass fort St. Philip. His loss since the debarkation of his troops, as stated by all the last prisoners and deserters, and as confirmed by many additional circumstances, exceed in the whole four thousand men, and was greater in the action of the 8th, than from the most correct data then in his power, was estimated by the inspector-general, whose report has been forwarded you. I am more and more satisfied in the belief, that had the arms reached us which was destined for us, the whole British army in this quarter would, before this time, have been captured or destroyed. We succeeded, however, on that day, in getting from the enemy about one thousand stand of arms of various descriptions. Since that action I have allowed the enemy very little respite. My artillery from both sides of the river, being constantly employed till the night and the hour of their retreat, in annoying them. It was time to quit a position in which so little rest could be enjoyed.

I am advised by major Overton, who commands fort St. Philip, in a letter of the 18th, that the enemy having bombarded his fort for eight or nine days, with some thirteen-inch shells, without producing any important effect, had on the morning of that day retired. Giving the proper weight to all these considerations, I believe you will not think me too sanguine in the belief that Louisiana is now clear of its enemy.

I hope I need not assure you, however, that wherever I command, such a belief shall not occasion any relaxation in the preparations for resistance. I am but too sensible, that the moment when the enemy is opposing us, is not the most proper for making any preparation.

I have the honour to be, &c.
ANDREW JACKSON.

NO. XXXIII.

Letter from major-general Jackson to the Rev. Abbé Dubourg.

H.Q. seventh military district, January 19, 1815.

Reverend Sir,

The signal interposition of Heaven, in giving success to our arms against the enemy, who so lately landed on our shores; an enemy as powerful as inveterate in his hatred; while it must excite in every bosom attached to the happy government under which we live, emotions of the liveliest gratitude, requires at the same time some external manifestation of those feelings.

Permit me, therefore, to entreat, that you will cause the service of public thanksgiving to be performed in the cathedral, in token of the great assistance we have received from the *Ruler of all events*, and of our humble sense of it.

With the greatest respect,
ANDREW JACKSON.

NO. XXXIV.

DEFENCE OF FORT. ST. PHILIP.

Extract of a letter from major-general Andrew Jackson, to the secretary of war, dated

Head Quarters, Seventh Military District New Orleans, 17th February, 1815.

I have the honour to enclose you major Overton's report of the attack of fort St. Philip, and of the manner in which it was defended.

The conduct of that officer and of those who acted under him, merits, I think, great praise. They nailed their own colours to the standard and placed those of the enemy underneath them, determined never to surrender the fort.

Copy of a letter from major Overton, commanding fort St. Philip, during the late bombardment of it, to major-general Jackson.

Fort St. Philip, January 19th, 1815.

Sir,

On the 1st of the present month, I received information that the enemy intended passing this fort to co-operate with their land forces, in the subjugation of Louisiana, and the destruction of the city of New Orleans. To effect this with more facility, they were first with their heavy bomb-vessels to bombard this place into compliance. On the grounds of this information, I turned my attention to the security of my command: I erected small magazines in different parts of the garrison, that if one blew up I could resort to another; built covers for my men to secure them from the explosion of the shells, and removed the combustible matter without the work. Early in the day of the 8th instant, I was advised of their approach, and on the 9th at a quarter past ten A.M. hove in sight two bomb-vessels, one sloop, one brig, and one schooner; they anchored two and a quarter miles below. At half past eleven, and at half past twelve they advanced two barges, apparently for the purpose of sounding within one and a half mile of the fort; at this moment I ordered my water battery, under the command of lieutenant Cunningham, of the navy, to open upon them; its well directed shot caused a precipitate retreat. At half past three o'clock, P.M. the enemy's bomb-vessels opened their fire from four sea-mortars, two of thirteen inches, two of ten, and to my great mortification I found they were without the effective range of my shot, as many subsequent experiments proved; they continued their fire with little intermission during the 10th, 11th; 12th, 13th, 14th, 15th, 16th, and 17th. I occasionally opened my batteries on them with great vivacity, particularly when they showed a disposition to change their position. On the 17th in the evening, our heavy mortar was said to be in readiness. I ordered that excellent officer captain Wolstonecraft of the artillerists, who previously had charge of it, to open a fire, which was done with great effect, as the enemy from that moment became disordered, and at daylight on the 18th commenced their retreat, after having thrown upwards of a thousand heavy shells, besides small shells from howitzers, round shot and grape, which he discharged from boats under cover of the night.

Our loss in this affair has been uncommonly small, owing entirely to the great pains that was taken by the different officers to keep their men under cover; as the enemy left scarcely ten feet of this garrison untouched.

The officers and soldiers through this whole affair, although nine days and nights under arms in the different batteries, the consequent fatigue and loss of sleep, have manifested the greatest firmness and the most zealous warmth to be at the enemy. To distinguish individuals would be a delicate task as merit was conspicuous every where.

Lieutenant Cunningham of the navy, who commanded my water battery, with his brave crew, evinced the most determined bravery and uncommon activity throughout, and in fact, sir, the only thing to be regretted is that the enemy was too timid to give us an opportunity of destroying him.

I herewith enclose you a list of the killed and wounded.

I am, sir, very respectfully,
W. H. OVERTON.

A list of the killed and wounded during the bombardment of fort St. Philip, commencing on the 9th and ending on the 18th of January, 1815.

Captain Wolstonecraft's artillery—Wounded 3.
Captain Murry's artillery—Killed 2; wounded 1.
Captain Bronten's infantry—Wounded 1.
Captain Wade's infantry—Wounded 2.
Total killed 2; wounded 7.

NO. XXXV

An address delivered to the commander-in-chief of the seventh military district, major-general Andrew Jackson, at the ceremony of solemn thanksgiving, after his brilliant defence of New Orleans. By the reverend W. Dubourg, administrator apostolic of the diocese of Louisiana.

General,

Whilst the state of Louisiana, in the joyful transports of her gratitude, hails you as her deliverer, and the asserter of her menaced liberties—whilst grateful America, so lately wrapped up in anxious suspense, on the fate of this important city, the emporium of the wealth of one half of her territory, and the true bulwark of its independence, is now re-echoing from shore to shore your splendid achievements, and preparing to inscribe your name on her immortal rolls, among those of her Washingtons—whilst history, poetry, and the monumental arts will vie in consigning to the admiration of the latest posterity, a triumph perhaps unparalleled in their records—whilst thus raised by universal acclamation to the very pinnacle of fame and ascending clouds of incense, how easy it had been for you, general, to forget the prime Mover of your wonderful successes, and to assume to yourself a praise which must essentially return to that exalted source whence every sort of merit is derived. But better acquainted with the nature of true glory, and justly placing the summit of your ambition in approving yourself the worthy instrument of Heaven's merciful designs, the first impulse of your religious heart was to acknowledge *the signal interposition of Providence*—your first step is a solemn display of *your humble sense of His favours.*

Still agitated at the remembrance of those dreadful agonies from which we have been so miraculously rescued, it is our pride also to acknowledge that the Almighty has truly had the principal hand in our deliverance, and to follow you, general, in attributing to his infinite goodness the homage of our unfeigned gratitude. Let the infatuated votary of a blind chance deride our credulous simplicity; let the cold-hearted atheist look up for the explanation of such important events to the mere concatenation of human causes; to us, the whole universe is loud in proclaiming a supreme Ruler, who as he holds the hearts of man in his hands, holds also the thread of all contingent occurrences. "Whatever be His intermediate agents," says an illustrious prelate, "still on the secret orders of His all-ruling providence, depend the rise and prosperity, as well as the decline and downfall of empires. From His lofty throne above he moves every scene below, now curbing, now letting loose the passions of men; now infusing His own wisdom into the leaders of nations; now confounding their boasted prudence, and spreading upon their councils a spirit of intoxication, and thus executing his uncontrollable judgements on the sons of men, according to the dictates of His own unerring justice."

To *Him*, therefore, our most fervent thanks are due for our late unexpected rescue, and it is *Him* we chiefly intend to praise, when considering you, general, as the *man of his right hand*, whom he has taken pains to fit out for the important commission of our defence; we extol that fecundity of genius, by which, in an instant of the most discouraging distress, you created unforeseen resources, raised as it were, from the ground, hosts of intrepid warriors, and provided every vulnerable point with ample means of defence. To *Him* we trace that instinctive superiority of your mind, which at once rallied around you universal confidence; impressed one irresistible movement to all the jarring elements of which this political machine is composed; aroused their slumbering spirits, and diffused through every rank that noble ardour which glowed in your bosom. To *Him* in fine, we address our acknowledgments for that consummate prudence which defeated all the combinations of a sagacious enemy, entangled him in the very snares which he had spread before us, and succeeded in effecting his utter destruction, without once exposing the lives of our citizens. Immortal thanks be to His supreme majesty, for sending us such an instrument of his bountiful designs! A gift of that value is the best token of the continuance of his protection—the most solid encouragement to us to sue for new favours. The first which it emboldens us humbly to supplicate as it is the nearer to our throbbing hearts, is that you may long enjoy, general, the honour of your grateful country, of which you will permit us to present you a pledge in this wreath of laurel, the prize of victory, the symbol of immortality. The next is a speedy and honourable termination of the bloody contest in which we are engaged. No one has so efficaciously laboured as you, general, for the acceleration of that blissful period; may we soon reap that sweetest fruit of your splendid and uninterrupted victories.

GENERAL JACKSON'S ANSWER.

Reverend sir,—I receive with gratitude and pleasure the symbolical crown which piety has prepared. I receive it in the name of the brave men who have so effectually seconded my exertions for the preservation of their country—they well deserve the laurels which their country will bestow.

For myself, to have been instrumental in the deliverance of such a country, is the greatest blessing that heaven could confer. That it has been effected with so little loss—that so few tears should cloud the smiles of our triumph, and not a cypress leaf be interwoven in the wreath which you present, is a source of the most exquisite enjoyment.

I thank you, reverend sir, most sincerely for the prayers which you offer up for my happiness. May those your patriotism dictates for our beloved country, be first heard. And may mine for your individual prosperity as well as that of the congregation committed to your care, be favourably received—the prosperity, the wealth, the happiness of this city, will then be commensurate with the courage and other qualities of its inhabitants.

NO. XXXVI.

To Nicholas Girod, Esq. Mayor of the City of New Orleans.

Head-quarters, 7th military district, January 27, 1815.

Sir,

Deeply impressed since my arrival with the unanimity and patriotic zeal displayed by the citizens over whom you so worthily preside, I should be inexcusable if any other occupation than that of providing for their defence had prevented my public acknowledgment of their merits. I pray you now, sir, to communicate to the inhabitants of your respectable city, the exalted sense I entertain of their patriotism, love of order, and attachment to the principles of our excellent constitution. The courage they have shown in a period of no common danger, and the fortitude with which they have rejected all the apprehensions which the vicinity of the enemy was calculated to produce, are not more to be admired than their humane attention to our own sick and wounded, as well as to those of that description among the prisoners. The liberality with which their representatives in the city council provided for the families of those who were in the field, evinced an enlightened humanity, and was productive of the most beneficial effects. Seldom in any community, has so much cause been given for deserved praise; while the young were in the field, and arrested the progress of the foe, the aged watched over the city, and maintained its internal peace; and even the softer sex encouraged their husbands and brothers to remain at the post of danger and duty. Not content with exerting for the noblest purpose that powerful influence which is given them by nature (and which in your countrywomen is rendered irresistible by accomplishments and beauty) they showed themselves capable of higher efforts, and, actuated by humanity and patriotism, they clothed by their own labour, and protected from the inclemency of the season the men who had marched from a distant state to protect them from insults. In the name of those brave men, I beg you, sir, to convey to them the tribute of our admiration and thanks; assure them that the distant wives and daughters of those whom they have succoured will remember them in their prayers; and that for myself no circumstance of this important campaign touches me with more exquisite pleasure than that I have been enabled to lead back to them, with so few exceptions, the husbands, brothers, and other relatives of whom such women only are worthy.

I anticipate, sir, with great satisfaction, the period when the final departure of the enemy will enable you to resume the ordinary functions of your office, and restore the citizens to their usual occupations—they have merited the blessings of peace by bravely facing the dangers of war.

I should be ungrateful or insensible, if I did not acknowledge the marks of confidence and affectionate attachment with which I have personally been honoured by your citizens; a confidence that has enabled me with greater success to direct the measures for their defence, an attachment which I sincerely reciprocate, and which I shall carry with me to the grave.

For yourself, Mr. Mayor, I pray you to accept my thanks for the very great zeal, integrity, and diligence with which you have conducted the arduous department of the police committed to your care, and the promptitude with which every requisition for the public service has been carried into effect.

Connected with the United States, your city must become the greatest emporium of commerce that the world has known. In the hands of any other power it can be nothing but a wretched colony. May your citizens always be as sensible of this great truth as they have shown themselves at present: may they always make equal efforts to preserve the important connexion, and may you, sir, long live, to witness the prosperity, wealth and happiness that will then inevitably characterize the great seaport of the western world.

I have the honour to be, &c.

(Signed) ANDREW JACKSON.

NO. XXXVII.

Letter from governor Claiborne to major-general Thomas.

New Orleans, February 25th, 1815.

Sir,

I have the honour to enclose you a resolution of the general assembly of Louisiana, from which you will perceive the grateful sense which is entertained of the services rendered to this state, "by our brave brother soldiers from Tennessee, Kentucky and the Mississippi Territory, and their gallant leaders."

It is the pride of America to see her brave defenders guide the plough or front her enemies, as the national interest and safety shall advise. To such citizen soldiers do we chiefly commit the protection of our dearest rights—the defence of our beloved country: and that we may continue to do so, and with confidence, the glorious termination of the campaign in which you have borne a distinguished part, affords a pleasing proof. From the prospect now before us, we may be permitted to hope, sir, that the calm of peace will soon authorize you to rest from the toils of war, and to lead back your patriotic division to their families and friends. The best wishes of the Louisianians will always accompany you and them. The spirit of union, of mutual affection and confidence, which now happily exists between the people of this state and their brothers of the sister states, will, I trust, be forever cherished—it is the surest pledge of our national glory.

I tender to you, sir,

The assurances of my respectful attachment,

(Signed) Wm. C.C. CLAIBORNE.

ANSWER.

Camp Dupre, two miles below New Orleans, Feb. 27th, 1815.

Sir,

Through the politeness of colonel Fortier I had the honour of receiving yours of the 25th inst. enclosing the resolution of the general assembly of the state of Louisiana, which I have had published to the troops under my command. Next to the pleasure derived from a consciousness of having discharged our duty, must be that which arises from the testimonials of gratitude conferred upon us by our brothers in arms, who alike with us, shared the dangers of the field, and the toils and hardships of the camp; and for the protection of whom we have left our homes and wives, our children, our friends, and every thing dear to us, and for whom we cherish that brotherly love and affection which is the cement of the union, and which alone endears man to man and state to state. For myself and my division, permit me to tender you and the honourable legislature of the state of Louisiana, an assurance of the grateful sensations we feel for the honour they have conferred upon us; and for myself accept, dear sir, the highest sentiments of esteem from.

Yours very respectfully,
JOHN THOMAS,
Com. Div. Ky. Militia.

Letter from governor Claiborne to major-general Carrol.

New Orleans, February 26th, 1815.

Sir,

I take great pleasure in communicating to you a resolution of the general assembly of this state, expressive of gratitude and thanks to you and your gallant comrades, "for the brilliant share they have had in the defence of Louisiana, and the happy harmony they have maintained with the inhabitants and militia of this state."

Under a leader, young in years, but old in deeds of valour, our brethren of Tennessee hastened to our relief; they arrived in time to participate in all the conflicts with the advancing foe, and *greatly to contribute* to his final overthrow. It must be pleasing to you, to contemplate the present comparative security of Louisiana. It cost you and your brave associates some toilsome days and watchful nights. But it is not to the gratitude of this state only, that you have acquired a title. The whole union must feel indebted to those whose faithful services have conduced to the preservation of one of its important members.

I tender to you, sir, &c.

(Signed) Wm. C.C. CLAIBORNE

ANSWER.

Camp Henderson, above New Orleans, March 2, 1815.

Sir,

I had the honour of receiving your letter of the 24th ult. covering the resolution of the legislature of the state of Louisiana, expressing in a very flattering manner their thanks to the troops of Tennessee, and to me individually, for the share we have taken in the defence of this country.

I hope you will convey to the legislature the grateful sentiments with which I am impressed for the honour done me and the troops whom I command.

I cannot withhold the expressions of gratitude due to the people of New Orleans for their benevolence in furnishing our suffering soldiers with warm clothing during the inclemency of winter, and at a time when the enemy were before our works.

They have administered to our sick and wounded every friendly attention, and extended to them all the rights of humanity.

The bright beams of peace appear ready to burst around us, and I hope soon to offer to you and the people of this country my congratulations for this glorious event.

If the report of peace be correct, the presence of the Tennessee arms will be no longer necessary, and our soldiers in returning home, will carry with them the impressions of friendship to the citizens of this country, which I hope may be cherished as their intercourse becomes more frequent, and perpetuated as long the Mississippi continues to flow.

I offer you the salutations of my friendly esteem,

Wm. CARROLL,
Maj. Gen. Com. Div. Tenn. Militia.

Letter from governor Claiborne to general Adair.

New Orleans, February 25th, 1815.

Sir,

To a soldier who has done his duty in all the conflicts in which his country has been involved, from the war of independence to the present moment, it must be matter of great exultation to notice the valour and firmness of the children of his old friends—to be convinced that they are the true descendants of the original stock. That the young men of your brigade should have looked up to you in the hour of battle, as their guide and their shield, is only a continuation of that confidence which their fathers had in a chief whose arm had so often, and so successfully, been raised against the foe. The enclosed resolution of the general assembly of Louisiana, will show you the high sense which is entertained in this state of your services, and those of your brothers in arms. Be towards them the vehicle of our sentiments, and receive for yourself, the assurances of my respect, and best wishes for your health and happiness.

(Signed) Wm. C.C. CLAIBORNE.

ANSWER.

Camp Dupre, February 26th, 1815.

Sir,

I have the honour of acknowledging the receipt of your excellency's note of yesterday (politely handed by colonel Leblanc) inclosing a resolution of the legislature of the state of Louisiana, generously awarding the thanks of the state to the militia from her sister states, who aided in the late successful struggle to expel a powerful invading enemy from her shores.

To a proud American, citizen or soldier, the consciousness of having faithfully discharged his duty to his country, must ever be his highest and most lasting consolation. But when to this is added the approbation, the gratitude of the wisest, the most respectable part of the community, with whom and under whose eye it has been his fortune to act, it will ever be esteemed, not only the highest reward for his services, but the most powerful incentive to his future good conduct.

Accept, sir, for the legislature, my warmest acknowledgment for the honourable mention they have made of the corps to which I belong; and for yourself the esteem and respect so justly due from me for your polite and highly interesting note of communications, and my best wishes for your health and happiness.

(Signed) JOHN ADAIR.

Letter from governor Claiborne to general Coffee.

New Orleans, February 25th, 1815.

Sir,

It affords me the greatest pleasure to enclose you a resolution of the general assembly of Louisiana, acknowledging the faithful and useful services of our western brothers, and tendering their thanks to you among other distinguished of officers.

The love of country, which induced you to change the calm of domestic life for the privations incident to a camp, is no less ardent in the brave volunteers whom you lead, than the gratitude which the people of Louisiana bear towards you and them; a heroic band, whose firmness in the field has alike contributed to avert from our settlements the horrors of an Indian warfare, and to the entire defeat and discomfiture of the powerful foe, who so arrogantly menaced the safety of this great and growing city. Receive for yourself, and be towards your companions in arms the organ of expressing my highest confidence and sincerest good will.

(Signed) W.C.C. CLAIBORNE.

ANSWER.

Camp Coffee, near New Orleans, March 4th, 1815.

Sir,

I have the honour to acknowledge the receipt of your letter of the 25th ult. and the resolution it enclosed of the legislature of Louisiana, presenting the thanks of that honourable body, to their brother soldiers from the west, for "the share they have taken in the defence of this country, and the harmony they have maintained with the inhabitants and militia of the state."

To know that we have contributed, in any degree, to the preservation of our common country, is to myself and the brave men under my immediate command the most pleasing reflection. To have received so flattering and distinguished a testimonial of our services adds to the pleasure which that consciousness alone would have afforded.

While we indulge the pleasing emotions that are thus produced, we should be guilty of great injustice, as well to merit as to our own feelings, if we withheld from the commander-in-chief, to whose wisdom and exertions we are so much indebted for our successes, the expression of our highest admiration and applause. To his firmness, his skill, his gallantry—to that confidence and unanimity among all ranks produced by those qualities, we must chiefly ascribe the splendid victories in which we esteem it a happiness and an honour to have borne a part.

We enter with sensibility into the feelings of the legislature, and of your excellency, on occasion of the harmony which has been so happily preserved with the inhabitants and militia of the state—May the same spirit of brotherhood always unite us when contending against a common enemy in defence of our best rights.

I tender the assurances of my own and of my companions' thanks, for the distinguished manner in which you and the legislature have been pleased to notice and honour our exertions.

I have the honour to be, sir, &c.

(Signed) JOHN COFFEE,
Brig. Gen. T.V.M.G. Men.

Letter from governor Claiborne to colonel Hinds.

New Orleans, February 26th, 1815.

Sir,

The enclosed vote of thanks of the general assembly of Louisiana, which I now have the honour to transmit you, brings to my recollection the satisfaction I experienced more than twelve years ago, on signing the commission which ushered your military talents into light. At that early period of your life, the highest hopes of your future usefulness were entertained by your friends, and to them and to you it must be alike pleasing to know that these hopes have been fully realized. Your gallant conduct, and that of the corps under your command during the last campaign, was indeed "the astonishment of one army and the admiration of the other." It will be gratefully remembered by your country, and has afforded for me an occasion to renew to you the assurances of my respect and esteem.

(Signed) Wm. C.C. CLAIBORNE.

ANSWER.

Cavalry Camp, above New Orleans, February 28th, 1815.

Sir,

I have had the honour to receive your communication covering a vote of thanks from the general assembly of the state of Louisiana. The very handsome terms in which your excellency and the general assembly have thought proper to speak of the humble efforts of the corps which it has been my good fortune to command, cannot be otherwise than acceptable to their feeling and flattering to their pride, for which we are more indebted to your excellency's partiality than to any extraordinary merit of our own, and which we are well aware consists principally in a great share of zeal for our country's service, kindled into action by the presence of a base and brutal invader. That the same unity of sentiment which gave force to our arms may continue, and that the people of Louisiana may long enjoy the substantial benefits resulting from the late most glorious conflict, in which they so honourably shared, is confidently to be expected and devoutly to be wished.

Accept, sir, for yourself, and through your excellency I tender the thanks of the corps I have the honour to command, for the honourable testimony borne of its services, and at the same time assurances of my individual respect and esteem.

(Signed) THO: HINDS,

Lieut. Col. Com. Vol. Cavalry

NO. XXXVIII.

Letter from general John Lambert to major General Jackson.

February 8th, 1815.

Sir,

I am just favoured with your letter of the 4th. I can assure you that every American prisoner that was present when I embarked on board the Tonnant has been sent into the Rigolets, and sir A. Cochrane has taken steps for the arrival of an equivalent number to the British prisoners now with you.

Under any circumstances I positively promise that your liberality shall not be in any way but reciprocal on my part, and I will not lose sight for a moment of hastening, if it is possible, the arrival of American prisoners, especially those who were taken on the 14th December last.

I am obliged to you for the allowing of two British officers to return on parole, and what you intimate on the subject shall be assented to.

What I said respecting the slaves regard those that I could not prevent coming to us when I was on shore. I am not at the anchorage where Mr. Livingston and Mr. White have been received; and indeed I have nothing to say to it. I did all I could to persuade them to return at the time, but not one was willing, as will be testified by Mr. Celestin, a proprietor whom I had detained until the British forces had evacuated their last position: this gentleman saw the slaves that were present, and did all he could to urge them to go back.

I am, sir, your very obedient servant,

(Signed) JOHN LAMBERT

Letter from admiral Cochrane to general Jackson.

H.B.M. ship Tonnant, off Mobile Bay, 12th February, 1815.

Sir,

In consequence of the style which captain Patterson thought proper to adopt in a letter that he addressed to me on the 23d January (a copy of which I beg leave to inclose) with some remarks upon the margin, I find myself precluded from making him any reply thereto, or of holding with that officer any further correspondence. (See Appendix, No. 22-a.)

But to prevent our respective prisoners suffering any unnecessary detention, I do myself the honour to communicate to you, that in order to fulfil the agreement for an exchange of prisoners, entered into by major Smith (aid-de-camp to major general Lambert) upon the 27th ultimo, I sent his majesty's ship Nymphe to the Havanna, to receive from his majesty's ship Ramilies one hundred of the American prisoners taken in the gun-vessels, which she had carried to sea.

These, with five seamen, who, for the purpose of being examined in the vice-admiralty court respecting the capture of the gun-vessels, I have been obliged to send to Bermuda, but who are to be returned the moment the legal forms have been complied with, will complete the number of American prisoners which have to be accounted for by the British forces under the agreement of the 17th ultimo, and they shall be forwarded to you without any delay so soon as they arrive in the squadron.

As it has been found very inconvenient, the sending of vessels to the Rigolets (those last sent not having yet returned, and are reported to be on shore) colonel Livingston and myself have agreed that the prisoners expected in the Nymphe shall proceed to the mouth of the Mississippi, and be delivered to the officer commanding at Plaquemines.

Having by this arrangement fulfilled the stipulations of our before-mentioned treaty, in which we agreed to the restoration of all the prisoners that our forces had made before we received from you any British prisoners, it is but just that you should follow the same principle with respect to the prisoners who have fallen into our hands by the surrender of Fort Bowyer, all of whom major general Lambert and myself are ready to exchange as they stand upon the lists (copies of which are inclosed) for such British prisoners as you may cause to be delivered at the mouth of the Mississippi, after the first account has been finally settled. And on my part, I will engage to send to the same place an equivalent of American prisoners, so soon as I am informed of the number and qualities of the British prisoners received.

I have the honour to be, sir, &c.

(Signed) ALEX. COCHRANE.

Letter from admiral Cochrane to general Jackson.

H.B.M. ship Tonnant, off Mobile Bay, 13th February, 1815.

Sir,

I have exceeding satisfaction in sending to you a copy of a bulletin that I have this moment received from Jamaica, proclaiming that a treaty of peace was signed between our respective plenipotentiaries at Ghent, on the 24th December, 1814, upon which I beg leave to offer you my sincere congratulations.

I have the honour to be, sir, &c.

(Signed) ALEX. COCHRANE.

Letter from general John Lambert to general Jackson.

Head Quarters, British army, February 19th, 1815.

Sir,

I am just informed by admiral Malcolm that the American prisoners made on the 14th of December are arrived in the fleet, and that they will sail immediately for the Mississippi, as it was settled with colonel Livingston, aid-de-camp.

I confidently trust there will be now no impediment to an equal number of British prisoners being immediately returned to us.

I beg leave to congratulate you on the prospect of peace, and hope I shall soon have to communicate to you the notice of the ratification being exchanged.

I have the honour to be, sir, &c.

(Signed) JOHN LAMBERT.

Letter from general Jackson to admiral Cochrane.

Head-Quarters, 7th Military District, New Orleans, February 20th, 1815.

Sir,

I am honoured by your letter of the 12th instant, by the return of my flag, inclosing a copy of commodore Patterson's to you, with some marginal strictures on its contents. The navy and military departments in our service being totally independent, I am not permitted to defend, still less to censure the conduct or correspondence of that officer at the head of the former; his distinguished merit, and general correctness of conduct, make it presumable that he will be able to justify his proceedings to the government, to whom alone he is accountable.

On the subject of the exchange, your assurance that the one hundred men sent off in the Ramilies, as well as the five detained for the condemnation of the gun-boats, will be delivered on their return, is satisfactory to myself and to commodore Patterson; and I now despatch all the prisoners in a situation to be removed as by the enclosed list; the residue, to the amount of——now at Natchez, are sent for, and will be forwarded to the Balize as soon as they shall arrive.

You will perceive by this, sir, that I perfectly acquiesce in the propriety of your remark, that justice requires me to follow the example of confidence given by yourself and general Lambert, in the delivery of the prisoners belonging to my army previous to the receipt of those taken from you, a confidence always mutually due from enemies who respect each other, and peculiarly proper between those who, in the probable course of events, may soon cease to be such.

There is another subject, on which a passage in general Lambert's last letter renders it necessary for me to address you; I mean that of the negroe slaves belonging to several inhabitants on the Mississippi, now in your fleet. I had written to general Lambert on this head two successive letters, in consequence of his informing me that these persons would be delivered to their masters on their application. To the first I received no answer, to the last I am informed that general Lambert *"has nothing to do with it."* Mr. White, to whom an order was given to receive such as were willing to return to their masters, having reported to me that he found several who were ready to accompany him, but that he was not permitted to take them; I am now obliged, sir, explicitly to ask whether the property thus taken is intended to be restored, and if it be, that a time and place may be appointed for its delivery.

The prisoners from Natchez will arrive in less than ten days; they will immediately sail for the Balize, and it is hoped that the prisoners taken at fort Bowyer may meet them there, to be conveyed back in the same vessels.

I have the honour to be, sir, &c.

(Signed) ANDREW JACKSON.

Letter from General Jackson to admiral Cochrane.

Head-Quarters, 7th Military District, New Orleans, 21st February, 1815.

Sir,

I have the honour to acknowledge the receipt of your letter of the 13th instant. It came to hand only this day by the way of the Balize, though purporting to have been sent by my aid-de-camp, Mr. Livingston, who arrived two days since from your fleet, and who, from a conversation he had with you, was disappointed in not finding it inclosed in the despatch he brought.

I sincerely reciprocate your congratulations on the important event you announced to me, that a treaty of peace has been signed between our two countries. This communication, connected with an expression in the bulletin you inclose, that captain Stirling of his majesty's ship Brazen was charged with despatches announcing the termination of hostilities between Great Britain and America, naturally leads to an inquiry, how far you consider this event as authorizing and requiring a cessation of hostilities between the military and naval forces of Great Britain and those of the United States in this district.

The prisoners in my possession at this place will sail for the Balize at eight o'clock on the morning of tomorrow. Those at Natchez, upwards of a hundred in number, will be forwarded to the same place as soon as they arrive here. They have been ordered down, and are expected shortly.

I have the honour to be, &c.

(Signed) ANDREW JACKSON.

NO. XXXIX.

Letter from brigadier general Winchester to the secretary at War.

Mobile, February 17th, 1815.

Sir,

It becomes my duty to communicate to you the unpleasant news of the loss of Fort Bowyer. It was closely invested by land, as well as water, on the 8th inst. On the l0th and 11th, passed a detachment over the bay with a view to divert the enemy from his object: but it arrived about twenty-four hours too late, though time enough to capture one of the enemy's barges with seventeen seamen, who say the garrison capitulated on the 12th; that the besiegers had advanced their works on the land side to within certain musket shot of the fort; that the loss on either side in killed is inconsiderable. I am in possession of no other account but that which comes from the prisoners. About thirty of the enemy's vessels, besides boats and barges, are lying within the bar, and above Mobile Point, and several ships of the line on the south and west of Dauphin Island. The wind is fair, and I expect the honour of seeing them here every night; if I do, I have great confidence my next will be on a pleasanter subject.

I have the honour to be, &c.

J. WINCHESTER,
Brig. Gen. Com. E. Sec. 7th Mil. Dis.

P.S. The garrison consisted of about three hundred and sixty men, including officers. Three small schooners, in which the detachment was transported over the bay, were captured by the enemy's barges after the troops had landed.

Letter from lieutenant colonel Lawrence to general Jackson.

Fort Bowyer, February 12th, 1815.

Sir,

Imperious necessity has compelled me to enter into articles of capitulation with major general John Lambert, commanding his Britannic majesty's forces in front of Fort Bowyer, a copy of which I forward you for the purpose of effecting an immediate exchange of prisoners. Nothing but the want of provisions, and finding myself completely surrounded by thousands—batteries erected on the sand-mounds which completely commanded the fort—and the enemy having advanced, by regular approaches, within thirty yards of the ditches, and the utter impossibility of getting any assistance or supplies, would have induced me to adopt this measure. Feeling confident, and it being the unanimous opinion of the officers, that we could not retain the post, and that the lives of many valuable officers and soldiers would have been uselessly sacrificed, I thought it most desirable to adopt this plan. A full and correct statement will be furnished you as early as possible.

Captain Chamberlin, who bears this to E. Livingston, Esq. will relate to him every particular, which will, I hope, be satisfactory.

I am with respect, &c.
(Signed) W. LAWRENCE,
Lieut. Col. Com'g.

ARTICLES OF CAPITULATION

Agreed upon between lieutenant colonel Lawrence and major general Lambert for the surrender of Fort Bowyer,

on the Mobile Point, 11th of February, 1815.

1. That the fort shall be surrendered to the arms of his Britannic majesty in its existing state as to the works, ordnance, ammunition, and every species of military stores.

2. That the garrison shall be considered as prisoners of war, the troops marching out with their colours flying and drums beating, and ground their arms on the glacis—the officers retaining their swords, and the whole to be embarked in such ships as the British naval commander in chief shall appoint.

3. All private property to be respected.

4. That a communication shall be made immediately of the same to the command-

ing officer of the 7th military district of the United States, and every endeavour made to effect an early exchange of prisoners.

5. That the garrison of the United States remain in the fort until twelve o'clock to-morrow, a British guard being put in possession of the inner gate at three o'clock to-day, the body of the guard remaining on the glacis, and that the British flag be hoisted at the same time—an officer of each service remaining at the head-quarters of each commander until the fulfilment of these articles.

H.C. SMITH, *major and military secretary.*

Agreed on the part of the royal navy,

T.H. BICKETTS, *Capt. H.M. ship Vengeant.*
R. CHAMBERLAIN, *2d Regt. U.S. Infantry.*
WM. LAWRENCE, *Lt. Col. 2d Inf'y. Com'g.*

Approved,

A. COCHRANE, *Com. in Chief H.M. Shipping.*
JOHN LAMBERT, *major general commanding.*

A true copy—Test,

JOHN REID, *Aid-de-Camp.*

NO. XL.

GENERAL ORDERS.

Head-Quarters, Western Section, 7th Military District, Assistant Adjutant-General's Office, New Orleans, April 7th, 1815.

At the request of lieutenant-colonel William Lawrence, of the 2d regiment United States' infantry, a court of inquiry was ordered on the 25th ultimo to assemble in this city, to inquire into the conduct of the lieutenant-colonel touching the defence and surrender of fort Bowyer, and to give an opinion thereon. The court, whereof lieutenant colonel Arbuckle was president, major Peyre and captain Humphrey members, commenced its proceedings on the 28th March last, and continued by adjournment from day to day up to the 5th instant, when it delivered the following opinion:

"The court of inquiry, after mature deliberation, are of opinion that fort Bowyer was defended in the best manner that the circumstances of the siege admitted of—that the conduct of colonel Lawrence on that occasion was honourable and becoming a good officer—that the fort, when it was surrendered, was in a situation which rendered a longer defence impracticable, and that no blame ought to attach, either to colonel Lawrence or to the garrison, for having surrendered fort Bowyer at the time they did."

The major-general feels much pleasure in observing, that the whole of the testimony in this case, and particularly that of major Woodruff of the 3d infantry, lieutenant Alexis of the navy, and major Chamberlain and captain Brownlow of the 2d infantry, (the two former as to the *position* and *strength* of fort Bowyer, and the two latter as to the *approaches of the enemy* and the *defence of the fort*) fully support the opinion of the court of inquiry in favour of lieutenant-colonel Lawrence.

The court of inquiry, whereof lieutenant-colonel Arbuckle is president, is dissolved.

E.P. GAINES, *major-general commanding.*

NO. XLI.

Address of general Jackson to the Soldiers and Citizens at New Orleans.

Head-Quarters, 7th Military District, New Orleans, 19th February, 1815.

Fellow-Citizens and Soldiers,

The flag-vessel which was sent to the enemy's fleet has returned, and brings with it intelligence, extracted from a London paper, that on the 24th of December articles of peace were signed at Ghent, by the American commissioners and those of his Britannic majesty.

We must not be thrown into false security by hopes that may be delusive. It is by holding out such that an artful and insidious enemy too often seeks to accomplish what the utmost exertions of his strength will not enable him to effect. To place you off your guard and attack you by surprise, is the natural expedient of one who, having experienced the superiority of your arms, still hopes to overcome you by stratagem—Though young in the "trade" of war, it is not by such artifices that he will deceive us.

Peace, whenever it shall be re-established on fair and honourable terms, is an event in which both nations ought to rejoice; but whether the articles which are said to have been signed for its restoration will be approved by those whose province it is to give to them their final confirmation, is yet uncertain. Until they shall be ratified by the prince regent and the president of the United States, peace, though so much desired, may be still distant. When that shall be done, the happy intelligence will be publicly and speedily announced. In the mean time, every motive that can operate on men who love their country, and are determined not to lose it, calls upon us for increased vigilance and exertion.

If peace be near at hand, the days of our watchfulness, of our toils, and our privations, will be proportionably few; if it be distant, we shall at any rate hasten its arrival, by being constantly and every where prepared for war.

Whatever be the designs of the enemy, we must be ready to meet them. Should they have the temerity to assail us again, we will once more drive him ignominiously from our shore; if he places his hopes of success on stratagem, our watchfulness will disappoint him; if on an exertion of his strength, we have proved how successfully that can be resisted.

It is true fort Bowyer has fallen, but it must and will be speedily regained. We will expel the invader from every spot on our soil, and teach him, if he hopes for conquest, how vain it is to seek it in a land of freedom.

ANDREW JACKSON.

Copy of a letter from the secretary of war to the governor of Kentucky.

Department of War,
February 13, 1815.

His Excellency The Governor of Kentucky,

Sir,

I have the honor to acknowledge the receipt of your letter of the 29th ultimo, and am happy to find such a coincidence in opinion, as it respects the necessity of vigorous efforts against the enemy, in the event of their being able to maintain their position at Orleans. But this brilliant achievement of General Jackson, and the consequent evacuation of the Island of Orleans by the enemy, will enable us to dispense with the greater part, if not the whole of the militia lately called from your state. You will therefore only call out two thousand men, which may be held in readiness, but not marched to the relief of those who are now in service at Orelans, until further orders.

I have the honor to be
JAMES MONROE.

Copy of a letter from the secretary of war to the governor of Tennessee.

Department of War
February 13, 1815

His Excellency The Governor of Tennessee,

Sir,

The brilliant achievement of General Jackson and the consequent evacuation of the Island of Orleans, will enable us to dispense with the late call for militia from the state of Tennessee. That portion of the militia of your state now in service at New Orleans and which are so eminently entitled to the thanks of their country, will be discharged by General Jackson, so soon as circumstances may in his opinion make it compatible with the public interest.

I have the honor to be
JAMES MONROE.

NO. XLII.

Letter from general Keane to general Jackson,

H.B.M. ship Tonnant, off Mobile, February 8th, 1815.

Major-General Keane presents his best respects to general Jackson, and feels particularly thankful for the kindness he has experienced from him through the medium of colonel Livingston—He is still further obliged for general Jackson's kind wishes for his recovery.

NOS. XLIII–XLIV.

Letter from general Jackson to the secretary at war.

Head-Quarters, 7th Military District, New Orleans, 17th February, 1815.

Sir,

I have the honour to inclose you a copy of major Overton's report of the attack on fort St. Philip, and of the manner in which it was defended.

The conduct of this officer, and of those who acted under him, merits, I think, great praise. They nailed their own colours to the standard, and placed those of the enemy underneath them, determined never to surrender the post.

The flag-vessel which I sent to the enemy's fleet a fortnight ago, for the purpose of ascertaining the causes that had prevented the delivery of a hundred of our seamen (taken on board the gun-boats) in violation of the articles entered into for the exchange of prisoners, has not yet returned, and I am apprehensive is detained by the enemy to prevent the discovery of some designs he may still hope to execute. Whatever their views may be, I am persuaded they will be disappointed in them.

A copy of the articles agreed upon for the exchange I herewith send you, and I beg leave to accompany it with the assurance of my determination, to restore no more of the British prisoners until those articles are complied with by the British commanders.

Major-general Keane, having lost his sword in the action of the 8th January, and having expressed a great desire to regain it, valuing it as the present of an esteemed friend, I thought proper to have it restored to him; thinking it more honourable to the American character to return it, after the expression of those wishes, than to retain it as a trophy of victory. I believe, however, it is a singular instance of a British general soliciting the restoration of his sword fairly lost in battle.

Some entire Congreve-rockets have been found, and a rest from which they are fired, which it is my intention to forward to the seat of government whenever a proper opportunity shall offer, as also the instruments of the British band of music, and their quarter flag.

General Keane's trumpet, as well as that which was used on the right column of the enemy, were taken in the action of the 8th January. Those instruments are in the possession of general Coffee's brigade, where I hope they will be permitted to remain.

I have the honour to be, &c.

(Signed) ANDREW JACKSON.

Letter from general Lambert to General Jackson.

Head-Quarters, Isle Dauphine, February 27th, 1815.

Sir,

I have this moment received your letter, dated the 20th inst, I have taken every step to bring the exchange to a speedy conclusion.

On the subject of the concluding paragraph, I have only to remark, that honourable and feeling conduct which has characterized every transaction in which I have had the honour to be concerned in with you.

You may rely upon it, I shall take no retrospective view of the conduct of any of the men returned, and shall find reasons in discountenancing an inquiry, should it be brought before me, or come to my knowledge through any other channel.

With regard to the negroes that have left their masters and are with this force, any proprietor or person deputed, that chooses to present himself to me will be received, and every facility afforded him to communicate with those people; and I shall be very happy if they can be persuaded all to return, but to compel them is what I cannot do.

With respect (which I inclose) to an address from major-general Villeré to the commandant of this force, I am at a loss to understand the purport. The commissary-general's orders are to purchase cattle wherever he can meet with them. Amongst receipts in that neighbourhood for beasts procured, is that for those belonging to the major-general. I should have been glad to have known the major-general's sentiments previous, as I certainly should not have troubled myself about his concerns, or endeavoured to render as little painful as I was able, not living in his house, the unavoidable circumstances attending the immediate theatre of war towards his son whom he had left unprotected.

I have the honour to be, &c.

(Signed) JOHN LAMBERT.

Letter from general Jackson to general Lambert.

Head-Quarters, 7th Military District, New Orleans, March 4th, 1815.

Sir,

I am gratified to find by the letter with which you have honoured me, that my confidence in your humanity and delicacy, of conduct with respect to the prisoners was not misplaced. My request was merely dictated by the plainest principles of justice. It is your ready, frank, and obliging compliance, that merits the flattering epithet you have been pleased to bestow on my conduct.

I am extremely sorry that the very high winds, which have prevailed ever since I sent for the British prisoners to Natchez, have prevented their arrival at this place. Vessels are ready to receive and carry them to the Balize the instant they shall arrive.

Having been just informed that Mr. Shields, who commanded a launch on Lake Borgne, has been made prisoner, I hope he may be sent in on parole for exchange.

The prisoners taken from your advanced post at Mobile Point are directed to be sent down to fort Bowyer, to be delivered to you, and included in the general exchange.

I am sorry that I cannot advise you, sir, of the ratification of the treaty signed at Ghent. At the date of my last advices it had not arrived at the seat of government.

I have the honour to be, &c.

(Signed) ANDREW JACKSON.

Letter from general Jackson to general Lambert.

Head-Quarters, 6th March, 1815.

Sir,

I have just received intelligence from Washington which leaves little doubt in my mind that the treaty signed at Ghent between the United States and Great Britain has been ratified by the president and senate of the United States, but by some unaccountable accident a despatch on another subject has been substituted for the one intended to give me an official notice of this event. The one I have received however, is accompanied by an order from the postmaster-general directing his deputies to forward the express carrying intelligence of the recent peace. Of this order I enclose a copy. And from other sources, to which I give credit, I learn that the same express brought official notice of the treaty to the governor of Tennessee. I have deemed it a duty, without loss of time, to communicate the exact state of those circumstances, that you might determine whether they would not justify you in agreeing, by a cessation of all hostilities, to anticipate the happy return of peace between our two nations, which the first direct intelligence must bring to us in an official form. The prisoners from Natchez, after having been long detained by adverse winds, are now within a short distance of the city, and will certainly proceed to-morrow morning to the Balize, to be delivered to your officer according to my promise.

I pray you, with the assurance of high respect, to receive that of the satisfaction I feel in reflecting that our correspondence, begun as commanders of hostile armies, should terminate as officers of nations in amity.

I have the honour to be, &c.

(Signed) ANDREW JACKSON.

Letter from major Woodruff to admiral Cochrane.

Dauphine Island, March 17th, 1815.

Sir,

I am instructed by his excellency major-general Andrew Jackson, commanding the United States 7th military district, to inform you of his having received notification of a treaty of peace between the United States of America and the government of Great Britain having been signed and exchanged at the city of Washington on the 17th February, 1815. By the first article of that treaty, "all territory, places and possessions whatsoever, taken by either party from the other during the war, or which may be taken after the signing of this treaty, excepting only the islands herein after mentioned shall be restored without delay, and without carrying any distinction, or carrying away any of the artillery, or other public property, originally captured in the said forts or places, and which shall remain therein upon the exchange of the ratifications of this treaty, or any slaves or other private property." I am also commanded by his excellency, major-general Andrew Jackson, to receive such forts, garrisons, artillery, munitions of war, or other property, as may be embraced by said first article. You will please therefore to make such arrangements as may be most convenient for carrying into effect the said first article of said treaty.

Such *slaves* as may be within your control, belonging to any inhabitant or citizen of the United States, I am also instructed to receive, to the end that their owners may again obtain possession of them.

I have the honour to be, &c.

Letter from general Lambert to major Woodruff.

Dauphine Island, March 17th, 1815.

Sir,

In answer to yours of this day's date, communicating to me that his excellency major-general Jackson had received notification of a treaty of peace between the United States of America and the government of Great Britain having been signed and exchanged at the city of Washington on the 17th February, 1815, and requiring you to carry into execution, on the part of the American government, the fulfilment of the first article of the treaty, I have to request that you will inform his excellency that immediately I receive the same from the person charged by the British government to transmit it to all its naval and military commanders serving in America, I shall give him immediate notice of it and be prepared to fulfil the treaty in every respect.

I have the honour to be, &c.

(Signed) JOHN LAMBERT.

Letter from general Lambert to general Jackson.

Isle of Dauphine, March 19th, 1815.

Sir,

Since I had the pleasure of writing to you yesterday, I am informed that every thing will be embarked (weather permitting) by the 25th. I have, in consequence, written to major-general M'Intosh, to inform him that the commandant of fort Bowyer has orders to deliver it up agreeable to the first article of the treaty of peace on that day.

The time of and preparations for a long voyage may detain the troops here a few days longer, but no exertion will be wanting to embark the whole as soon as possible.

As I may not have another opportunity of addressing you, permit me to avail myself of the present to wish you health and happiness, and to express my regret that circumstances will not allow me to assure you personally of the same.

I have the honour to be, &c.

(Signed) JOHN LAMBERT.

Letter from general Lambert to major Woodruff.

Isle Dauphine, March 20th, 1815.

Sir,

I answer to that part of your letter which touches upon the negroes who have come into the British force previous to the ratification of the peace, that is, on the 18th February last, I do not feel myself authorized to deliver them up under the treaty, without their consent.

I have the honour to be, &c.

(Signed) JOHN LAMBERT.

NO. XLV.

Letter from general Jackson to James Monroe, secretary of war.

Head-Quarters, 7th military district, New Orleans 24th February, 1815.

Sir,

The flag-vessel which I sent to the enemy's fleet returned a few days ago, with assurances from admiral Cochrane, that the American prisoners taken in the gun-boats and sent to Jamaica, shall be returned as soon as practicable. The Nymphe has been despatched for them.

Through the same channel I received the sad intelligence of the surrender of fort Bowyer: this is an event which I little expected to happen, but after the most gallant resistance; that it should have taken place, without even a fire from the enemy's batteries is as astonishing as it is mortifying.

In consequence of this unfortunate affair, an addition of three hundred and sixty-six has been made to the list of American prisoners; to redeem these and the seamen, I have, in conformity with propositions held out by admiral Cochrane, forwarded to the mouth of the Mississippi upwards of four hundred British prisoners; others will be sent, to complete the exchange, as soon as they arrive from Natchez, to which place I had found it expedient to order them.

Major Blue, who had been ordered by general Winchester to the relief of fort Bowyer, succeeded in carrying one of the enemy's picquets, consisting of seventeen, but was too late to effect the whole purpose for which he had been detached—the fort having capitulated twenty-four hours before his arrival. I learn from the bearer of my last despatches to the enemy's fleet, who was detained during the operations against fort Bowyer, that his loss on that occasion, by the fire from the garrison was between twenty and forty.

I have the honour to be, &c,

A.J.

NO. XLVI.

Letter from general Jackson to major-general Lambert.

Head-Quarters, 7th military district, New Orleans, 26th February, 1815.

Sir,

I have the honour to acknowledge the receipt of your letter of the 19th inst.

In conformity with arrangements entered into with admiral Cochrane by my aid-de-camp, Mr. Livingston, I despatched from this place on the 22nd inst. four hundred British prisoners to be delivered at the mouth of the Mississippi, to the officer appointed on the part of his B.M. to receive them. Others will be sent to complete the exchange, as soon as they arrive from Natchez.

It is expected that the American prisoners made at fort Bowyer will be forwarded to the same point, as soon as practicable, and in time to return by the vessels that will convey the British prisoners now on their way from Natchez.

I take the liberty to enclose you copies of two letters, which I did myself the honour to address to admiral Cochrane on the 20th and 2lst inst. in doing which you will perceive both my motive and my object.

I have the honour to be, &c.
A.J.

NO. XLVII.

Letter from general Jackson to major-general Lambert.

Head-Quarters, 7th military district, March 7th, 1815.

Sir,

In consequence of the intimation contained in your formal letters, that every facility will be given to the proprietors of slaves now with your forces, to induce them to return, I have given permission to M.M. Jumonville, Lanergue, Lacoste, Forstall, Philipan, Delphin, Velez and Quarron to pass under a flag in the schooner Louisa, captain Pierre Etienne, to the fleet, for the purpose of seeing and reclaiming their slaves, to whom I pray that they (the slaves) may be delivered.

I have the honour to be, &c.
A.J.

NO. XLVIII.

GENERAL ORDERS.

Head-Quarters, 7th military district, adjutant-general's office, New Orleans, 8th March, 1815.

Although the commanding general has not received official advice that the state of war has ceased by the ratification of the treaty of peace between the United States and

Great Britain, he has persuasive evidence of the fact, and credits it, at the risk of being misguided by his wishes. Under this impression, his first act is to release from actual service the body of the militia of this state, who have taken the field in obedience to the orders for a levy *en masse*. In discharging them from the noble duty which they were called to perform, the general does justice to the alacrity with which they have in general obeyed the call—to the enthusiasm which animated them on the first invasion of the enemy, and the unanimity and patriotism which disappointed his insolent hopes. He thanks them, in the name of their common country, for the noble defence they have made, and he congratulates them in his own, on the consequences it has produced. Louisiana, though not called on for any exertion in assuming her independence, has shown, by her courage in its support, that she knows how to prize the inestimable blessing; her sons have not only ensured safety, but have acquired even a greater good—national reputation. Preserve this as the best reward of your exertions, and hand it down untarnished, together with your example, to your posterity. Let no designing men induce you to destroy it, by exciting jealousies of your best friends, or divisions among yourselves—by preaching party spirit in peace, insubordination in war, injustice to your brave companions in arms, blindness to your own interests and to the true character of those enemies of your peace. Guard against these evils as you hope to enjoy the blessings you have so bravely won; and before you yield to such perfidious counsels, examine scrupulously whether those from whom they proceed, deserve your confidence, by any exertion they have made in your defence. A zealous wish for the prosperity of the interesting country, in whose defence he has been, by the blessing of heaven, instrumental, has induced the commanding general to give this admonitory caution, which those who court popularity, may tell you is unnecessary. He, however, values no popularity but that which arises from a faithful discharge of duty. In performing it, his object has been to secure your happiness; and he will always consider it as one of the most fortunate incidents in his life, to have contributed, by his exertions, to the prosperity of your country.

By command, ROBERT BUTLER.

NO. XLIX

Letter from general Jackson to general Lambert.

Head-Quarters, 7th Military District,
New Orleans, March 13th, 1815.

Sir,

It is with great satisfaction that I inform you of my having received this day official advice of the ratification and interchange of the treaty of peace between the United States and Great Britain.

A copy of the treaty and of the ratification will be presented to you by major Woodruff, of the 3d infantry, who will express you more fully than I can in the compass of a letter, those sentiments which the new state of things between the two nations inspire.

I have, by special direction of the secretary of war, ordered an immediate cessation of hostilities, and by the like order make this communication to you.

Mr. Livingston is empowered to make such arrangements for the restoration required by the first article of the treaty, and to receive all places, now in your possession, as well as the slaves mentioned in your former letters, and all public property, conformably to the provisions of the said treaty.

Any facility or accommodation that may be required for your supplies, or the comforts of your sick or wounded in my power, will be given with the greatest pleasure.

I have the honour to be, &c.
ANDREW JACKSON.

Letter from general Jackson to major Woodruff.

New Orleans, March 13th, 1815.

Major Woodruff will inform captain Newman at Petites Coquilles of the restoration of peace, and direct him to permit the British flag, now waiting at that place, to come up to the city. He will also instruct captain Newman that all vessels are, in future, to be permitted to pass and repass freely.

He will then proceed to the British fleet and deliver the despatches with which he is charged to the commander-in-chief. He will receive the surrender of the posts and public property agreeable to the treaty, and require the delivery of slaves taken from hence.

General M'Intosh will furnish the troops necessary for the occupation of the fort on his requisition.

A. JACKSON.

Copy of a letter from the secretary of war to general Jackson.

Department of War,
March 13, 1815.

Major General Andrew Jackson,

Sir,

You will have received my communication, informing you that a treaty had been signed, on the 24 December, at Ghent, by the commissioners on the part of the United States & Great Britain; and that the exchange of the ratification took place here on the 17 ultimo. It is expected that you have already taken the necessary measures for carrying into effect, within your military district, the stipulations of the first article of the treaty, as were respecting the surrender of the ports and places held by the British forces, as the slaves, and other private property, stipulated to be delivered up.

The movements of the British forces against Mobile, and their previous conduct at Pensacola, give some cause to apprehend that there may have been some arrangement between the British & Spanish governments, respecting the occupation of West

Florida. Should the British forces have obtained possession of any part of that country, formerly claimed as part of West Florida, west of the Perdido River, and refuse to deliver it up, under the stipulations of the first article of the treaty, you will make use of the forces under your command to expel them from it. All that part of West Florida being considered as a part of the United States, it must be defended as such.

I have the honor to be
JAMES MONROE.

NO. L.

GENERAL ORDERS.

Head-Quarters, 7th Military District, adjutant-general's Office,
New Orleans, March 13, 1815.

The commanding general, with the most lively emotions of joy, and of gratitude to Heaven, announces to the troops under his command, that a treaty of peace between the United States and Great Britain was ratified and exchanged at Washington, on the 17th of February last.

In consequence whereof, he loses not an instant in revoking and annulling the general order issued on the 15th day of December last, proclaiming martial law, which is hereby revoked, annulled, countermanded; and he orders all hostilities immediately to cease against the troops and subjects of the united kingdom of Great Britain and Ireland.

And in order that the general joy attending this event may extend to all manner of persons, the commanding general proclaims and orders a pardon for all military offences heretofore committed in this district, and orders that all persons in confinement, under such charges, be immediately discharged.

By order, ROBERT BUTLER, *Adjutant-General.*

Head-Quarters, 7th Military District, Adjutant-General's Office,
New Orleans, March 13, 1815.

The commanding general communicates with great satisfaction to the troops under his command, the following testimonial of the just sense which the president of the United States entertains of their patriotism, valour, and good conduct. He congratulates them particularly on their being able to receive his applause with a consciousness of having deserved it; and takes a singular pleasure in conveying to the brave citizens of this state, who took up arms in its defence, the assurance that their exertions are appreciated as they deserve by the executive of the United States.

"The president requests that you will express to the troops who have acted under you, the very favourable sentiments which he entertains of their conduct. The alacrity with which they repaired to the standard of their country, exposed, in many instances, to distressing privations; the patience with which they have borne the fatigues of the campaign, and their bravery in action, have been seen by him with great satisfaction. To our newly adopted fellow citizens of Louisiana, you will give assurance of his great sensibility to the decided and honourable proof which they have given of their attachment and devotion to the union, and of the manly support of the rights of their country.

(Signed) "JAMES MONROE, *Secretary of State*."

By command, ROBERT BUTLER, *Adj. Gen.*

NO. LI.

GENERAL ORDERS.

Head-Quarters, 7th Military District, Adjutant-general's Office,
New Orleans, March 14th, 1815.

The major-general is at length enabled to perform the pleasing task of restoring to Tennessee, Kentucky, Louisiana and the territory of the Mississippi, the brave troops who have acted such a distinguished part in the war which has just terminated. In restoring these brave men to their homes, much exertion is expected of, and great responsibility held on the commanding officers of the different corps. It is required of major-generals Carroll and Thomas, and brigadier-general Coffee, to march their commands without unnecessary delay to their respective states, and have them mustered for payment and discharged. The troops from the Mississippi territory and state of Louisiana, both militia and volunteers, will be immediately mustered out of service by major Davis, assistant-inspector-general, paid and discharged. Every arrangement will be made through the department of war, to have the troops of Tennessee and Kentucky paid off the soonest possible after their return. All public arms, accoutrements, camp equipage, and military stores of every description, now in the possession of the different troops herein directed to be discharged, will be immediately deposited with the deputy-commissary of ordnance and quarter-master-general, except such camp equipage as is absolutely necessary for the troops on their return march, which must be delivered to some public agent on their dismissal. The quarter-master-general is hereby ordered to furnish transportation for all invalids belonging to the different corps. Those who cannot be moved without imminent danger of their lives, must be well accommodated, and supplied with hospital stores, and a sufficient number of surgeons retained to attend them. The contractor will furnish provisions for the troops herein named, on their return march, on the requisition of the respective commanding officers; who, it is expected, will use every care and attention that no depredations are committed on private property; and are held personally responsible to remunerate, agreeably to the regulations of the war department, all damages of property injured or destroyed by their commands.

The major-general has again the satisfaction of announcing the approbation of the president of the United States to the conduct of the troops under his command, expressed in flattering terms through the honourable the secretary at war.

In parting with those brave men, whose destinies have been so long united with his own, and in whose labours and glories it is his happiness and his boast to have participated, the commanding general can neither suppress his feelings nor give utterance to them as he ought. In what terms can he bestow suitable praise on merit so extraordinary, so unparallelled! Let him in one burst of joy, gratitude and exultation exclaim—"these are the saviours of their country—these the patriot soldiers who triumphed over the invincibles of Wellington, and conquered the conquerors of Europe!" With what patience did you submit to privations—with what fortitude did you endure fatigue—what valour did you display in the day of battle! You have secured to America a proud name among the nations of the earth—a glory which will never perish.

Possessing those dispositions, which equally adorn the citizen and the soldier, the expectations of your country will be met in peace as her wishes have been gratified in war. Go then, my brave companions, to your homes; to those tender connexions and those blissful scenes which render life so dear—full of honour, and crowned with laurels which will never fade. With what happiness will you not, when participating in the bosoms of your families the enjoyment of peaceful life, look back to the toils you have borne—to the dangers you have encountered? How will all your past exposures be converted into sources of inexpressible delight? Who, that never experienced your sufferings, will be able to appreciate your joys? The man who slumbered ingloriously at home, during your painful marches, your nights of watchfulness and your days of toil, will envy you the happiness which these recollections will afford—still more will he envy the gratitude of that country which you have so eminently contributed to save.

Continue, fellow soldiers, on your passage to your several destinations, to preserve that subordination, that dignified and manly deportment which have so ennobled your character.

While the commanding-general is thus giving indulgence to his feeling towards those brave companions who accompanied him through difficulties and danger, he cannot permit the names of Blount, and Shelby, and Holmes, to pass unnoticed. With what a generous ardour of patriotism have these distinguished governors contributed all their exertions to provide the means of victory! The memory of these exertions, and of the success with which they were attained, will be to them a reward more grateful than any which the pomp of title or the splendour of wealth can bestow.

What a happiness it is to the commanding-general that, while danger was before us, he was, on no occasion, compelled to use, towards his companions in arms, either severity or rebuke. If, after the enemy had retired, improper passions began to show their empire in a few unworthy bosoms, and rendered a resort to energetic measures necessary for their suppression, the commanding-general has not confounded the innocent with the guilty,—the seduced with the seducers. Towards you, fellow-soldiers, the most cheering recollections exist, blended, alas! with regret, that disease and war should have ravished from us so many worthy companions. But the memory of the cause in which they perished, and of the virtues which animated them while living, must occupy the place where sorrow would claim to dwell.

Farewell, fellow-soldiers. The expression of your general's thanks is feeble; but the gratitude of a country of freemen is yours—yours the applause of an admiring world.

ANDREW JACKSON.

NO. LII.

TREATY OF PEACE.

JAMES MADISON, PRESIDENT OF THE UNITED STATES,

To all and singular to whom these presents shall come, greeting:

Whereas a treaty of peace and amity between the United States of America and his Britannic majesty was signed at Ghent, on the twenty-fourth day of December, one thousand eight hundred and fourteen, by plenipotentiaries respectively appointed for that purpose; and the said treaty having been, by and with the advice and consent of the senate of the United States; duly accepted, ratified and confirmed, on the seventeenth day of February, one thousand eight hundred and fifteen; and ratified copies thereof having been exchanged agreeably to the tenor of the said treaty, which is in the words following, to wit:

TREATY OF PEACE AND AMITY BETWEEN HIS BRITANNIC MAJESTY AND THE UNITED STATES OF AMERICA.

His Britannic majesty and the United States of America, desirous of terminating the war which has unhappily subsisted between the two countries, and of restoring, upon principles of perfect reciprocity, peace, friendship, and good understanding between them, have, for that purpose, appointed their respective plenipotentiaries, that is to say: his Britannic majesty, on his part, has appointed the right honourable James lord Gambier, late admiral of the white, now admiral of the red squadron of his majesty's fleet, Henry Goulbourn, esq. member of the imperial parliament, and under secretary of state, and William Adams, esq. doctor of civil laws:—and the president of the United States, by and with the advice and consent of the senate thereof, has appointed John Quincy Adams, James A. Bayard, Henry Clay, Jonathan Russel, and Albert Gallatin, citizens of the United States, who, after a reciprocal communication of their respective full powers, have agreed upon the following articles:

ART. I.—There shall be a firm and universal peace between his Britannic majesty and the United States, and between their respective countries, territories, cities, towns and people, of every degree, without exception of places or persons. All hostilities, both by sea and land, shall cease as soon as this treaty has been ratified by both parties, as hereinafter mentioned. All territories, places, and possessions whatsoever, taken from either party by the other, during the war, or which may be taken after the signing of this treaty, excepting only the islands hereinafter mentioned, shall be restored without delay, and without causing any destruction, or carrying away any of the artillery or other public property originally captured in the said forts or places, and which shall remain therein, upon the exchange of the ratifications of this treaty, or any slaves or other private property, and all archives, records, deeds, and papers, either of a public nature, or belonging to private persons, which, in the course of the war, may have fallen into the hands of the officers of either party, shall be, as far as may be practicable, forthwith restored and delivered to the proper authorities and persons to whom they respectively belong. Such of the islands in the bay of Passamaquoddy as are claimed by both parties, shall remain in the possession of the party in whose occupation they may be at the time of the exchange of the ratifications of this treaty, until the decision respecting the title to the said islands shall have been made, in conformity with the fourth article of this treaty. No disposition made by this treaty, as to such possession of the islands and territories claimed by both parties, shall, in any manner whatever, be construed to affect the right of either.

ART. II.—Immediately after the ratification of this treaty by both parties, as hereinafter mentioned, orders shall be sent to the armies, squadrons, officers, subjects and citizens of the two powers to cease from all hostilities: and to prevent all causes of complaint which might arise on account of the prizes which may be taken at sea after the ratifications of this treaty, it is reciprocally agreed, that all vessels and effects which may be taken after the space of twelve days from the said ratifications, upon all parts of the coast of North America, from the latitude of twenty-three degrees north, to the latitude of fifty degrees north, as far eastward in the Atlantic ocean, as the thirty-sixth degree of west longitude from the meridian of Greenwich, shall be restored on each side: That the time shall be thirty days in all other parts of the Atlantic ocean, north of the equinoxial line or equator, and the same time for the British and Irish channels, for the gulf of Mexico, and all parts of the West Indies: forty days for the North Seas, for the Baltic, and for all parts of the Mediterranean. Sixty days for the Atlantic ocean south of the equator as far as the latitude of the Cape of Good Hope: ninety days for every part of the world south of the equator: and one hundred and twenty days for all other parts of the world, without exception.

ART. III.—All prisoners of war taken on either side, as well by land as by sea, shall be restored as soon as practicable after the ratification of this treaty, as hereinafter mentioned, on their paying the debts which they may have contracted during their captivity. The two contracting parties respectively engage to discharge, in specie, the advances which may have been made by the other, for the sustenance and maintenance of such prisoners.

ART. IV.—Whereas it was stipulated by the second article in the treaty of peace of one thousand seven hundred and eighty three, between his Britannic majesty and the United States of America, that the boundary of the United States should comprehend all islands within twenty leagues of any part of the shores of the United States, and lying between lines to be drawn due east from the points where the aforesaid boundaries between Nova-Scotia, on the one part, and East Florida on the other, shall respectively touch the Bay of Fundy, and the Atlantic ocean, excepting such islands as now are, or heretofore have been within the limits of Nova-Scotia: and whereas the several islands in the Bay of Passamaquoddy, which is part of the Bay of Fundy, and the Island of Grand Menan, in the said Bay of Fundy, are claimed by the United States as being comprehended within their aforesaid boundaries, which said islands are claimed as belonging to his Britannic majesty as having been at the time of, and previous to, the aforesaid treaty of one thousand seven hundred and eighty three, within the limits of the province of Nova Scotia: in order, therefore, finally to decide upon these claims, it is agreed that they shall be referred to two commissioners, to be appointed in the following manner, viz. One commissioner shall be appointed by his Britannic majesty, and one by the president of the United States, by and with the advice and consent of the senate thereof, and the said two commissioners so appointed shall be sworn impartially to examine and decide upon the said claims according to such evidence as shall be laid before them on the part of his Britannic majesty and of the United States respectively. The said commissioners shall meet at St. Andrews, in the province of New Brunswick, and shall have power to adjourn to such other place or places as they shall think fit. The said commissioners shall, by a declaration or report under their hands and seals, decide to which of the two contracting parties the several islands aforesaid do respectively belong, in conformity with the true intent of the said treaty of peace of one thousand seven hundred and eighty-three. And if the said commissioners shall agree in their decision, both parties shall consider such decision as final and conclusive. It is further agreed, that in the event of the two commissioners differing upon all or any of the matters so referred to them, or in the event of both or either of the said commissioners refusing or declining, or wilfully omitting, to act as such, they shall make jointly or separately, a report or reports, as well to the government of his Britannic majesty, as to that of the United States, stating in detail the points on which they differ, and the grounds upon which their respective opinions have been formed, or the grounds upon which they, or either of them, have so refused, declined, or omitted to act. And his Britannic majesty, and the government of the United States, hereby agree to refer the report or reports of the said commissioners, to some friendly sovereign state, to be then named for that purpose, and who shall be requested to decide on the differences which may be stated in the said report or reports, or upon the report of one commissioner, together with the grounds upon which the other commissioner shall be refused, declined, or omitted to act, as the case may be. And if the commissioner so refusing, declining, or omitting to act, shall also wilfully omit to a state the grounds upon which he has so done, in such manner that the said statement may be referred to such friendly sovereign or state, together with the report of such other commissioner, then such sovereign or state, shall decide exparte upon the said report alone. And his Britannic majesty and the government of the United States engage to consider the decision of some friendly sovereign or state to be final and conclusive, on all matters so referred.

ART. V.—Whereas neither that point of the high lands lying due north from the source of the river St. Croix, and designated in the former treaty of peace between the two powers as the northwest angle of Nova Scotia, now the northwesternmost head of Connecticut river, has yet been ascertained; and whereas that part of the boundary line between the dominion of the two powers which extends from the source of the river St. Croix directly north to the above mentioned northwest angle of Nova Scotia, thence along the said high lands which divide those rivers that empty themselves into the river St. Lawrence from those which fall into the Atlantic ocean, to the northwesternmost head of Connecticut river, thence down along the middle of that river to the forty-fifth degree of north latitude: thence by a line due west on said latitude until it strikes the river Iroquois or Cataraguy, has not yet been surveyed: it is agreed, that for these several purposes, two commissioners shall be appointed, sworn, and authorized, to act exactly in the manner directed with respect to those mentioned in the next preceding article, unless otherwise specified in the present article. The said commissioners shall meet at St. Andrews, in the province of New Brunswick, and shall have power to adjourn to such other place or places as they shall think fit. The said commissioners shall have power to ascertain and determine the points above mentioned, in conformity with the provisions of the said treaty of peace of one thousand seven hundred and eighty-three, and shall cause the boundary aforesaid, from the source of the river St. Croix, to the river Iroquois or Cataraguy, to be surveyed and marked according to the said provisions. The said commissioners shall make a map of the said boundary, and annex it to a declaration under their hands and seals, certifying it to be the true map of the said boundary, and particularizing the latitude and longitude of the northwest angle of Nova Scotia, of the northwesternmost head of Connecticut river, and of such other points of the said boundary as they may deem proper. And both parties agree to consider such map and declaration as finally and conclusively fixing the said boundary. And in the event of the said two commissioners differing, or both, or either of them, refusing or declining, or wilfully omitting to act, such reports, declarations, or statements, shall be made by them, or either of them, and such reference to a friendly sovereign or state, shall be made, in all respects as in the latter part of the fourth article is contained, and in as full a manner as if the same was herein repeated.

ART. VI.—Whereas by the former treaty of peace, that portion of the boundary of the United States from the point where the forty-fifth degree of north latitude strikes the river Iroquois or Cataraguy to the lake Superior, was declared to be "along the middle of said river into lake Ontario, through the middle of said lake until it strikes the communication by water between that lake and lake Erie, thence along the middle of said communication into lake Erie, through the middle of said lake until it arrives at the water communication into the lake Huron, thence through the middle of said lake to the water communication between that lake and lake Superior." And whereas doubts have arisen what the middle of said river, lakes, and water communications, and whether certain islands lying in the same were within the dominions of his Britannic majesty or of the United States: in order, therefore, finally to decide these doubts, they shall be referred to two commissioners, to be appointed, sworn, and authorized to act exactly in the manner directed with respect to those mentioned in the next preceding article, unless otherwise specified in this present article. The said commissioners shall meet, in the first instance at Albany, in the state of New York, and shall have power to adjourn to such other place or places as they shall think fit. The said commissioners shall, by a report or declaration, under their hands and seals, designate the boundary through the said river, lakes, or water communications, and decide to which of the two contracting parties the several islands lying within the said river, lakes, and water communications, do respectively belong, in conformity with the true intent of the said treaty of one thousand seven hundred and eighty-three. And both parties agree to consider such designation and decision as final and conclusive. And in the event of the said two commissioners differing, or both, or either of them, refusing, declining, or wilfully omitting to act, such reports, declarations, or statements, shall be made by them, or either of them; and such reference to a friendly sovereign or state shall be made in all respects as in the latter part of the fourth article is contained, and in as full a manner as if the same was herein repeated.

ART. VII—It is further agreed that the said two last mentioned commissioners, after they shall have executed the duties assigned to them in the preceding article, shall be, and they are hereby authorized, upon their oaths, impartially to fix and determine, according to the true intent of the said treaty of peace of one thousand seven hundred and eighty-three, that part of the boundary between the dominions of the two powers, which extends from the water communication between lake Huron and lake Superior, to the most northwestern point of the lake of the Woods, to decide to which of the two parties the several islands lying in the lakes, water communications and rivers, forming the said boundary, do respectively belong, in conformity with the true intent of the said treaty of peace of one thousand seven hundred and eighty-three; and to cause such parts of the said boundary, as require it, to be surveyed and marked. The said commissioners shall, by a report or declaration under their hands and seals, designate the boundary line aforesaid, state their decisions on the points thus referred to them, and particularize the latitude and longitude of the most northwestern point of the lake of the Woods, and of such other parts of the said boundary, as they may deem proper. And both parties agree to consider such designation and decision as final and conclusive. And in the event of the said two commissioners differing, or both, or either of them, refusing, declining, or wilfully omitting to act, such reports, declarations, or statements, shall be made by them, or either of them, and such reference to a friendly sovereign or state, shall be made in all respects, as in the latter part of the fourth article is contained, and in as full a manner as if the same was herein repeated.

ART. VIII—The several boards of two commissioners mentioned in the four preceding articles, shall respectively have power to appoint a secretary, and to employ such surveyors or other persons as they shall judge necessary. Duplicates of all their respective reports, declarations, statements, and decisions, and of their accounts and of the journal of their proceedings, shall be delivered by them to the agents of his Britannic majesty, and to the agents of the United States, who may be respectively appointed and authorized to manage the business on behalf of their respective governments. The said commissioners shall be respectively paid in such manner as shall be agreed between the two contracting parties, such agreement being to be settled at the time of the exchange of the ratifications of this treaty; and all other expenses attending said commissioners shall be defrayed equally by the two parties. And in case of death, sickness, resignation, or necessary absence, the place of every such commissioner respectively shall be supplied in the same manner as such commissioner was first appointed, and the new commissioner shall take the same oath or affirmation, and do the same duties. It is further agreed between the two contracting parties, that in case any of the islands mentioned in any of the preceding articles, which were in the possession of one of the parties prior to the commencement of the present war between the countries, should, by the decision of any of the boards of commissioners aforesaid, or of the sovereign or state so referred to, as in the four next preceding articles contained, fall within the dominions of the other party, all grants of land made previous to the commencement of the war, by the party having had such possession, shall be as valid as if such island or islands, had by such decision or decisions, been adjudged to be within the dominions of the party having such possession.

ART. IX.—The United States of America engage to put an end, immediately after the ratification of the present treaty, to hostilities with all the tribes or nations of Indians, with whom they may be at war at the time of such ratification; and forthwith to restore to such tribes or nations, respectively, all the possessions, rights, and privileges, which they may have enjoyed or been entitled to in one thousand eight hundred and eleven, previous to such hostilities: *Provided always*, that such tribes or nations shall agree to desist from all hostilities against the United States of America, their citizens and subjects, upon the ratification of the present treaty being notified to such tribes or nations, and shall so desist accordingly. And his Britannic majesty engages, on his part, to put an end immediately after the ratification of the present treaty, to hostilities with all the tribes or nations of Indians with whom he may be at war at the time of such ratification, and forthwith to restore to such tribes or nations respectively, all the possessions, rights, and privileges, which they may have enjoyed, or been entitled to in one thousand eight hundred and eleven, previous to such hostilities: *Provided always*, that such tribes or nations shall agree to desist from all hostilities against his Britannic majesty, and his subjects, upon the ratification of the present treaty being notified to such tribes or nations, and shall so desist accordingly.

ART. X.—Whereas the traffic in slaves is irreconcilable with the principles of humanity and justice, and whereas both his Britannic majesty and the United States are desirous of continuing their efforts to promote its entire abolition, it is hereby agreed that both the contracting parties shall use their best endeavours to accomplish so desirable an object.

ART. XI.—This treaty, when the same shall have been ratified on both sides, without alteration by either of the contracting parties and the ratifications mutually exchanged, shall be binding on both parties, and the ratifications shall be exchanged at Washington, in the space of four months from this day, or sooner if practicable.

In faith whereof, we the respective plenipotentiaries, have signed this treaty, and have thereunto affixed our seals.

Done, in triplicate, at Ghent, the twenty-fourth day of December, one thousand eight hundred and fourteen.

(L.S.) GAMBIER,
(L.S.) HENRY GOULBOURN,
(L.S.) WILLIAM ADAMS,
(L.S.) JOHN QUINCY ADAMS,
(L.S.) J. A. BAYARD,

(L.S.) H. CLAY,
(L.S.) JONATHAN RUSSELL,
(L.S.) ALBERT GALLATIN.

Now, therefore, to the end that the said treaty of peace and amity may be observed with good faith, on the part of the United States, I, JAMES MADISON, president as aforesaid, have caused the premises to be made public: and I do hereby enjoin all persons bearing office, civil or military, within the United States, and all others, citizens or inhabitants thereof, or being within the same, faithfully to observe and fulfil the said treaty and every clause and article thereof.

In testimony whereof I have caused the seal of the United States to be affixed to these presents, and signed the same with my hand.

Done at the city of Washington, this eighteenth day of February, in the year of our Lord one thousand eight hundred and fifteen, and of the sovereignty and independence of the United States the thirty-ninth.

By the President,

JAMES MADISON.
JAMES MONROE.

NO. LIII.

ADDRESS

From the city battalion of uniform companies to major-general Jackson.

New Orleans, 16th March, 1815.

GENERAL,

We have delayed until this moment the expression of our feelings towards you, less the honest emotions of our hearts should be ascribed to a desire of propitiating the favour of our commander. At this moment, when neither hope nor fear can be supposed to have influenced us, we pray you to receive the sincere tribute of our thanks—as soldiers, for the confidence you have reposed in us; for the paternal care with which you have watched over our comforts, and above all, for that justice you have done to our zeal in assigning us on every occasion a post of *danger* and of *honour*—as citizens, for the wisdom of the measures you devised to protect our country; for the skill and bravery with which they were executed; and for that indispensable *energy* to which we owe our safety. Leaving to others the task of declaiming about *privileges* and constitutional rights, we are content with having fought in support of them—we have understanding enough to know when they are wantonly violated: and no false reasoning shall make us ungrateful to the man whose wisdom and valour have secured them to us and to our posterity! We do not deal in professions; we pray you, general, to be assured, that in the officers and men of this battalion you have *soldiers* who have been and are always ready to affront every danger under your command—*fellow-citizens*, grateful for your services—*friends*, personally attached to your fortunes, and ready to promote your happiness at the risk of their own. You have allowed us the endearing title of your *brothers in arms*—it was given to us on this field, strewed then with the bodies of our enemies; and we feel a noble pride in the consciousness that allows us to accept it. That fraternity, cemented in hostile blood, shall be the pride of our lives; and in aftertimes will secure to our children the respect of posterity. General, common phrases cannot express the emotions which agitate us at the moment of our separation—but we pray heaven to watch over your safety; and we trust to a grateful country for the honours and advancement which your services have merited.

J.B. PLAUCHE,
STE. GEME, captain.
M. WHITE, captain.
A. GUIBERT, captain.
HUDRY, captain.
P. ROCHE, captain.
JOHN ST. JEAN, lieutenant.
COEUR DE ROY.
DE ST. ROMES, lieutenant.
N. THOMPSON, lieutenant.
C. FREMONT, lieutenant.
DUHULQUOD, lieutenant.
L. PILIE, lieutenant.
BENETAUD.
BERTEL, lieutenant.
HUET, lieutenant.
LE MOUNIER, serjeant-major.

GENERAL'S ANSWER.

FELLOW-SOLDIERS,

Although born and bred in a land of freedom, popular favour has always been with me a secondary object. My first wish, in political life, has been to be useful to my country. Yet, I am not insensible to the good opinion of my fellow-citizens; I would do much to obtain it; but I cannot, for this purpose, sacrifice my own conscience or what I conceive to be the interests of my country.

These principles have prepared me to receive, with just satisfaction, the address you have presented. The first wish of my heart, the safety of your country, has been accomplished; and it affords me the greatest happiness to know that the means taken to secure this object have met the approbation of those who have had the best opportunities of judging of their propriety, and who, from their various relations, might be supposed the most ready to censure any which had been improperly resorted to. The distinction you draw, gentlemen, between those who only declaim about civil rights and those who fight to maintain them, shows how just and practical a knowledge you have of the true principles of liberty—without such knowledge all theory is useless or mischievous.

Whenever the invaluable rights which we enjoy under our happy constitution are threatened by invasion, privileges the most dear, and which, in ordinary times, ought to be regarded as the most sacred, may be required to be infringed for their security. At such a crisis, we have only to determine whether we will suspend, for a time, the exercise of the latter, that we may secure the permanent enjoyment of the former. Is it wise, in such a moment, to sacrifice the spirit of the laws to the letter, and by adhering too strictly to the letter, lose the *substance* forever, in order that we may, for an instant, preserve the *shadow*? It is not to be imagined that the express provisions of any written law can fully embrace emergencies which suppose and occasion the suspension of all law, but the highest and the last, that of self-preservation. No right is more precious to a freeman than that of suffrage; but had your election taken place on the 8th of January, would your declaimers have advised you to abandon the defence of your country in order to exercise this inestimable privilege at the polls? Is it to be supposed that your general, if he regarded the important trust committed to his charge, would have permitted you to preserve the constitution by an act which would have involved constitution, country and honour in one undistinguished ruin?

What is more justly important than personal liberty; yet how can the civil enjoyment of this privilege be made to consist with the order, subordination and discipline of a camp? Let the sentinel be removed by *subpoena* from his post, let writs of *habeas corpus* carry away the officers from the lines, and the enemy may conquer your country by only employing lawyers to defend your constitution.

Private property is held sacred in all good governments, and particularly in our own, yet, shall the fear of invading it prevent a general from marching his army over a corn-field, or burning a house which protects the enemy?

These and a thousand other instances might be cited to show that laws must sometimes be silent when necessity speaks. The only question with the friend of his country will be, have these laws been made to be silent wantonly and unnecessarily? If necessity dictated the measure, if a resort to it was important for the preservation of those rights which we esteem so dear, and in defence of which we had so willingly taken up arms, surely it would not have been becoming in the commander-in-chief to have shrunk from the responsibility which it involved. He did not shrink from it. In declaring martial law, his object, and his only object, was to embody the whole resources of the country, for its defence. That law, while it existed, necessarily suspended all rights and privileges inconsistent with its provisions. It is matter of surprise that they who boast themselves the champions of those rights and privileges should not, when they were first put in danger by the proclamation of martial law, have manifested that lively sensibility of which they have since made so ostentatious a display. So far, however, was this from being the case, that this measure not only met, then, the open support of those who when their country was invaded thought resistance a virtue, and the silent approbation of *all*; but even received the particular recommendation and encouragement of many who now inveigh the most bitterly against it. It was not until a victory, secured by that very measure, had lessened the danger which occasioned a resort to it, that the present *feeling guardians of our rights* discovered that the commanding-general ought to have suffered his posts to be abandoned through the interference of a foreign agent—his ranks to be thinned by desertion, and his whole army to be broken to pieces by mutiny; while yet a powerful force of the enemy remained on your coast, and within a few hours sail of your city.

I thought and acted differently. It was not until I discovered that the civil power stood no longer in need of the military for its support, that I restored to it its usual functions; and the restoration was not delayed a moment after that period had arrived.

Under these circumstances, fellow-soldiers, your resolution to *let others declaim about privileges and constitutional rights*, will never draw upon you the charge of being indifferent to those inestimable blessings; your attachment to them has been proved by a stronger title—that of having nobly fought to preserve them.—You who have thus supported them against the open pretensions of a powerful enemy, will never, I trust, surrender them to the underhand machinations of men who stand aloof in the hour of peril, and who, when the danger is gone, claim to be the *"defenders of your constitution."*

An honourable peace has dissolved our military connexion; and, in a few days, I shall quit a country endeared to me by the most pleasing recollections. Among the most prominent of these, gentlemen, are those I shall ever entertain of the distinguished bravery, the exact discipline, the ardent zeal, and the important services of your corps. The offered friendship of each individual composing it, I receive with pleasure, and with sincerity reciprocate. I shall always pride myself on a fraternity with such men, created in such a cause.

ANDREW JACKSON.

NO. LIV.

Letter from general Jackson to the secretary of war.
Head-quarters, 7th military district,

New Orleans, March 16, 1815.

Sir,

I have the honour to acknowledge the receipt of your letter of the 16th ult. advising me of the ratification of the treaty of peace between Great Britain and the United States.

In conformity with your directions, I have forwarded to the officer commanding his Britannic majesty's forces, in this quarter, information of that event.

The Tennessee and Kentucky militia will be immediately marched to their respective states, and discharged without receiving any pay beforehand. The Louisiana and Mississippi militia will be discharged and paid here. It is hoped that funds will be provided for the payment of the former in suitable time.

Difficulties are experienced from the want of means to procure forage, and transportation on the return march, colonel Knight having not yet arrived. On this account I have offered my bills on the governor of Tennessee, payable in treasury notes at Nashville.

I have received no intelligence of colonel Knight, except by your letter of the 7th ult.

The greater portion of the regulars in this quarter having enlisted to serve during the war, expect to be immediately discharged. As you have not mentioned them in your instructions, I shall be glad to hear from you on the subject as soon as possible.

It is my intention, so soon as I get the troops mustered out of service here, to remove my head-quarters to Nashville, where I shall expect to receive the orders of the government.

Major-general Gaines is placed in the immediate command of this section of the district, and I am happy to commit it to one in whom the government has such high and deserved confidence.

I have the honour to be, &c.
A. JACKSON.

NO. LV.

Letter from major Woodruff to general Jackson.

New Orleans, March 23d, 1815.

Sir—In compliance with your orders of the 14th inst. I left the bayou St. Johns at twelve o'clock of the same day, and arrived at Dauphine island on the night of the 16th, the head-quarters of the British army.

I immediately informed major-general Lambert of your having received official notice of a treaty of peace having been signed and exchanged at the city of Washington, on the 17th of February, 1815, between the United States of America and the government of Great Britain; (a copy of which I handed him)—and that I was ordered by you to receive all forts, places, artillery, munitions of war, or other public or private property captured during the war, embraced by the first article of said treaty; and that I was particularly instructed to receive all *slaves*, belonging to any inhabitant or citizen of the United States, captured or protected by the British army.

General Lambert informed me that he could not give up fort Bowyer until he received official information, from an authorized agent of his government, that the treaty had been confirmed by *ours*;—that then he would be prepared to execute, on the part of his government, every article of said treaty, except that part relating to *slaves*, as it was totally incompatible with the spirit and constitution of his government to recognize *slavery* at all—that he would use his influence, in persuading them to return to their masters, by every argument in his power; but that he would not use force in compelling their obedience, or permit it to be used within the British lines. That I might stand acquitted of having discharged my duty, I addressed a note to the British commander on the 16th instant, marked No.1. His note in return, No.2, you will perceive is evasive, and by no means a satisfactory answer to mine. I again requested a categorical answer, particularly to that part of my note relating to slaves. His answer you will find marked No. 3.

I flatter myself, sir, I have done all in my power to effect your wishes, and regret my exertions were not attended with more success.

I have the honour to be, &c.
J. WOODRUFF.

NO. LVI.

Letter from general Lambert to general Jackson.

Head-Quarters, Isle Dauphine, March 18, 1815.

SIR—I received with great pleasure, by the hands of major Woodruff, on the evening of the 16th, about nine o'clock, yours of the 13th instant. I communicated the contents immediately to rear admiral Malcolm, and orders were issued for the cessation of hostilities, and to all detached posts and ships to be withdrawn in our respective commands. I daily expect an official communication (similar to what you have received) from Mr. Baker. In the meantime every preparation is making for the embarkation of this force, and ships are now sent away, when we are able to put sufficient provisions on board to take them to Bermuda. Victuallers from Jamaica must be here in a very few days, when every thing will be put on board as quickly as possible; and should I by that time not have received any intelligence, the admiral and myself will have no hesitation in putting to sea directly. I have requested major Woodruff, who went up to Mobile yesterday, to acquaint the commanding officer that I would let him know the moment we were prepared to give up the fort, which would be when the transports could get out of the bay. The fort would be restored in every respect as when it fell into our possession, with the exception only of a brass mortar, cast in George the Second's reign, which had been sent away the day after.

In the fulfilling the first article of the treaty, I cannot consider the meaning of "not causing any destruction, or carrying away any artillery, or other public property, *originally* captured in the said forts or places, and to *which* shall *remain therein* upon the exchange of the ratification of this treaty, or any slave, or other property," having reference to any antecedent period to the 18th of February, the day of the exchange of ratifications; because it is only from that time that the article could be fulfilled in a long war. If those negroes (the matter now in question) belonged to the *territory* or *city* we were *actually* in *occupation* of, I should conceive we had no right to take them away; but by their coming away, they are virtually the same as deserters or property taken away at any time of the war. I am obliged to say so much in justification of the right; but I have from the first done all I could to prevent, and subsequently, together with admiral Malcolm, have given every facility, and used every persuasion that they should return to their masters, and many have done so; but I could not reconcile it to myself to abandon any, who, from false reasoning perhaps, joined us during the period of hostilities and have thus acted in violation of the laws of their country, and besides become obnoxious to their masters.

Had it been an object to take the negroes away, they could have been embarked in the first instance; but they have been permitted to remain in the hopes that they might return.

I am much obliged to you for your offer of supplies, and comforts for the sick and wounded. I send a commissary, to make a few purchases, and have directed him to call on Mr. Livingston with this letter.

I have the honour to be, &c.
JOHN LAMBERT, *Maj. Gen. Com'g.*

NO. LVII.

CONGRESS OF THE UNITED STATES.

The following resolutions, expressive of the high sense entertained by congress of the patriotism and good conduct of the people of Louisiana and of New Orleans, were unanimously adopted:

Resolved, by the senate and house of representatives of the United States of America in congress assembled, That congress entertain a high sense of the patriotism, fidelity, zeal and courage with which the people of the state of Louisiana promptly and unanimously stepped forth, under circumstances of imminent danger from a powerful invading army, in defence of all the individual, social, and political rights held dear by man. Congress declare and proclaim, that the brave Louisianians deserve well of the whole people of the United States.

Resolved, That congress entertain a high sense of the generosity, benevolence, and humanity, displayed by the people of New Orleans, in voluntarily offering the best accommodations in their power, and giving the kindest attention to the wounded, not only of our own army, but also to the wounded prisoners of a vanquished foe.

Resolved, That the president of the United States be requested to cause the foregoing resolutions to be communicated to his excellency the governor of Louisiana, accompanied with a request that he cause the greatest possible publicity to be given to them, for the information of the whole people of Louisiana.

Resolutions expressive of the thanks of congress to major-general Jackson, and the troops under his command, for their gallantry and good conduct in the defence of New Orleans:

Resolved, by the senate and house of representatives of the United States of America in congress assembled, That the thanks of congress be, and they are hereby given to major-general Jackson, and through him to the officers and soldiers of the regular army, of the militia, and of the volunteers, under his immediate command, and the officers and soldiers charged with the defense of fort St. Philip, for their uniform gallantry and good conduct conspicuously displayed against the enemy from the time of his landing before New Orleans until his final expulsion from the state of Louisiana: and particularly for their valour, skill and good conduct on the 8th of January last, in repulsing, with great slaughter, a numerous British army of chosen veteran troops, when attempting by a bold and daring attack to storm and carry the works hastily thrown up for the defence of New Orleans, and thereby obtaining a most signal and complete victory over the enemy, with a disparity of loss on his part unexampled in military annals.

Resolved, That the president of the United States be requested to cause to be struck a gold medal, with devices emblematical of this splendid achievement, and presented to major-general Jackson, as a testimony of the high sense entertained by congress of his judicious and distinguished conduct on that memorable occasion.

Resolved, That the president of the United States be requested to cause the foregoing resolutions to be communicated to major-general Jackson, in such terms as he may deem best calculated to give effect to the objects thereof.

Resolved, That congress entertain a high sense of the valour and good conduct of commodore D.T. Patterson, of the officers, petty officers, and seamen attached to his command, for their prompt and efficient co-operation with general Jackson, in the late gallant and successful defence of the city of New Orleans, when assailed by a powerful British force.

Resolved, That congress entertain a high sense of the valour and good conduct of major Daniel Carmick, of the officers, non-commissioned-officers and marines, under his command, in the defence of said city, on the late memorable occasion.

NO. LVII-a.

Copy of a letter from the secretary of war to general Jackson.

Department of War,
February 5, 1815.

Major General
Andrew Jackson,

Sir,

I have just had the honor to receive your letter of the 9 & 13th ultimo. communicating an account of the brilliant victory obtained by the troops under your command, near New Orleans, over the very superior force of the veteran troops of Great Britain, which attacked you on the 8th. It is particularly gratifying to find, that in so signal a success, attended with the slaughter and captivity of so many of the invading foe, it has pleased providence, to extend a protecting arm over our fellow citizens. History records no example of so glorious a victory, obtained with so little bloodshed on the part of he victorious.

I am instructed by the President to convey to you in strong terms, his approbation of your conduct and that of the troops acting under you, who have rendered such important services to their country. Your arrangements for the defense of the city in selecting and fortifying the proper points, at which to oppose the enemy, and the disposition of your force in action, afford proof of a talent for command, which do you honor. By the example of your personal energy and distinguished gallantry in the field, the more necessary and commendable with young troops, it is believed that the happiest effect was produced. By these important services you have merited, in an eminent degree the approbation of the Government, and the gratitude of the your fellow citizens.

The President requests that you will express to the troops, who have acted under you, the very favorable sentiments which he entertains of their conduct. The alacrity with which they repaired to the standard of their country, exposed in many instances to distressing privations; the patience with which they have borne the fatigues of the campaign, and their bravery in action have been seen by him with great satisfaction. To our newly adopted fellow citizens of Louisiana, you will give assurance of his great sensibility, to the decided and honorable proof which they have afforded, of their attachment and devotion to the union, and of their manly support of the rights of their country. [Little—perhaps] did the enemy expect, in their invasion of New Orleans, to meet the forces of such distant states assembled in its defense or such firm, faithful and zealous cooperation, on the part of our newly adopted brethren there.

Every effort which the government could make to reinforce you, by troops, and to supply you with arms, and with every munitions of war, has been made and is still making. I send you a statement of these supplies and of the times of which they were forwarded. You will investigate the conduct of those to whose charge they were committed, and if guilty of criminal neglect, inflict on them the punishment which their conduct merits, and the law will justify.

It will be gratifying to you to know, that 5000 additional troops, are ordered to your aid from Kentucky, and 2,500 from Tennessee; and that the most effectual measures have been taken for their transportation, provision and accommodation. Orders have also been given for the supply of these troops with arms, and a further supply to you of munitions of war.

Major General Gaines was ordered sometime since to repair to New Orleans, to take a command under you, with an understanding, that he should proceed slowly on account of the weak state of his health, proceeding from his wounds, which were still open. I hope however that he will soon be with you if he has not yet arrived.

I have the honor to be
JAMES MONROE.

NO. LVIII.

Letter from general Jackson to general Lambert. Head-Quarters, 7th Military District,

New Orleans, 20th February, 1815.

SIR,

By my letter of this date, addressed to sir Alexander Cochrane you will perceive that I have fully acquiesced in your ideas relative to the delivery and exchange of prisoners, and you will herewith receive all those now here in a state to be removed.

As you intimate that you do not consider the slaves as under your control, I have addressed the only further demand I shall make on that subject to sir Alexander Cochrane.

Some of my officers, under a mistaken idea that deserters were confined with the prisoners, have, as I have understood, made improper applications to some of the latter to quit your service. It is possible they may have in some instances succeeded in procuring either a feigned or a real consent to this effect, the whole of the transaction, however, met my marked reprehension, and all the prisoners are now restored to you. But as improper allurements may have been held out to these men, it will be highly gratifying to my feelings to learn that no investigation will be made, or punishment inflicted, in consequence of the conduct of those who may, under such circumstances, have swerved from their duty. As the transaction might not have been otherwise disclosed to you, the notice I now take of it shows the confidence I feel that you will not make use of any implied presumption to be drawn from it.

ANDREW JACKSON.

NO. LIX.

RESOLUTIONS OF THE LEGISLATURE OF LOUISIANA.

Be it resolved by the senate and house of representatives of the state of Louisiana in general assembly convened, That the legislature of the state of Louisiana deem it their duty to proclaim the facts herein after stated, as bearing testimony to the zeal and patriotism that were displayed by the citizens in every part of this state, during the late invasion of the British.

At the first news of our danger, the militia, together with a vast number of volunteers, flocked into New Orleans from every county in this state. The planters on both sides of the river, within a space of several leagues, either above or below town, furnished thousands of their slaves, and sent them to every particular place where their labour was thought necessary; it was through the means which were voluntarily granted by the planters, that most of the artillery, ammunition and provisions were transported; and whenever detachments occasionally stopped at their plantations, the latter met them with the most cordial reception, and were supplied with both food and forage as the same was wanting or could possibly be procured.

It should be remarked, that even those planters, whose estates had already been destroyed by the enemy, or had fallen into his possession, far from being dismayed by the sad prospect before them, had only been brought to that pitch of misfortune that their love of their country might appear with a greater lustre. Thus at the same time that MM. Villeré's, Delaronde's, Lacoste's and Bienvenu's sugar estates were laid waste, and made a prey to conflagration, M. Villeré, senior, major-general of our gallant militia, went on a survey of the upper counties for the purpose of hastening re-enforcements, which, at the first call, presented themselves in readiness to march; and when, after his return to camp, he had once taken charge at the second line of the post that had been assigned him, he was seen there invariably to fulfil his duties with that wonderful tranquillity of mind which a man, having nothing to lose, would have hardly been capable of: yet this gentleman, the head of a numerous family, could not but know, that one hundred slaves of his own were on his plantation at the mercy of the British, and that all his moveable property had already been either plundered or destroyed.

His son, M. Villeré, jun. major of the 3d regiment, after having, at the peril of his life, effected his escape from the British army, who had surprised him at his house, joined the forces that marched to repel the enemy on the 23d of December, and has ever since performed an active duty.

The important position of Chef-Menteur was protected by major Lacoste at the head of his corps, consisting of free men of colour, whilst his sugar estate was set to ruin and devastation. M. Lacoste, jun. his son, though deprived of the use of one arm, nevertheless shared constantly with his brother soldiers the toils and dangers of war.

Mr. Delaronde, colonel of the third regiment, though he abstained from claiming that part of the service which his rank entitled him to, did not disdain to serve as a guide, and with imminent peril continued scouting in woods almost impracticable, both in the flank and rear of the British, for the purpose of reconnoitring and making known their position.

In town, colonel Fortier, sen. contributed in a great measure to the more prompt departure for Chef-Menteur of the free men of colour, already embodied, by furnishing them, at his own cost, with such articles as they stood in need of. To him also the country owes the forming and organizing a second corps of free men of colour, to whom the brave Savary was appointed a captain. At his call, both captain and soldiers repaired to his house to be enlisted. He personally attended to the arming and equipping of them; and through his exertions that company under the command of major Daquin, was enabled to take the field and to face the enemy a few hours after its formation. M. Fortier caused also several hundred of muskets unfit for use to be repaired.

No sooner was it reported that a British squadron had arrived on our coast, than the uniform companies of the militia of New Orleans, under the command of major Plauché, and captains P. Roche, St. Geme, Hudry, White and Guibert, and the rifle corps under the command of captain Beale, who had some time before tendered their services, were placed at the bayou St. John, to which point it was expected the enemy would attempt to penetrate. It was from that position those gallant companies marched, with the rapidity of lightning, to the plains of Villeré, on the 23d of December, at the first appearance of the British. They travelled nearly twelve miles with wonderful rapidity, and fought with a bravery and resolution that would have done credit even to experienced soldiers. The first and second regiments of the militia of New Orleans, under the command of colonel Dejan and Zenon Cavelier, have conducted themselves in the several posts they were called upon to defend, with zeal and courage. They have borne with patience the fatigue of painful marches, occasioned by their being successively sent from one position to another. The fourth regiment, commanded by Mr. G.W. Morgan, their colonel, was entrusted with the defence of Chef-Menteur, upon major Lacoste's corps being withdrawn therefrom: they discharged their duty in a manner that bade defiance to all possible attempt, on the part of the enemy, to force that important pass. Three volunteer troops of horse, the one of them from the Attakapas, under the command of captain Dubuclay, and the other from Feliciana, commanded by captain Smith, and the last from Bayou Sarah, under command of captain Griffith, had already arrived in town, prior to the landing of the British. Two more troops of horse were immediately formed at New Orleans, headed by captains Chaveau and Ogden. The conduct of those several corps, upon every occasion where their services have been called for, deserves particular notice: and they were extremely useful. Captain Dubuclay was wounded in the head by a musket-ball, while in the act of rallying some men in an engagement on the right bank of the river.

General Thomas, general Hopkins and general M'Causland, at the head of the gallant militia under their command, hastened by forced marches from their respective counties in order to assist in defending the country.

General Garrigues Flaujac, by his patriotism and the talents he displayed, whilst the capital was threatened by the enemy, has earned the honour of being ranked among those who deserved well of their country.

Whilst our gallant militia were employed in the defence of the country at the several posts which had been assigned them, the citizens more advanced in years, having voluntarily formed themselves into companies of veterans, attended to the preservation of police and civil order in town. They greatly contributed by their good countenance, to dissipate the alarm created by the approach of the enemy; and by their unwearied exertions they insured the speedy and faithful conveyance to the camp of such articles as were to be sent there. They were also usefully employed in overseeing that the many donations made by our fellow-citizens, should be both applied properly and without confusion. At the head of these respectable veterans appeared Mr. Debuys, sen. their captain.

General Labatut had the command of the town. He performed his task with a zeal and activity that have done him infinite honour.

The mayor and city council of New Orleans, by the adoption of measures that indicate their foresight and humanity, have maintained our internal peace, and so far prevented a scarcity of provisions to be felt in town, as to make it doubtful whether the presence of the enemy in our neighbourhood had diminished our supplies.

The attention of Mr. Nicholas Girod, the mayor of New Orleans, in the meanwhile, was extended, with great benefit, to each part of the service. All the means placed at his disposal were applied in a manner that told a skilful administrator. Such families as were in actual distress, were relieved, and furnished with provisions agreeably to a decree of the city council appropriating a sum fully adequate to this purpose of benevolence.

The fair sex of New Orleans, without exception, eagerly undertook a variety of needle-work, for the use of the army. Many of them, who till then had been accustomed to do none but the nicest work, did not disdain sewing cloaks of the coarsest woollens. They gave both lint and linen for the use of the sick and wounded.

The Ursuline nuns are also entitled to a particular notice. They gave admittance within the walls of their monastery to as many of the sick as could be conveniently lodged therein, and afforded them every aid, conformably to the dictates of true charity.

All the practicing surgeons and physicians in the town have acted so as to do the highest honour to their profession. Their readiness in bestowing assistance to the military who wanted it, was such as did not permit them to wait till an application should be made for their services. A sympathetic feeling led them several miles below town to meet the wounded on the way and give them immediate attendance.

A committee named by the same veterans above mentioned, whose patriotism was not merely confined to the performance of the military duties they had willingly submitted to,—on which committee they had appointed namely, Messrs. Fortier, sen. Jh. Soulie, and Mr. Louaillier, a member of the house of representatives,—was affording relief to the sick and wounded with an indefatigable zeal; procuring subscriptions for the purchase of clothing, intended for our fellow-soldiers, who had left their homes, unprovided for a winter campaign. A sum exceeding fourteen thousand dollars was actually laid out for that laudable object, including in it the appropriation of six thousand dollars made by the legislature.

Every member on that committee deserves the highest praise for their perseverance and assiduity in fulfilling their task.

The enumeration of the corps and individuals who have given so many proofs of patriotism and devotion to their country, ought not to be closed without mentioning the governor of this state, whose efforts have constantly been directed towards cherishing the happy dispositions of the inhabitants, and whose authority to its utmost extent has been employed in securing the success of the measures adopted for the defence of this country.

Be it further resolved by the authority aforesaid, That each and every person and collection of persons mentioned in the foregoing statement are justly entitled to the gratitude of their country.

Be it further resolved by the authority aforesaid, That it shall be the duty of the governor of the state of Louisiana, in the name of the said state, to present the corps of veterans of New Orleans with a stand of colours bearing the following inscription, "*Our sons were repelling the foe, we attended to the safety of their mothers, and wives;*" and on the other side thereof will be seen a river, with an eagle hovering over the same, and this inscription on the river's bank "*for common use, and the benefit of all.*"

MAGLOIRE GUICHARD, *Speaker of the House of Representatives.*
FULWAR SKIPWITH, *President of the Senate.*

NO. LX.

By the President of the United States of America.

A PROCLAMATION.

Among the many evils produced by the wars, which, with little intermission, have afflicted Europe, and extended their ravages into other quarters of the globe, for a period exceeding twenty years, the dispersion of a considerable portion of the inhabitants of different countries, in sorrow and in want, has not been the least injurious to human happiness, nor the least severe in the trial of human virtue.

It had been long ascertained that many foreigners, flying from the dangers of their own home, and that some citizens, forgetful of their duty, had co-operated in forming an establishment on the island of Barataria, near the mouth of the river Mississippi, for the purpose of a clandestine and lawless trade. The government of the United States caused the establishment to be broken up and destroyed; and, having obtained the means of designating the offenders of every description, it only remained to answer the demands of justice by inflicting an exemplary punishment.

But it has since been represented that the offenders have manifested a sincere penitence; that they have abandoned the prosecution of the worst cause for the support of the best, and, particularly, that they have exhibited, in the defence of New Orleans, unequivocal traits of courage and fidelity. Offenders, who have refused to become the associates of the enemy in the war, upon the most seducing terms of invitation; and who have aided to repel his hostile invasion of the territory of the United States, can no longer be considered as objects of punishment, but as objects of a generous forgiveness.

It has therefore been seen, with great satisfaction, that the general assembly of the state of Louisiana earnestly recommend those offenders to the benefit of a full pardon: And in compliance with that recommendation, as well as in consideration of all the other extraordinary circumstances of the case, I *James Madison*, president of the United States of America, do issue this proclamation, hereby granting, publishing and declaring, a free and full pardon of all offences committed in violation of any act or acts of the congress of the said United States, touching the revenue, trade and navigation thereof, or touching the intercourse and commerce of the United States with foreign nations, at any time before the eighth day of January, in the present year one thousand eight hundred and fifteen, by any person or persons whatsoever, being inhabitants of New Orleans and the adjacent country, or being inhabitants of the said island of Barataria, and the places adjacent: *Provided*, that every person, claiming the benefit of this full pardon, in order to entitle himself thereto, shall produce a certificate in writing from the governor of the state of Louisiana, stating that such person has aided in the defence of New Orleans and the adjacent country, during the invasion thereof as aforesaid.

And I do hereby futher authorize and direct all suits, indictments, and prosecutions, for fines, penalties, and forfeitures, against any person or persons, who shall be entitled to the benefit of this full pardon, forth with to be stayed, discontinued and released: And all civil officers are hereby required, according to the duties of their respective stations, to carry this proclamation into immediate and faithful execution.

Done at the city of Washington, the sixth day of February, in the year one thousand eight hundred and fifteen, and of the independence of the United States the thirty-ninth.

JAMES MADISON.

By the president, JAMES MONROE,
Acting Secretary of State.

NO. LXI.

DECISION OF THE COURT MARTIAL IN THE CASE OF MAJOR VILLERÉ.

Head-Quarters, Adjutant-General's Office, New Orleans, March 15, 1815.

After a full examination of all the testimony for and against the prosecution, the court find the said major Villeré "not guilty" of the charges and specifications exhibited against him, and do acquit him of all and every one of them.—And the court consider it due to the accused, further to declare, that "major Villeré appears to have performed his duty, from the moment he was left in command under the orders of major-general Villeré, with zeal and fidelity; and that the circumstance of his surprise and capture by the enemy, though much to be regretted, might have occurred to the most vigilant officer, and must be attributed to the loss of the whole of his picquet or advanced guard, and the extraordinary rapidity with which the enemy moved from that point."The major-general commanding approved the foregoing sentence of the general court martial, and ordered major Villeré to resume his sword without delay.

By order, ROBERT BUTLER, *Adj.Gen.*

NOTE.—Major Villeré did not introduce any testimony in his behalf.

NO. LXII.

COURT OF INQUIRY.

Extracts of the Proceedings of a Court of Inquiry relative to the Retreat on the Right Bank of the Mississippi, on the 8th of January, 1815.

THE court, on mature deliberation, are of opinion that the conduct of colonel Daris, Dijan and Cavallier, in the action and retreat on the 8th of January, on the western bank of the Mississippi, is not reprehensible, nor do they know of any misconduct, as officers, in either since that time.

The causes of the retreat are attributed to the shameful flight of the command of major Arnaud, sent to oppose the landing of the enemy;—the retreat of the Kentucky militia, which, considering their position, the deficiency of their arms, and other causes, may be excusable;—and the panic and confusion introduced in every part of the line, thereby occasioning the retreat and confusion of the Orleans and Louisiana drafted militia.

Whilst the court find much to applaud in the zeal and gallantry of the officer immediately commanding, they believe that a farther reason for the retreat may be found in the manner in which the force was posted on the line, which they consider exceptionable. The commands of colonels Dijan, Cavallier and Declauett, composing five hundred men, supported by three pieces of artillery, having in front a strong breastwork, occupying only a space of two hundred yards, whilst the Kentucky militia, only one hundred and seventy men strong, without artillery, occupied more than three hundred yards, covered by a small ditch only.

WM. CARROLL, *Maj.Gen.* President of the Court.

NO. LXIII.

COURT OF INQUIRY.

At a Court of Inquiry assembled in the Naval arsenal, at New Orleans, by order of commodore Daniel T. Patterson, commanding the naval forces of the United States, on the New Orleans station, and continued by adjournment from day to day,—from Monday the 15th, until Friday the 19th of May, 1815— Present—Master commandant, Louis Alexis, president—

Lieutenant commandant Charles C. B. Thompson, and lieutenant Charles E. Crawley, *members*—for the purpose of investigating the conduct of the officers and men of the late division of United States' gun vessels, under the command of lieutenant commandant Thomas Ap C. Jones, captured by a flotilla of British barges and lanches, on the 14th of December, 1814. The court being organized, agreeably to form, commenced with the examination of the testimony in relation to the conduct of the commanding officer of the division; and after hearing attentively all the evidence that could be produced on that subject, proceeded to a minute investigation of the whole affair.

It appears to the court, that on the 12th of December last, the British fleet first made its appearance off Cat and Ship islands—that lieutenant commandant Jones, after having reconnoitred with his division of gun-vessels, five in number, and ascertained the state of the enemy's force, on the 13th, a flotilla of the enemy's barges appearing to advance, attempted to reach the fort at the Petty Coquilles, but that in consequence of the current being ahead, and the wind failing, he was prevented from getting any further than the Malheureux islands, where he anchored his gun-vessels between twelve and two at night.

It appears to the court, that on the morning of the 14th, the enemy's flotilla being perceived to be still advancing, he placed his division in the best position to receive them, and to oppose their passage—that the enemy advanced to the attack in the course of the forenoon, and that the number of the barges and lanches to which the gun-vessels were opposed was between forty-five and fifty.

It appears to the court, that about one-third of this number attacked the flag-vessel No. 156, while the others surrounded chiefly No. 162 and 163, and that after lieutenant commandant Jones had been very severely wounded, Mr. George Parker, his master's mate, continued the action until overpowered by numbers, to which no effectual resistance could be made; during which time several of the enemy's barges were sunk alongside, and great slaughter done in others.

It appears to the court, that gun-vessel No. 163 was the second vessel carried, after a gallant opposition, having previously kept off the enemy for some time, and being entirely surrounded.

It appears to the court, that gun-vessel No. 162, was the vessel next carried; that this was not effected, however, until her commander, lieutenant Spedden, had been most severely wounded (who, nevertheless, remained on deck and continued to give orders to the last,) nor until she was completely surrounded by the enemy, who suffered greatly in the contest.

It appears to the court, that No.5, sailing-master Ferris, was the next vessel that fell into the hands of the enemy—that the enemy succeeded in boarding her at a time, when further resistance was rendered ineffectual by the dismounting of her twenty-four pounder, and when the fire from the other gun-vessels had been turned upon her, after their capture.

It appears to the court, that No.23, lieutenant M'Keever, was the last vessel captured, and that this was effected at about half past twelve o'clock, after the enemy had succeeded in turning the fire of the other gun-vessels, previously captured, upon her.

It also appears to the court, that the barges and launches of the enemy were all mounted with cannon, and had from a thousand to twelve hundred men on board, armed in the best possible manner.

And, lastly, it further appears to the court, that after gun-vessel No. 156 had been captured by the enemy, her fire was turned upon the other gun vessels, and continued for a considerable time under the American colours.

The result of this inquiry is, a unanimous opinion, that lieutenant commandant Jones evinced by his movements, previous to the action, a judgement highly creditable to his character—that when an attack had become certain, he availed himself of every means to gain the best position for his squadron; and that, during the subsequent engagement, when opposed to a force of at least nine times his number, in large, well-appointed boats, formidably armed, he evinced a firmness and intrepidity worthy the emulation of his countrymen, and reflecting the highest honour on the service to which he belongs.

The court likewise conceive, that midshipman Parker, who acted as master's-mate during the action, on board the flag-vessel, displayed, in his determined resistance to the enemy, after the fall of his commander, the most signal bravery; and that he merits, in an especial degree, the notice of his government.

The court feels gratified in expressing the opinion, that the brave crew of the gun-vessel No. 156 forcibly felt the example of their officers; and that, under its influence, they maintained a most unequal conflict, with unparalleled destruction to the enemy, until they were borne down by numbers to which no opposition could be made.—Nor did the fall of this vessel, by which the enemy's force was not only increased, but, by her position, in a great measure covered, check the ardour of the gallant defenders of the rest of the squadron; for we find them contending as long as the least prospect of annoying the enemy lasted; their exertions unimpaired by their loss, and yielding at last, in succession only, to the concentrated force of the enemy, brought to act against each vessel.

With the clearest evidence for their guide, the court experience the most heartfelt gratification in declaring the opinion, that lieutenant commandant Jones, and his gallant supporters, lieutenants Spedden and M'Keever, sailing-masters Ulrich and Ferris, their officers and men, performed their duty on this occasion in the most able and gallant manner, and that the action has added another and distinguished honour to the naval character of our country.

LOUIS ALEXIS,
Master Commandant U.S. Navy.
G. DAVIS,
Officiating Judge Advocate.

In approving the proceedings and opinion of the court of inquiry, I avail myself with pleasure of the favourable occasion thus afforded me to express my admiration of the gallantry and skill displayed by lieutenant Jones, and his brave companions, in the defence made by them against so overwhelming a force as not to afford a prospect of success, to which the enemy were astonished to find a resistance offered. In this unequal contest I trust it will be found, that the national and naval character has been nobly sustained—that the resistance of the attack of so very superior a force has contributed, in no small degree, to the eventual safety of this city.

The proceedings and opinion of the court of inquiry, of which master commandant Louis Alexis is president, are approved.

DANIEL T. PATTERSON,
Captain U.S. Navy, com'g. N.O. Station.

NO. LXIV.

A list of the several corps composing the British army at the time of its landing on the shores of the Mississippi, with an estimate of their respective force.

4th regiment, king's own, lieutenant-colonel Francis Brooke	750 strong
7th do. Royal Fusiliers, lieutenant-colonel E. Blakeney	850
14th do. Duchess of York's own (light dragoons) lieutenant-colonel C. M. Baker	350
21st* do. Royal North Britain fusiliers, lieutenant-colonel W. Patterson	900
40th do. Sommersetshire, lieutenant-colonel H. Thornton	1000
43d do. Monmouth (light infantry) lieutenant-colonel Patrickson	850
44th do. East Essex, lieutenant-colonel honourable Thomas Mullen	750
85th do. Buck volunteers (light infantry) lieutenant-colonel William Thornton	650
93d do. Highland, lieutenant-colonel Robert Dale	1100
95th† do. Rifle corps, major Samuel Mitchell	500

*Of this regiment we have seen two returns signed by D. Dervan, adjutant, of the 17th December and 5th January, each of which justify the amount here given—its establishment was one thousand two hundred and eight.

†This regiment consists of three battalions, of one thousand men each, of which only a demi-battalion was sent to Louisiana.

1st do. West India, lieutenant-colonel C. W. Whitby	700
5th do. West India, lieutenant-colonel A.M.K. Hamilton	700
A detachment from the 62d regiment	350
Rocket brigade, artillery, drivers, engineers, sappers and miners	1500
Royal marines	1500
Sailors taken from the fleet	2000
Total	14,450

Staff of the British Army.

Sir Edward M. Packenham, colonel of the 7th regiment of foot, lieutenant-general commander-in-chief of the expedition.
Major-general Samuel Gibbs, colonel of the 59th regiment of foot, commanding the first division.
Major-general John Lambert, colonel 1st regiment foot-guards, commanding the second division.
Major-general John Keane, colonel 60th regiment of foot, commanding the third division.
Lieutenant-colonel John Dixon of the royal artillery, commanding the artillery.
Lieutenant-colonel Burgoyne, of the royal engineers, commanding the engineer department.
Lieutenant-colonel Steven, adjutant-general.
Lieutenant-colonel Bell, quarter-master-general.
Lieutenant-colonel Bradford and major Smith, military secretaries.
Mr. Soane, purveyor-general.
Mr. Hunter, pay master-general.
Mr. Moody, commissary-general.
Doctor John Robb, inspector-general of hospitals.
Doctor Thomson, inspector of hospitals.

In addition to the above, I give the following letter as corroborating the above statement.

Letter from Robert Morrell, M.D. to major Latour.

New Orleans, April 8, 1815.

Sir,

During my detention in the British fleet, the officers, both naval and military, with whom I had the opportunity to converse, always estimated their force here on the 8th January, at ten thousand regular troops at least. An incident occurred relating to this subject on the evening of the 7th January, which you may think worth communicating; This day I had accidentally omitted to wear uniform: while at supper with the ward-room officers of the Gorgon frigate, a military officer, (whose name I disremember) was introduced as coming directly from camp; he took a seat at table, and began to talk freely about the situation of the army, his business in the fleet, and addressing himself principally to me, he having taken up the idea I was first lieutenant of the ship. After various inquiries about the two lines, I asked the number of British he supposed might be on shore, he replied, when the last re-enforcements would be landed (which he had met three days before near Villere's canal) there would be, marines and sailors inclusive, from thirteen to fifteen thousand men; he was certain of this, for he had seen some returns previous to his departure; this was an intelligent officer, having the grade of captain, who had been sent by the commander-in-chief to ascertain the quantity of provisions in the fleet.

I am, &c.
ROBERT MORRELL, M.D.
United States Navy

NO. LXVI.

No. 1.

London, Admiralty Office, March 9, 1815.

Despatches addressed by Vice-Admiral the honourable Alexander Cochrane, G.C.B. &c. to John Wilson Croker, Esq.

Armide, off Isle au Chat, Dec.16, 1814.

Sir—Having arrived at the anchorage off Chandeleur islands, on the 8th inst. captain Gordon, of the Seahorse, (which ship, with the Armide and Sophie, I had sent on from off Pensacola to the anchorage within Isle au Vaisseau) reported to me that two gun-vessels of the enemy, apparently large sized sloops, of very light draught of water, had fired at the Armide, upon her way down from within the chain of small islands that run parallel to the coast from Mobile towards Lac Borgne, and having afterwards joined three others, cruising in the lake, were then visible from his mast head.

The Bayone Catalan, (or des Pecheurs) at the head of Lac Borgne, being the contemplated point of disembarkation, the distance from the inner anchorage of the frigates and troop-ships to the Bayone full sixty miles, and our principal means of transport open boats, it became impossible that any movement of the troops could take place till this formidable flotilla was either captured or destroyed.

Rear-admiral Malcolm joined me with the fleet upon the 11th instant, and upon the 12th I placed the lanches, barges, and pinnaces of the squadron, with captain Montressor, of the Manly, and captain Roberts, of the Meteor, under the command of captain Lockyer, of the Sophie, and sent them into Lac Borgne, in pursuit of the enemy, while the frigates, troop-ships, and smaller vessels, moved into the inmost anchorage, each vessel proceeding on until she took the ground.

After an arduous row of thirty-six hours, captain Lockyer had the good fortune to close with the flotilla, which he attacked with such judgment and determined bravery, that, notwithstanding their formidable force, their advantage of a chosen position, and their studied and deliberate preparation, he succeeded in capturing the whole of the vessels, in so serviceable a state as to afford at once the most essential aid to the expedition.

For the particulars of this brilliant affair, I refer their lordships to the accompanying copy of captain Lockyer's letter, detailing his proceedings, which, I am fully aware, their lordships will duly appreciate.

Captain Lockyer's conduct on this occasion, in which he has been severely wounded, and his long and actual services as a commander, justly entitling him to their lordship's protection, and finding it expedient to place this flotilla collectively upon the establishment of a thirty-six gun frigate, I have appointed him to the command thereof.

Captain Montressor, whom I have placed in the command of the gun-vessels until captain Lockyer's wounds will admit of his serving, and captain Roberts, whom I have before had occasion to mention to their lordships, together with lieutenants Tatnell and Roberts, and the officers mentioned by captain Lockyer, I trust will not fail to meet their lordship's notice.

Our loss has been severe, particularly in officers: but, considering that this successful enterprise has given us the command of Lac Borgne, and considerably reduced our deficiency of transports, the effort has answered my fullest expectations.

I have the honour to be, &c.
ALEXANDER COCHRANE,
Vice-admiral and Commander-in-chief.

Letter from Nicholas Lockyer to admiral Cochrane.

H.M. sloop Sophie, Cat Island Roads, December 17, 1814.

Sir—I beg leave to inform you, that in pursuance of your orders the boats of the squadron, which you did me the honour to place under my command, were formed into three divisions, (the first headed by myself, the second by captain Montressor, of the Manly, and the third by captain Roberts, of the Meteor) and proceeded, on the night of the 12th instant, from the frigates anchorage in quest of the enemy's flotilla.

After a very tedious row of thirty-six hours, during which the enemy attempted to escape from us, the wind fortunately obliged him to anchor off St. Joseph's island, and nearing him, on the morning of the 14th, I discovered his force to consist of five gun vessels of the largest dimensions, which were moored in a line abreast, with springs on their cables, and boarding nettings triced up, evidently prepared for our reception.

Observing also, as we approached the flotilla, an armed sloop* endeavouring to join them, captain Roberts, who volunteered to take her with part of his division, succeeded in cutting her off and capturing her, without much opposition.

*This "armed sloop," which required a division of barges to capture mounted one four-pounder, and carried eight men.

About ten o'clock, having closed to, within long gun-shot, I directed the boats to come to a grapnel, and the people to get their breakfasts; and as soon as they had finished we again took to our oars, and pulling up to the enemy against a strong current, running at the rate of nearly three miles an hour, exposed to a heavy and destructive fire of round and grape, about noon I had the satisfaction of closing with the commodore in the Seahorse's barge.

After several minutes' obstinate resistance, in which the greater part of the officers and crew of this boat were either killed or wounded, myself among the latter, severely, we succeeded in boarding, and being seconded by the Seahorse's first barge, commanded by Mr. White, midshipman, and aided by the boats of the Tonnant, commanded by lieutenant Tatnell, we soon carried her, and turned her guns with good effect upon the remaining four.

During this time captain Montressor's division was making every possible exertion to close with the enemy, and, with the assistance of the other boats, then joined by captain Roberts, in about five minutes we had possession of the whole of the flotilla.

I have to lament the loss of many of my brave and gallant companions, who gloriously fell in this attack; but considering the great strength of the enemy's vessels, (whose force under-neath described) and their state of preparation, we have by no means suffered so severely as might have been expected.

I am under the greatest obligations to the officers, seamen and marines, I had the honour to command on this occasion, to whose gallantry and exertions the service is indebted for the capture of these vessels; any comments of mine would fall short of the praise due to them. I am especially indebted to captains Montressor and Roberts, for their advice and assistance. They are entitled to more than I can say of them, and have my best thanks for the admirable style in which they pushed on with their divisions to the capture of the remainder of the enemy's flotilla.

In an expedition of this kind, where so many were concerned, and so much personal exertion and bravery was displayed, I find it impossible to particularize every individual who distinguished himself, and deserves to be well-spoken of; but I feel it my duty to mention those whose behaviour fell immediately under my own eye.

Lieutenant George Pratt, second of the Seahorse, who commanded that ship's boats, and was in the same boat with me, conducted himself to that admiration which I cannot sufficiently express. In his attempt to board the enemy he was several times severely wounded, and at last so dangerously, that I fear the service will be deprived of this gallant and promising young officer.

I cannot omit to mention also the conduct of lieutenants Tatnell and Roberts, of the Tonnant, particularly the former, who, after having his boat sunk alongside, got into another, and gallantly pushed on to the attack of the remainder of the flotilla. Lieutenant Roberts was wounded in closing with the enemy.

I have the honour to be, &c.
NICHOLAS LOCKYER, *Captain.*

No. 1—Gun-vessel, 1 long twenty-four-pounder, 4 twelve-pound carronades, and 4 swivels, with a complement of 45 men; captain Jones, commodore.
No. 2—Gun-vessel, 1 long thirty-two-pounder, 6 long six-pounders, a five-inch howitzers, and 4 swivels, with a complement of 45 men; lieutenant M'Ives [M'Keever.]
No. 3—Gun-vessel, 1 long twenty-four-pounder, 4 long six-pounders, and 4 swivels, with a complement of 45 men.
No. 4—Gun-vessel, 1 long twenty-four-pounder, 4 twelve-pound carronades, with a complement of 45 men.
No. 5—Gun-vessel, 1 long twenty-four-pounder, 4 twelve-pound carronades, with a complement of 45 men.
No. 6—Armed sloop, 1 long six-pounder, 2 twelve-pound carronades, with a complement of 20 men.

NICHOLAS LOCKYER, *Captain.*

A list of killed and wounded in the boats of his majesty's ships, at the capture of the American gun vessels, near New Orleans.

Tonnant—1 able seaman, 2 ordinary seamen, killed; 1 lieutenant, 4 midshipmen, 4 able seamen, 4 ordinary seamen, 2 landsmen, 3 private marines, wounded.
Norge—1 quarter-master, killed; 1 master's-mate, 4 able seamen, 3 ordinary seamen, 1 private marine, wounded.
Bedford—1 seamen, killed; 2 lieutenants, 1 master's-mate, 2 seamen, wounded.
Royal Oak—1 seaman, wounded.
Ramilies—4 seamen, killed; 9 seamen, wounded.
Armide—1 seaman, killed.
Cydnus—1 midshipman, 1 seaman, 2 private marines, wounded.
Seahorse—1 midshipman, 1 volunteer of the first class, 1 able seaman, 1 ordinary seaman, 1 landman, 4 private marines, killed; 1 lieutenant of marines, 7 able seamen, 7 ordinary seamen, 1 landman, 4 private marines, wounded.
Traave—1 volunteer of the first class, 1 captain of the foretop, killed; 1 private marine, wounded.
Sophie—1 captain, wounded.
Meteor—3 seamen, wounded.
Belle Poule—2 seamen, wounded.
Gorgon—1 master's mate, wounded.

Total—3 midshipmen, 13 seamen, 1 private marine, killed; 1 captain, 4 lieutenants, 1 lieutenant of marines, 3 master's-mates, 7 midshipmen, 50 seamen, 11 marines, wounded.

No. 2.

Letter from major-general Keane to major-general Packenham.

Camp on the left bank of the Mississippi, nine miles from New Orleans, December 26, 1814.

Sir,

I have the honour to inform you, that between the 17th and 22d inst. the troops destined for the attack of New Orleans, were collected at Isle aux Poix, which is at the entrance of the Pearl river.

Having learnt that it was possible to effect a landing at the head of the bayou Catalan, which runs into lake Borgne, I directed major Forrest, assistant quarter-master-general, to have it reconnoitered. Lieutenant Peddic, of that department, accompanied by the hon. captain Spenser, of the navy, ascertained on the night of the 18th, that boats could reach the head of the bayou, from which a communication might be made to the high road on the left bank of the Mississippi, leading to New Orleans.

On the morning of the 23d, every arrangement being made by vice-admiral the hon. sir Alexander Cochrane, I determined to attempt it. The light brigade, composed of the 85th and 95th regiments, captain Lane's rocketeers, one hundred sappers and miners, and the 4th regiment as a support, the whole under the command of colonel Thornton, were placed in the boats, and the 21st, 44th, and 93d regiments, under colonel Brooke, and a large proportion of artillery, under major Munro, were embarked in small vessels.

At ten A.M. on the 22d, we sailed from Pearl river, and reached the head of the bayou at day-light next morning. A landing was immediately effected without any other opposition than the country presented. Captain Blanchard, of the royal engineers, in the course of two hours opened a communication through several fields of reeds, intersected by deep muddy ditches, bordered by a low swampy wood. Colonel Thornton then advanced and gained the high road, taking up a position with the right resting on the road, and the left on the Mississippi. In this situation I intended to remain until the boats returned for the rest of the troops to the vessels, some of which grounded at a great distance.

At about eight o'clock in the evening, when the men, much fatigued by the length of time they had been in the boats, were asleep in their bivouac, a heavy flanking fire of round and grape shot was opened upon them, by a large schooner and two gun-vessels, which had dropped down the river from the town, and anchored abreast of our fires;—immediate steps were necessary to cover the men, and colonel Thornton in the most prompt and judicious manner, placed his brigade under the inward slope of the bank of the river, as did also lieutenant-colonel Brooke, of the 4th regiment; behind some buildings which were near that corps. This movement was so rapid that the troops suffered no more than a single casualty.

The three-pounders, being the only guns up, the success of a few twelve-pound rockets, directed by captain Lane, was tried against these vessels; but the ground on which it was necessary to lay them not being even, they were found not to answer, and their firing was ceased.

A most vigorous attack was then made on the advanced front and right flank picquets, the former of the 95th under captain Hallan, the latter the 85th under captain Schaw; these officers and their respective picquets, conducted themselves with firmness, and checked the enemy for a considerable time; but renewing their attack with a large force, and pressing at these points, colonel Thornton judged it necessary to move up the remainder of both corps. The 85th regiment was commanded by brevet major Gubbins, whose conduct cannot be too much commended; on the approach of his regiment to the point of attack, the enemy, favoured by the darkness of the night, concealed themselves under a high fence which separated the fields, and calling to the men as friends, under pretence of being part of their own force, offered to assist them in getting over, which was no sooner accomplished, than the 85th found itself in the midst of very superior numbers, who, discovering themselves, called on the regiment immediately to surrender—the answer was an instantaneous attack; a more extraordinary conflict has perhaps never occurred, absolutely hand to hand both officers and men. It terminated in the repulse of the enemy, with the capture of thirty prisoners. A similar finesse was attempted with the 95th regiment, which met the same treatment.

The enemy finding his reiterated attacks were repulsed by colonel Thornton, at half past ten o'clock advanced a large column against our centre; perceiving his intention, I directed colonel Stovin to order lieutenant-colonel Dale, with one hundred and thirty men of the 93d regiment, who had just reached the camp, to move forward and use the bayonet, holding the 4th regiment in hand, formed in line, as my last reserve. Colonel Dale endeavoured to execute the orders, but the crafty enemy would not meet him, seeing the steadiness of his small body, gave it a heavy fire, and quickly retired. Colonel Brooke, with four companies of the 21st regiment, fortunately appeared at that moment on our right flank, and sufficiently secured it from further attack. The enemy now determined on making a last effort, and collecting the whole of his force, formed an extensive line, and moved directly against the light brigade. At first this line drove in all the advanced posts, but colonel Thornton, whose noble exertions had guaranteed all former success, was at hand; he rallied his brave comrades round him, and moving forward with a firm determination of charging, appalled the enemy, who, from the lesson he had received on the same ground in the early part of the evening, thought it prudent to retire, and did not again dare to advance. It was now twelve o'clock, and the firing ceased on both sides.

From the best information I can obtain, the enemy's force amounted to five thousand men, and was commanded by major-general Jackson; judging from the number left on the field, his loss must have been severe. I now beg leave to enclose a list of our casualties on that night, and have only to hope it will appear to you that every officer and soldier on shore did his duty.

To sir Alexander Cochrane I feel particularly obliged for his very friendly counsel and ready compliance with every wish I expressed respecting the service or welfare of the troops.

To rear-admiral Malcom, and the several captains employed in the landing, &c. I confess the greatest obligation. I must leave it to the vice-admiral to do them the justice they so much deserve, for I cannot find words to express the exertions made by every branch of the navy, since the period of our arrival on this coast.

In the attack made on the centre, lieutenant-colonel Stovin, assistant adjutant-general, received a severe wound, which deprived me of his able services; to him and major Forrest, assistant quarter-master-general, I feel greatly indebted; they are both officers of great merit; colonel Brooke is entitled to every praise for securing our right flank.

To colonel Thornton I feel particularly grateful; his conduct on the night of the 23d, I shall ever admire and honour. He headed his brigade in the most spirited manner, and afforded it a brilliant example of active courage and cool determination.

I have every reason to be satisfied with lieutenant-colonel Brooke, commanding the 4th regiment; as also with major Mitchell, of the 95th, who was unfortunately taken prisoner at the close of the affair.

The exertions of major Monro of the royal artillery, were unremitting; to him, and the officers under his command, I feel every obligation. The assistance given by captain Blanchard, and the officers of the royal engineers, was most conspicuous, and entitle them to my best thanks.

Brevet major Hooper, acting deputy-assistant adjutant-general, was attached to the light brigade. Colonel Thornton states, that he derived the greatest benefit from his activity, zeal, and judgment. I regret to have to add, that he was very severely wounded, and had his leg amputated in the course of the night.

The indefatigable zeal and intelligence displayed by lieutenants Peddie and Evans, of the quarter-master-general's department, entitle them to the most favourable consideration.

Assistant commissary-general Wemyss's arrangements were satisfactory, and deputy-inspector Thompson claims my best acknowledgments, for the care and attention shown the wounded, the whole of whom were collected, dressed, and comfortably lodged before two in the morning.

Major Mills, of the 14th light dragoons, accompanied me on shore; from him, captain Persse, my aid-de-camp, and the hon. lieutenant Curzon, naval aid-de-camp, I received every assistance.

Trusting that the steps I pursued, while in command, will meet your approbation,

I have the honour to be, &c.

(Signed) JOHN KEANE, major-general.

No. 3.

Extract from the Journal of the movements of the army employed on the southern coast of North America.

On the evening of the 25th December, 1814, major-general sir E. Pakenham arrived and assumed the command of the army.

On the 26th at daylight our batteries opened on the enemy's schooner, then lying on the opposite bank of the river, and which had occasionally cannonaded our line the preceding days. The effect was such as to set her on fire, and at 9 A.M. she blew up. A ship armed with sixteen long twenty-four pounders, which came down the day before to a position abreast of our advance, no sooner saw the fate of the schooner than she got under way and ran up the river.

On the 27th at daylight the troops moved forward in two columns, driving in the enemy's pickets to within six miles of the town, where their main body was discovered strongly posted behind a canal, having a breastwork in their front, the extent from right to left being about one thousand yards; their right rested on the Mississippi, and was further protected by the armed ship moored in a position to enfilade our columns as they advanced—their left touched the wood. This wood extends in a parallel direction with the river, and is, in general, distant from it one thousand to fifteen hundred yards. The intermediate space is intersected by strong horizontal railings and a wet ditch or drain, and is principally planted with sugar-canes. Considerable houses, with large out-buildings and negro huts attached, are scattered at irregular distances along this tract.

The left column, under major-general Keane, advanced along the main road to within about eight hundred yards of the enemy's right, when he opened from two guns upon the head of our column; upon this it was moved off the road to the right, under cover of some houses. The ship at the same time opened an enfilading fire upon our left, and kept up an incessant cannonade for above an hour. The columns were now deployed, and the line ordered to lie down, our right pickets touching the wood. The enemy cannonaded us from four guns in his line, and from the ship during the day, but with little effect. In the evening the troops were retired beyond reach of the enemy's guns, and directed to hut themselves. Ground was also marked out for a redoubt of our flank, and the guns on our left covered them from the enemy's fire.

From the 28th to the 31st every exertion was made to get up from the ships ten eighteen-pound and four twenty-four-pound carronades, with the ammunition and stores. These were brought up the canal in boats to within a quarter of a mile of the main road, and thence transported on carriages of the country or our own limbers, by the seamen, with incredible labour. The weather was fortunately fair, and the road consequently good.

The enemy, during this period, established two batteries of one gun each on the opposite bank of the river, and occasionally threw shot into our camp with some effect.

Four eighteen-pounders were placed in a battery formed with hogsheads of sugar, on the main road, to fire upon the ship if she dropped down the river.

Preparations were also made to establish batteries, one of six eighteen-pounders to break the enemy's line, and the four twenty-four-pound carronades, and the field-gun and howitzers were to keep the fire of the enemy under, whilst the troops were to be moved forward to storm the works so soon as a practicable breach was effected.

On the night of the 31st December working parties were employed in throwing up the batteries and getting in the guns. In this they were most materially assisted by the seamen under captain sir Thomas Troubridge: before daylight the whole was completed, and the batteries ready to open.

The morning of the 1st January was foggy, and objects could not be discerned at any distance until nine o'clock, when our batteries opened. The enemy soon returned our fire, and a mutual cannonade took place:—Our batteries made little impression upon the enemy's parapet. The order for the assault was therefore not carried into effect. The troops remained in this advanced position, and orders were given to retire the guns in the night. The evening changed to wet, and the ground became in consequence so deep, that it required the exertions of the whole army as a working party, aided by the seamen, to retire the guns a short distance before daylight. The army then fell back to the position it occupied on the 31st.

C. R. FORREST, *A.Q.R.M.G.*

No. 4.

DESPATCH FROM GENERAL LAMBERT TO LORD BATHHURST.

Camp in front of the enemy's line before New Orleans, January 10, 1815.

My Lord,

It becomes my duty to lay before your lordship the proceedings of the force lately employed on the coast of Louisiana, under the command of major-general sir E.M. Pakenham, K.B. and acting in concert with vice-admiral the honourable sir A. Cochrane, K. B.

The report which I enclose from major-general Keane will put your lordship in possession of the occurrences which took place until the arrival of major-general the hon. sir E. M. Pakenham, to assume the command: from that period I send an extract of the journal of major Forrest, assistant-quarter-master-general, up to the time of joining the troops (which sailed on the 26th October last under my command) and which was on the 6th January; and from that period I shall detail, as well as I am able, the subsequent events.

I found the army in position, in a flat country, with the Mississippi on its left, and a thick extensive wood on its right, and open to its front, from which the enemy's line was quite distinguishable.

It seems sir E. Pakenham had waited for the arrival of the fusileers and the 43d regiment, in order to make a general attack upon the enemy's line; and on the 8th the army was formed for that object.

In order to give your lordship as clear a view as I can, I shall state the position of the enemy. On the left bank of the river it was simply a straight line of a front of about one thousand yards, with a parapet, the right resting on the river and the left on a wood, which had been rendered impracticable for any body of troops to pass. This line was strengthened by flank works, and had a canal of four feet deep, but not always of an equal width; it was supposed to narrow towards their left. About eight heavy guns were in position on this line. The Mississippi is here about eight hundred yards wide, and they had on the right bank a heavy battery of twelve guns, which enfiladed the whole front of the position on the left bank.

Preparations were made on our side with very considerable labour, to clear out and widen a canal that communicated with a stream by which the boats had passed up to the place of disembarkation, to open it into the Mississippi, by which means troops could be got over to the right bank, and the co-operation of armed boats would be secured.

The disposition for the attack was as follows: a corps consisting of the 85th light infantry, two hundred seamen, and four hundred marines, the 5th West-India regiment, and four pieces of artillery, under the command of colonel Thornton of the 85th, was to pass over during the night, and move along the right bank towards New Orleans, clearing its front, until it reached the flanking battery of the enemy on that side, which it had orders to carry.

The assailing of the enemy's works in front of us was to be made by the brigade composed of the 4th, 21st and 44th, under major-general Gibbs, and the 3d brigade, consisting of the 93d, two companies of the 95th, and two companies of the fusileers, and the 43d, under major-general Keane. Some black troops were destined to skirmish in the wood on the right;—the principal attack to be made by major-general Gibbs;—the first brigade and the 43d formed the reserve;—the attacking columns were to be provided with scaling-ladders and rafts;—the whole to be at their stations by daylight. An advanced battery in our front of six eighteen-pounders was thrown up during the night, about eight hundred yards from the enemy's line. The attack was to be made at the earliest hour. Unlooked for difficulties, increased by the falling of the river, occasioned considerable delay in the entrance of the armed boats; and those destined to land colonel Thornton's corps, by which four or five hours were lost, and it was not until half past five in the morning that the first division, consisting of five hundred men, were over. The ensemble of the general movement was lost, and in a point which was of the last importance to the attack of the left bank of the river, although colonel Thornton, as your lordship will see by his report, which I enclose, ably executed in every particular his instructions, and fully justified the confidence the commander of the forces placed in his abilities. The delay attending that corps occasioned some on the left bank, and the attack did not take place till the columns were discernible from the enemy's line at more than two hundred yards distance. As they advanced a continued and most galling fire was opened from every part of their line, and from the battery on the right bank.

The brave commander of the forces, who never in his life could refrain from being at the post of honour, and sharing the danger to which the troops were exposed, as soon as from his station he had made the signal for the troops to advance, galloped on to the front to animate them by his presence, and he was seen with his hat off encouraging them on the crest of the glacis; it was there (almost at the same time) that he received two wounds, one in his knee, and another, which was almost instantly fatal, in his body: he fell in the arms of major M'Dougall, aid-de-camp. The effect of this in the sight of the troops, together with major-general Gibbs and major-general Keane being both borne off wounded at the same time, with many other commanding officers, and further, the preparations made to aid in crossing the ditch not being so forward as they ought to have been, from, perhaps, the men being wounded who were carrying them, caused a wavering in the column, which in such a situation became irreparable; and as I advanced with the reserve, at about two hundred and fifty yards from the line, I had the mortification to observe the whole falling back upon me in the greatest confusion. In this situation, finding that there had been no impression made,—that though many men had reached the ditch, and were either drowned or obliged to surrender, and that it was impossible to restore order in the regiments where they were,—I placed the reserve in position,* until I could obtain such information as to determine me how to act to the best of my judgment, and whether or not I should resume the attack, and if so, I felt it could be done only by the reserve. The confidence I have in the corps composing it would have encouraged me greatly, though not without loss, which might have made the attempt of serious consequence, as I know it was the opinion of the late distinguished commander of the forces, that the carrying of the first line would not be the least arduous service. After making the best reflections I was capable of, I kept the ground the troops then held, and went to meet vice-admiral sir A. Cochrane, and to tell him that under all the circumstances, I did not think it proper to renew the attack on that day. At about ten o'clock I learnt of the success of colonel Thornton's corps on the right bank. I sent the commanding officer of the artillery, colonel Dickson, to examine the situation of the battery, and report if it was tenable; but informing me that he did not think it could be held with security by a smaller corps than two thousand men, I consequently ordered lieutenant-colonel Gubbins, on whom the command had devolved (colonel Thornton being wounded) to retire.

The army remained in position until night, in order to gain time to destroy the eighteen-pounder battery we had constructed the preceding night in advance, I then gave orders for the troops to resume the ground they had occupied previous to the attack.

Our loss has been very severe, but I trust it will not be considered, notwithstanding the failure, that this army has suffered the military character to be tarnished. I am satisfied, had I thought it right to renew the attack, that the troops would have advanced with cheerfulness. The services of both army and navy, since their landing on this coast, have been arduous beyond any thing I have ever witnessed, and difficulties have been got over with an assiduity and perseverance beyond all example by all ranks, and the most hearty co-operation has existed between the two services.

It is not necessary for me to expatiate to you upon the loss the army has sustained in major-general the hon. sir E. Pakenham, commander-in-chief of this force, nor

*This position was *supine* one. The reserve, and all those of the advanced columns, who escaped slaughter, were ordered to crouch down in the stubble, where they lay flat upon their faces till night. This new evolution was executed in order to avoid the fire of our artillery.

could I in adequate terms. His services and merits are so well known, that I have only, in common with the whole army, to express my sincere regret, and which may be supposed at present to come peculiarly home to me.

Major-general Gibbs, who died of his wounds the following day, and major-general Keane, who were both carried off the field within twenty yards of the glacis, at the head of their brigades, sufficiently speak at such a moment how they were conducting themselves. I am happy to say major-general Keane is doing well.

Captain Wylly, of the fusileers, military secretary of the late commander of the forces, will have the honour of delivering to your lordship these despatches. Knowing how much he enjoyed his esteem, and was in his confidence from a long experience of his talents, I feel I cannot do less than pay this tribute to what I conceive would be the wishes of his late general, and to recommend him strongly to your lordship's protection.

I am, &c.

(Signed) JOHN LAMBERT.

Return of casualties on the 8th January, 1815.

General staff—1 captain, 1 lieutenant; wounded one major-general.
Royal artillery—5 rank and file killed; 10 rank and file wounded.
Royal engineers, sappers and miners—3 rank and file wounded.
4th foot—l ensign, 2 serjeants, 39 rank and file killed; 1 lieutenant-colonel, 1 major, 5 captains, 11 lieutenants, 4 ensigns, 1 staff, 9 serjeants, 222 rank and file wounded; 1 lieutenant, 1 serjeant, 53 rank and file missing.
7th foot—1 major, 1 captain, 1 serjeant, 38 rank and file killed; 2 captains, 2 lieutenants, 2 serjeants, 47 rank and file wounded.
21st foot—1 major, 1 captain, 1 lieutenant, 2 serjeants, 65 rank and file killed; 1 lieutenant-colonel, 1 major, 2 lieutenants, 6 serjeants, 1 drummer, 144 rank and file wounded; 2 captains, 7 lieutenants, 8 serjeants, 2 drummers, 217 rank and file missing.
43d foot—2 serjeants, 1 drummer, 8 rank and file killed; 2 lieutenants, 3 serjeants, 3 drummers, 34 rank and file wounded; 1 captain, 5 rank and file missing.
44th foot—1 lieutenant, 1 ensign, 1 serjeant, 32 rank and file killed; 1 captain, 5 lieutenants, 3 ensigns, 5 serjeants, 149 rank and file wounded; 1 lieutenant, 2 serjeants, 1 drummer, 76 rank and file missing.
85th foot—2 rank and file killed; 1 lieutenant-colonel, 1 lieutenant, 3 serjeants, 2 drummers, 34 rank and file wounded; 1 rank and file missing.
93d foot—1 lieutenant-colonel, 2 captains, 2 serjeants, 58 rank and file killed; 4 captains, 5 lieutenants, 17 serjeants, 3 drummers, 348 rank and file wounded; 3 lieutenants, 2 serjeants, 1 drummer, 99 rank and file missing.
95th foot—1 serjeant, 10 rank and file killed, 2 captains, 5 lieutenants, 5 serjeants, 89 rank and file wounded.
Royal marines—2 rank and file killed; 1 captain, 2 lieutenants, l serjeant, 12 rank and file wounded.

Royal navy—2 seamen killed; 1 captain, 18 seamen wounded.
1st West-India regiment—5 rank and file killed; 1 captain, 2 lieutenants, 2 ensigns, 2 serjeants, 16 rank and file wounded; l rank and file missing.
5th West-India regiment—1 serjeant wounded.
Total loss—1 major-general, 1 lieutenant-colonel, 2 majors, 5 captains, 2 lieutenants, 2 ensigns, 11 serjeants, 1 drummer; 266 rank and file killed; 2 major-generals, 3 lieutenant-colonels, 2 majors, 18 captains, 38 lieutenants, 9 ensigns, 1 staff, 54 serjeants, 9 drummers, 1,126 rank and file wounded; 3 captains, 12 lieutenants, 13 serjeants, 4 drummers, 452 rank and file missing.

Names of officers killed, wounded and missing.

KILLED.

General staff—Major-general the honourable sir Edward Pakenham, K.B. commander of the forces; captain Thomas Wilkinson, 85th regiment, major of brigade.
4th foot—Ensign William Crowe.
7th foot—Major George King, captain George Henry.
21st foot—Major John Anthony Whittaker, captain Robert Renny (lieutenant colonel,) and lieutenant Donald M'Donald.
44th foot—Lieutenant Rowland Davies, ensign M. M'Loskey.
93d foot—Lieutenant-colonel Robert Dale, captain Thomas Hickins, and captain Alexander Mairhead.

WOUNDED

General staff—Major-general Gibbs, severely (since dead;) major-general Keane, severely; captain Henry Thomas Shaw, 4th foot (brigade-major) slightly; lieutenant Delacy Evans (3d dragoons, deputy-assistant-quarter-master-general) severely.
4th foot—lieutenant-colonel Francis Brooke, slightly; major A.D. Faunce (lieutenant-colonel) severely; captain J. Williamson (major) severely; captain T. Jones (lieutenant-colonel) severely, (since dead;) captain J.W. Fletcher, severely; captain R. Erskine severely; captain D.S. Craig slightly; lieutenants Ellis, Parnal, Hopkins, and J. Salvin, slightly; lieutenants W.H. Brook, B. Martin, and G. Richardson, severely; lieutenant P. Boulby and G.H. Hearn, slightly; lieutenants W. Squire, C.H. Farrington, J. Marshall, and H. Andrews, severely; ensign Alexander Gerard, slightly; ensign Thomas Benwell, severely; ensigns J. S. Fernandaz, and E. Newton, slightly; lieutenant and adjutant W. Richardson, slightly.
7th foot—captain J.J.A Mullins, slightly; captain W.E. Page, severely; lieutenant M. Higgins, severely; lieutenant C. Lorentz, slightly.
21st foot—Lieutenant-colonel W. Patterson (colonel) severely (not dangerously;) major A.J. Ross, severely; lieutenant J. Waters, severely; second-lieutenant A. Geddes, severely.

43d foot—lieutenant J. Meyricke, severely (left leg amputated;) lieutenant D. Campbell, severely.
44th foot—Captain H. Debbieg (lieutenant-colonel) slightly; lieutenant W. Maclean, slightly; lieutenants R. Smith, H. Brush, R. Phelan, and W. Jones, severely; ensigns J. White, B. L. Hayden, and J. Donaldson, severely.
85th foot—Lieutenant-colonel W. Thornton (colonel) severely, (not dangerously;) lieutenant B.C. Urquhart, severely (not dangerously.)
93d foot—captains; R. Ryan, P.O.K. Boulger, A. M'Kenzie, and H. Ellis, severely; lieutenants H.H. M'Lean, R. Spark, and D. Macpherson, slightly; C. Gordon, and J. Hay, severely.
95th foot—Captain J. Travers, severely; captain N. Travers, slightly; lieutenants J. Reynolds, sir J. Ribton, J. Gosset, W. Blackhouse, and Barker, severely.
Royal marines—Captain G. Elliott, slightly; lieutenants H. Elliott, and C. Morgan, slightly.
1st West-India regiment—Captain Isles, severely; lieutenants M'Donald and Morgan, severely; ensign Millar, slightly; ensign Pilkington, severely.
Royal navy—Captain Money, of H.M. ship Trave, severely; midshipman M. Woolcombe, Tonnant, severely.
93d foot—Volunteer John Wilson, slightly.

MISSING.

4th foot—Lieutenant E. Field, severely wounded and taken prisoner.
21st foot—Captain J. M'Haffie (major;) captain A. Kidd; lieutenants J. Stewart and A. Armstrong, taken prisoners; lieutenants J. Brady, wounded and taken prisoner; lieutenant J. Leavock, taken prisoner; lieutenant R. Carr, wounded and taken prisoner; lieutenant J.S.M. Fonhlangue, taken prisoner; second lieutenant P.Quin, wounded and taken prisoner.
43d foot—Captain R. Simpson, severely wounded and taken prisoner.
44th foot—Lieutenant W. Knight.
93d foot—Lieutenants G. Munro, J. M'Donald and Graves, severely wounded; volunteer B. Johnson.

FRED. STOVEN, *Lieut. Col. Dep. Adjt.Gen.*

RETURN OF CASUALTIES BETWEEN THE 9TH AND 26TH JANUARY, 1815.

43d foot—l rank and file killed; 1 lieutenant, (E.D'Arcy, severely, both legs amputated,) 1 serjeant, 2 rank and file wounded.
85th foot—1 rank and file wounded.
Total—1 rank and file killed; 1 lieutenant, 1 serjeant, 3 rank and file wounded.

FRED. STOVEN, *Lieut. Col. Dep. Adjt. Gen.*

RETURN OF THE ORDNANCE

Taken from the enemy by a detachment of the army acting on the right bank of the Mississippi, under the command of colonel Thornton.

Redoubt, Right Bank of the Mississippi, Jan. 8th, 1815.

1 brass ten-inch howitzer, 2 brass four-pounder field-pieces, 3 twenty-four-pounders, 3 twelve-pounders, 6 nine-pounders, 1 twelve-pounder carronade, not mounted.

On the howitzer is inscribed, "Taken at the surrender of York-Town, 1781."

J. MITCHELL, *Major, Capt. Royal Art.*

No. 5.

Letter from lieutenant-colonel Thornton to major-general Pakenham.

Redoubt on the right bank of the Mississippi, January 8, 1815.

Sir,

I lose no time in reporting to you the success of the troops which you were yesterday pleased to place under my orders, with the view of attacking the enemy's redoubt and position on this side of the river.

It is within your own knowledge, that the difficulty had been found so extremely great of dragging the boats through the canal, which had been lately cut with so much labour, to the Mississippi, that, notwithstanding every possible exertion for the purpose, we were unable to proceed across the river until eight hours after the time appointed, and even then, with only a third part of the force which you had allotted for the service.

The current was so strong, and the difficulty, in consequence of keeping the boats together, so great, that we only reached this side of the river at day-break, and by the time the troops were disembarked, which was effected without any molestation from the enemy, I perceived by the flashes of the guns that your attack had already commenced.

This circumstance made me extremely anxious to move forward, to prevent the destructive enfilading fire, which would, of course, be opened on your columns from the enemy's batteries on this side; and I proceeded with the greatest possible expedition, strengthened and secured on my right flank by three gun-boats, under captain Roberts of the navy, whose zeal and exertions on this occasion were as unremitted as his arrangements in embarking the troops, and in keeping the boats together in crossing the river, were excellent.

The enemy made no opposition to our advance, until we reached a piquet, posted behind a bridge, at about five hundred paces from the house in the Orange Grove, and secured by a small work, apparently just thrown up.

This picquet was very soon forced and driven in by a division of the 85th regiment, under captain Schaw, of that regiment, forming the advanced-guard, and whose mode of attack for the purpose was prompt and judicious to a degree.

Upon my arrival at the Orange Grove, I had an opportunity of reconnoitring, at about seven hundred yards, the enemy's position, which I found to be a very formidable redoubt on the bank of the river, with the right flank secured by an intrenchment extending back to a thick wood, and its line protected by an incessant fire of grape. Under such circumstances it seemed to me to afford the best prospect of success, to endeavour to turn his right at the wood; and I accordingly detached two divisions of the 85th regiment, under brevet lieutenant-colonel Gubbins, to effect that object; which he accomplished with his usual zeal and judgment; whilst one hundred sailors, under captain Money, of the royal navy, who, I am sorry to say, was severely wounded, but whose conduct was particularly distinguished on the occasion, threatened the enemy's left, supported by the division of the 85th regiment, under captain Schaw.

When these divisions had gained their proper position, I deployed the column composed of two divisions of the 85th regiment, under major Deshon, whose conduct I cannot sufficiently recommend, and about one hundred men of the royal marines, under major Adair, also deserving of much commendation, and moved forward in line, to the attack of the centre of the intrenchment.

At first the enemy, confident in his own security, showed a good countenance, and kept up a heavy fire, but the determination of the troops which I had the honour to command, to overcome all difficulties, compelled him to a rapid and disorderly flight, leaving in our possession his redoubts, batteries, and position, with sixteen pieces of ordnance, and the colours of the New Orleans regiment of militia.

Of the ordnance taken, I enclose the specified return of major Mitchell, of the royal artillery, who accompanied and afforded me much assistance, by his able directions of the firing of some rockets, it not having been found practicable, in the first instance, to bring over the artillery attached to his command.

I shall have the honour of sending you a return of the casualties that have occurred, as soon as it is possible to collect them, but I am happy to say they are extremely inconsiderable when the strength of the position, and the number of the enemy are considered, which our prisoners (about thirty in number) agree in stating from fifteen hundred to two thousand men, commanded by general Morgan.

I should be extremely wanting both in justice and in gratitude, were I not to request your particular notice of the officers whose names I have mentioned, as well as of major Blanchard, of the royal engineers, and lieutenant Peddie, of the 27th regiment, deputy assistant-quarter-master-general, whose zeal and intelligence I found of the greatest service.

The wounded men are meeting with every degree of attention and humanity by the medical arrangements of staff surgeon Baxter.

The enemy's camp is supplied with a great abundance of provisions, and a very large store of all sorts of ammunition.

On moving to the attack I received a wound, which shortly after my reaching the redoubt, occasioned me such pain and stiffness, that I have been obliged to give over the command of the troops on this side to lieutenant-colonel Gubbins, of the 85th light infantry; but as he has obtained some re-enforcement since the attack, of sailors and marines, and has taken the best precautions to cover and secure his position, I will be answerable, from my knowledge of his judgment and experience, that he will retain it, until your pleasure and further orders shall be communicated to him.

I have the honour to be, &c.

(Signed) W. THORNTON.

No. 6.

Letter from vice-admiral Cochrane to John Wilson Croker, esq.

Armide, off Isle au Chat, January 1815.

Sir,

An unsuccessful attempt to gain possession of the enemy's lines near New Orleans on the 8th instant, having left me to deplore the fall of major-general the hon. Sir Edward Pakenham, and major-general Gibbs, and deprived the service of the present assistance of major-general Keane, who is severely wounded, I send the Plantagenet to England, to convey a despatch from major-general Lambert, upon whom the command of the army has devolved, and to inform my lords commissioners of the admiralty of the operations of the combined forces since my arrival upon this coast.

The accompanying letters, Nos. 163 and 169, of the 7th and 16th ultimo, will acquaint their lordships of the proceedings of the squadron to the 15th December.

The great distance from the anchorage of the frigates and troop-ships to the bayou Catalan, which, from the best information we could gain, appeared to offer the most secure, and was, indeed, the only unprotected spot whereat to effect a disembarkation; and our means, even with the addition of the captured enemy's gun-vessels, only affording us transport for half the army, exclusive of the supplies that were required, it became necessary, in order to have support for the division that would first land, to assemble the whole at some intermediate position, from whence the second division could be re-embarked in light vessels brought into the lake, as near the bayou as might be practicable, and remain there until the boats could land the first division and return.

Upon the 16th, therefore, the advance, commanded by colonel Thornton, of the 85th regiment, was put into the gun-vessels and boats, and captain Gordon of the Seahorse proceeded with them, and took post upon the Isle aux Poix, a small swampy spot at the mouth of the Pearl river, about thirty miles from the anchorage, and nearly the same distance from the bayou, where major-general Keane, rear-admiral Codrington, and myself, joined them on the following day; meeting the gun-vessels and boats returning to the shipping for troops and supplies of stores and provisions.

The hon. captain Spencer, of the Carron, and lieutenant Peddy of the quarter-master-general's department, who were sent to reconnoitre the bayou Catalan, now returned with a favourable report of its position for disembarking the army; having, with their guide, pulled up in a canoe to the head of the bayou, a distance of eight miles, and landed within a mile and a half of the high road to, and about six miles below New Orleans, where they crossed the road without meeting with any interruption, or perceiving the least preparation on the part of the enemy.

The severe changes of the weather, from rain to fresh gales and hard frost, retarding the boats in their repeated passages to and from the shipping, it was not until the 21st that (leaving on board the greater part of the two black regiments and the dragoons) we could assemble troops and supplies sufficient to admit of our proceeding; and on that day we recommenced the embarkation of the second division in the gun-vessels, such of the hired craft as could be brought into the lakes, and the Anaconda, which by the greatest exertions had been got over the shoal passage.

On the 22d these vessels being filled with about two thousand four hundred men, the advance, consisting of about one thousand six hundred men, got into the boats, and at eleven o'clock the whole started, with a fair wind, to cross Lac Borgne. We had not, however, proceeded above two miles when the Anaconda grounded, and the hired craft and gun-vessels taking the ground in succession before they had got within ten miles of the bayou; the advance pushed on, and at about midnight reached the entrance.

A piquet, which the enemy had taken the precaution to place there, being surprised and cut off, mayor-general Keane, with rear-admiral Malcolm and the advance, moved up the bayou, and having effected a landing at day-break, in the course of the day was enabled to take up a position across the main road to New Orleans, between the river Mississippi and the bayou.

In this situation, about an hour after sun-set, and before the boats could return with the second division, an enemy's schooner of fourteen guns, and an armed ship of sixteen guns, having dropped down the Mississippi, the former commenced a brisk cannonading, which was followed up by an attack of the whole of the American army. Their troops were, however, beaten off, and obliged to retire with considerable loss, and major-general Keane advanced somewhat beyond his former position. As soon as the second division was brought up, the gun-vessels and boats returned for the remainder of the troops, the small armed seamen and marines of the squadron, and such supplies as were required.

On the 26th, major-general sir E. Pakenham and major-general Gibbs arrived at head-quarters, when the former took command of the army.

The schooner which had continued at intervals to annoy the troops, having been burnt on the 27th by hot shot from our artillery, and the ship having warped farther up the river, the following day the general moved forward to within gun-shot of an intrenchment which the enemy had newly thrown up, extending across the cultivated ground from the Mississippi to an impassable swampy wood on his left, a distance of about one thousand yards.

It being thought necessary to bring heavy artillery against this work, and also against the ship which had cannonaded the army when advancing, guns were brought up from the shipping, and on the 1st instant batteries were opened; but our fire not having the desired effect, the attack was deferred until the arrival of the troops under major-general Lambert, which were daily expected.

Major-general Lambert, in the Vengeur, with a convoy of transports, having on board the 7th and 43d regiments, reached the outer anchorage on the 1st, and this re-enforcement was all brought up to the advance on the 6th instant, while preparations were making for a second attack, in the proposed plan for which it was decided to throw a body of men across the river to gain possession of the enemy's guns on the right bank. For this purpose the canal by which we were enabled to conduct provisions and stores towards the camp, was widened and extended to the river, and about fifty barges, pinnaces, and cutters, having, in the day of the 7th, been tracked under cover and unperceived, close up to the bank, at night the whole were dragged into the Mississippi, and placed under the command of captain Roberts, of the Meteor.

The boats having grounded in the canal, a distance of three hundred and fifty yards from the river, and the bank being composed of wet clay thrown out of the canal, it was not until nearly daylight that, with the utmost possible exertions, this service was completed.

The 85th regiment, with a division of seamen under captain Money, and a division of marines under major Adair, the whole amounting to about six hundred men, commanded by col. Thornton, of the 85th regiment, were embarked and landed on the right bank of the river without opposition, just after daylight; and the armed boats moving up the river as the troops advanced, this part of the operations succeeded perfectly; the enemy having been driven from every position, leaving behind him seventeen pieces of cannon.

The great loss however sustained by the principal attack having induced general Lambert to send orders to colonel Thornton to retire after spiking the guns and destroying the carriages, the whole were re-embarked and brought back, and the boats, by a similar process of hard labour, were again dragged into the canal, and from thence to the bayou, conveying at the same time such of the wounded as it was thought requisite to send off to the ships.

Major-general Lambert having determined to withdraw the army, measures were taken to re-embark the whole of the sick and wounded that it was possible to move, and the stores, ammunition, ordnance, &c. with such detachments of the army, seamen, and marines, as were not immediately wanted; in order that the remainder of the army may retire unincumbered, and the last division be furnished with sufficient means of transport.

This arrangement being in a forward state of execution, I quitted head-quarters on the 14th instant, leaving rear-admiral Malcolm to conduct the naval part of the operations in that quarter, and I arrived at this anchorage on the 16th, where I am arranging for the reception of the army, and preparing the fleet for further operations.

I must, in common with the nation, lament the loss which the service has sustained by the death of major-general the hon. sir Edward Pakenham, and major-general Gibbs. Their great military qualities were justly estimated while living, and their zealous devotion to our country's welfare, will be cherished as an example to future generations.

In justice to the officers and men of the squadron under my command who have been employed upon this expedition, I cannot omit to call the attention of my lords commissioners of the admiralty to the laborious exertions and great privations which have been willingly and cheerfully borne, by every class, for a period of nearly six weeks.

From the 12th of December, when the boats proceeded the attack of the enemy's gun vessels, to the present time, but very few of the officers or men have ever slept on board their ships.

The whole of the army, with the principal part of its provisions, its stores, artillery, ammunition, and the numerous necessary appendages, have been all transported from the shipping to the head of the bayou, a distance of seventy miles, chiefly in open boats, and are now re-embarking by the same process. The hardships, therefore, which the boats crews have undergone, from their being kept day and night continually passing and repassing in the most changeable and severe weather, have rarely been equalled; and it has been highly honourable to both services, and most gratifying to myself, to observe the emulation and unanimity which has pervaded the whole.

Rear-admiral Malcolm superintended the disembarkation of the army, and the various services performed by the boats; and it is a duty that I fulfil with much pleasure, in assuring their lordships that his zeal and exertions upon every occasion could not be surpassed by any one. I beg leave also to offer my testimony to the unwearied and cheerful assistance afforded to the rear-admiral by captains sir Thomas M. Hardy, Dashwood, and Gordon, and the several captains and other officers. Rear-admiral Codrington accompanied me throughout the service, and I feel much indebted for his able advice and assistance.

Captain sir Thomas Troubridge, and the officers and seamen attached, under his command, to the army, have conducted themselves much to the satisfaction of the generals commanding. Sir Thomas Troubridge speaks in the highest terms of the captains and other officers employed under him, as named in his letter (a copy of which is enclosed) reporting their services. He particularly mentions captain Money, of the Trave, who I am much concerned to say, had both bones of his leg broken by a musket shot, advancing under a heavy fire to the attack of the battery that was afterwards carried.

The conduct of captain Money at Washington and near Baltimore, where he was employed with the army, having before occasioned my noticing him to their lordships, I beg leave now to recommend him most strongly to their protection. The wound that he has received not affording him any probability of his being able to return to his duty for a considerable time, I have given him leave to go to England; and shall intrust to him my despatches.

I have not yet received any official report from the captain of the Nymph, which ship, with the vessels named in the margin,* were sent into the Mississippi, to create a diversion in that quarter.

The bombs have been for some days past throwing shells into fort Plaquemine, but I fear without much effect. I have sent to recall such of them as are not required for the blockade of the river.

I have the honour to be, &c.
ALEXANDER COCHRANE.

Letter from capt. Thomas Troubridge to vice-admiral Cochrane.

Head-quarters near New Orleans, January 12, 1815.

Sir,

The conduct and exertions of the officers and seamen which you did me the honour to place under my command to serve with the army on shore, having been such as to meet very general approbation, I feel it a duty I owe to them to make such known to you, and to particularize the exertions of captains Money, Rogers, and Westphall.

I cannot sufficiently express the high sense I entertain of the zeal and activity of lieutenant Scott, of the Tonnant, and lieutenant Fletcher, of the Norge, who, on all occasions, have shown themselves most deserving officers.

Captains Money and Rogers, who were detached across the river, again report the exertion and gallantry of lieutenant Scott, and also of Mr. Woolcombe, midshipman of his majesty's ship Tonnant, who particularly distinguished themselves in leading their men under a heavy fire to the battery that was carried. It is with infinite regret that I report the severe wound captain Money received while on this service. To lieutenants Wroote, of the Royal Oak, and Franklin, of the Bedford, with the many other officers employed, every praise is due.

I have the honour to be, &c.
THOMAS TROUBRIDGE.

No. 7.

Letter from general Lambert to earl Bathurst.

His Britannic Majesty's ship Tonnant, off Chandeleur's island, January 28th, 1815.

My Lord,

After maturely deliberating on the situation of this army, after the command had unfortunately devolved upon me, on the 8th instant, and duly considering what probability now remained of carrying on with success, on the same plan, an attack against New Orleans, it appeared to me that it ought not to be persisted in. I immediately

*Nymph, Herald, Aetna, Meteor, Thistle, Pigmy.

communicated to vice-admiral sir A. Cochrane that I did not think it would be prudent to make any further attempt at present, and that I recommended re-embarking the army as soon as possible, with a view to carry into effect the other objects of the force employed upon this coast; from the 9th inst. it was determined that the army should retreat, and I have the satisfaction of informing your lordship that it was effected on the night of the 18th inst. and ground was taken up on the morning of the 19th on both sides of the bayone, or creek, which the troops had entered on their disembarkation, fourteen miles from their position before the enemy's line, covering New Orleans, on the left bank of the Mississippi, and one mile from the entrance into Lac Borgne: the army remained in bivouac until the 27th instant, when the whole were re-embarked.

In stating the circumstances of this retreat to your lordship, I shall confidently trust that good order and discipline ever existed in this army, and that zeal for the service, and attention was ever conspicuous in officers of all ranks. Your lordship is already acquainted with the position the army occupied, its advanced post close up to the enemy's, and the greater part of the army were exposed to the fire of the batteries which was unremitting day and night since the 1st of January, when the position in advance was taken up. The retreat was effected without being harassed in any degree by the enemy; all the sick and wounded (with the exception of eighty, whom it was considered dangerous to remove), field artillery, ammunition, hospital and other stores of every description, which had been landed on a very large scale, were brought away, and nothing fell into the enemy's hands, excepting six iron eighteen-pounders, mounted on sea carriages, and two carronades, which were in position on the left bank of the Mississippi; to bring them off at the moment the army was retiring was impossible, and to have done it previously would have exposed the whole force to any fire the enemy might have sent down the river. These batteries were of course destroyed, and the guns rendered perfectly unserviceable; only four men were reported absent next morning, and those, I suppose, must have been left behind and have fallen into the hands of the enemy: but when it is considered the troops were in perfect ignorance of the movement, until a fixed hour during the night, that the picquets did not move off till half-past three o'clock in the morning, and that the whole had to retire through the most difficult new made road, cut marshy ground, impassable for a horse, and where, in many places, the men could only go in single files, and that the absence of men might be accounted for in so many ways, it would be rather a matter of surprise the number was so few.

An exchange of prisoners has been effected with the enemy upon very fair terms, and their attention to the brave prisoners, and wounded, that have fallen into their hands, has been kind and humane, I have every reason to believe.

However unsuccessful the termination of the late service the army and navy have been employed upon, has turned out, it would be injustice not to point out how much praise is due to their exertions; ever since the 13th December, when the army began to move from the ships, the fatigue of disembarking and bringing up artillery and supplies from such a distance has been incessant; and I must add, that owing to the exertions of the navy, the army has never wanted provisions. The labour of the seamen and soldiers was particularly conspicuous on the night of the 7th inst. when fifty boats were dragged through a canal into the Mississippi, in which there were only eighteen inches of water, and I am confident that the vice-admiral sir Alexander Cochrane, who suggested the possibility of this operation, will be equally ready to admit this, as well as the hearty co-operations of the troops of all occasions.

From what has come under my own observation since I joined this army, and from official reports that have been made to me, I beg to call your lordship's attention to individuals who, from their station, have rendered themselves peculiarly conspicuous. Major Forrest, at the head of the quarter-master-general's department, I cannot say too much of. Lieutenant Evans and Peddie of the same, have been remarkable for their exertions and indefatigability; sir John Tylden, who had acted in the field as assistant adjutant-general with me (lieutenant-colonel Stovin having been wounded on the 23d ult. though doing well, not as yet being permitted to take active service), has been very useful; on the night of the 7th, previous to the attack, rear-admiral Malcolm reports the great assistance he received from him in forwarding the boats into the Mississippi; captain Wood, of the 4th regiment, deputy assistant adjutant-general, has filled that situation since the first disembarkation of the troops with zeal and attention.

During the action of the 8th inst. the command of the 2d brigade devolved upon lieutenant-colonel Brooke, 4th regiment, that of the 3d upon colonel Hamilton, 5th West India regiment, and the reserve upon colonel Blayken, royal fusileers; to all these officers I feel much indebted for their service. Lieutenant-colonel Dickson, royal artillery, has displayed his usual abilities and assiduity; he reports to me his general satisfaction of all the officers under his command, especially major Munro, senior officer of the royal artillery, previous to his arrival, and of the officers commanding companies.

Lieutenant-colonel Burgoyne, royal engineers, afforded me every assistance that could be expected from his known talents and experience; that service lost a very valuable and much esteemed officer in lieutenant Wright, who was killed when reconnoitring on the evening of the 31st ultimo.

Lieutenant-colonel Mein, of the 43d, and lieutenant colonel Gubbins, 85th regiment, field officers of the piquets on the 18th, have great credit for the manner in which they withdrew the outposts on the morning of the 19th under the direction of colonel Blakeney, royal fusileers.

I request in a particular manner to express how much this army is indebted to the attention and diligence of Mr. Robb, deputy inspector of hospitals, and their immediate removal, with such excellent arrangement, that the wounded were all brought off with very favourable circumstance, except such cases as would have rendered their removal dangerous.

Captain sir Thomas Troubridge, royal navy, who commanded a battalion of seamen, and who was attached to act with the troops, rendered the greatest service by his exertions in whatever way they were required; colonel Dickson, royal artillery, particularly mentions how much he was indebted to him.

The conduct of two squadrons of the 14th light dragoons, latterly under the command of lieutenant-colonel Baker, previously of major Mills, has been the admiration of every one, by the cheerfulness with which they have performed all descriptions of service. I must also mention the exertions of the royal staff corps under major Todd so reported by the deputy-quarter-master-general.

Permit me to add the obligations I am under to my personal staff. Lieutenant the honourable Edward Curzon, of the royal navy, who was selected as a naval aid-de-camp to the commanding officer of the troops on their first disembarkation, each of whom have expressed the satisfaction they had in his appointment, to which I confidently add my own.

Major Smith, of the 95th regiment, now acting as military secretary, is so well known for his zeal and talents, that I can with great truth say, that I think he possesses every qualification to render him hereafter one of the brightest ornaments of his profession.

I cannot conclude without expressing how much the army is indebted to rear-admiral Malcolm, who had the immediate charge of landing and re-embarking the troops; he remained on shore to the last, and by his abilities and activity smoothed every difficulty.

I have the honour to be, &c.

(Signed) JOHN LAMBERT.

P.S. I regret to have to report that during the night of the 25th, in very bad weather, a boat containing two officers, viz. lieutenant Brydges and cornet Hammond, and thirty-seven of the 14th light dragoons, unfortunately fell into the hands of the enemy, off the mouth of the Rigolets. I have not been able to ascertain correctly the particular circumstances.

Return of casualties in action with enemy near New Orleans, on the 23d and 24th December, 1814.

General staff—1 lieutenant-colonel, 1 major, 1 lieutenant wounded.

Royal artillery—2 rank and file killed; 1 lieutenant, 7 rank and file missing.

Royal engineers, sappers and miners—1 rank and file missing.

4th foot—1 captain, 1 lieutenant, 1 sergeant, 1 drummer, 1 rank and file killed; 1 sergeant, 2 drummers, 8 rank and file wounded; 2 rank and file missing.

35th ditto—2 captains, 11 rank and file, killed; 1 captain, 3 lieutenants, 4 sergeants, 2 drummers, 57 rank and file, wounded; 1 lieutenant, 1 ensign, 1 sergeant, 16 rank and file, missing.

93d do—1 rank and file, wounded.

95th foot—6 sergeants, 17 rank and file, killed; 1 captain, 2 lieutenants, 6 sergeants, 34 rank and file, wounded; 1 major, 2 sergeants, 39 rank and file, missing.

Total—4 captains, 1 lieutenant, 7 sergeants, 1 drummer, 33 rank and file, killed; 1 lieutenant-colonel, 1 major, 2 captains, 8 lieutenants, 10 sergeants, 4 drummers, 141 rank and file, wounded, 1 major, 1 lieutenant, 1 ensign, 3 sergeants, 58 rank and file, missing.

NAMES OF OFFICERS KILLED, WOUNDED, AND MISSING.

KILLED.

4th foot—captain F.J. Johnstone, lieutenant John Southerland.

21st do—captain W. Conran.

85th do—captains C. Grey and C. Harris.

WOUNDED.

General staff—lieutenant-colonel Stovin, 28th foot, assistant adjutant-general, severely but not dangerously; major Hooper, 87th foot, deputy assistant adjutant-general severely (leg amputated), lieutenant D. Evans, 3d dragoons, deputy assistant quarter-master-general, severely.

Royal artillery—lieutenant J. Christie, severely.

4th foot—lieutenant T. Moody, severely.

89th foot—captain James Knox, lieutenants G. Willings, F. Maunsell, and W. Hickson, severely.

95th foot—captain W. Hallen, lieutenant D. Forbes, severely; lieutenant W.J.G. Farmer, slightly.

MISSING.

85th do—lieutenant W. Walker, and ensign G. Ashton.

95th do—major Samuel Mitchell.

FRED. STOVIN.

RETURN OF CASUALTIES BETWEEN THE 25TH AND 31ST DECEMBER, 1814.

Royal artillery—4 rank and file killed; 1 lieutenant, 5 rank and file wounded.

Royal engineers, sappers and miners, 1 rank and file wounded.

4th foot—4 rank and file wounded.

21st do—1 rank and file killed, 1 rank and file wounded.

44th do—2 rank and file wounded; 1 rank and file missing.

85th do—1 drummer, 3 rank and file killed; 2 ensigns, 11 rank and file wounded.

93d do—2 rank and file killed; 5 rank and file wounded.

95th do—3 rank and file killed; 1 sergeant, 3 rank and file wounded; 1 rank and file missing.

1st West India regiment—1 captain, killed.

5th do—1 rank and file killed; 2 rank and file wounded.

Total—1 captain, 1 drummer, 14 rank and file killed; 1 lieutenant, 2 ensigns, 4 sergeants, 34 rank and file wounded; 2 rank and file missing.

NAMES OF OFFICERS KILLED AND WOUNDED.

KILLED.

1st West India regiment—captain F. Collings.

WOUNDED.

Royal artillery—lieutenant B.L. Poynter, slightly.

85th foot—ensign sir Fred. Eden, Bart. severely (since dead) ensign T. Ormsby, slightly.

FRED. STOVEN.

RETURN OF CASUALTIES BETWEEN THE 1ST AND 5TH JANUARY, 1815.

Royal artillery—1 lieutenant, 1 sergeant, 9 rank and file, killed; 12 rank and file, wounded.

Royal engineers, sappers and miners-1 lieutenant, killed.

21st foot—1 rank and file killed; one lieutenant, 4 rank and file wounded.

44th do—1 lieutenant, 1 rank and file killed; 3 rank and file wounded.

85th do—2 rank and file killed; 2 lieutenants, 4 rank and file wounded.

93d do. foot—1 sergeant, 8 rank and file killed; 1 lieutenant, 10 rank and file wounded.

95th do—l rank and file killed; 2 rank and file missing.

5th West India regiment—4 rank and file killed; 2 rank and file wounded.

Total—3 lieutenants, 2 sergeants, 27 rank and file killed; 4 lieutenant, 40 rank and file wounded; 2 rank and file missing.

NAMES OF THE OFFICERS KILLED AND WOUNDED.

KILLED.

Royal artillery—lieutenant A. Ramsay.

Royal engineers—lieutenant P. Wright.

44th foot—lieutenant John Blakeney.

WOUNDED.

21st foot—lieutenant J. Leavock, slightly.

85th do—lieutenant R. Carlton, severely; lieutenant J.W. Boys, slightly.

93d do—lieutenant A. Phaup, severely, (since dead.)

FRED. STOVIN.

No. 8.

Letter from general Lambert to earl Bathurst.

Head-Quarters, Isle Dauphine, February 14th, 1815.

My Lord,

My despatch, dated January 29th, will have informed your lordship of the re-embarkation of this force, which was completed on the 30th; the weather came on so bad on that night, and continued so until the 5th of February, that no communication could be held with the ships at the inner anchorage, a distance of about seventeen miles.

It being agreed between vice-admiral sir Alexander Cochrane and myself that operations should be carried towards Mobile, it was decided that a force should be sent against fort Bowyer, situated on the eastern point of the entrance of the bay, and from every information that could be obtained, it was considered a brigade would be sufficient for this object, with a respectable force of artillery. I ordered the second brigade, composed of the 4th, 21st and 44th regiments, for this service, together with such means in the engineer and artillery departments as the chief and commanding officer of the royal artillery might think expedient. The remainder of the force had orders to disembark on Isle Dauphine, and encamp; and major-general Keane, whom I am truly happy to say has returned to his duty, superintended their arrangement.

The weather being favourable on the 7th for the landing to the eastward of Mobile Point, the ships destined to move on that service sailed under the command of captain Ricketts, of the Vengeur, but did not arrive in sufficient time that evening to do more than determine the place of disembarkation, which was about three miles from fort Bowyer.

At daylight the next morning the troops got into the boats, and six hundred men were landed under lieutenant-colonel Debbeig, of the 44th, without opposition, who immediately threw out the light companies under lieutenant Bennett, of the 4th regiment, to cover the landing of the brigade. Upon the whole being disembarked, a disposition was made to move on towards the fort, covered by the light companies. The enemy was not seen until about one thousand yards in front of their works; they gradually fell back, and no firing took place until the whole had retired into the fort, and our advance had pushed on nearly to within three hundred yards. Having reconnoitred the forts with lieutenant-colonels Burgoyne and Dickson, we were decidedly of opinion, that the work was formidable only against an assault; that batteries being once established, it must speedily fall. Every exertion was made by the navy to land provisions, and the necessary equipment of the battering train and engineer stores. We broke ground on the night of the 8th, and advanced a firing party to within one hundred yards of the fort during the night. The position of the batteries being decided upon the next day, they were ready to receive their guns on the night of the 10th, and on the morning of 11th the fire of a battery of four eighteen-pounders on the left, and two eight-inch howitzers on the right, each about one hundred yards distance, two six-pounders at about three hundred yards, and eight small cohorns advantageously placed on the right, with intervals between of one hundred and two hundred yards, all furnished to keep up an incessant fire for two days, were prepared to open. Preparatory to commencing, I summoned the fort, allowing the commanding officer half an hour for decision upon such terms as were proposed. Finding he was inclined to consider them, I prolonged the period, at his request, and at three o'clock the fort was given up to a British guard, and British colours hoisted; the terms being signed by major Smith, military secretary, and captain Ricketts, R.N. and finally approved of by the vice-admiral and myself, which I have the honour to enclose.

I am happy to say our loss was not very great; and we are indebted for this, in a great measure, to the efficient means attached to this force. Had we been obliged to resort to any other mode of attack, the fall could not have been looked for under such favourable circumstances.

We have certain information of a force having been sent from Mobile, and disembarked about twelve miles off, in the night of the 10th, to attempt its relief; two schooners with provisions, and an intercepted letter, fell into our hands, taken by captain Price, R.N. stationed in the bay.

I cannot close this despatch without naming to your lordship again lieutenant-colonels Dickson, royal artillery, and Burgoyne, royal engineers, who displayed their usual zeal and abilities; and lieutenant Bennet, of the 4th, who commanded the light companies and pushed up close to the enemy's works.

Captain hon. R. Spencer, R.N. who had been placed with a detachment of seamen under my orders, greatly facilitated the service in every way by his exertions.

From captain Ricketts, of the R.N. who was charged with the landing and the disposition of the naval force, I received every assistance.

JOHN LAMBERT.

Fort Bowyer, February 14th, 1815.

Return of ordnance, ammunition and stores, captured from the enemy in this place, on the 12th instant:

GUNS.

1 twenty-four-pounder, 2 nine-pounders, outside the fort.
Iron—3 thirty-two-pounders, 8 twenty-four-pounders, 6 twelve-pounders, 5 nine-pounders.
Brass—1 four-pounder.
Mortar—1 eight-inch.
Howitzer—l five-and-a-half-inch.

SHOT.

Thirty-two-pounder—856 round, 64 grape, 11 case.
Twenty-four-pounder—851 round, 176 bar, 286 grape, 84 case.
Twelve-pounder—535 round, 74 grape, 439 case.
Nine-pounder—781 round, 208 grape, 429 case.
Six-pounder—15 round, 75 bar, 13 case.
Four-pounder—231 round, 38 grape, 147 case.
Shells—25 eight-inch, 74 five-and-a-half-inch.
183 hand-grenades.
5,519 pounds powder.
1 triangle gin, complete.
16,976 musket ball-cartridges.

500 flints.
351 muskets, complete, with accoutrements.

JAS. PERCIVAL, *Ass. Com. Royal Artillery.*
A. DICKINSON, *Lt. Col. Com. Royal Artillery.*

Return of casualties in the army under the command of major-general Lambert, employed before fort Bowyer, between the 8th and 12th of February, 1815.

Royal sappers and miners—1 rank and file wounded.
4th foot—8 rank and file killed; 2 serjeants, 13 rank and file wounded.
21st foot—2 serjeants, 2 rank and file killed; 1 rank and file wounded.
40th foot—1 rank and file killed; 1 rank and file wounded.
Total—13 killed, 18 wounded.

F. STOVEN, *D.A.G.*

Return of the American garrison of fort Bowyer, which surrendered to the force under major-general Lambert, 11th February, 1815.

1 field-officer, 3 captains, 10 subalterns, 2 staff, 16 serjeants, 16 drummers, 327 rank and file, 20 women, 16 children, 3 servants not soldiers.

F. STOVEN, *D.A.G.*

NO. LXVII.

LETTERS FOUND ON BOARD THE ST. LAWRENCE AT THE TIME OF HER SURRENDER TO THE CHASSEUR PRIVATEER.

From colonel Malcolm to rear-admiral Malcolm.

Cumberland Island, 5th February, 1815.

I received your letter of the 5th ult. it is written before your last attack on that place, but I most sincerely hope you will ultimately succeed. From all accounts New Orleans is very strong: the enemy will have gained a great confidence in themselves from their success. What a disappointment it will be in England should you fail—the chance of failure has not been calculated on, and from the force employed it has been made too sure at first. I have no opinion of either the Indians or *black new-raised corps*: the former in this country carry on a most furious war—murder and desolation mark their track—there is no hope but flying, or resistance to the last moment of life: this is what every one says of the Florida Indians, of course the inhabitants of all descriptions would fear to come near you. There is a report here that neither the 21st or 44th regiments behaved well, but as a report I treat it. I should be sorry to hear two British regiments slurred in an attack.*

*In this letter of the colonels there was a lamentation expressed that his share of the prize money at St. Mary's did not exceed *five hundred pounds!*

From colonel Malcolm to rear-admiral Malcolm.

Cumberland Island, 11th February, 1815.

I hope we may hear from you in a short time, and of your success against the place you are now before—(New Orleans.) *It will repay the troops for all their trouble and fatigues!* I do not expect, either war or peace, that we will move from this island this winter; if the war goes on, a garrison must be left here in charge of the island.

From sir Thomas Cochrane, of the Surprise frigate, to captain Pigot, off New Orleans.

Cumberland Island, February 12th, 1815.

I came here just two days too late to share in the good things going on. Old Somerville was senior, and ordered the attack on St. Mary's, which Barrie *executed.* The prize-money will be about thirty thousand pounds, *not more.* Had our force been sufficient, the next movement would have been against Savannah, but not mustering above a thousand bayonets, we were content to keep possession of this island, which we are placing in a state of defence. Our operations will, I suppose, be shortly put a stop to by our friend, *Jemmy Madison,* as peace or war now depends on him: the commissioners at Ghent having signed, and the prince regent ratified, the terms of a peace, and hostilities will cease as soon as he does the same. We hope, in the mean time, better luck will attend you at New Orleans than has hitherto done, and that you will have time to give general Jackson a trimming.

From sir Thomas Cochrane to sir Thomas Troubridge, off New Orleans.

North End Cumberland Island, February 12th, 1815.

I hope this will reach head-quarters in time for the St. Lawrence, who sails immediately for your part of the world with the news of peace being concluded with this country, but of which I should think you will receive earlier intelligence direct from England. We are in daily expectation of a flag of truce to inform us of Mr. Madison's having ratified the treaty, on his doing which hostilities will immediately cease. I confess myself by no means sorry for this event. I think we have had quite enough of war for some years to come, although I should have wished we had made the Yankees more sensible of our power and ability to punish them, should they again provoke us. *As it is, except the injury done to their trade, we have little to boast of.* We are all very much grieved to learn the disasters in your quarter. Our loss seems to have been immense; and from the reports we pick up, one is led to believe there was not much prospect of success at the commencement of the attack. We are most particularly unfortunate in our general officers on all occasions. I am afraid general Power and the regiment with him, will not be with you in time to render any service. He was at Bermuda on the 24th ult. at which period the Statira had not arrived.

I came here six weeks ago, and found St. Mary's had been taken two days before my arrival, which, of course, *cuts me out of what has been captured.* Barrie commanded the party landed; old Somerville was senior officer, the admiral having only arrived the day before me, in consequence of being blown off the coast by strong northwest gales on his way from the Chesapeake. It was at first supposed, as is usual on all these occasions, that a great deal of money would be made; but if they clear *thirty thousand pounds, it will be as much as they will do.*

From admiral Cockburn to captain Evans.

Head-Quarters, Cumberland Island, 11th February, 1815.

No general, however, as you now know, has come here; you have had them all your way, and though I have learnt by a few hasty lines the unfortunate result of our first endeavours against New Orleans, yet excepting as far as relates to the poor generals and to the gross numbers you lost, I know no particulars, not even which of my many friends amongst you are dead or alive, or which have broken bones or whole skins. I trust, however, it will prove that you are amongst the latter, and I hope you will when at leisure favour me with a detailed account of all that has passed in your neighbourhood.

We have been more fortunate here *in our small way*. We have taken St. Mary's, a *tolerably rich place*, and with little loss have managed to do much damage to the enemy, and we are now in tolerable security, upon a large fertile island in Georgia, *though an ugly account of peace* being signed (the particulars of which I have sent to sir admiral Cochrane) seems to promise a speedy dismissal to us from this coast.

From Mr. Swainson to lieutenant Douglas, of H.M. brig Sophie, off New Orleans.

9th February, 1815.

We had some fine fun at St. Mary's; the bombs were at the town, and had plenty of plunder. How are you off *for tables*, and *chests of drawers, &c?*

From J. Gallon to J. O'Reily, esq. on board H.M. ship Tonnant, off New Orleans.

Cumberland Island, 9th February, 1815.

We have had fine fun since I saw you. What with the Rappahannock and various other places, we have contrived *to pick up a few trifling things, such as mahogany tables, chests of drawers, &c.*

From John Miller to Mr. Thomas Miller, 75 Old Gravel Lane, St. George's, East London.

H.M. ship Lacedemonian, off land, February 12th, 1815.

We have lately been employed with the squadron under admiral Cockburn, and have taken Cumberland Island, and the town of St. Mary's, from the Yankees. Our troops and sailors behaved very well; part of the black regiment employed on this service acted with great gallantry. Blacky had *no idea of giving quarters*; and it was with difficulty the officers prevented their putting *the prisoners to death*. The Yankee riflemen fired at our men in ambush; blacky, on the impulse of the moment, left the ranks, and pursued them into the woods, fighting like *heroes*. A poor Yankee, *disarmed*, begged for mercy. Blacky replied, *"he no come in bush for mercy,"* and immediately shot him dead!

From J. R. Glover to captain Westful, of the Anaconda.

Head-Quarters, Cumberland Island, 1st February, 1815.

We have established our head-quarters here, after *ransacking* St. Mary's, from which we brought property to the amount of *fifty thousand pounds*, and had we two thousand troops, we might yet collect a *good harvest* before peace takes place. My forebodings will not allow me to anticipate either honour or profit to the expedition, of which you form a part, and I much fear the contrary, yet most fervently do I hope my forebodings may prove groundless. The admiral (Cockburn) is as active as ever, and success in general attends his undertakings.

From captain Napier, of the Euryalus frigate, to captain Gordon, of the Seahorse.

Off Cape Henry, January 24th, 1815.

Here I am in Lynhaven bay, the clippers sailing every day, and losing them for want of fast sailers. All our prizes are well disposed of. I have had a good deal to do with them, and not many thanks as you may suppose from the agents. I have petitioned the prince regent in behalf of the whole of us, for a *good slice* of prize-money, and I hope to succeed. You, I suppose, will not be displeased at it. Excuse this hasty scrawl, I am in a d—d bad humour, having just returned from an unsuccessful chase.

NO. LXVIII.

NEGRO STEALING, &C.

After the news of peace had reached the infamous Cockburn, at Cumberland Island, the following depredations were committed on St. Simons, by the British. The respectable editor of the Savannah Republican introduces the facts to the public by assuring us that "implicit reliance may be placed" on the following statement:

"St. Simons, February 13, 1815.

"As the only person, at present, capable of making a just representation of the losses sustained by the inhabitants of St. Simons, I beg leave to state them to you, with a view that it may be presented to the proper department.

Major Butler, (Hampton,) one hundred and fifty negroes: his dwelling-house rifled; groceries and every other article removed to head-quarters (Cumberland.)

James Hamilton will be ruined as to his negro property; his store pillaged; machinery employed in ginning the seed cotton destroyed; the whole of his packed cotton removed.

A. C. Wylly, forty negroes taken, with his cotton.

E. Matthews, twenty-six negroes and six bales of cotton.

J. H. Giekie, fifteen negroes, several bales of cotton.

John Couper, the number of negroes unknown.

In truth, it is impossible to state circumstantially the loss which the unfortunate inhabitants have sustained. Cattle slaughtered in every direction; property of every description held in requisition or destroyed. My feelings prevent my adding to this hateful catalogue of wo."

To the above I will subjoin a list of the negroes taken from the shores of the Mississippi by the British, whom they refused to surrender, under the pretext of considering them as deserters, as it has been seen in this work.

Messrs. Jumonville de Villiérs,	20
Kernion,	2
Ducros,	9
Beauregard,	2
Dufossat,	1
Mendez,	4
Delaronde,	7
Celestin Lachiapella,	43
Versailles,	2
Veillon and Solis,	2
Macarty,	1
Jacques and Gabriel Villeré,	52
LaCoste,	13
Delassize,	6
Bienvenu,	10
Delery,	1
Reggio,	3
Harang,	1
Philipon,	5
Bronier,	3
Leandre Lacoste,	8
Delino,	4
Total	199

Besides the loss of their negroes, some of the planters above named have experienced other heavy losses, such as the whole of their cattle, horses, buildings, furniture, &c. to the amount of more than two hundred thousand dollars.

NO. LXIX.

The following document was omitted in its proper place; it is deemed, however, of too much importance to be excluded entirely.

ADDRESS

Directed by major-general Jackson to be read at the head of each of the corps composing the line below New Orleans, Jan. 21, 1815.

CITIZENS AND FELLOW SOLDIERS,

The enemy has retreated, and your general has now leisure to proclaim to the world what he has noticed with admiration and pride your undaunted courage, your patriotism, and patience, under hardships and fatigues. Natives of different states, acting together, for the first time, in this camp; differing in habits and in language, instead of viewing in these circumstances the germ of distrust and division, you have made them the source of an honourable emulation, and from the seeds of discord itself have reaped the fruits of an honourable union. This day completes the fourth week since fifteen hundred of you attacked treble your number of men, who had boasted of their discipline, and their services under a celebrated leader, in a long and eventful war—attacked them in their camp, the moment they had profaned the soil of freedom with their hostile tread, and inflicted a blow which was a prelude to the final result of their attempt to conquer, or their poor contrivances to divide us. A few hours was sufficient to unite the gallant band, though at the moment they received the welcome order to march they were separated many leagues, in different directions from the city. The gay rapidity of the march, and the cheerful countenances of the officers and men, would have induced a belief that some festive entertainment, not the strife of battle, was the object to which they hastened with so much eagerness and hilarity. In the conflict that ensued, the same spirit was supported, and my communication to the executive of the United States have testified the sense I entertained of the merits of the corps and officers that were engaged. Resting on the field of battle, they retired in perfect order on the next morning to these lines, destined to become the scene of future victories, which they were to share with the rest of you, my brave companions in arms. Scarcely were your lines a protection against musket-shot, when on the 28th a disposition was made to attack them with all the pomp and parade of military tactics, as improved by those veterans of the Spanish war.

Their batteries of heavy cannon kept up an incessant fire; their rockets illuminated the air; and under their cover two strong columns threatened our flanks. The foe insolently thought that this spectacle was too imposing to be resisted, and in the intoxition of his pride he already saw our lines abandoned without a contest—how were those menacing appearances met?

By shouts of defiance, by a manly countenance, not to be shaken by the roar of his cannon, by the glare of his firework rockets; by an artillery served with superior skill, and with deadly effect. Never, my brave friends, can your general forget the testimonials of attachment to our glorious cause, of indignant hatred to our foe, of affectionate confidence in your chief, that resounded from every rank, as he passed along your line. This animating scene damped the courage of the enemy; he dropped his scaling ladders and fascines, and the threatened attack dwindled into a *demonstration*, which served only to show the emptiness of his parade, and to inspire you with a just confidence in yourselves.

The new year was ushered in with the most tremendous fire his whole artillery could produce: a few hours only, however, were necessary for the brave and skilful men who directed our own to dismount his cannon, destroy his batteries, and effectually silence his fire. Hitherto, my brave friends, in the contest on our lines, your courage had been passive only; you stood with calmness, a fire that would have tried the firmness of a veteran, and you anticipated a nearer contest with an eagerness which was soon to be gratified.

On the 8th of January the final effort was made. At the dawn of day the batteries opened and the columns advanced. Knowing that the volunteers from Tennessee and the militia from Kentucky were stationed on your left, it was there they directed their chief attack.

Reasoning always from false principles, they expected little opposition from men whose officers even were not in uniform, who were ignorant of the rules of dress, and who had never been caned into discipline—fatal mistake! a fire incessantly kept up, directed with calmness and with unerring aim, strewed the field with the bravest officers and men of the column which slowly advanced, according to the most approved rules of European tactics, and was cut down by the untutored courage of American militia. Unable to sustain this galling and unceasing fire, some hundreds nearest the entrenchment called for quarter, which was granted—the rest retreating, were rallied at some distance, but only to make them a surer mark for the grape and canister shot of our artillery, which, without exaggeration, mowed down whole ranks at every discharge; and at length they precipitately retired from the field.

Our right had only a short contest to sustain with a few rash men who fatally for themselves, forced their entrance into the unfinished redoubt on the river. They were quickly dispossessed, and this glorious day terminated with the loss to the enemy of their commander-in-chief and one major-general killed, another major-general wounded, the most experienced and bravest of their officers, and more than three thousand men killed, wounded and missing, while our ranks, my friends, were thinned only by the loss of six of our brave companions killed, and seven disabled by wounds—wonderful interposition of Heaven! unexampled event in the history of war!

Let us be grateful to the God of battles who has directed the arrows of indignation against our invaders, while he covered with his protecting shield the brave defenders of their country.

After this unsuccessful and disastrous attempt, their spirits were broken, their force was destroyed, and their whole attention was employed in providing the means of escape. This they have effected; leaving their heavy artillery in our power, and many of their wounded to our clemency. The consequences of this short, but decisive campaign, are incalculably important. The pride of our arrogant enemy humbled, his forces broken, his leaders killed, his insolent hopes of our disunion frustrated—his expectation of rioting in our spoils and wasting our country changed into ignominious defeat, shameful flight, and a reluctant acknowledgment of the humanity and kindness of those whom he had doomed to all the horrors and humiliation of a conquered state.

On the other side, unanimity established, disaffection crushed, confidence restored, your country saved from conquest, your property from pillage, your wives and daughters from insult and violation—the union preserved from dismemberment, and perhaps a period put by this decisive stroke to a bloody and savage war. These, my brave friends, are the consequences of the efforts you have made, and the success with which they have been crowned by Heaven.

These important results have been effected by the united courage and perseverance of the army; but which the different corps as well as the individuals that composed it, have vied with each other in their exertions to produce. The share they have respectively had, will be pointed out in the general order accompanying this address. But the gratitude, the admiration of their country, offers a fairer reward than that which any praises of the general can bestow, and the best is that of which they can never be deprived, the consciousness of having done their duty, and of meriting the applause they will receive.

GENERAL ORDERS.

Head-Quarters, 7th Military District, Camp below New Orleans, Adjutant general's Office, January 21.

Before the camp at these memorable lines shall be broken up, the general thinks it a duty to the brave army which has defended them, publicly to notice the conduct of the different corps which compose it. The behaviour of the regular troops, consisting of parts of the 7th and 44th regiments of infantry, and the corps of marines, all commanded by colonel Ross, has been such as to merit his warm approbation. The 7th regiment was led by major Peyre, and the 44th by captain Baker, in the action of the 23d, in a manner that does those officers the highest honour. They have continued through the campaign to do their duty with the same zeal and ability with which it was commenced. On that occasion the country lost a valuable officer in the death of lieutenant M'Clellan of the 7th infantry, who fell while bravely leading his company. Lieutenant Dupuy of the 44th, although severely wounded in this action, returned in time to take a share in all the subsequent attacks.

To the Tennessee mounted gunmen, to their gallant leader, brigadier-general Coffee, the general presents his warmest thanks, not only for their uniform good conduct in action, but for the wonderful patience with which they have borne the fatigue, and the perseverance with which they surmounted the difficulties of a most painful march, in order to meet the enemy—a diligence and zeal to which we probably owe the salvation of the country. Ordinary activity would have brought them too late to act the brilliant part they have performed in the defeat of our invaders. All the officers of that corps have distinguished themselves; but the general cannot avoid mentioning the name of lieutenant-colonel Lauderdale who fell on the night of the 23d—and those of colonels Dyer, Gibson and Elliott, who were wounded, but disdaining personal considerations, remained firm to their duty.

The cavalry from the Mississippi territory, under their enterprizing leader major Hinds, was always ready to perform every service which the nature of the country enabled them to execute. The daring manner in which they reconnoitred the enemy on his lines, excited the admiration of one army and the astonishment of the other.

Major-general Carrol, commanding the detachment of West Tennessee militia, has shown the greatest zeal for the service, a strict attention to duty, and an ability and courage that will always recommend him to the gratitude of his country. His troops have, since the lines were formed, occupied and defended the weakest part of them, and borne, without a murmur, an encampment on a marshy and unhealthy soil. In the memorable action, of the 8th January, the chief effort of the enemy was directed against them; but their valour, and that of the brave men who supported them, (general Coffee's brigade on the left, and a part of the Kentucky troops on the right) soon made it clear that a rampart of high-minded men is a better defence than the most regular fortification.

General Adair, who, owing to the indisposition of general Thomas, brought up the Kentucky militia, has shown that troops will always be valiant when their leaders are so. No men ever displayed a more gallant spirit than these did under that most valuable officer. His country is under obligations to him.

The general would be ungrateful or insensible to merit, if he did not particularly notice the conduct of the officers and men who so bravely supported and so skilfully directed his artillery. Colonel M'Rea, in the action of the 23d, showed, as he always does, great courage. Lieutenant Spotts, under whose immediate direction our artillery had been placed, led it to action with a daring courage worthy of admiration. Captain Humphrey commanded the first battery on our right—the service is greatly indebted to that officer, not only for the able and gallant manner in which he directed his fire, but for the general activity he displayed in his department.

Lieutenant Norris of the navy, with Mr. Walker Martin and a detachment of seamen, was stationed at the 2d battery; and lieutenant Crawley, with Mr. W. Livingston (master's mate) with a similar detachment, were stationed at a thirty-two-pounder, which was remarkably well directed—they performed their duty with the zeal and bravery which has always characterized the navy of the United States. Captains Dominique and Belluche, lately commanding privateers at Barataria, with part of their former crew and many brave citizens of New Orleans, were stationed at Nos. 3 and 4. The general cannot avoid giving his warm approbation of the manner in which these gentlemen have uniformly conducted themselves while under his command, and of the gallantry with which they have redeemed the pledge they gave at the opening of the campaign to defend the country. The brothers Lafitte have exhibited the same courage and fidelity; and the general promises that the government shall be duly apprized of their conduct. Colonel Perry, deputy quarter-master-general, volunteered his services at No. 6—he was ably aided by lieutenant Kerr of the artillery—his battery was well served, bravely supported, and greatly annoyed the enemy—Nos. 8 and 9 were directed by lieutenant Spotts with his usual skill and bravery, assisted by Mr. Cheaveau.

The general takes the highest pleasure in noticing the conduct of general Garrigue de Flaujac, commanding one of the brigades of militia of this state, and member of the senate. His brigade not being in the field as soon as the invasion was known, he repaired to the camp and offered himself as a volunteer for the service of a piece of artillery, which he directed with the skill which was to be expected from an experienced artillery officer: disdaining the exemption afforded by his seat in the senate, he continued in this subordinate but honourable station, and by his example as well as his exertion, has rendered essential services to his country. Mr. Sebastian Hiriard of the same body, set the same example, served a considerable time in the ranks of the volunteer battalion, and afterwards as adjutant of the coloured troops. Major Plauche's battalion of volunteers, though deprived of the valuable services of major Carmac, who commanded them, by a wound which that officer received in the attack of the 28th of December, have realized all the anticipations which the general had formed of their conduct. Major Plauche, and major St. Geme of that corps, have distinguished themselves by their activity, their courage, and their zeal; and the whole corps have greatly contributed to enable the general to redeem the pledge he gave, when at the opening of the campaign he promised the country, not only safety, but a splendid triumph over its insolent invaders. The two corps of coloured volunteers have not disappointed the hopes that were formed of their courage and perseverance in the performance of their duty. Majors Lacoste and Daquin, who commanded them, have deserved well of their country. Captain Savary's conduct has been noticed in the account rendered of the battle of the 23d, and that officer has since continued to merit the highest praise. Captain Beale's company of the city riflemen has sustained by its subsequent conduct the reputation it acquired in the action of the 23d. Colonel de la Ronde, of the Louisiana militia, has been extremely serviceable by his exertions, and has shown great courage, and an uniform attachment to the cause of the country.

General Humbert, who offered his services as a volunteer, has continually exposed himself to the greatest dangers, with his characteristic bravery, as has also the Mexican field-marshal, Don Juan de Anaya, who acted in the same capacity. The general acknowledges the important assistance he has received from commodore Patterson, as well by his professional exertion, as the zealous co-operation of his department during the whole course of the campaign. Captain Henley, on board of the Carolina, and afterwards in directing the erection of several batteries at the bayou and on the right bank of the river, was of great utility to the army. Lieutenant Alexis, of the navy, stationed in the navy arsenal, was indefatigable in exertions to forward to the army every thing which could facilitate its operations—his zeal and activity deserve the notice of the government. Major Nicks, who, by an accidental wound was deprived of the pleasure of commanding the 7th regiment during the campaign was continually employed in the fort, and furnished the ammunition and the artillery that was wanted with the greatest activity and promptitude. To the volunteers of the Mississippi territory, and to the militia of the remoter parts of this state, who have arrived since the decisive action of the 8th, the general tenders his thanks, and is convinced that nothing but opportunity was wanting to entitle them to the praises that have bean merited by the rest of the army. Captain Ogden's troop of horse was peculiarly useful by their local knowledge of the ground on which they acted; and the small detachment of the Attacapas dragoons, stationed near head-quarters, were indefatigable, in performing all the duties which devolved on them.

The general would not do justice to his staff if he did not bestow deserved praise on the adjutant-general, colonel Butler, and his assistant, major Chotard, for their zeal and activity in the important department of service confided to them, and for the bravery which led them wherever danger or duty required their presence. The vigilance, courage, and attention to duty, exhibited during the campaign by colonel Haynes, and his two assistants, majors Davis and Hampton, have been appreciated, as they deserved to be, by the general.

The general's aids-de-camp, Thomas L. Butler and captain John Reed, as well as his volunteer aids, Messrs. Livingston, Duncan, Grymes, Duplessis and major Davezac de Castera, the judge advocate, have merited the thanks of the general by the calm and deliberate courage they have displayed on every occasion, and in every situation that called it forth. The topographical engineer, major Tatum, exhibited all the ardour of youth in the hour of peril, united to the experience acquired by his long services. The chief engineer, major Lacarriere Latour, has been useful to the army by his talents and bravery. The same praises are due to his assistants, captain Lewis Livingston and Mr. Latrobe. Their medical staff has merited well of the country, and the general would not do justice to his own feelings were he to withhold from Dr. Kerr, hospital surgeon, who volunteered his services, and Dr. Flood, the just tribute of applause deserved by them for their medical skill and personal bravery. The quarter-master's department, though deprived of the personal exertions of colonel Piatt, who was wounded in the night action of the 23d, performed well their duties. Major-general Villeré and brigadier Morgan have merited the approbation of the general by their unwearied attention since they took the field.

The large mortar was ably directed by captain Lefebre and by Mr. Gilbert. Captain Blanchard was very useful as an engineer, and merits the general's praise for the celerity and skill with which he erected the battery which now commands the river, on the right of the camp. Mr. Busquet and Mr. Ducoin, of major St. Geme's company, displayed great knowledge and dexterity as artillerists. To the whole army the general presents the assurance of his official approbation, and of his individual regard. This splendid campaign will be considered as entitling every man who has served in it to the salutation of his brother in arms.

By command,
ROBERT BUTLER, Adjt. Gen.

INDEX